Waiting for Spring 3

Anashin

Waiting
for Spring
vol.3

Presented by
Anashin

CONTENTS

WAITING FOR SPRING
Harumatsu Bokura

Character & Story

To be like her role model Aya-chan, Mitsuki is determined to make some real friends in high school, but her days pass by without much success. She finds solace at the café where she works, but it doesn't stay a sanctuary for long... One day, the school's celebrities—the Elite Four Hotties of the basketball team— appear out of nowhere! Before she knows it, Mitsuki gets caught up in their silly hijinks. As she spends more time with the four of them, she begins to meet new people and make new friends, too. When she goes to a practice game to cheer the boys on, she is reunited with Aya-chan and is stunned to learn that her childhood best friend was actually a boy! What's more, he aggressively pursues her and makes a bet with Towa!

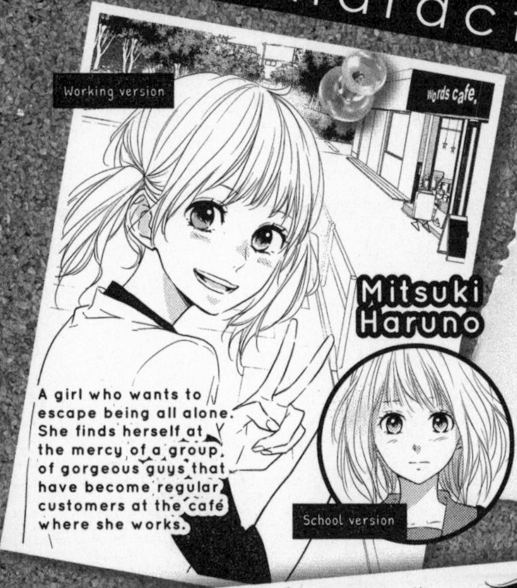

Working version
Words cafe.
Mitsuki Haruno
A girl who wants to escape being all alone. She finds herself at the mercy of a group of gorgeous guys that have become regular customers at the café where she works.
School version

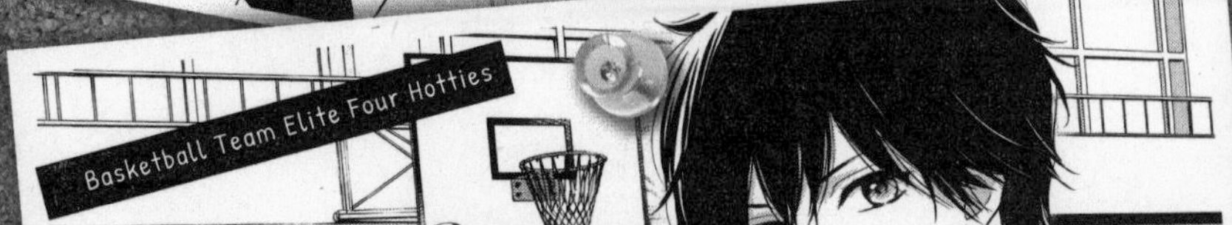

Basketball Team Elite Four Hotties
Ryūji Tada
A second-year. Comes off as a bad boy, but is rather naïve. He's crushing on the Boss's daughter, Nanase-san.
Kyōsuke Wakamiya
A second-year in high school. Mysterious and always cool-headed. He's like a big brother to everyone.
Rui Miyamoto
A first-year in high school. His innocent smile is adorable, but it hides a wicked heart?!
Towa Asakura
Mitsuki's classmate. He's quiet and a bit spacey, but he's always there to help her.

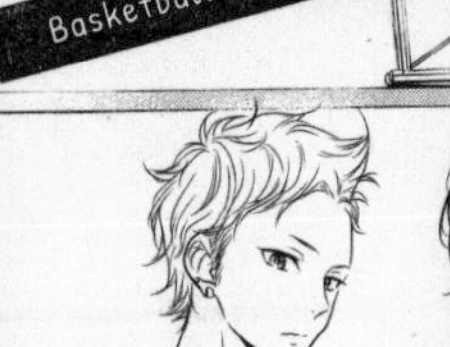

Aya-chan

Mitsuki's best friend from elementary school. When they finally meet again, she discovers he was a boy all along!

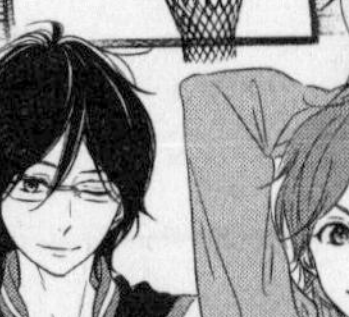

Reina Yamada

Mitsuki's first friend from her class. She has somewhat eccentric tastes?!

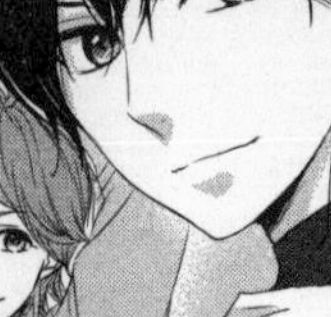

Boss

Runs the café where Mitsuki works and kindly watches over her.

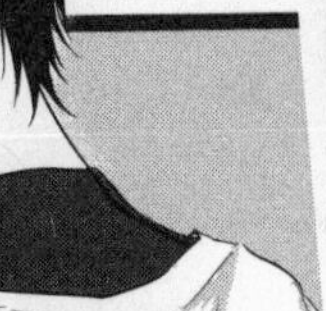

Nanase-san

"Nana-san" for short. The Boss's daughter. Straightforward and resolute, she's like a reliable big sister.

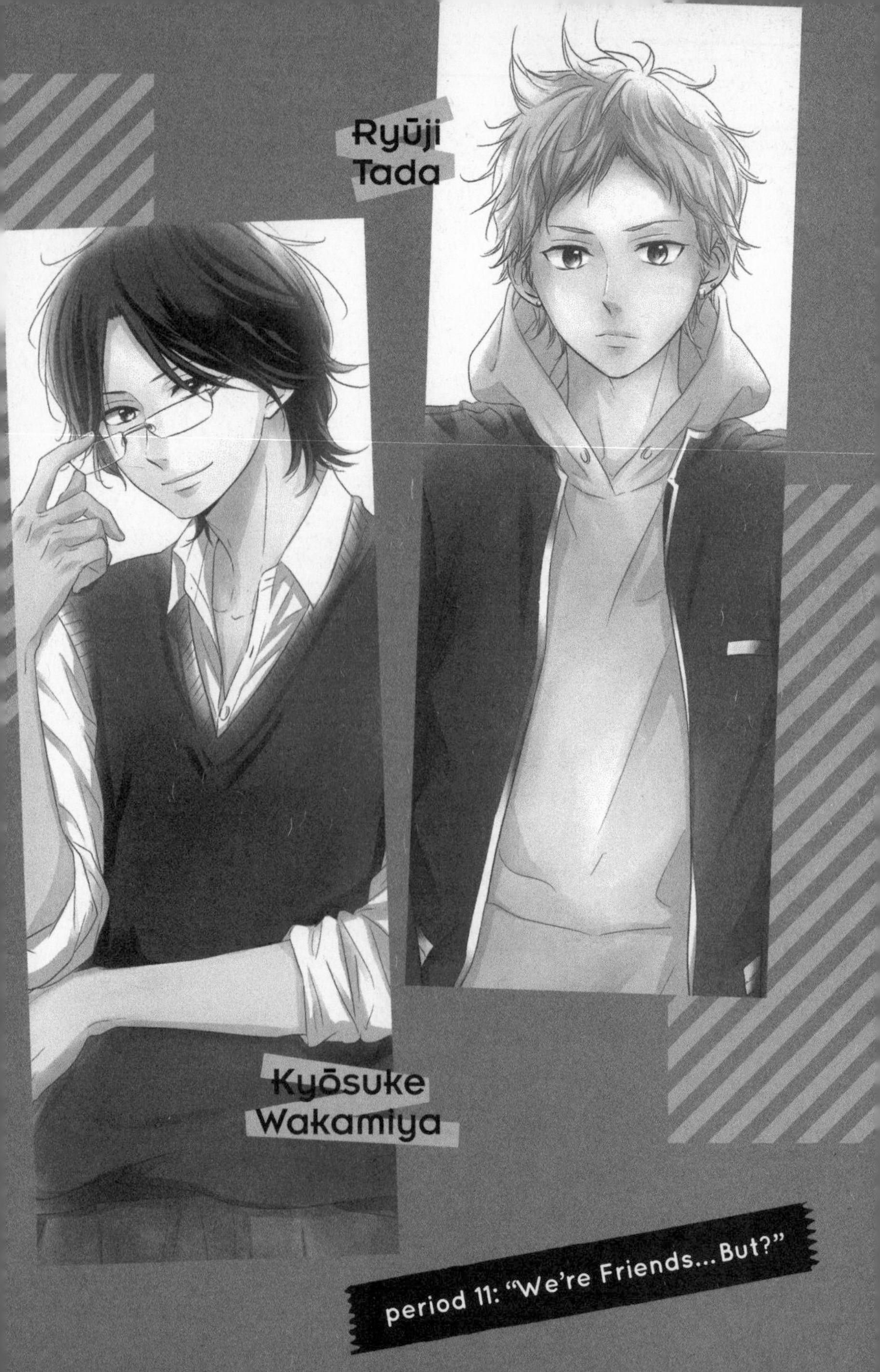
Ryūji Tada
Kyōsuke Wakamiya
period 11: “We’re Friends... But?”

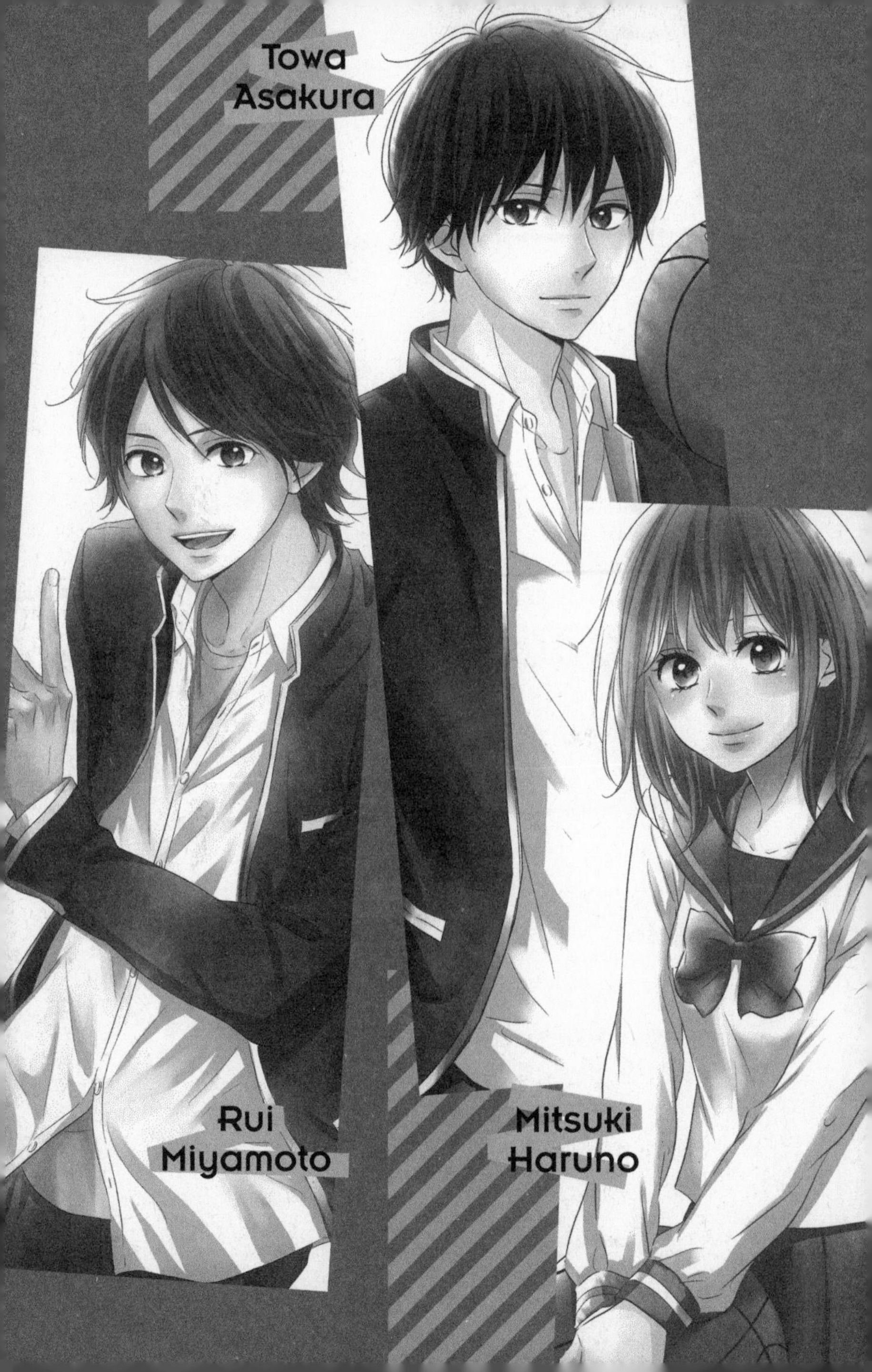
Towa Asakura
Mitsuki Haruno
Rui Miyamoto

Hello!
Anashin here!

Thank you so much for picking up Volume 3!
This is my first series that has lasted longer than two volumes,
and every day I'm overwhelmed with emotion and gratitude that
I get to draw so much manga.
And suddenly, I realize this series has been going on for more
than a year. (Of course, you could say it's **only** been a year.)
But personally, I don't feel like it's been that long at all....
I wonder if that's because only about two months have passed
in the story. Maybe that's how it feels to spend so much time
with your characters every day. Physically, though, I am clearly
getting weaker (ha ha). But emotionally, I'm still in my youth!
Right. So now that I've said my piece...

I want to keep doing my very best to present these
character's lives to you.
I hope you enjoy it!

Because of the way the pages worked out, the Silhouette
Pop Quiz is taking a break this time. My apologies to
anyone who was looking forward to it.
(Huh? There must be **some** of you, right?)

It will make a comeback in any future
volume that has extra pages.

Probably...
Hmm...

And so, let Volume 3 begin!!

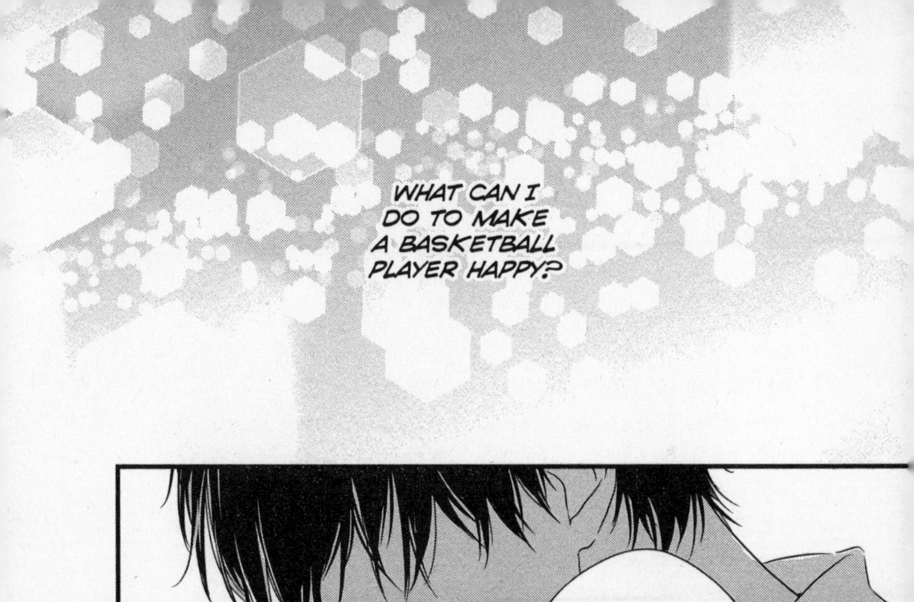
WHAT CAN I DO TO MAKE A BASKETBALL PLAYER HAPPY?
...GIVE HIM A HUG FROM THE GIRL HE LIKES.
GASP

This time, I would like to use these spaces to answer questions I get in letters and on Twitter.

Your comments and messages of support always make my day ♡

Thank you so much.

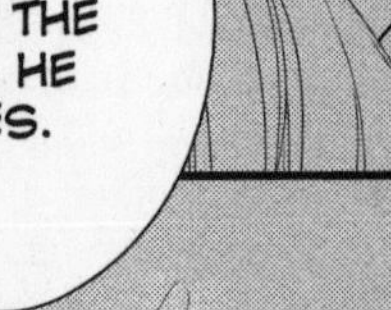

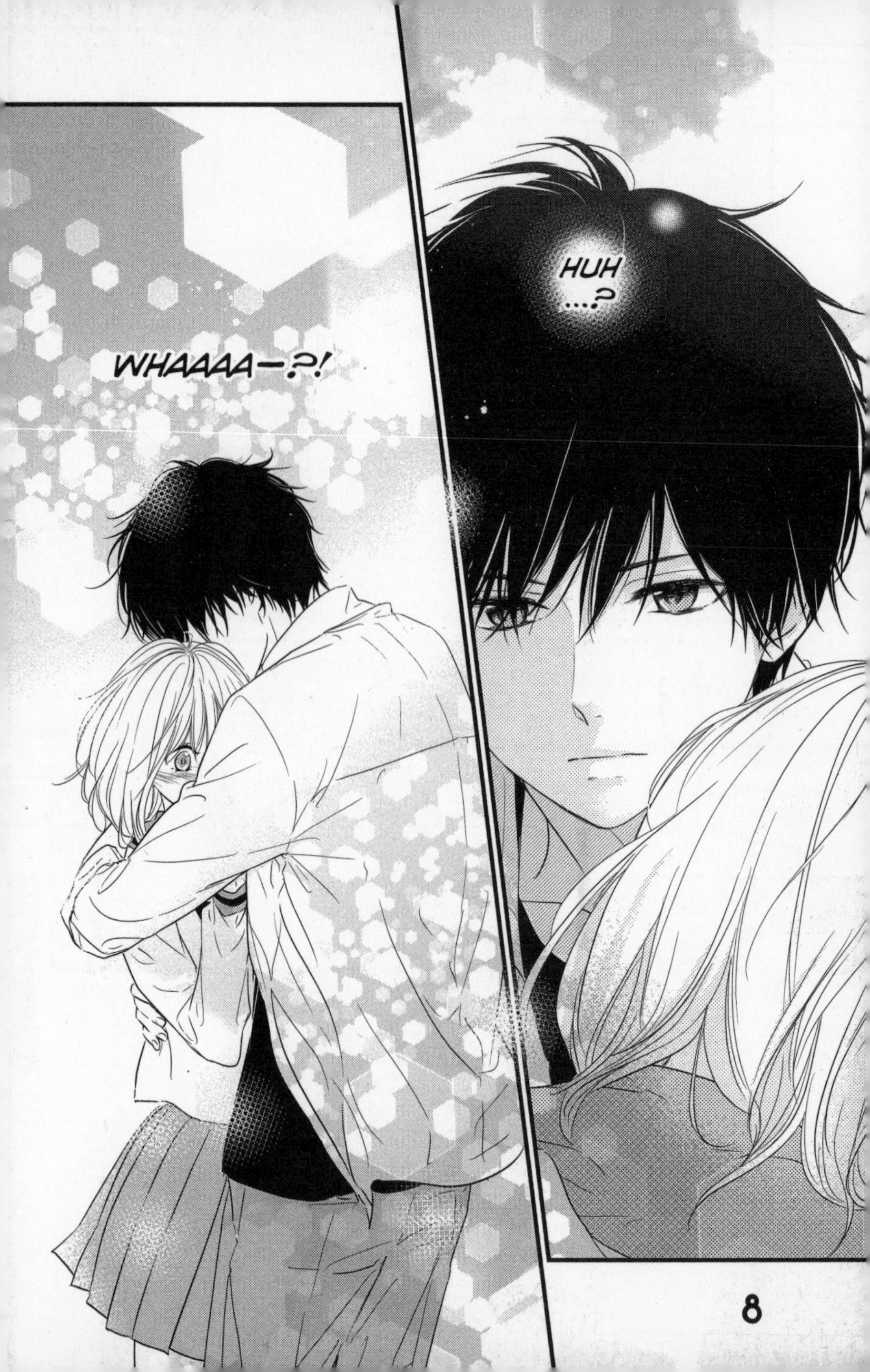
HUH ...?
WHAAAA—?!

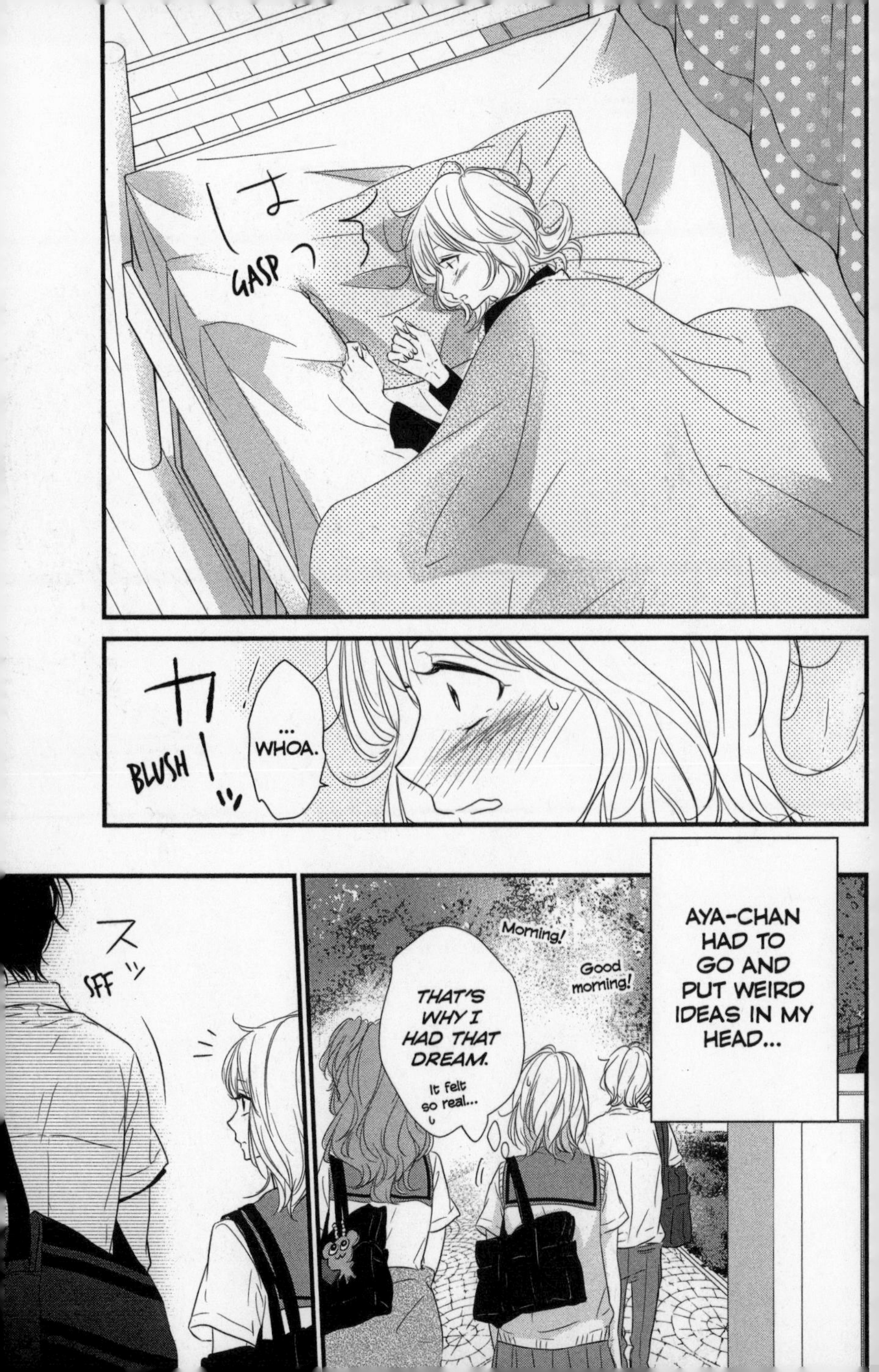
はっ
GASP
BLUSH
... WHOA.
AYA-CHAN HAD TO GO AND PUT WEIRD IDEAS IN MY HEAD...
Morning!
Good morning!
THAT'S WHY I HAD THAT DREAM.
It felt so real...
スッ
SFF

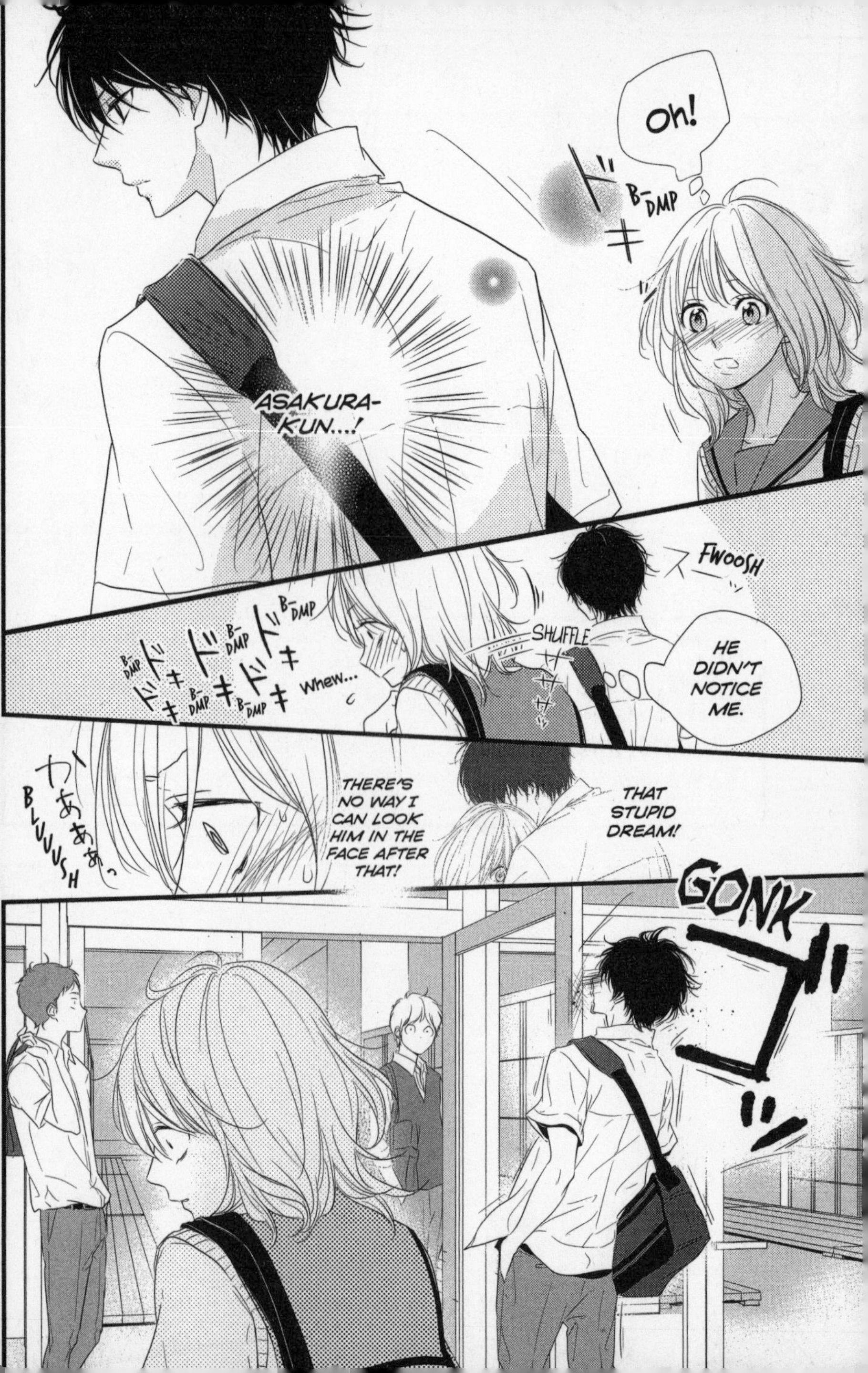
Oh!
B-DMP
ASAKURA-KUN...!
FWOOSH
HE DIDN'T NOTICE ME.
SHUFFLE
B-DMP
B-DMP
B-DMP
B-DMP
B-DMP
Whew...
THAT STUPID DREAM!
THERE'S NO WAY I CAN LOOK HIM IN THE FACE AFTER THAT!
BLUUUSH
GONK

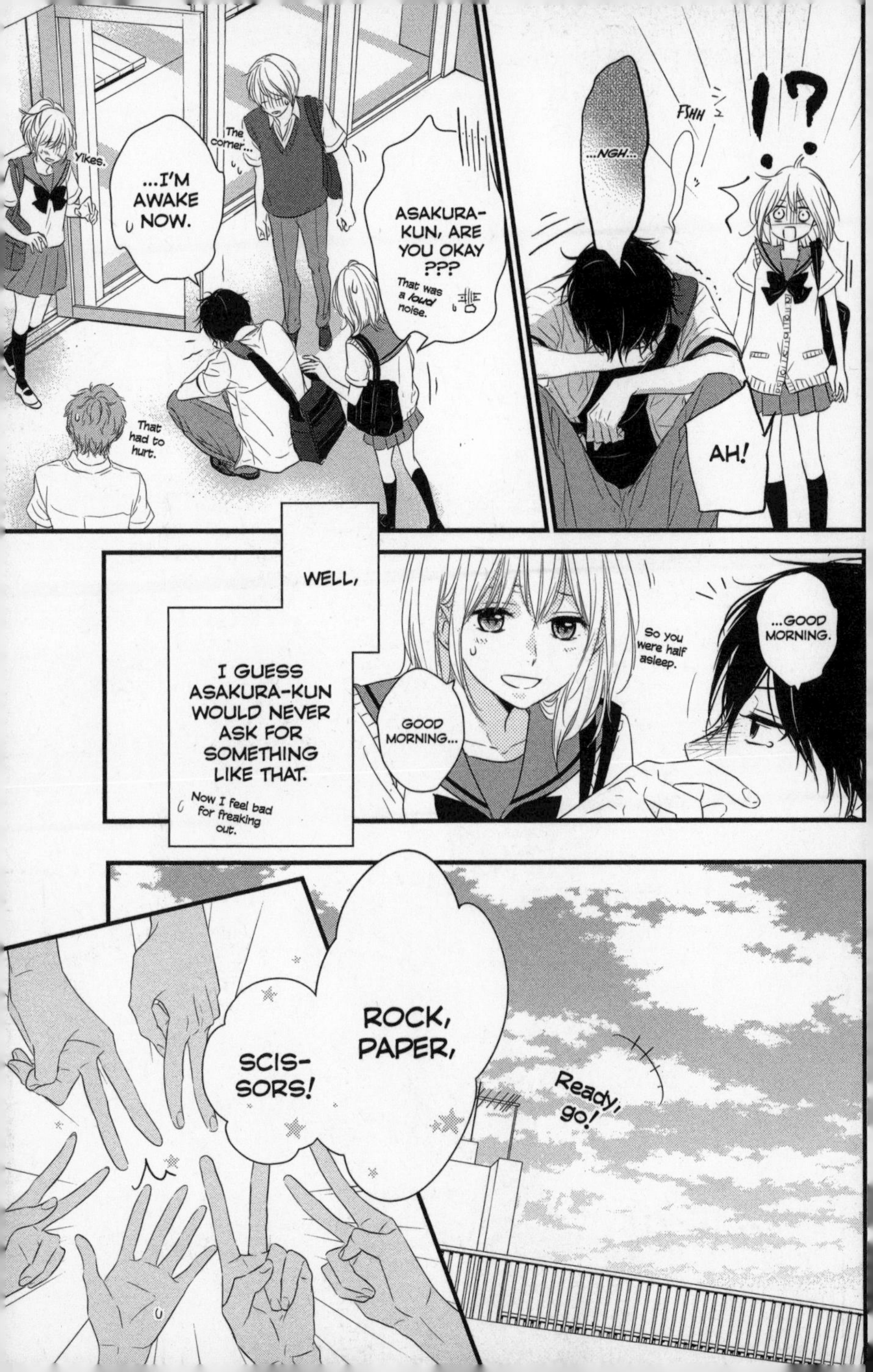
!?
FSHH
...NGH...
AH!
ASAKURA-KUN, ARE YOU OKAY ???
That was a loud noise.
The corner...
...I'M AWAKE NOW.
Yikes.
That had to hurt.
...GOOD MORNING.
So you were half asleep.
GOOD MORNING...
WELL,
I GUESS ASAKURA-KUN WOULD NEVER ASK FOR SOMETHING LIKE THAT.
Now I feel bad for freaking out.
Ready, go!
ROCK, PAPER,
SCIS-SORS!

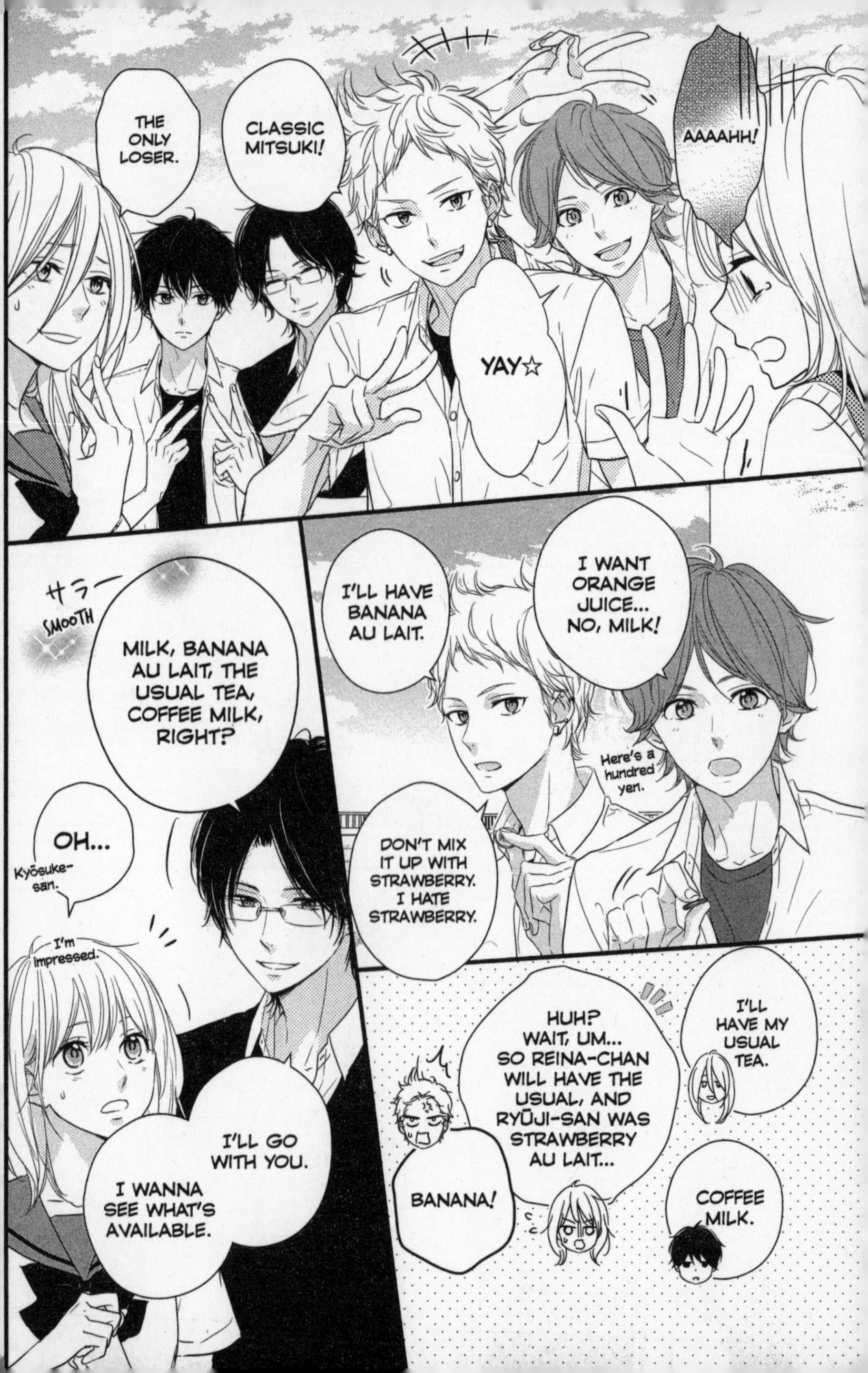
AAAAHH!
YAY☆
CLASSIC MITSUKI!
THE ONLY LOSER.
I WANT ORANGE JUICE... NO, MILK!
I'LL HAVE BANANA AU LAIT.
Here's a hundred yen.
DON'T MIX IT UP WITH STRAWBERRY. I HATE STRAWBERRY.
I'LL HAVE MY USUAL TEA.
HUH? WAIT, UM... SO REINA-CHAN WILL HAVE THE USUAL, AND RYŪJI-SAN WAS STRAWBERRY AU LAIT...
COFFEE MILK.
BANANA!
サラー
SMOOTH
MILK, BANANA AU LAIT, THE USUAL TEA, COFFEE MILK, RIGHT?
OH... Kyōsuke-san.
I'm impressed.
I'LL GO WITH YOU. I WANNA SEE WHAT'S AVAILABLE.

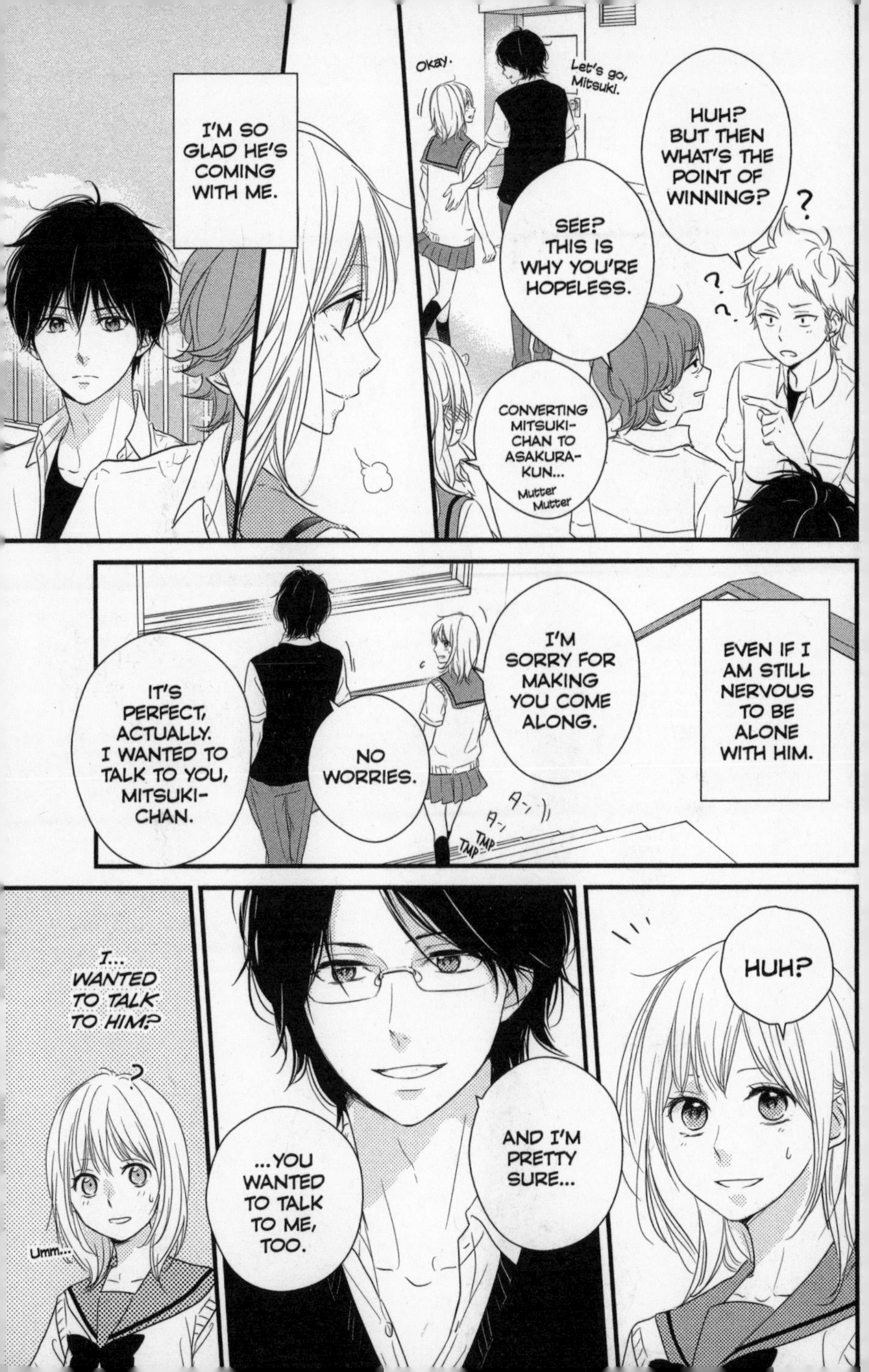
HUH? BUT THEN WHAT'S THE POINT OF WINNING?
Let's go, Mitsuki.
Okay.
SEE? THIS IS WHY YOU'RE HOPELESS.
CONVERTING MITSUKI-CHAN TO ASAKURA-KUN...
Mutter Mutter
I'M SO GLAD HE'S COMING WITH ME.
EVEN IF I AM STILL NERVOUS TO BE ALONE WITH HIM.
I'M SORRY FOR MAKING YOU COME ALONG.
TMP TMP
NO WORRIES.
IT'S PERFECT, ACTUALLY. I WANTED TO TALK TO YOU, MITSUKI-CHAN.
HUH?
AND I'M PRETTY SURE...
...YOU WANTED TO TALK TO ME, TOO.
I... WANTED TO TALK TO HIM?
Umm...

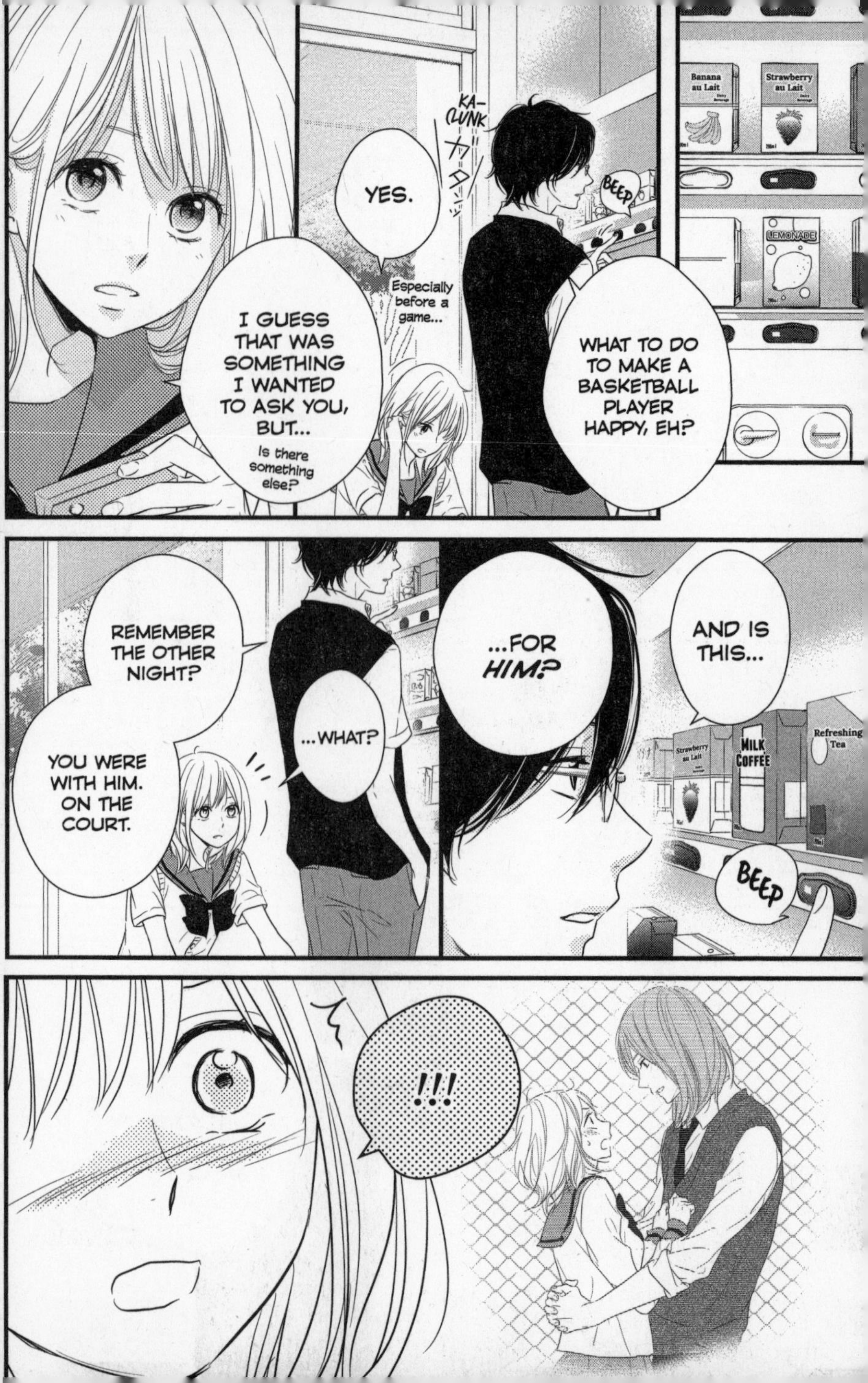
Banana au Lait
Strawberry au Lait
LEMONADE
BEEP
KA-CLUNK
WHAT TO DO TO MAKE A BASKETBALL PLAYER HAPPY, EH?
YES.
Especially before a game...
I GUESS THAT WAS SOMETHING I WANTED TO ASK YOU, BUT...
Is there something else?
AND IS THIS...
...FOR HIM?
Strawberry au Lait
MILK COFFEE
Refreshing Tea
BEEP
...WHAT?
REMEMBER THE OTHER NIGHT?
YOU WERE WITH HIM. ON THE COURT.
!!!

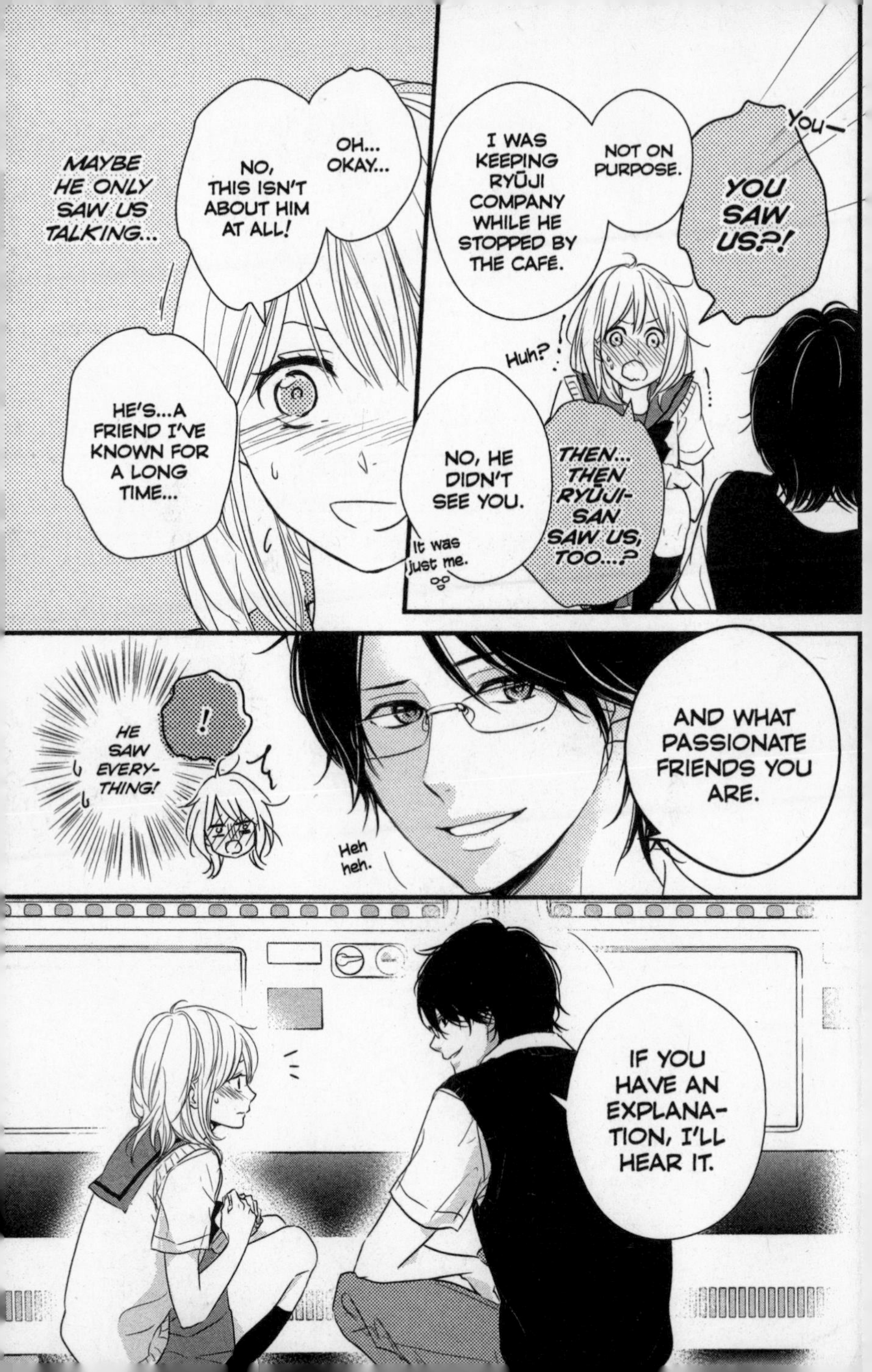
You—
YOU SAW US?!
NOT ON PURPOSE.
I WAS KEEPING RYŪJI COMPANY WHILE HE STOPPED BY THE CAFÉ.
Huh?
THEN... THEN RYŪJI-SAN SAW US, TOO...?
NO, HE DIDN'T SEE YOU.
It was just me.
OH... OKAY...
NO, THIS ISN'T ABOUT HIM AT ALL!
MAYBE HE ONLY SAW US TALKING...
HE'S...A FRIEND I'VE KNOWN FOR A LONG TIME...
AND WHAT PASSIONATE FRIENDS YOU ARE.
Heh heh.
!
HE SAW EVERYTHING!
IF YOU HAVE AN EXPLANATION, I'LL HEAR IT.

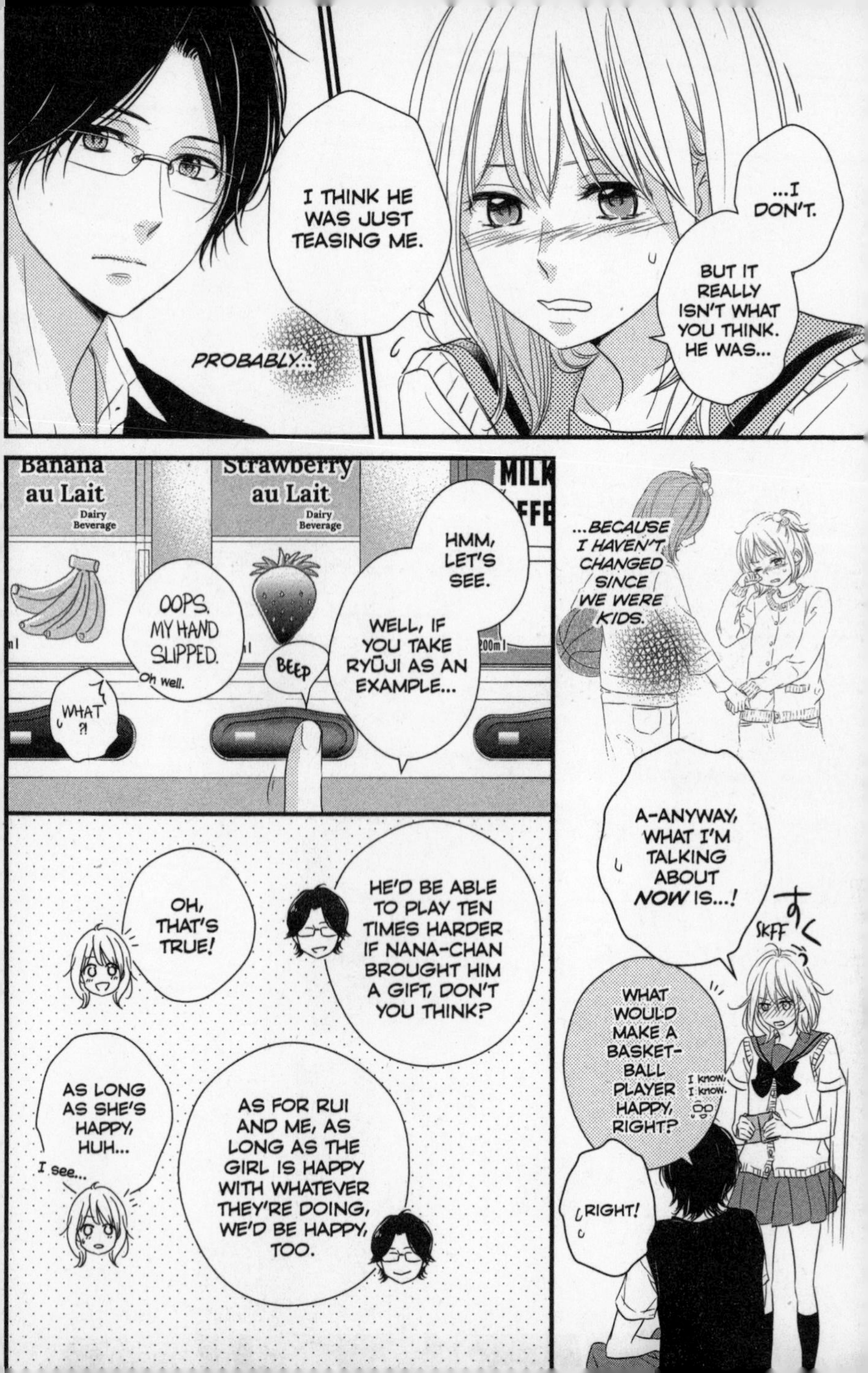
...I DON'T.
BUT IT REALLY ISN'T WHAT YOU THINK. HE WAS...
I THINK HE WAS JUST TEASING ME.
PROBABLY...
...BECAUSE I HAVEN'T CHANGED SINCE WE WERE KIDS.
A-ANYWAY, WHAT I'M TALKING ABOUT NOW IS...!
SKFF
すく
WHAT WOULD MAKE A BASKET-BALL PLAYER HAPPY, RIGHT?
I know. I know.
RIGHT!
Banana au Lait
Dairy Beverage
Strawberry au Lait
Dairy Beverage
HMM, LET'S SEE.
WELL, IF YOU TAKE RYŪJI AS AN EXAMPLE...
BEEP
OOPS. MY HAND SLIPPED.
Oh well.
WHAT ?!
HE'D BE ABLE TO PLAY TEN TIMES HARDER IF NANA-CHAN BROUGHT HIM A GIFT, DON'T YOU THINK?
OH, THAT'S TRUE!
AS FOR RUI AND ME, AS LONG AS THE GIRL IS HAPPY WITH WHATEVER THEY'RE DOING, WE'D BE HAPPY, TOO.
AS LONG AS SHE'S HAPPY, HUH...
I see...

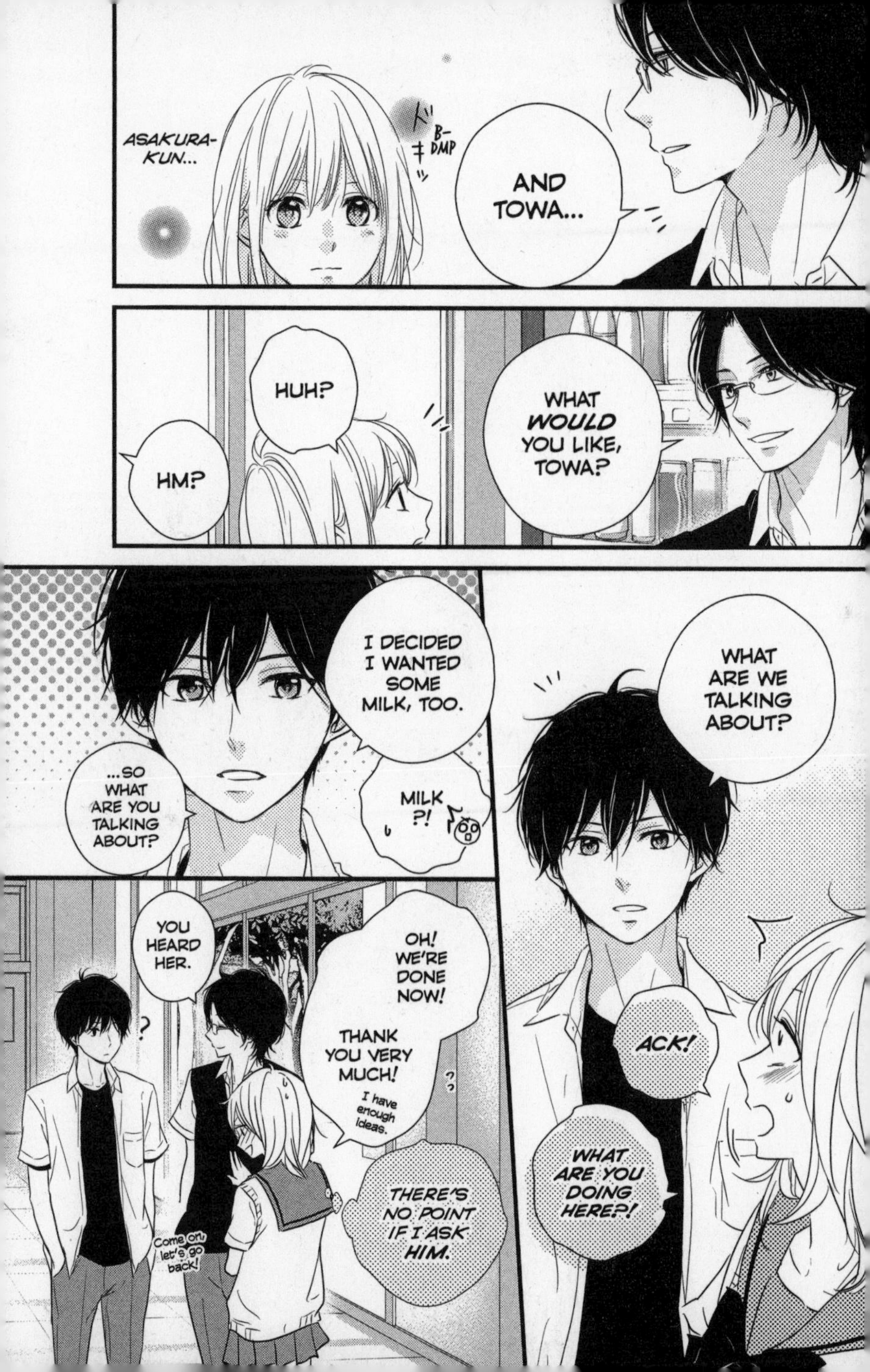
AND TOWA...
B-DMP
ASAKURA-KUN...
WHAT WOULD YOU LIKE, TOWA?
HUH?
HM?
WHAT ARE WE TALKING ABOUT?
ACK!
WHAT ARE YOU DOING HERE?!
I DECIDED I WANTED SOME MILK, TOO.
MILK?!
...SO WHAT ARE YOU TALKING ABOUT?
OH! WE'RE DONE NOW!
THANK YOU VERY MUCH!
I have enough ideas.
YOU HEARD HER.
THERE'S NO POINT IF I ASK HIM.
Come on, let's go back!

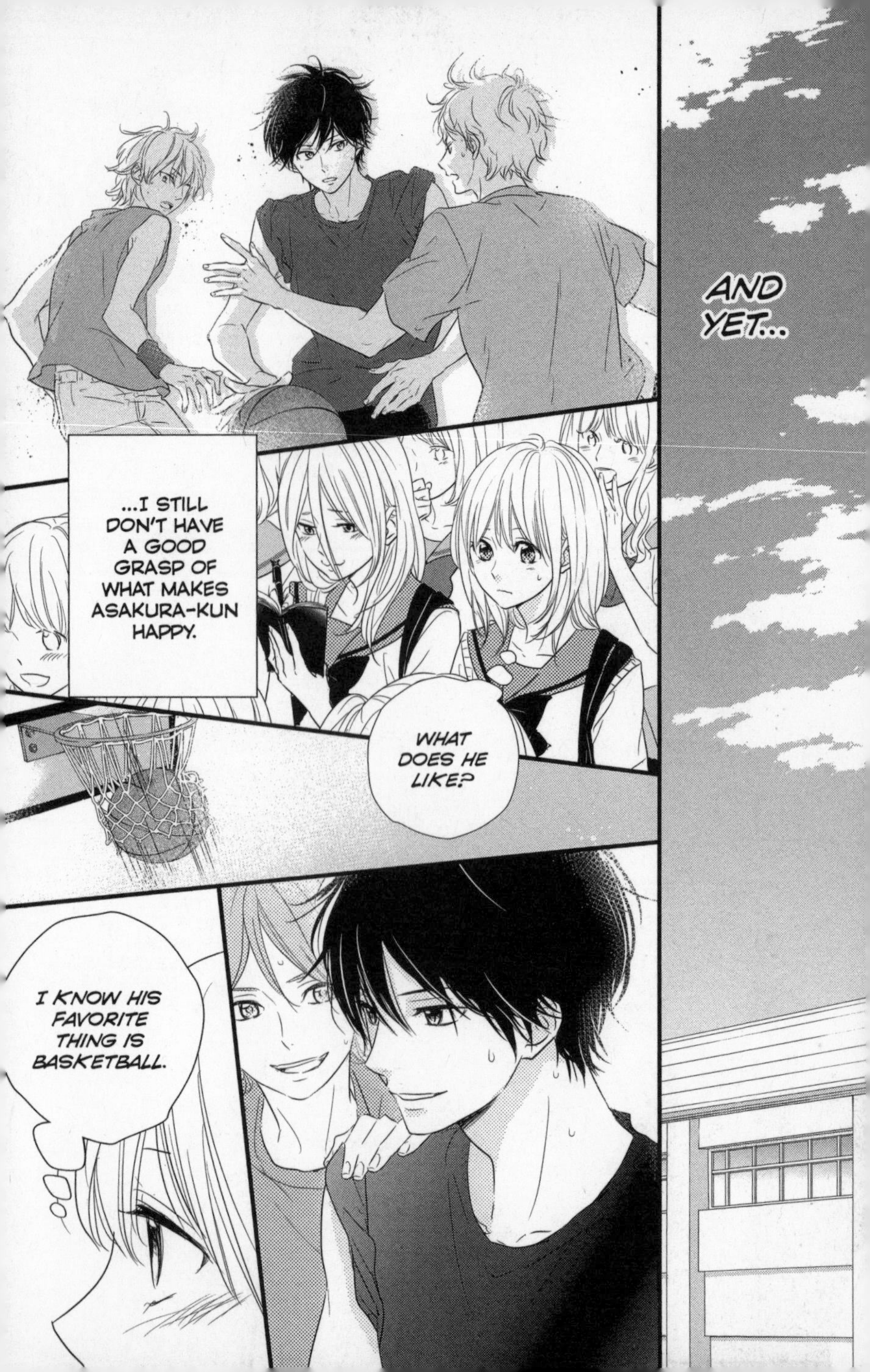

AND YET...
...I STILL DON'T HAVE A GOOD GRASP OF WHAT MAKES ASAKURA-KUN HAPPY.
WHAT DOES HE LIKE?
I KNOW HIS FAVORITE THING IS BASKETBALL.

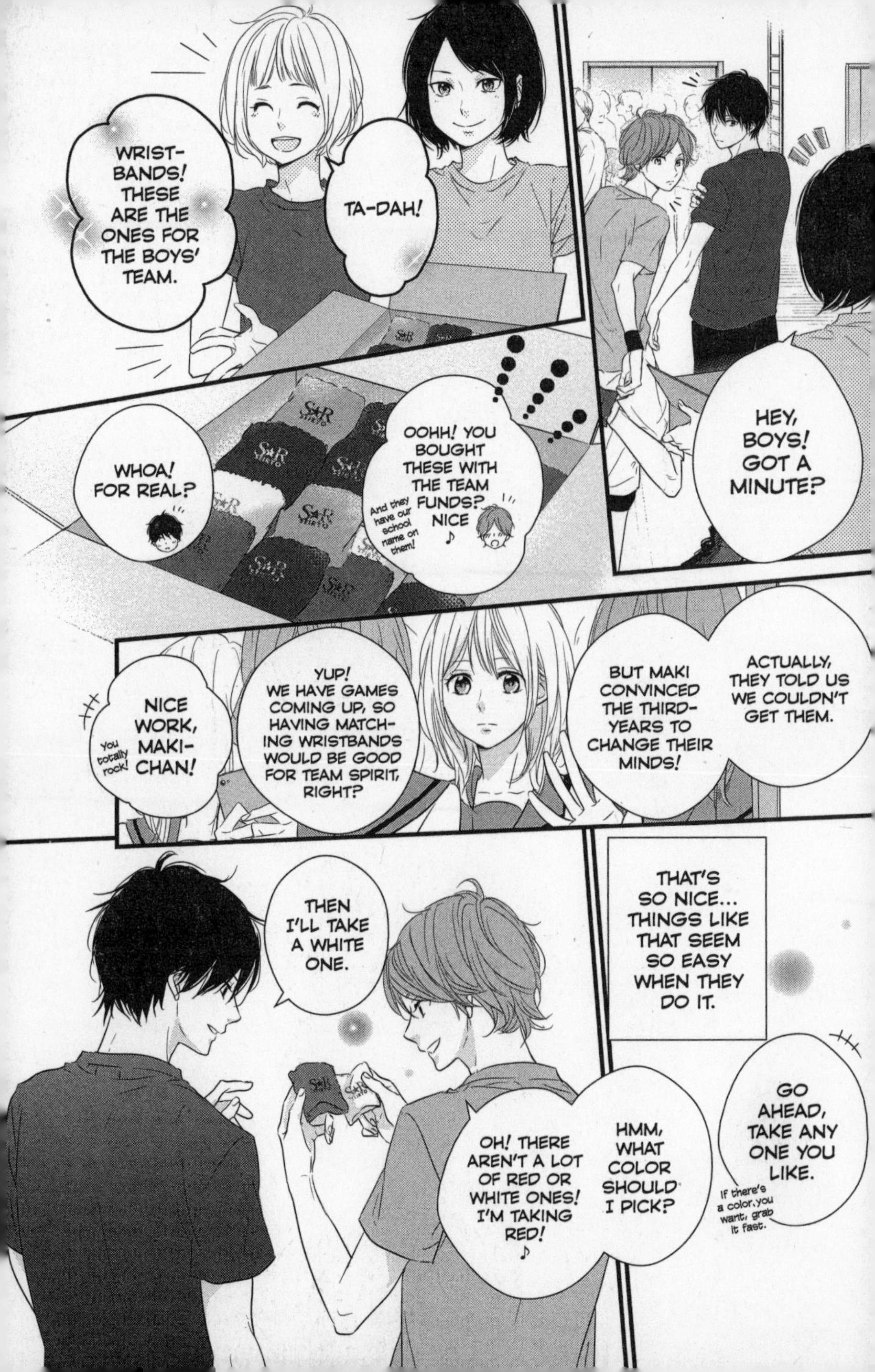
HEY, BOYS! GOT A MINUTE?
TA-DAH!
WRIST-BANDS! THESE ARE THE ONES FOR THE BOYS' TEAM.
OOHH! YOU BOUGHT THESE WITH THE TEAM FUNDS? NICE ♪
And they have our school name on them!
WHOA! FOR REAL?
ACTUALLY, THEY TOLD US WE COULDN'T GET THEM.
BUT MAKI CONVINCED THE THIRD-YEARS TO CHANGE THEIR MINDS!
YUP! WE HAVE GAMES COMING UP, SO HAVING MATCHING WRISTBANDS WOULD BE GOOD FOR TEAM SPIRIT, RIGHT?
NICE WORK, MAKI-CHAN!
You totally rock!
THAT'S SO NICE... THINGS LIKE THAT SEEM SO EASY WHEN THEY DO IT.
GO AHEAD, TAKE ANY ONE YOU LIKE.
If there's a color, you want, grab it fast.
HMM, WHAT COLOR SHOULD I PICK?
OH! THERE AREN'T A LOT OF RED OR WHITE ONES! I'M TAKING RED! ♪
THEN I'LL TAKE A WHITE ONE.

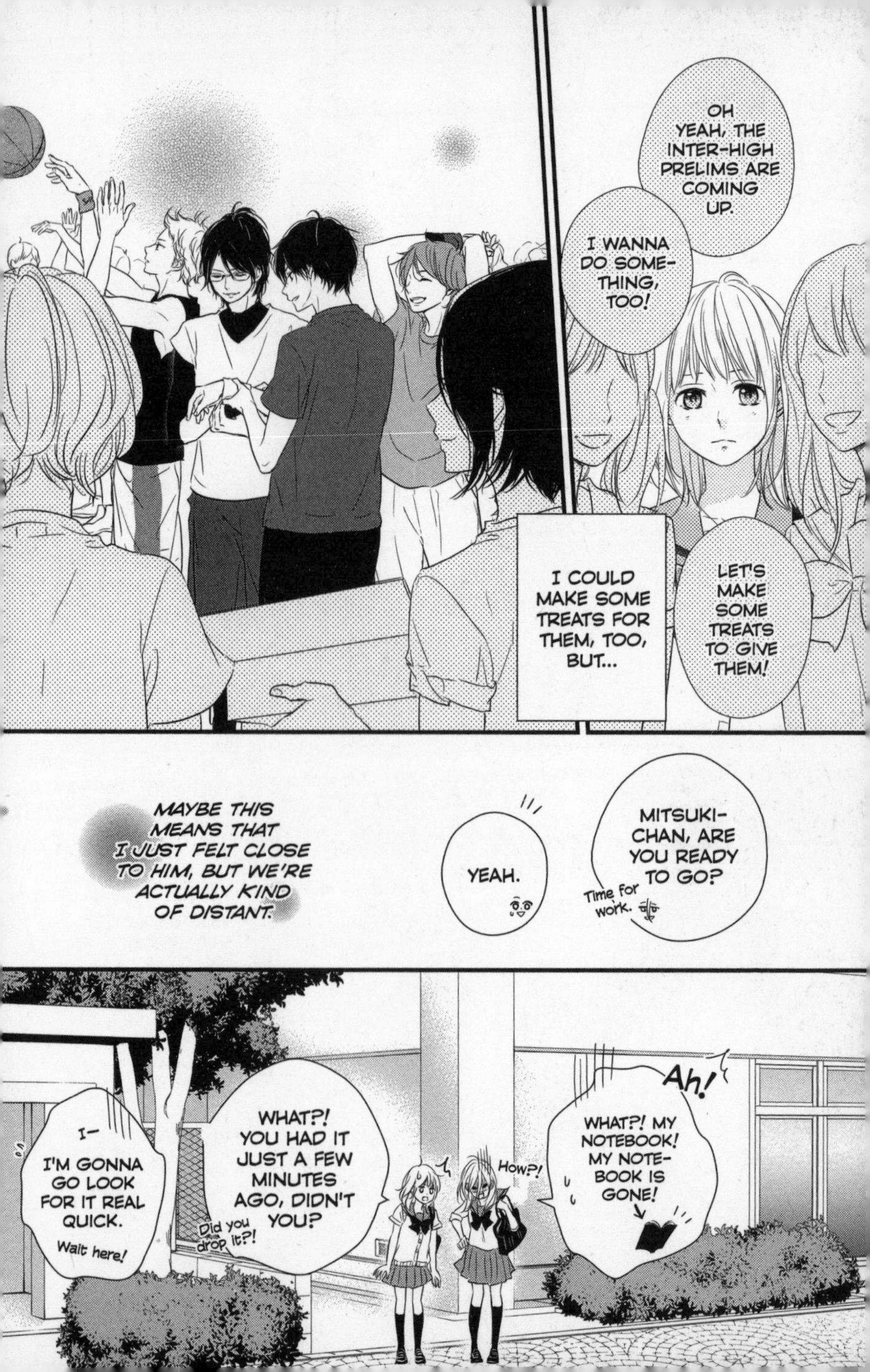
OH YEAH, THE INTER-HIGH PRELIMS ARE COMING UP.
I WANNA DO SOMETHING, TOO!
LET'S MAKE SOME TREATS TO GIVE THEM!
I COULD MAKE SOME TREATS FOR THEM, TOO, BUT...
MITSUKI-CHAN, ARE YOU READY TO GO?
Time for work.
YEAH.
MAYBE THIS MEANS THAT I JUST FELT CLOSE TO HIM, BUT WE'RE ACTUALLY KIND OF DISTANT.
Ah!
WHAT?! MY NOTEBOOK! MY NOTEBOOK IS GONE!
How?!
WHAT?! YOU HAD IT JUST A FEW MINUTES AGO, DIDN'T YOU?
Did you drop it?!
I—
I'M GONNA GO LOOK FOR IT REAL QUICK.
Wait here!

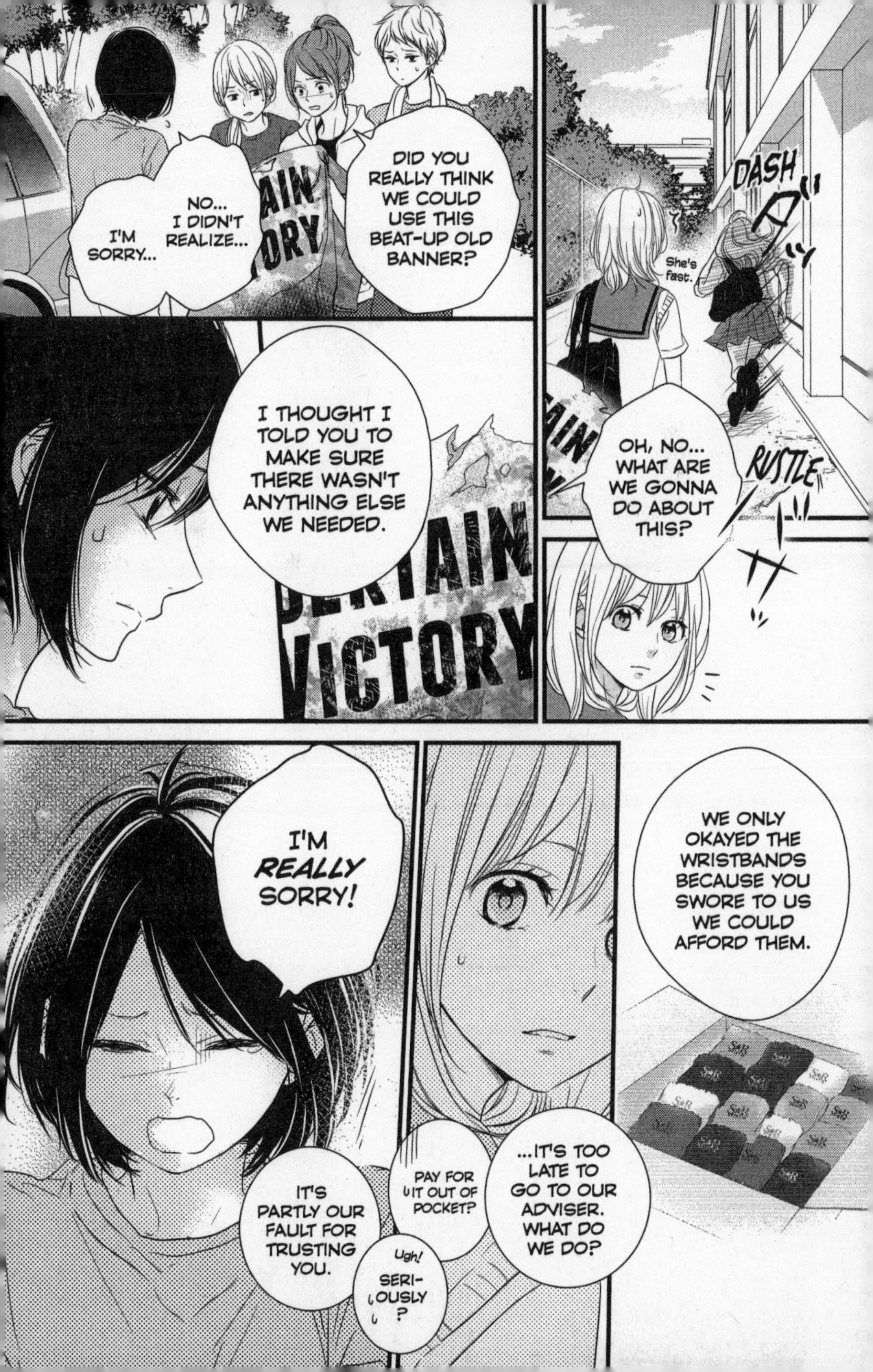
DASH
She's fast.
RUSTLE
DID YOU REALLY THINK WE COULD USE THIS BEAT-UP OLD BANNER?
NO... I DIDN'T REALIZE...
I'M SORRY...
I THOUGHT I TOLD YOU TO MAKE SURE THERE WASN'T ANYTHING ELSE WE NEEDED.
CERTAIN VICTORY
OH, NO... WHAT ARE WE GONNA DO ABOUT THIS?
WE ONLY OKAYED THE WRISTBANDS BECAUSE YOU SWORE TO US WE COULD AFFORD THEM.
...IT'S TOO LATE TO GO TO OUR ADVISER. WHAT DO WE DO?
PAY FOR IT OUT OF POCKET?
Ugh! SERI-OUSLY?
IT'S PARTLY OUR FAULT FOR TRUSTING YOU.
I'M *REALLY* SORRY!

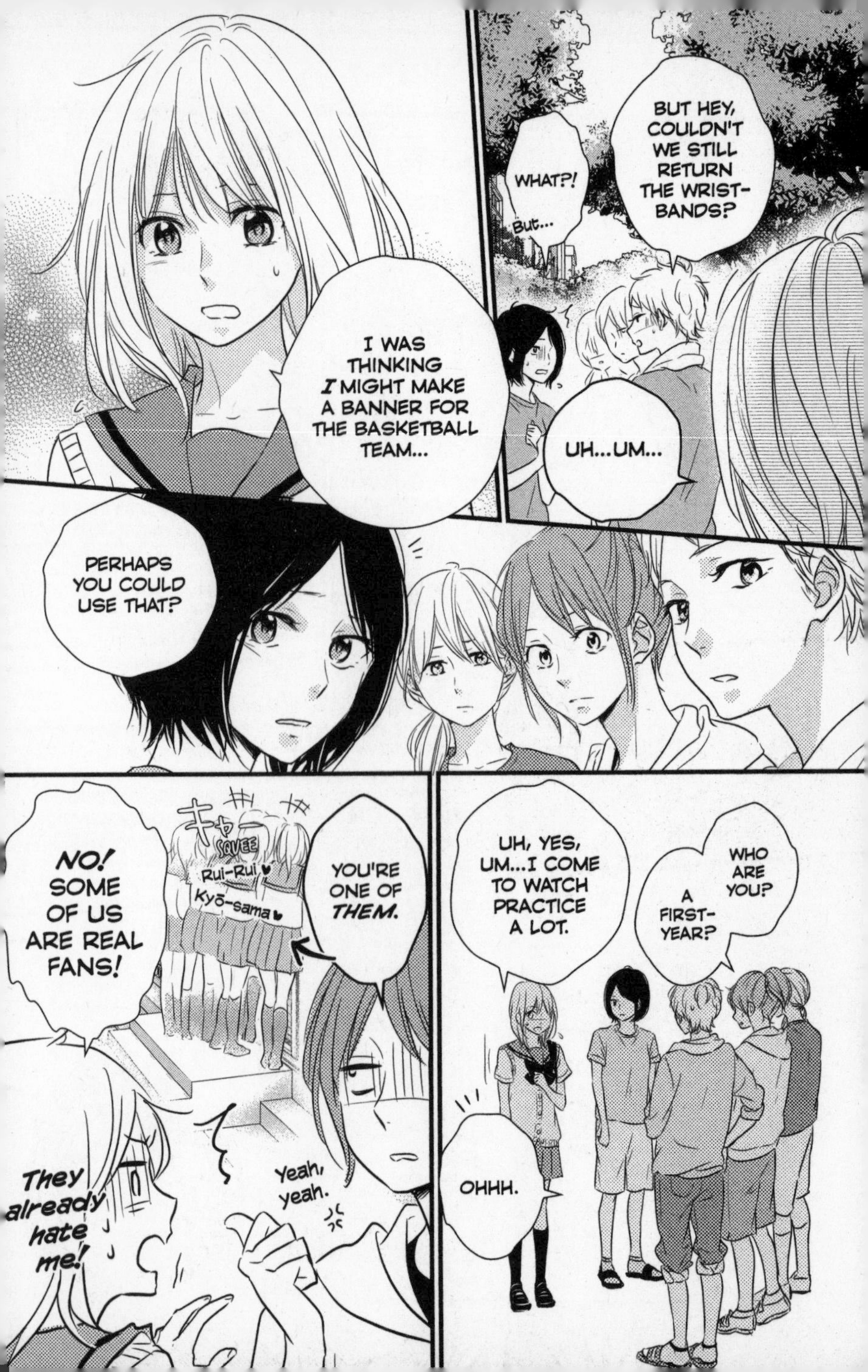
BUT HEY, COULDN'T WE STILL RETURN THE WRIST-BANDS?
WHAT?!
But...
UH...UM...
I WAS THINKING *I* MIGHT MAKE A BANNER FOR THE BASKETBALL TEAM...
PERHAPS YOU COULD USE THAT?
WHO ARE YOU?
A FIRST-YEAR?
UH, YES, UM...I COME TO WATCH PRACTICE A LOT.
OHHH.
YOU'RE ONE OF *THEM*.
キャー
SQUEE
Rui-Rui
Kyō-sama
NO! SOME OF US ARE REAL FANS!
Yeah, yeah.
They already hate me!

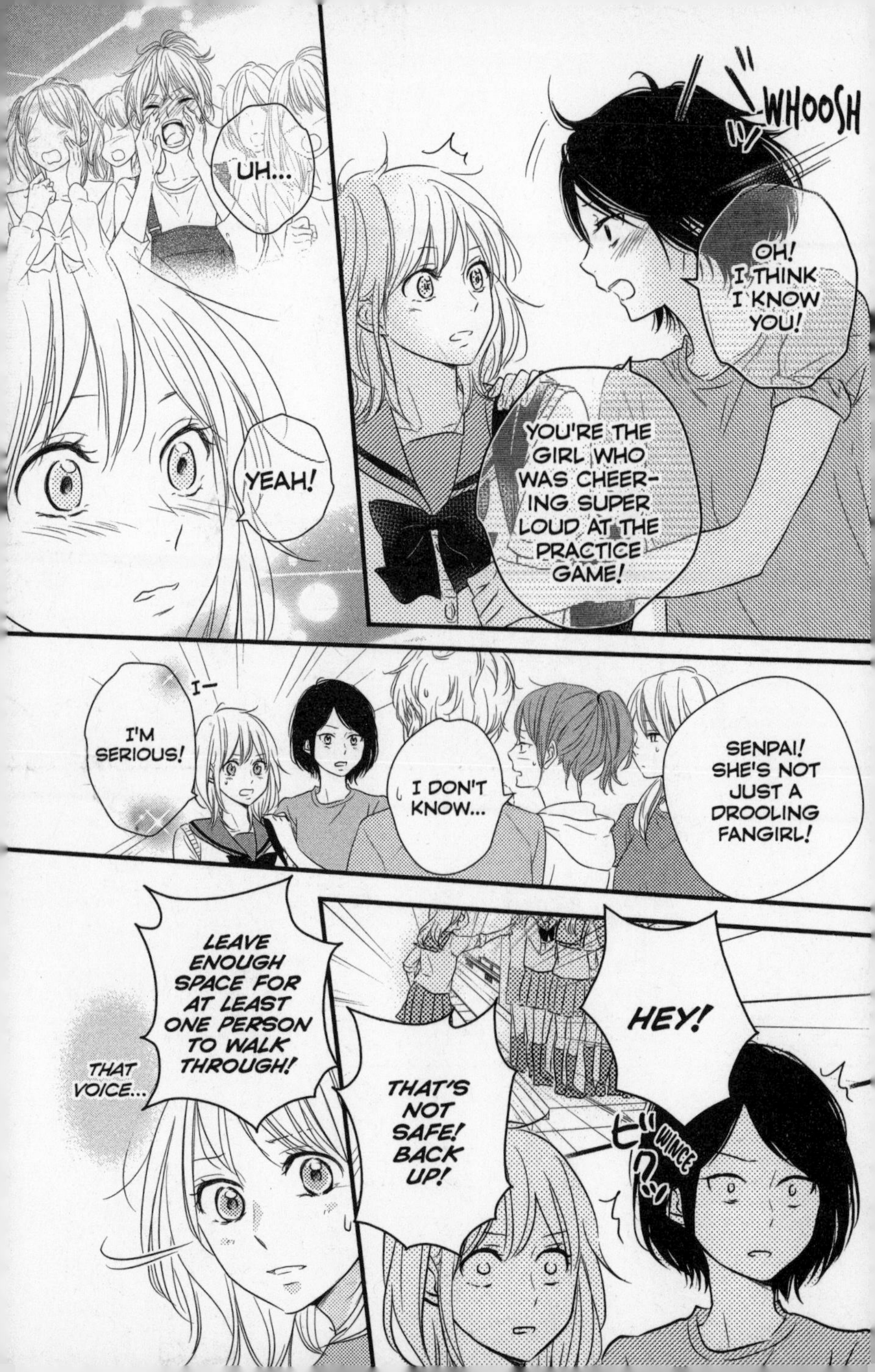
WHOOSH
OH! I THINK I KNOW YOU!
YOU'RE THE GIRL WHO WAS CHEER-ING SUPER LOUD AT THE PRACTICE GAME!
UH...
YEAH!
SENPAI! SHE'S NOT JUST A DROOLING FANGIRL!
I DON'T KNOW...
I—
I'M SERIOUS!
HEY!
WINCE
THAT'S NOT SAFE! BACK UP!
LEAVE ENOUGH SPACE FOR AT LEAST ONE PERSON TO WALK THROUGH!
THAT VOICE...

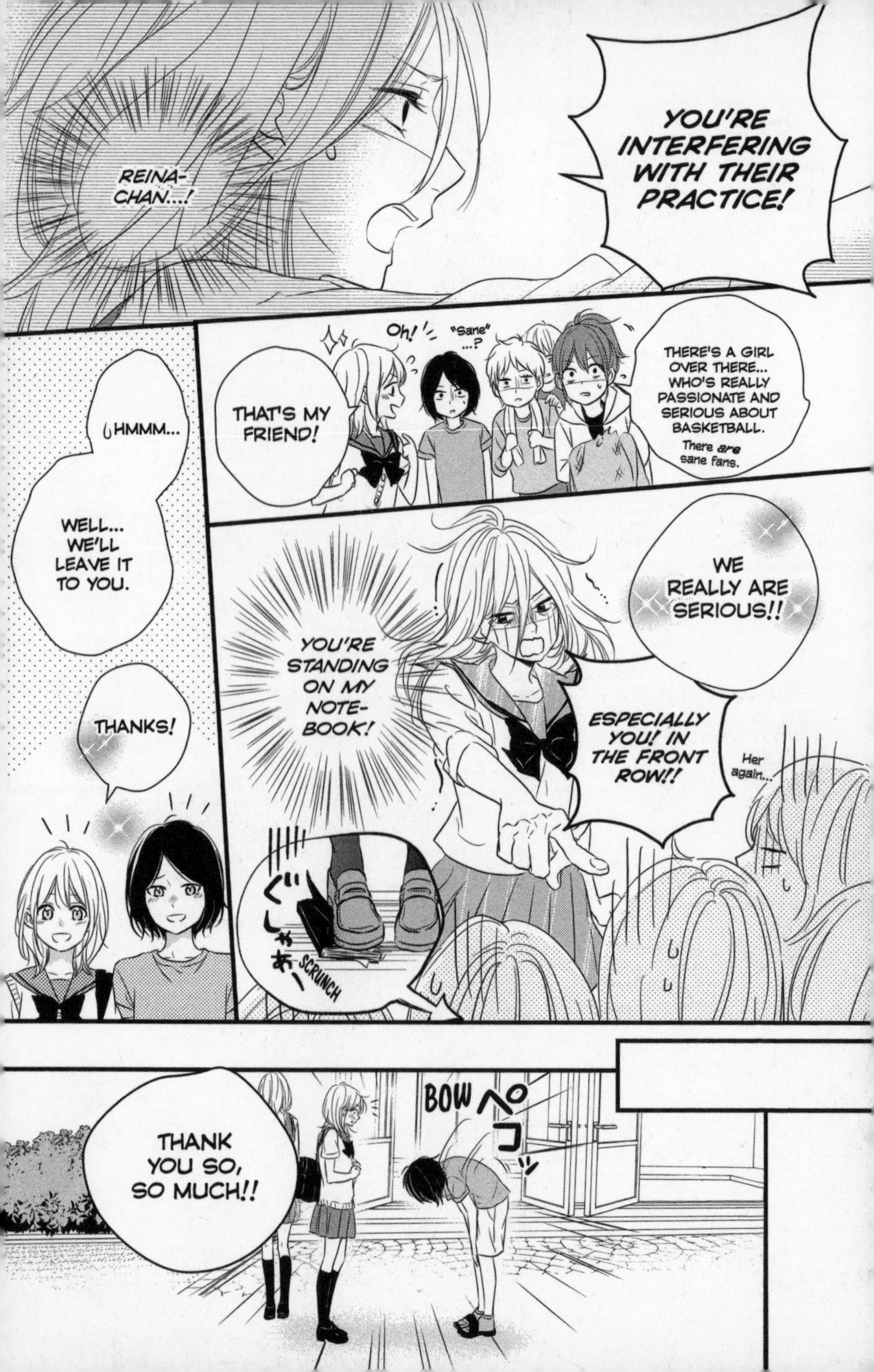
YOU'RE INTERFERING WITH THEIR PRACTICE!
REINA-CHAN...!
THERE'S A GIRL OVER THERE... WHO'S REALLY PASSIONATE AND SERIOUS ABOUT BASKETBALL.
There are sane fans.
"Sane" ...?
Oh!
THAT'S MY FRIEND!
WE REALLY ARE SERIOUS!!
ESPECIALLY YOU! IN THE FRONT ROW!!
Her again...
YOU'RE STANDING ON MY NOTE-BOOK!
ぐしゃあ
SCRUNCH
HMMM...
WELL... WE'LL LEAVE IT TO YOU.
THANKS!
ペコッ
BOW
THANK YOU SO, SO MUCH!!

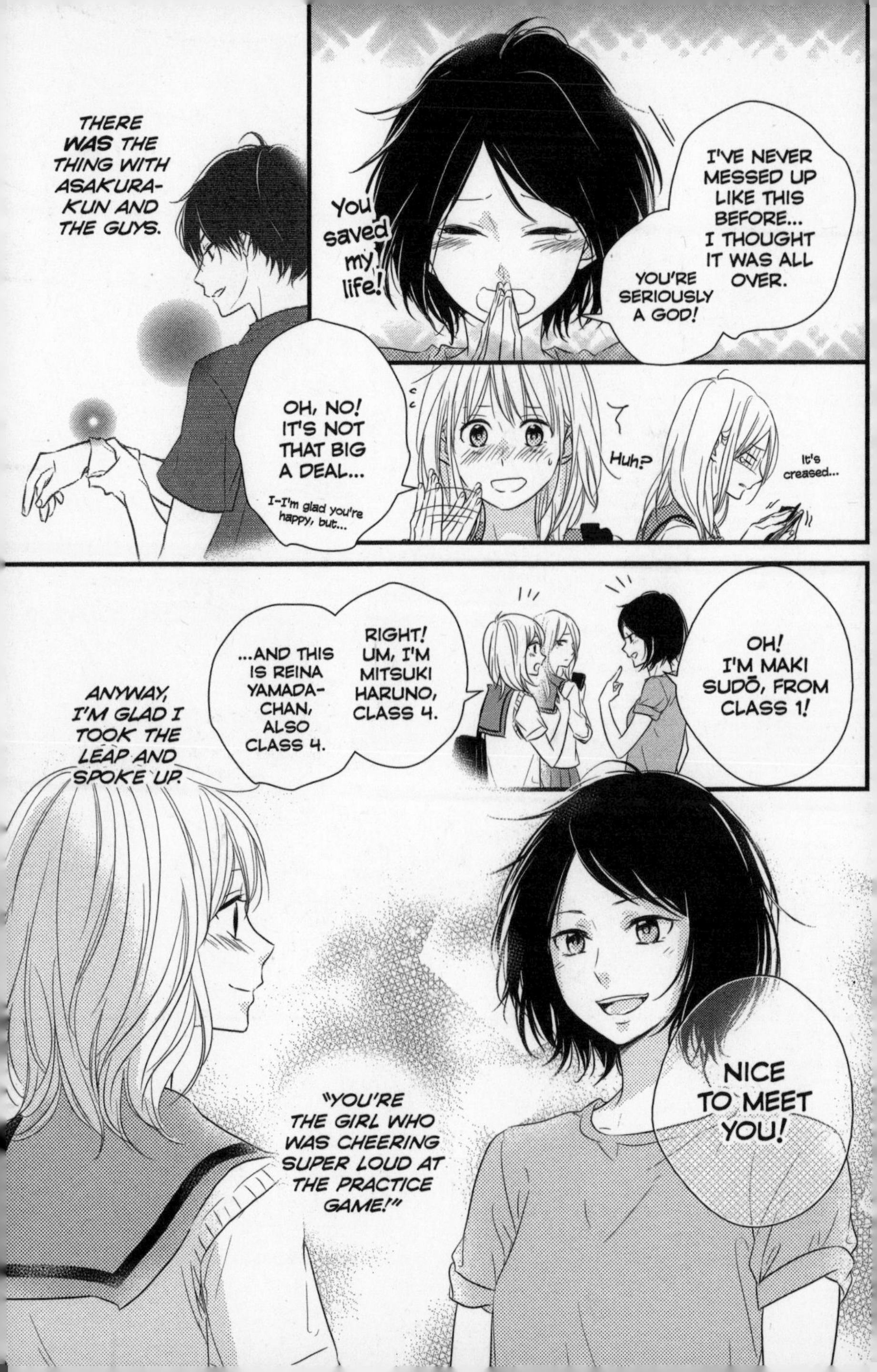
I'VE NEVER MESSED UP LIKE THIS BEFORE... I THOUGHT IT WAS ALL OVER.
YOU'RE SERIOUSLY A GOD!
You saved my life!
It's creased...
Huh?
OH, NO! IT'S NOT THAT BIG A DEAL...
I-I'm glad you're happy, but...
THERE WAS THE THING WITH ASAKURA-KUN AND THE GUYS.
OH! I'M MAKI SUDŌ, FROM CLASS 1!
RIGHT! UM, I'M MITSUKI HARUNO, CLASS 4.
...AND THIS IS REINA YAMADA-CHAN, ALSO CLASS 4.
ANYWAY, I'M GLAD I TOOK THE LEAP AND SPOKE UP.
NICE TO MEET YOU!
"YOU'RE THE GIRL WHO WAS CHEERING SUPER LOUD AT THE PRACTICE GAME!"

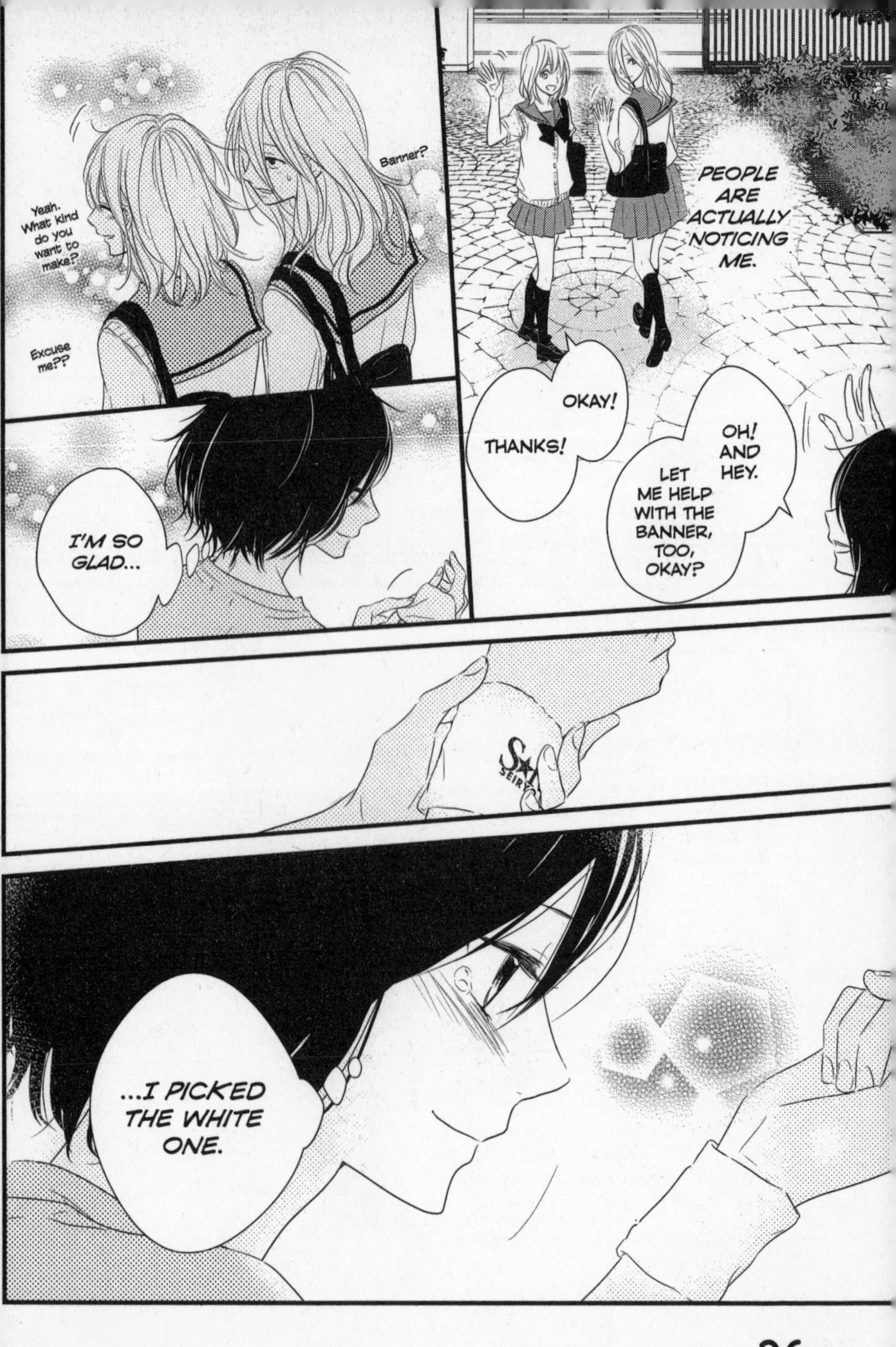
PEOPLE ARE ACTUALLY NOTICING ME.
OH! AND HEY. LET ME HELP WITH THE BANNER, TOO, OKAY?
OKAY! THANKS!
Banner?
Yeah. What kind do you want to make?
Excuse me??
I'M SO GLAD...
...I PICKED THE WHITE ONE.

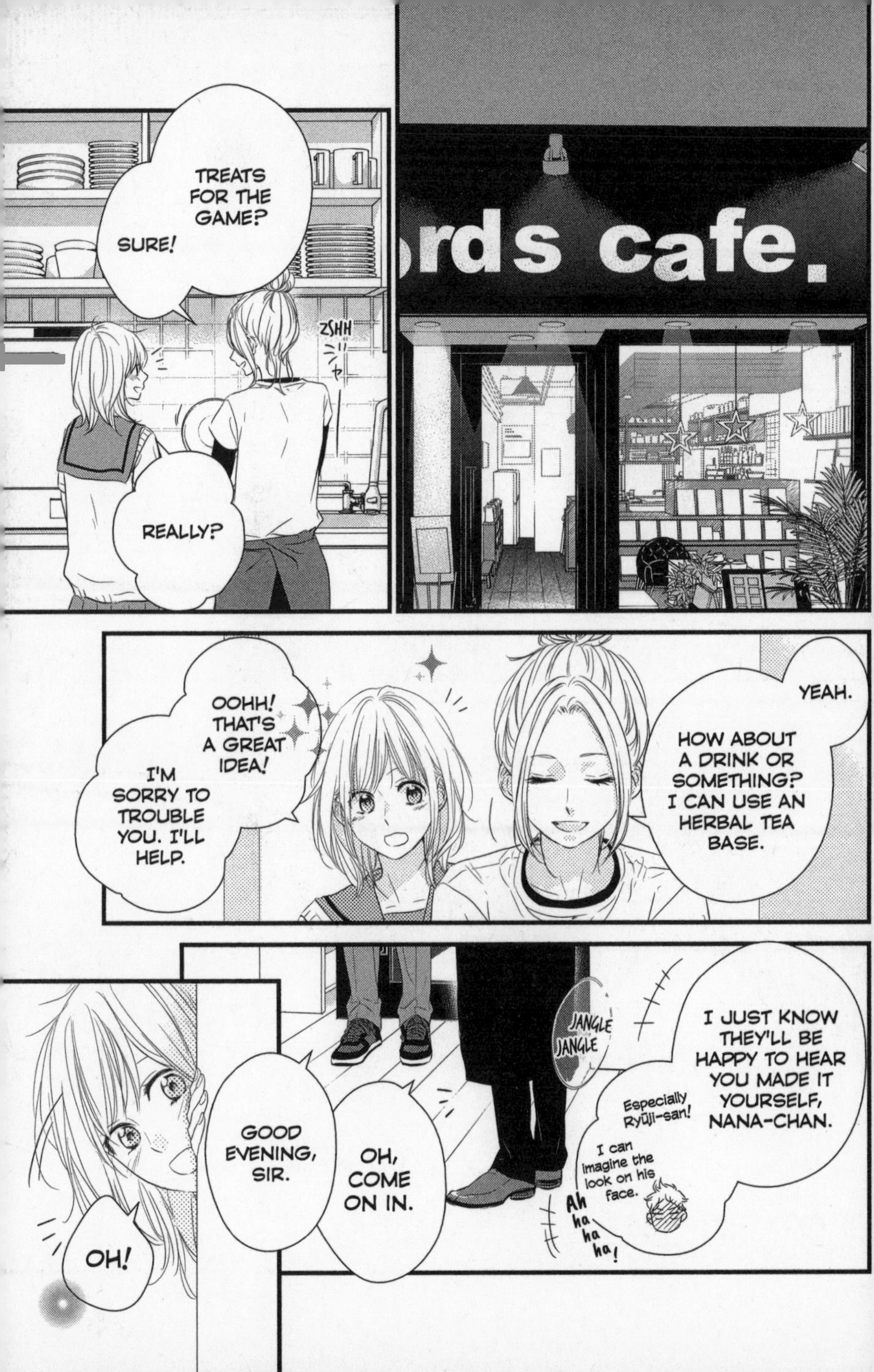
ords cafe.
TREATS FOR THE GAME?
SURE!
ZSHH
REALLY?
YEAH.
HOW ABOUT A DRINK OR SOMETHING? I CAN USE AN HERBAL TEA BASE.
OOHH! THAT'S A GREAT IDEA!
I'M SORRY TO TROUBLE YOU. I'LL HELP.
I JUST KNOW THEY'LL BE HAPPY TO HEAR YOU MADE IT YOURSELF, NANA-CHAN.
Especially Ryūji-san!
I can imagine the look on his face.
Ah ha ha ha!
JANGLE JANGLE
OH, COME ON IN.
GOOD EVENING, SIR.
OH!

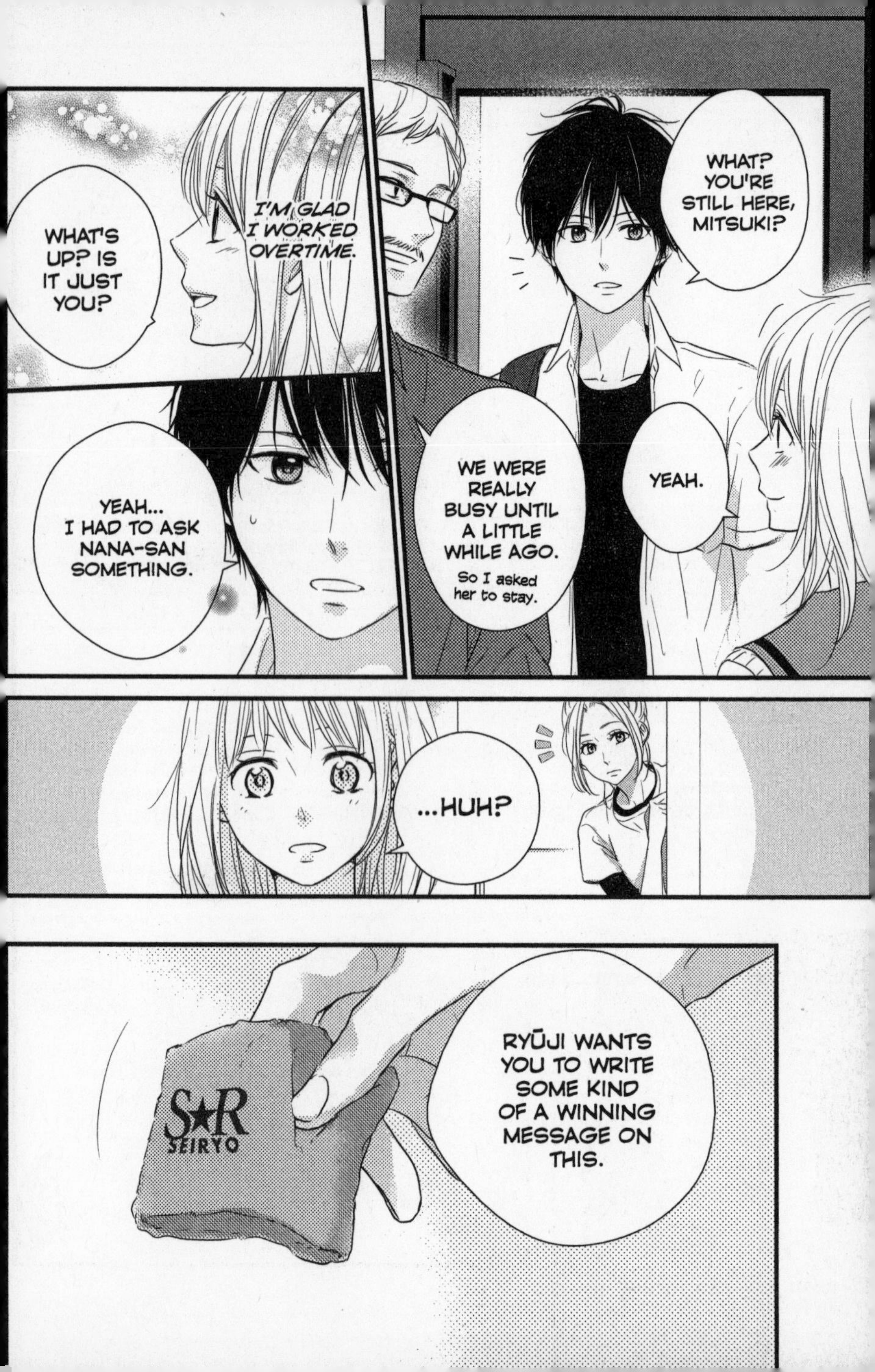

WHAT? YOU'RE STILL HERE, MITSUKI?
YEAH.
WE WERE REALLY BUSY UNTIL A LITTLE WHILE AGO.
So I asked her to stay.
WHAT'S UP? IS IT JUST YOU?
I'M GLAD I WORKED OVERTIME.
YEAH... I HAD TO ASK NANA-SAN SOMETHING.
...HUH?
RYŪJI WANTS YOU TO WRITE SOME KIND OF A WINNING MESSAGE ON THIS.
S★R SEIRYO

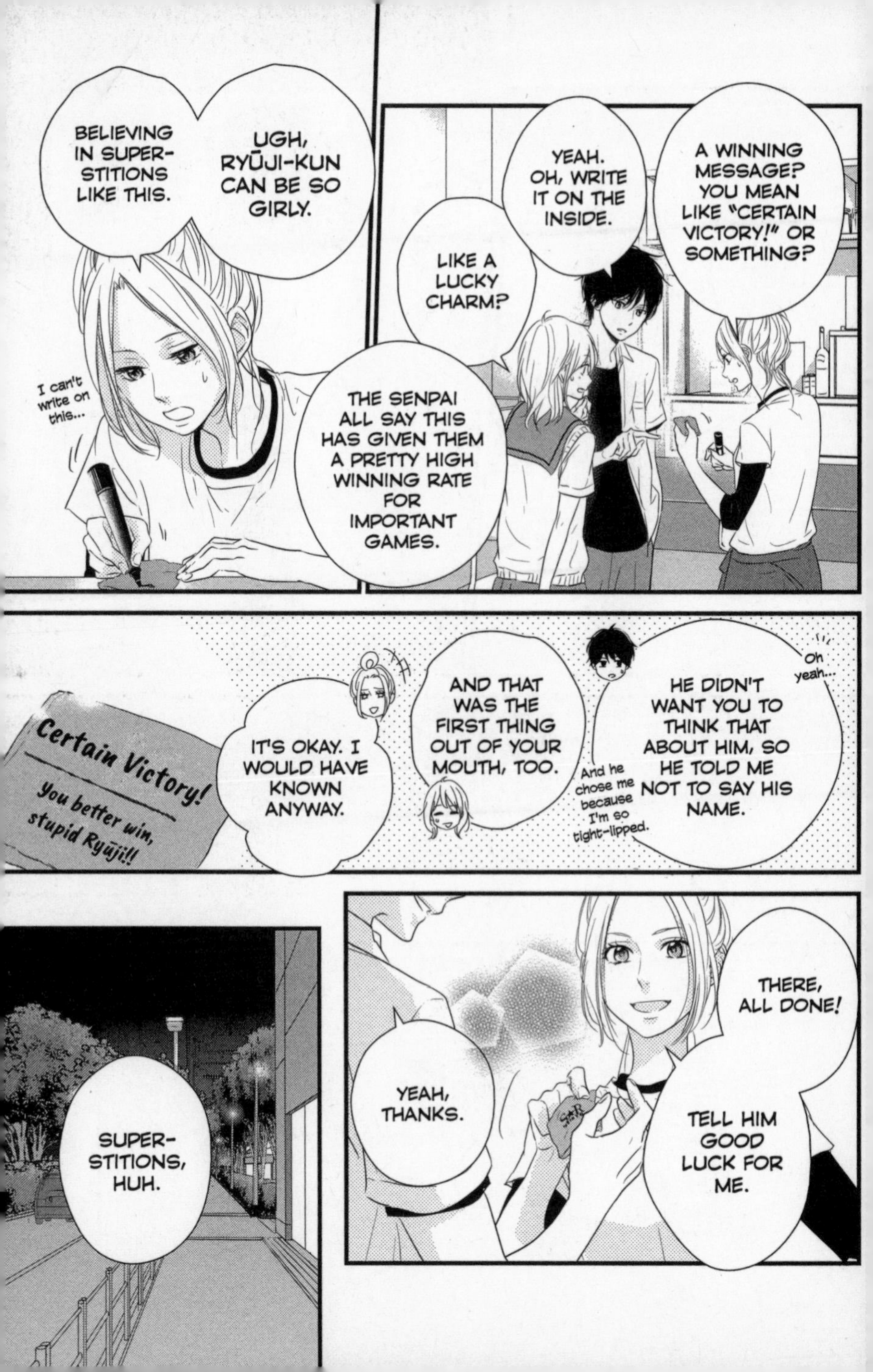
A WINNING MESSAGE? YOU MEAN LIKE "CERTAIN VICTORY!" OR SOMETHING?
YEAH. OH, WRITE IT ON THE INSIDE.
LIKE A LUCKY CHARM?
THE SENPAI ALL SAY THIS HAS GIVEN THEM A PRETTY HIGH WINNING RATE FOR IMPORTANT GAMES.
UGH, RYŪJI-KUN CAN BE SO GIRLY.
BELIEVING IN SUPER-STITIONS LIKE THIS.
I can't write on this...
Oh yeah...
HE DIDN'T WANT YOU TO THINK THAT ABOUT HIM, SO HE TOLD ME NOT TO SAY HIS NAME.
And he chose me because I'm so tight-lipped.
AND THAT WAS THE FIRST THING OUT OF YOUR MOUTH, TOO.
IT'S OKAY. I WOULD HAVE KNOWN ANYWAY.
Certain Victory!
You better win, stupid Ryūji!!
THERE, ALL DONE!
TELL HIM GOOD LUCK FOR ME.
YEAH, THANKS.
SUPER-STITIONS, HUH.

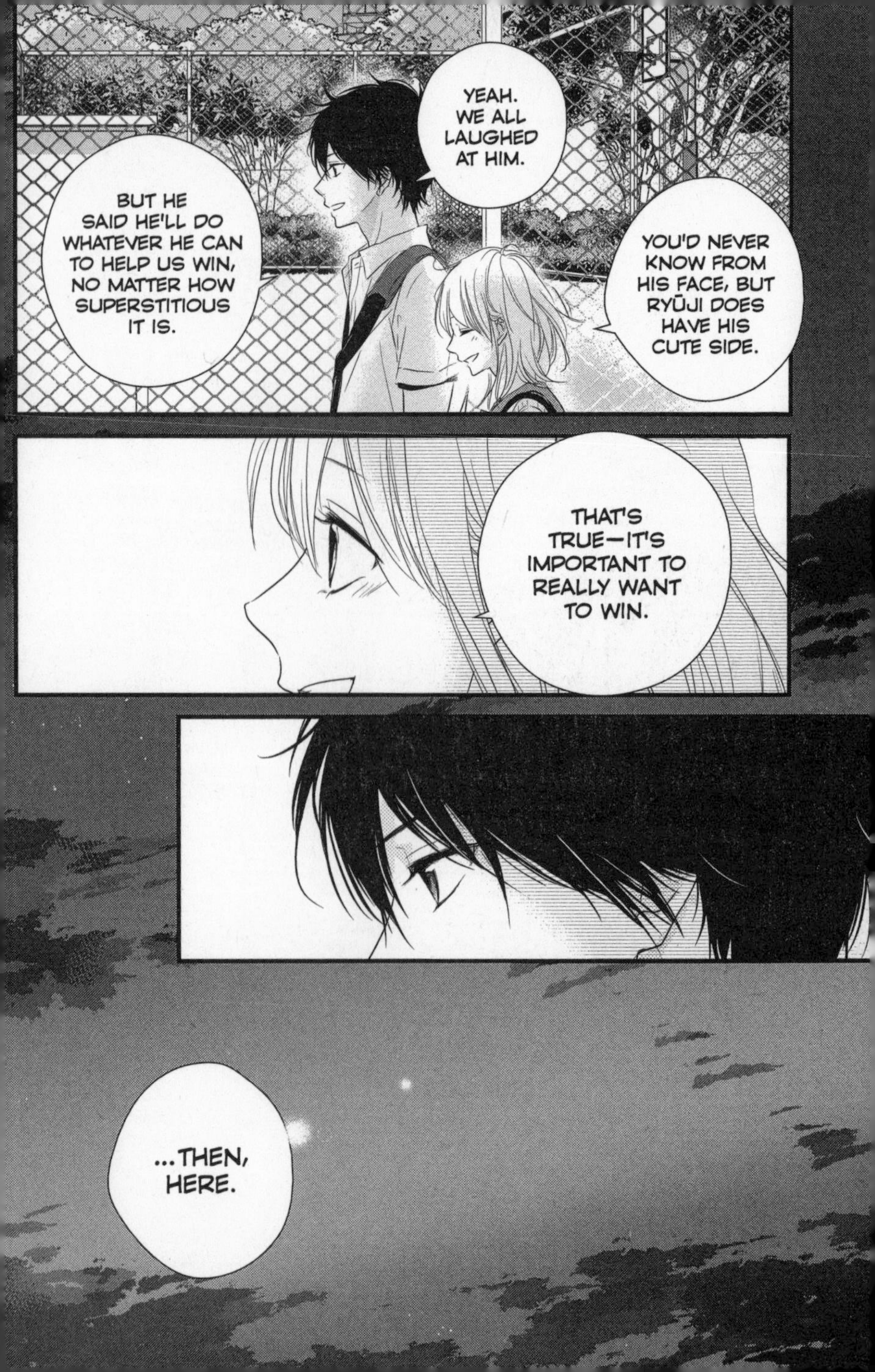
YEAH. WE ALL LAUGHED AT HIM.
BUT HE SAID HE'LL DO WHATEVER HE CAN TO HELP US WIN, NO MATTER HOW SUPERSTITIOUS IT IS.
YOU'D NEVER KNOW FROM HIS FACE, BUT RYŪJI DOES HAVE HIS CUTE SIDE.
THAT'S TRUE—IT'S IMPORTANT TO REALLY WANT TO WIN.
...THEN, HERE.

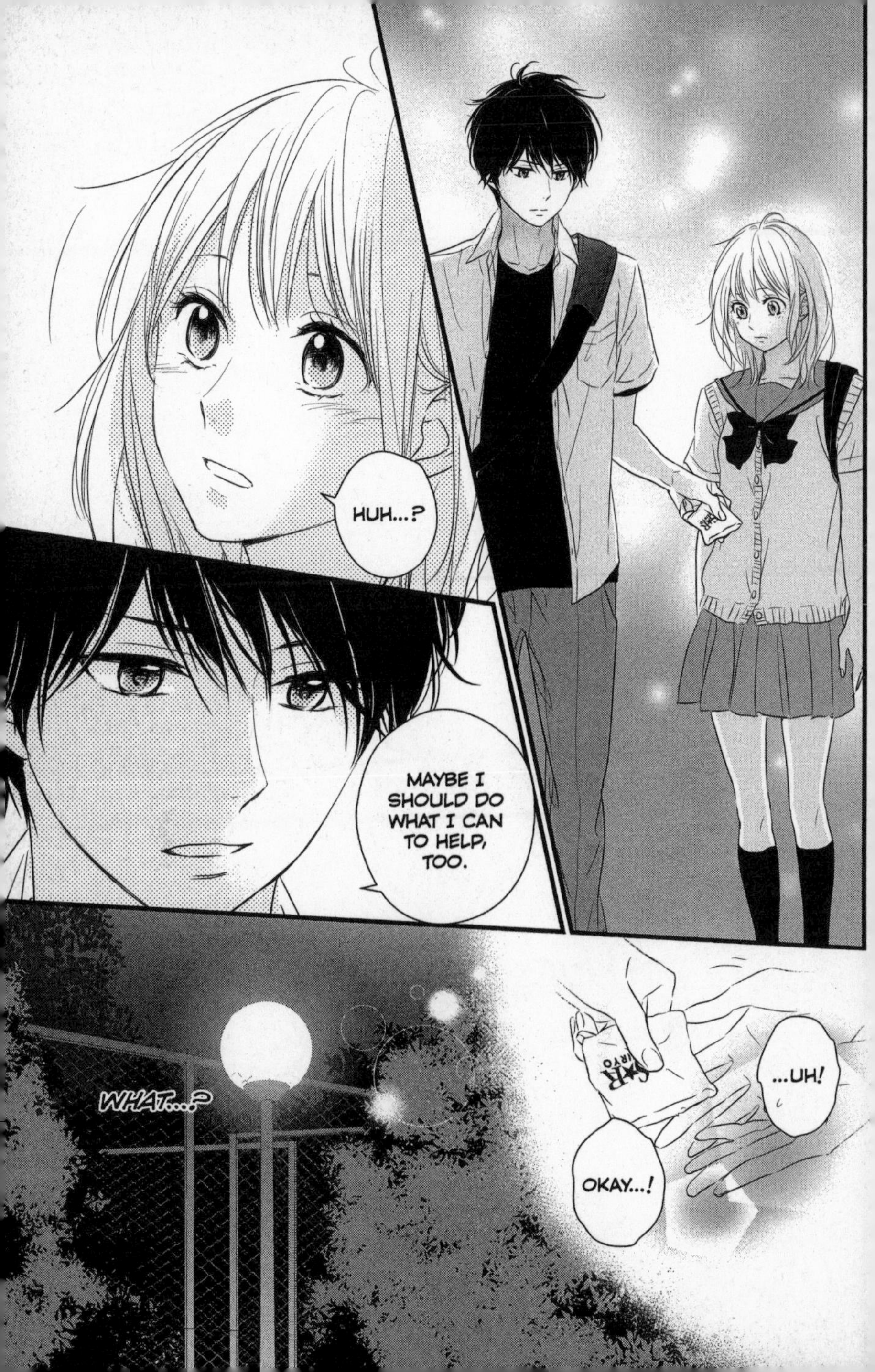
HUH...?
MAYBE I SHOULD DO WHAT I CAN TO HELP, TOO.
...UH!
OKAY...!
WHAT...?

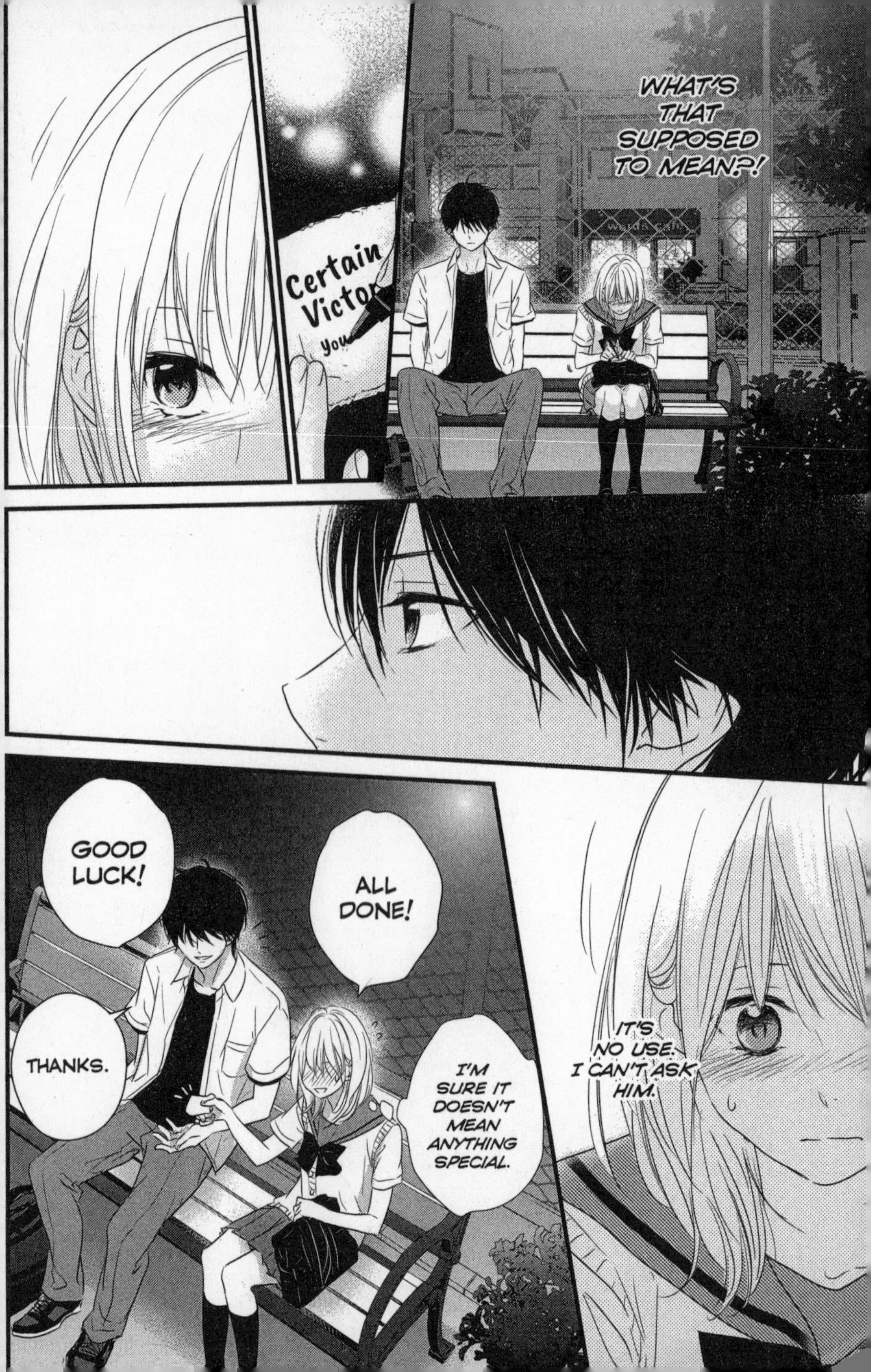
WHAT'S THAT SUPPOSED TO MEAN?!
Certain Victo
You
IT'S NO USE. I CAN'T ASK HIM.
ALL DONE!
GOOD LUCK!
I'M SURE IT DOESN'T MEAN ANYTHING SPECIAL.
THANKS.

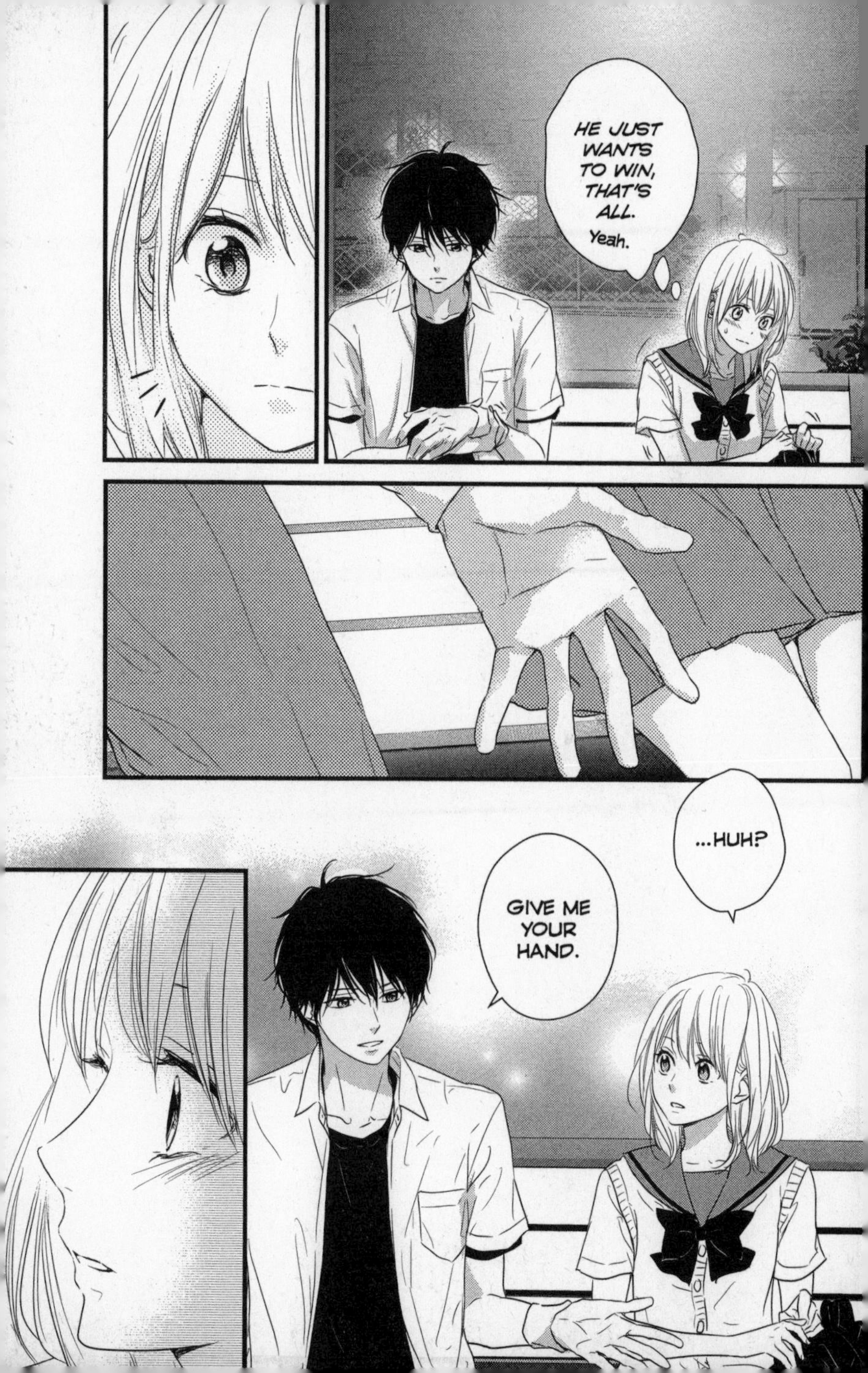
HE JUST WANTS TO WIN, THAT'S ALL.
Yeah.
...HUH?
GIVE ME YOUR HAND.

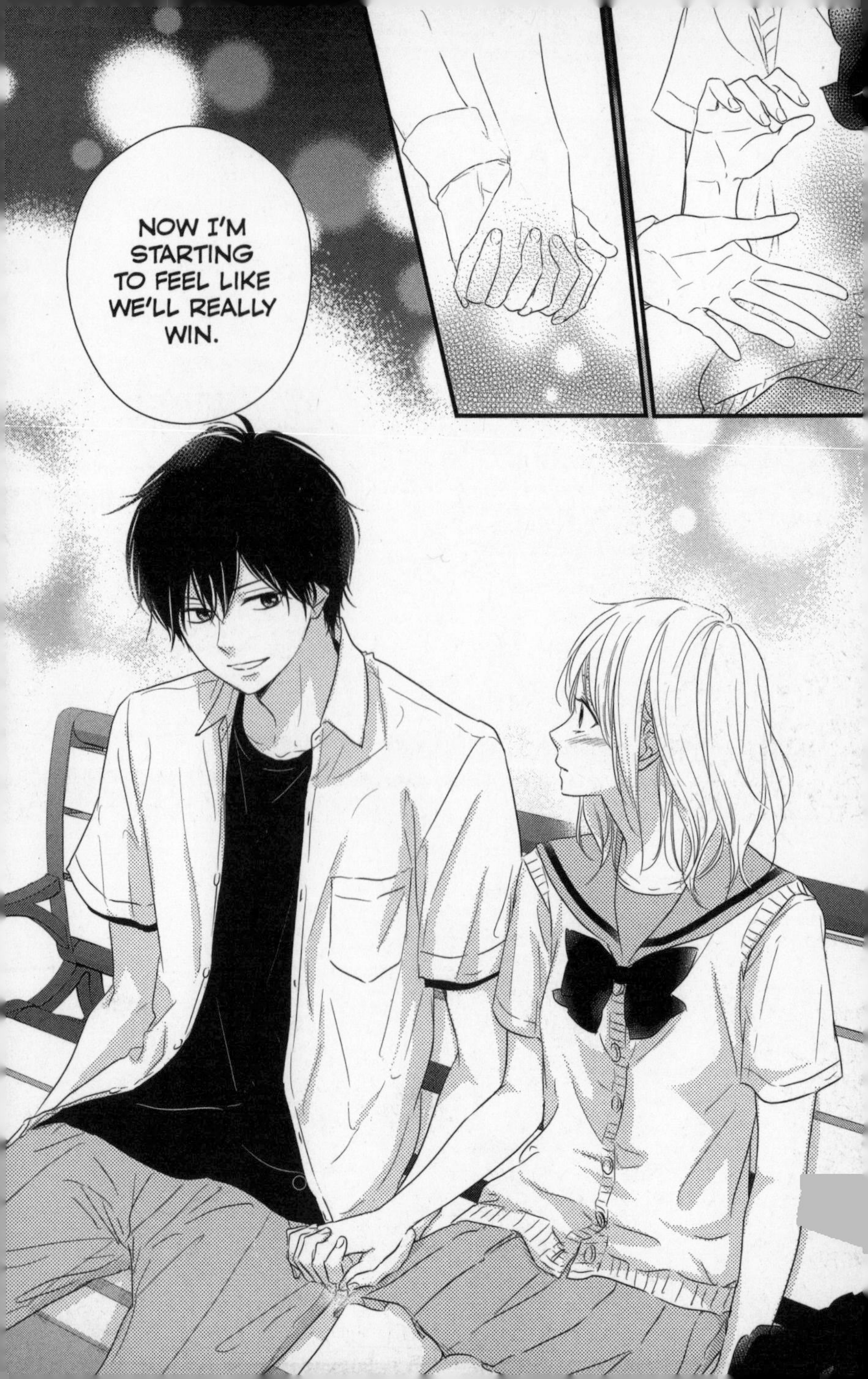
NOW I'M STARTING TO FEEL LIKE WE'LL REALLY WIN.

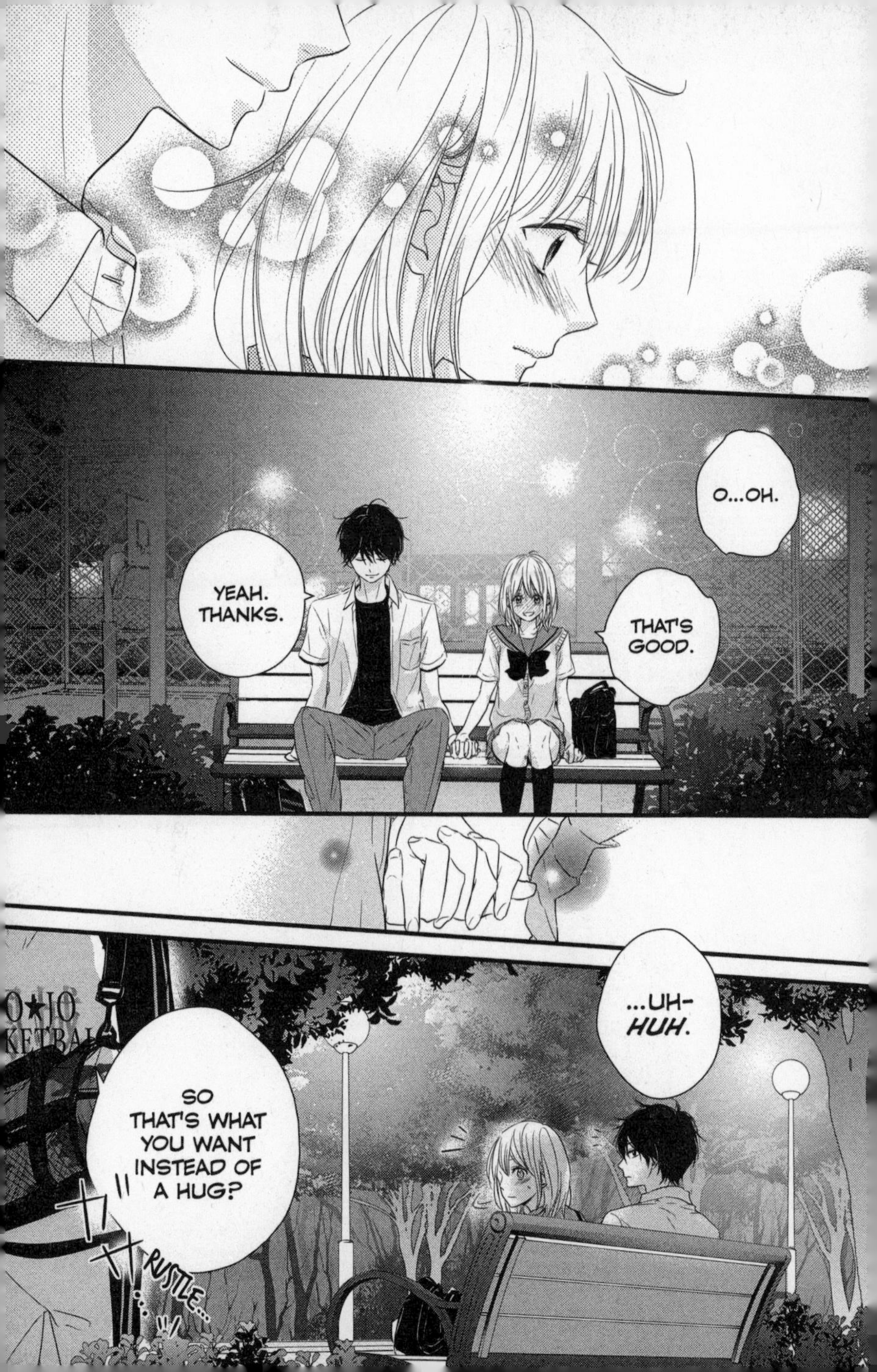
O...OH.
THAT'S GOOD.
YEAH. THANKS.
...UH-HUH.
SO THAT'S WHAT YOU WANT INSTEAD OF A HUG?
RUSTLE...

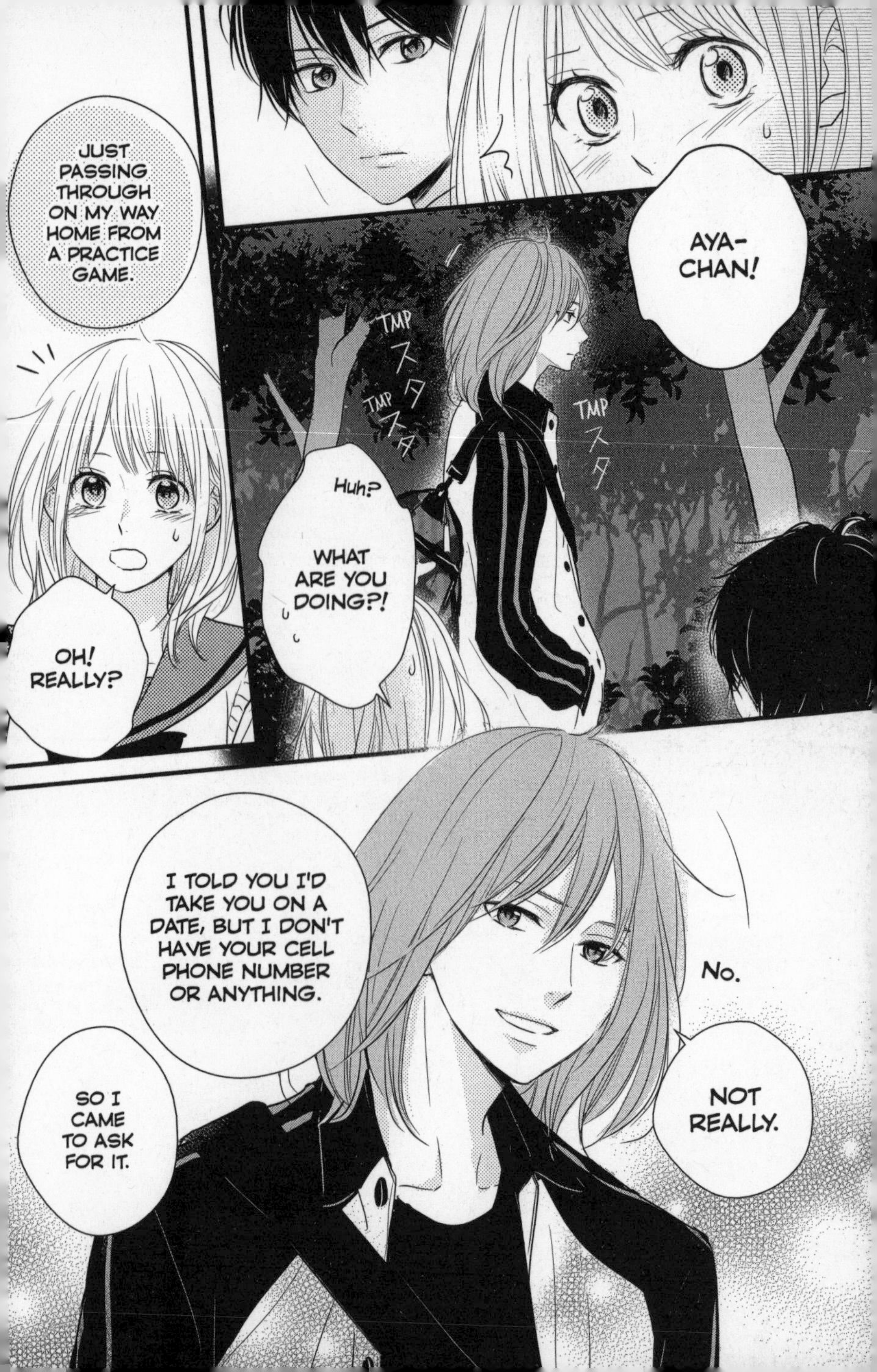
AYA-CHAN!
TMP スタ
TMP スタ
TMP スタ
Huh?
WHAT ARE YOU DOING?!
JUST PASSING THROUGH ON MY WAY HOME FROM A PRACTICE GAME.
OH! REALLY?
No.
NOT REALLY.
I TOLD YOU I'D TAKE YOU ON A DATE, BUT I DON'T HAVE YOUR CELL PHONE NUMBER OR ANYTHING.
SO I CAME TO ASK FOR IT.

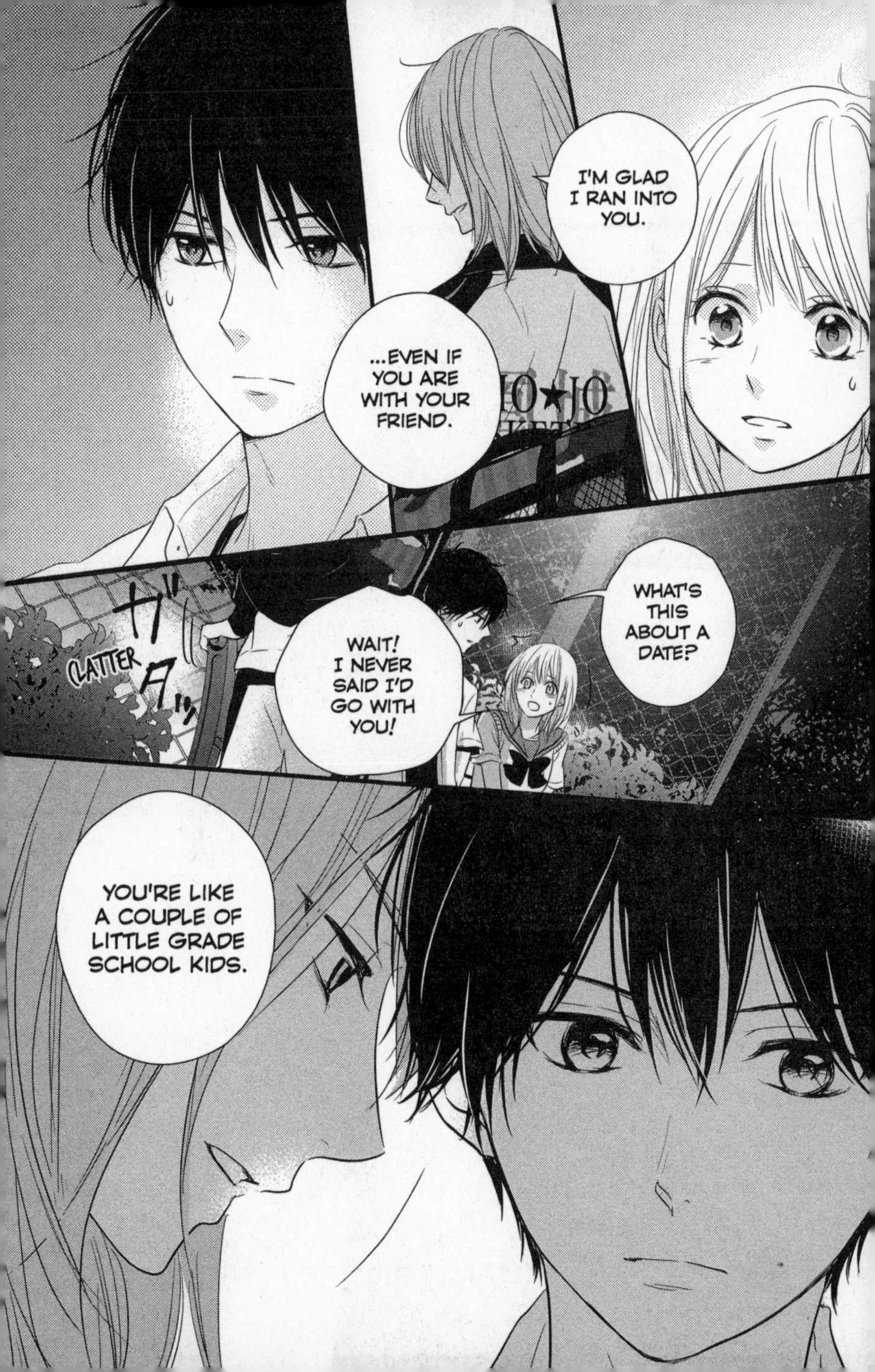
I'M GLAD I RAN INTO YOU.
...EVEN IF YOU ARE WITH YOUR FRIEND.
WHAT'S THIS ABOUT A DATE?
WAIT! I NEVER SAID I'D GO WITH YOU!
CLATTER
YOU'RE LIKE A COUPLE OF LITTLE GRADE SCHOOL KIDS.

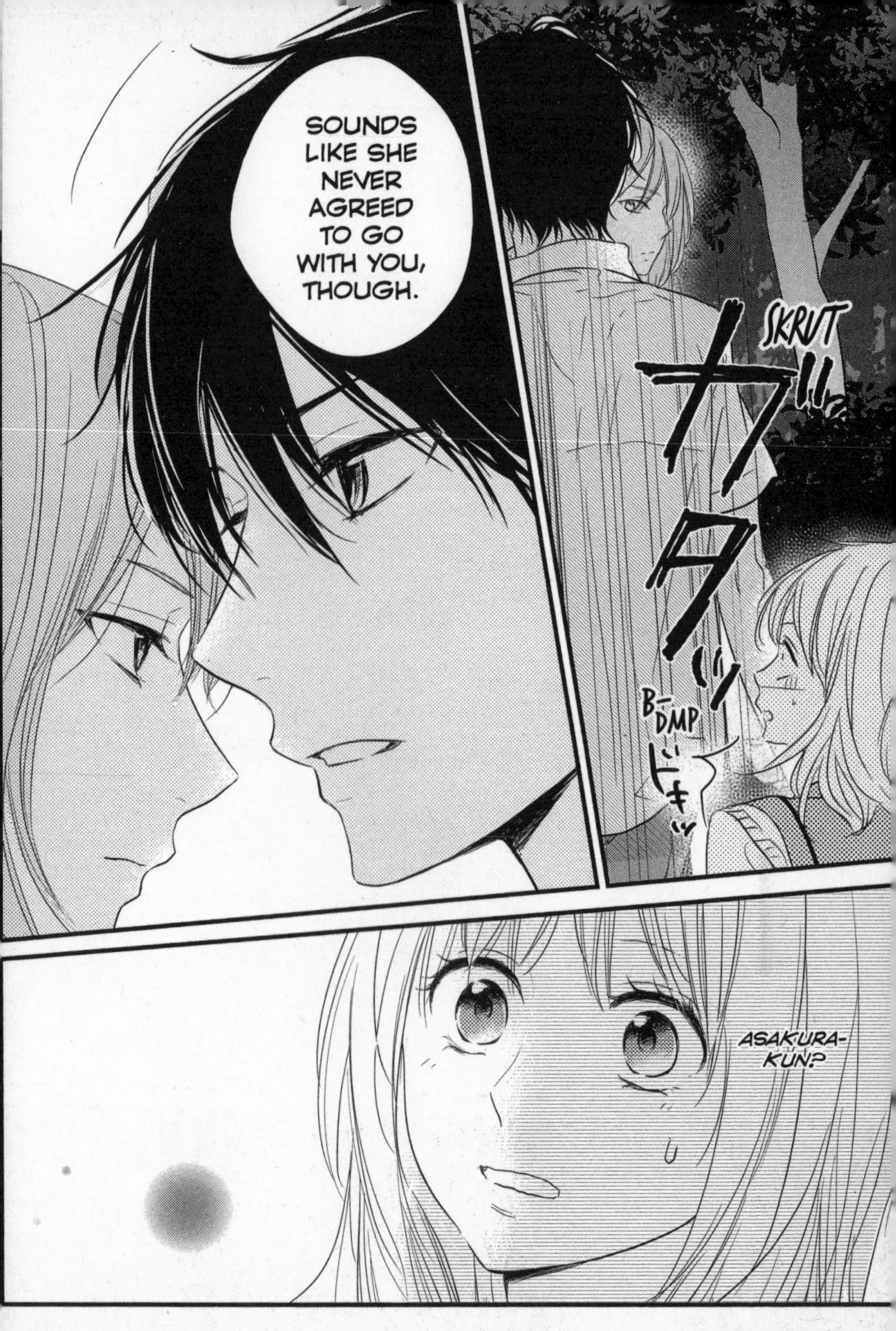
SKRUT
カタッ
B-DMP
ドキッ
SOUNDS LIKE SHE NEVER AGREED TO GO WITH YOU, THOUGH.
ASAKURA-KUN?

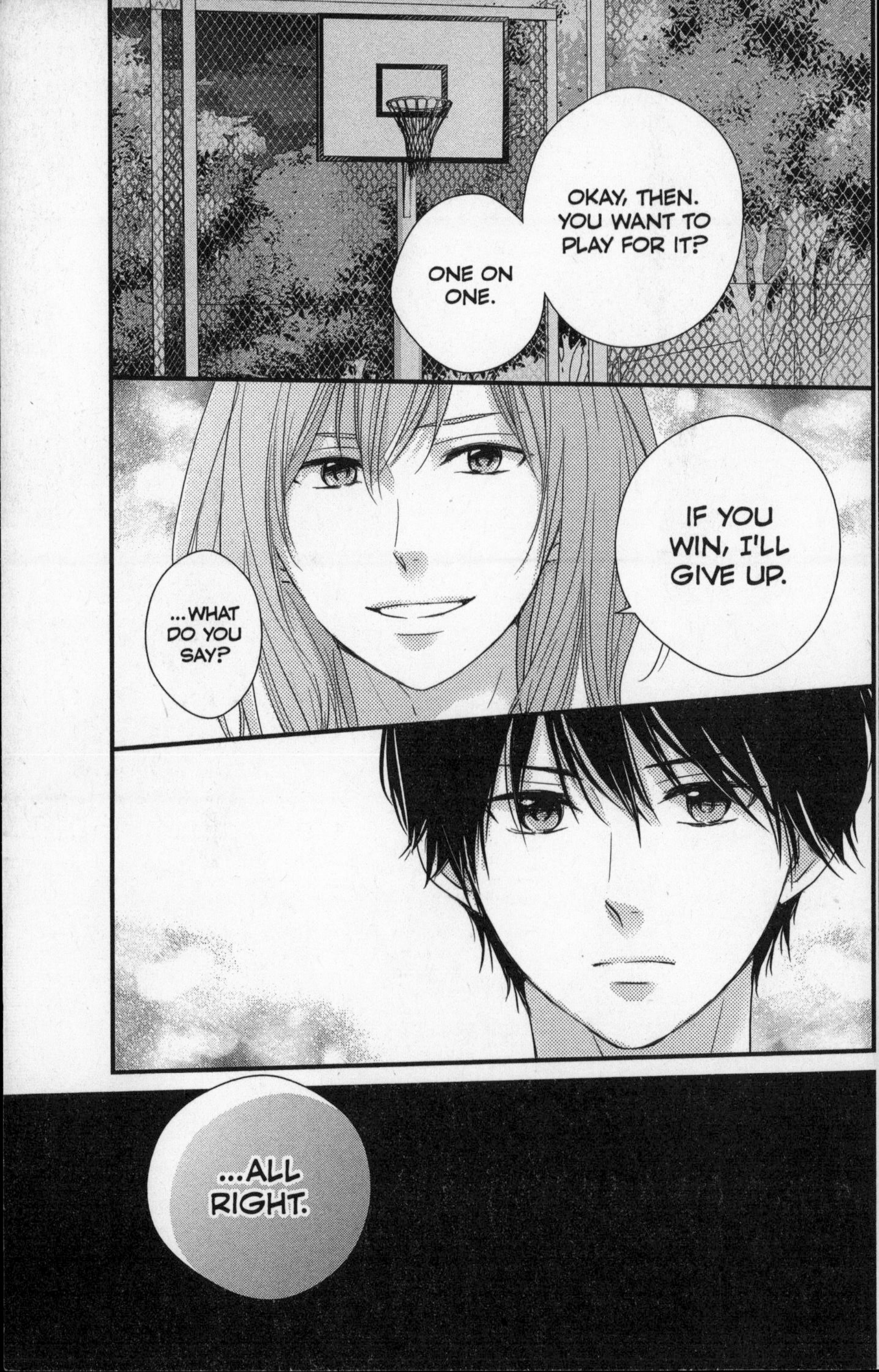
OKAY, THEN. YOU WANT TO PLAY FOR IT?
ONE ON ONE.
IF YOU WIN, I'LL GIVE UP.
...WHAT DO YOU SAY?
...ALL RIGHT.

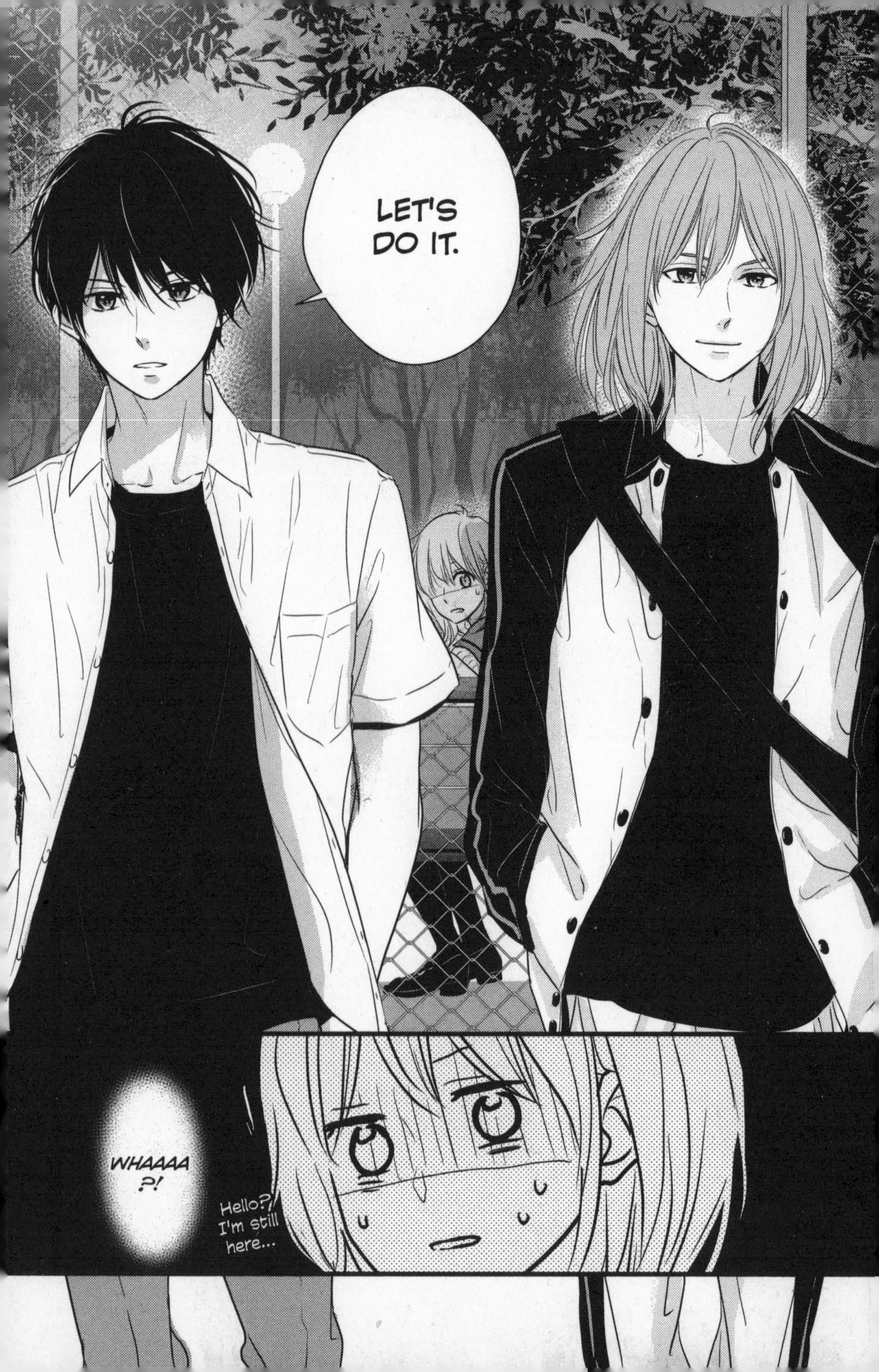
LET'S DO IT.
Hello?! I'm still here...
WHAAAA ?!

period 12: "Sense of Impending Troubles?"

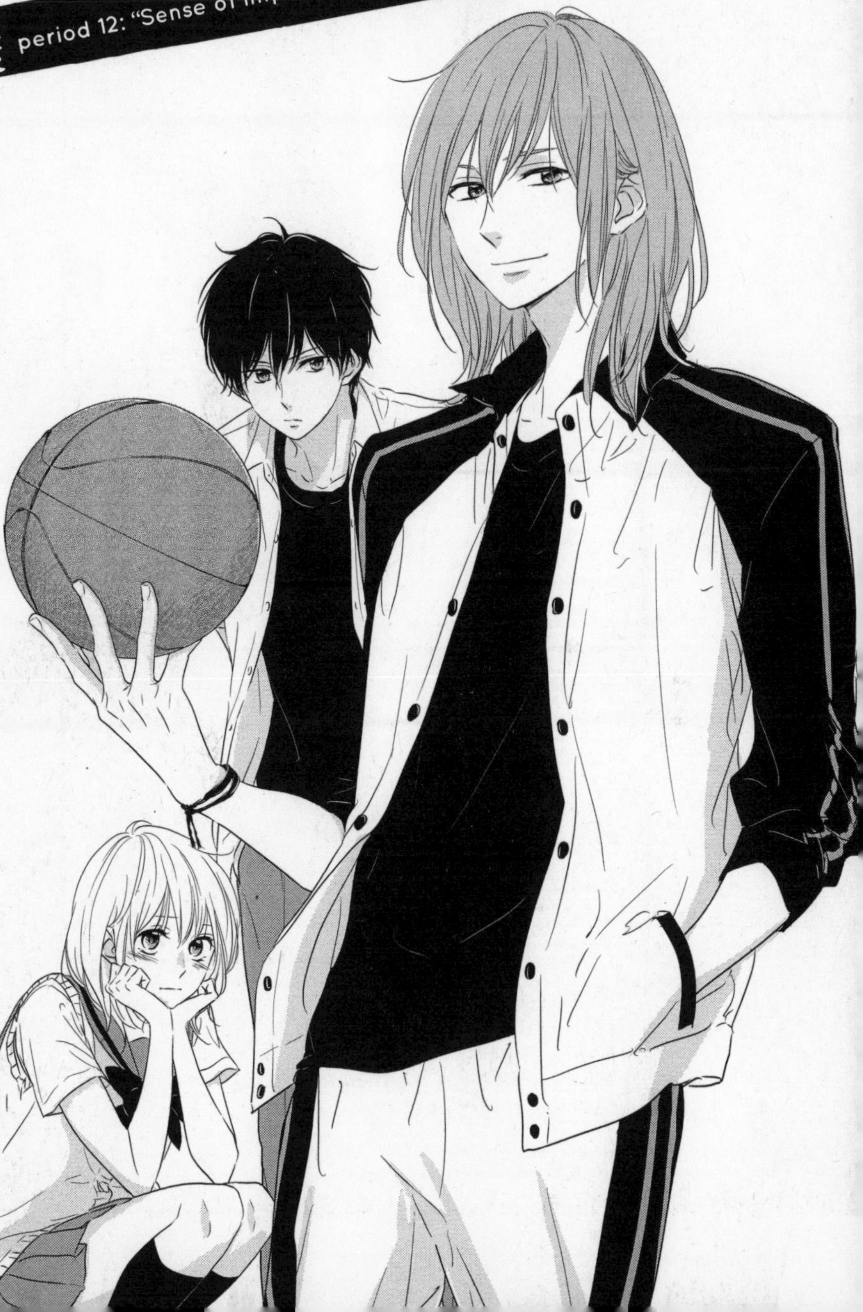

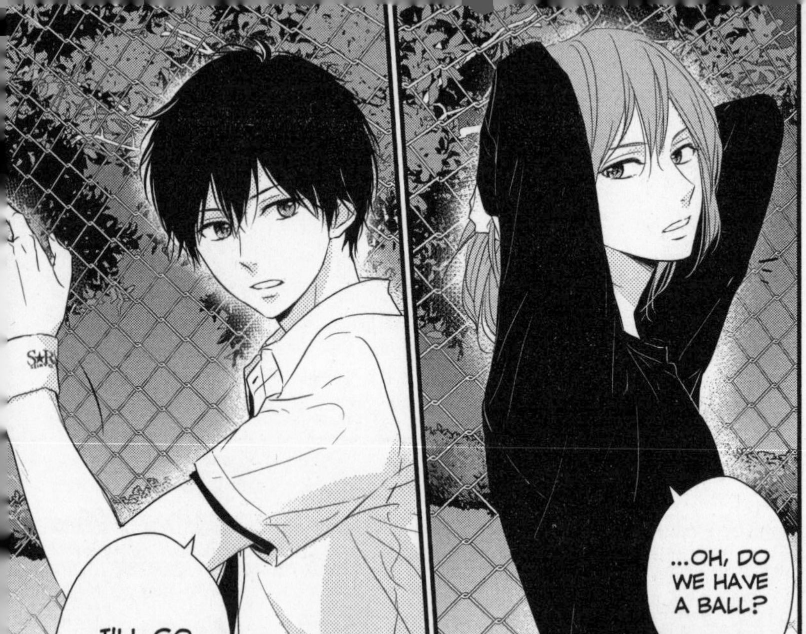
...OH, DO WE HAVE A BALL?
I'LL GO GET ONE.
"PLAY FOR IT"?
B-DMP ドクッ

Q. What do you focus on when choosing a character's name?

A. For this series, I didn't confine myself to anything, and I didn't base them on anything. I decided on names that suit the characters and are easy to say. Also, in every series, I think a little about how I don't want them to sound strange if I come back to it a few years later.

Except for Mitsuki. She's kind of named after Miu and Luna (*tsuki* in Japanese) from my last series, *Hiren Trip*... Just because!

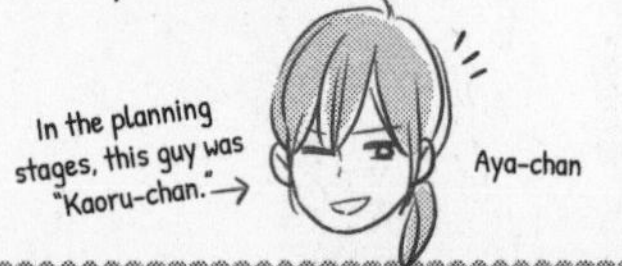
In the planning stages, this guy was "Kaoru-chan."
Aya-chan

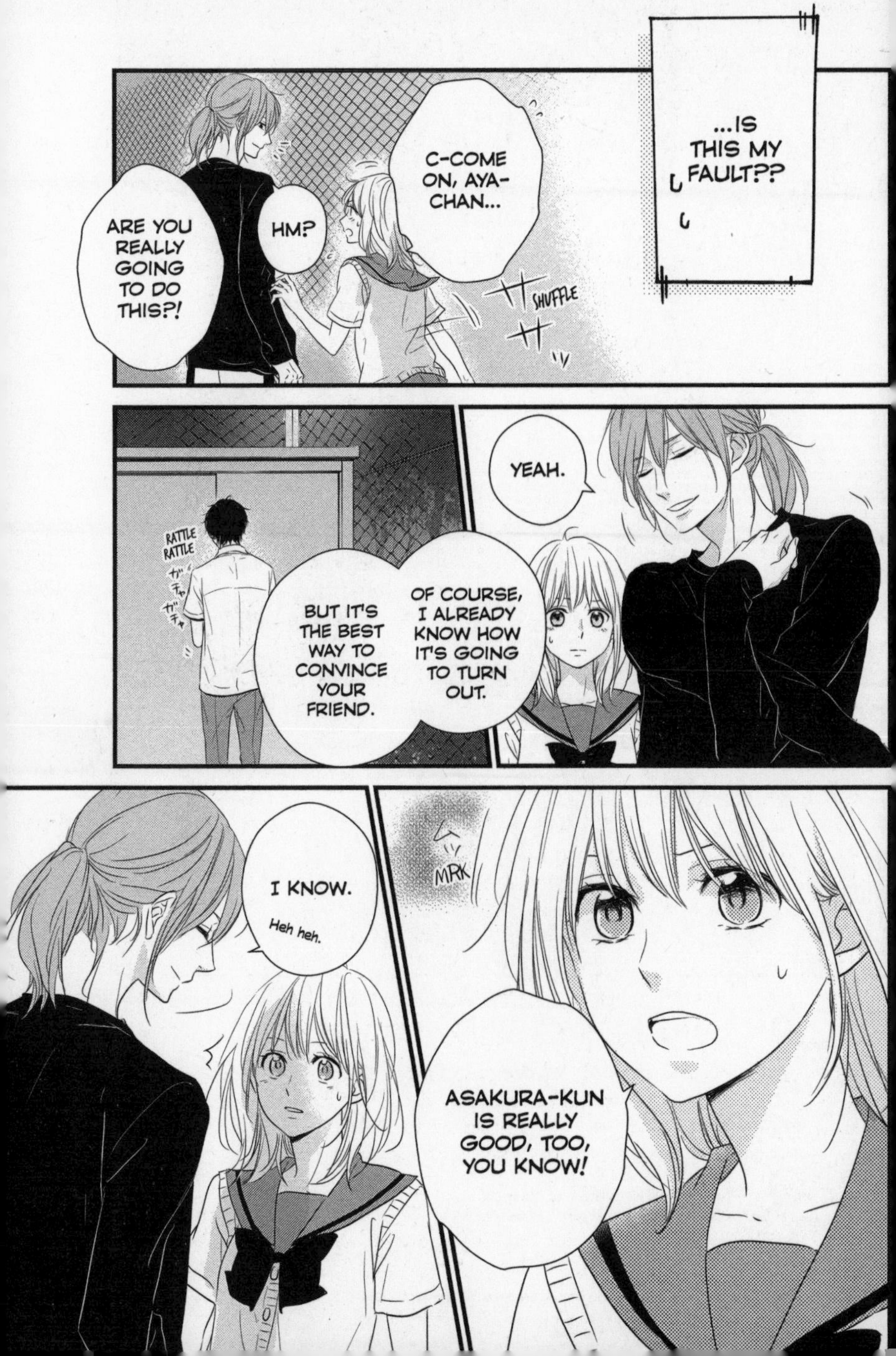
...IS THIS MY FAULT??
C-COME ON, AYA-CHAN...
HM?
ARE YOU REALLY GOING TO DO THIS?!
SHUFFLE
YEAH.
OF COURSE, I ALREADY KNOW HOW IT'S GOING TO TURN OUT.
BUT IT'S THE BEST WAY TO CONVINCE YOUR FRIEND.
RATTLE RATTLE
MRK
ASAKURA-KUN IS REALLY GOOD, TOO, YOU KNOW!
I KNOW.
Heh heh.

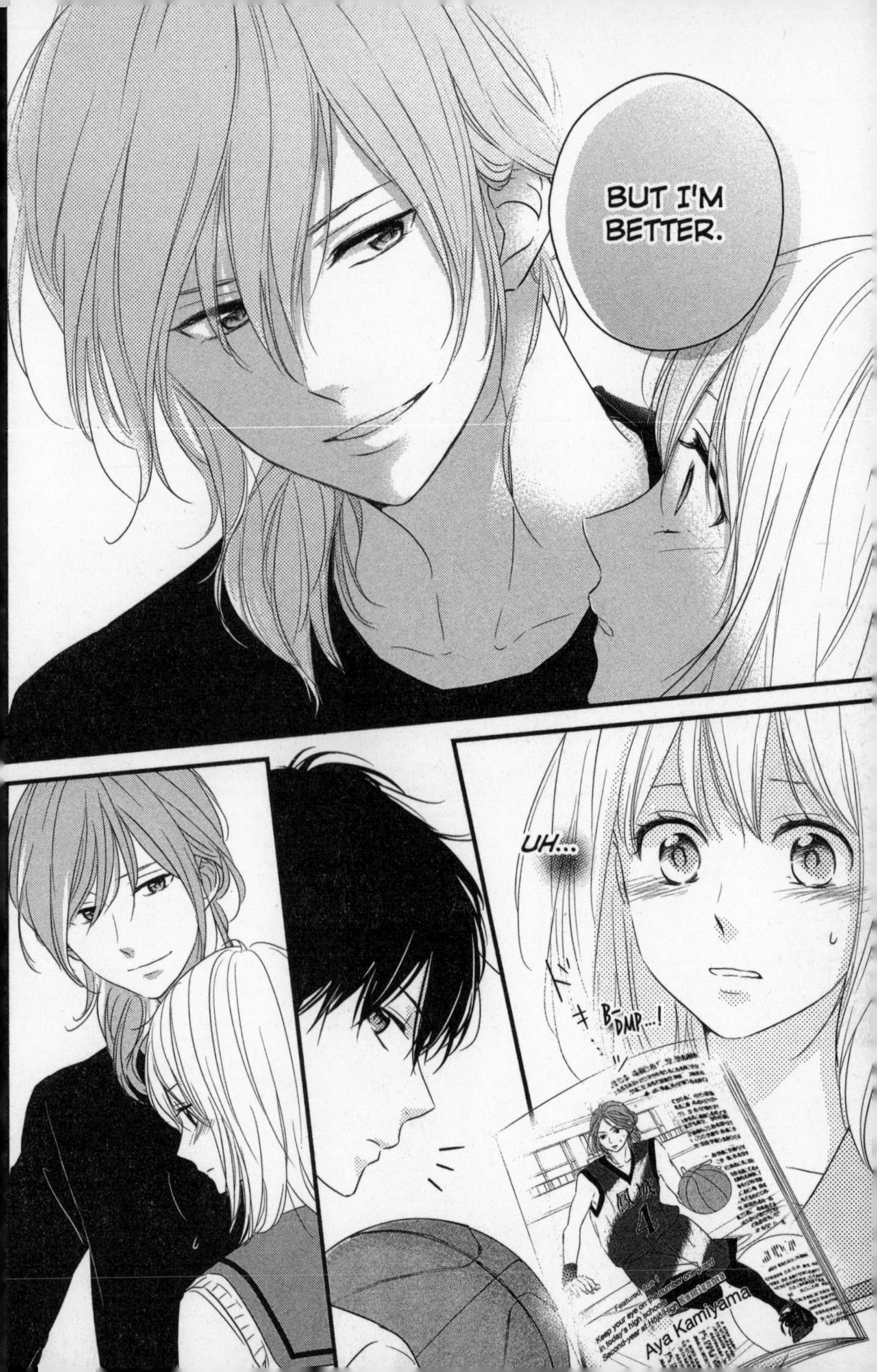
BUT I'M BETTER.
UH...
B-DMP...!
Featured Ace 1
Keep your eye on the number one guard in today's high schools
Second-year at Hōjō High
Aya Kamiyama

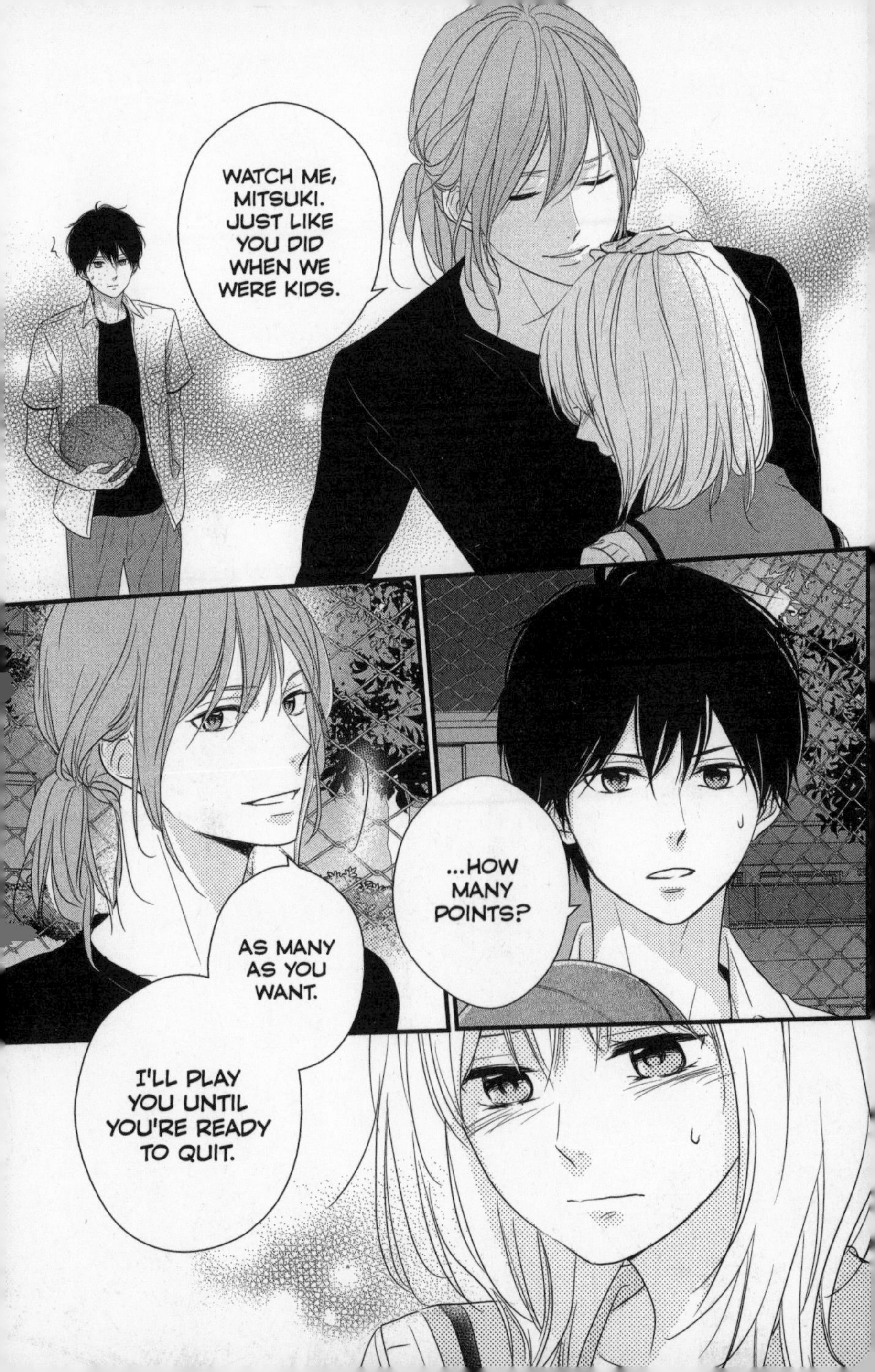
WATCH ME, MITSUKI. JUST LIKE YOU DID WHEN WE WERE KIDS.
...HOW MANY POINTS?
AS MANY AS YOU WANT.
I'LL PLAY YOU UNTIL YOU'RE READY TO QUIT.

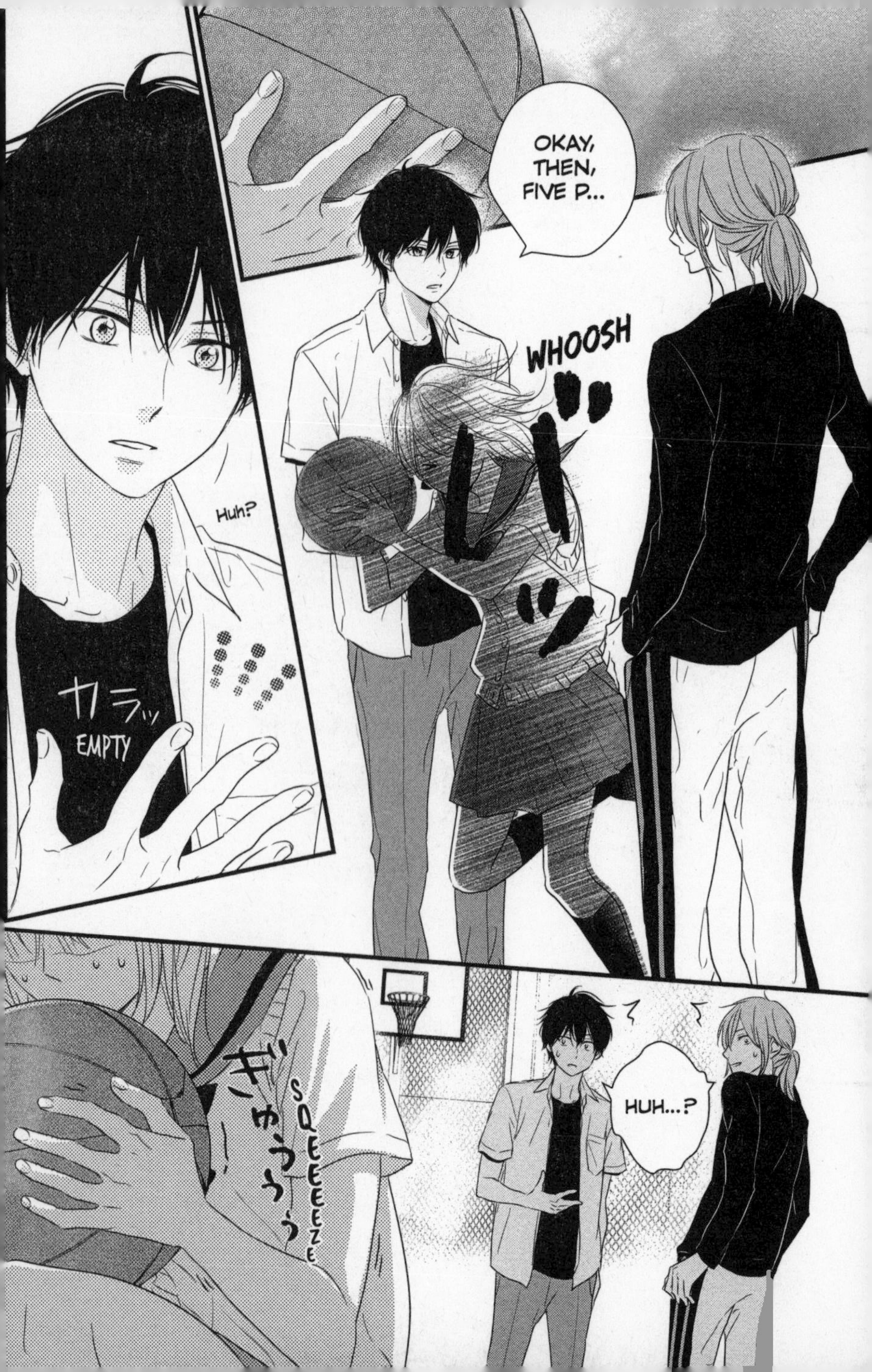
OKAY, THEN, FIVE P...
WHOOSH
Huh?
カラッ
EMPTY
HUH...?
ぎゅううう
SQEEEEZE

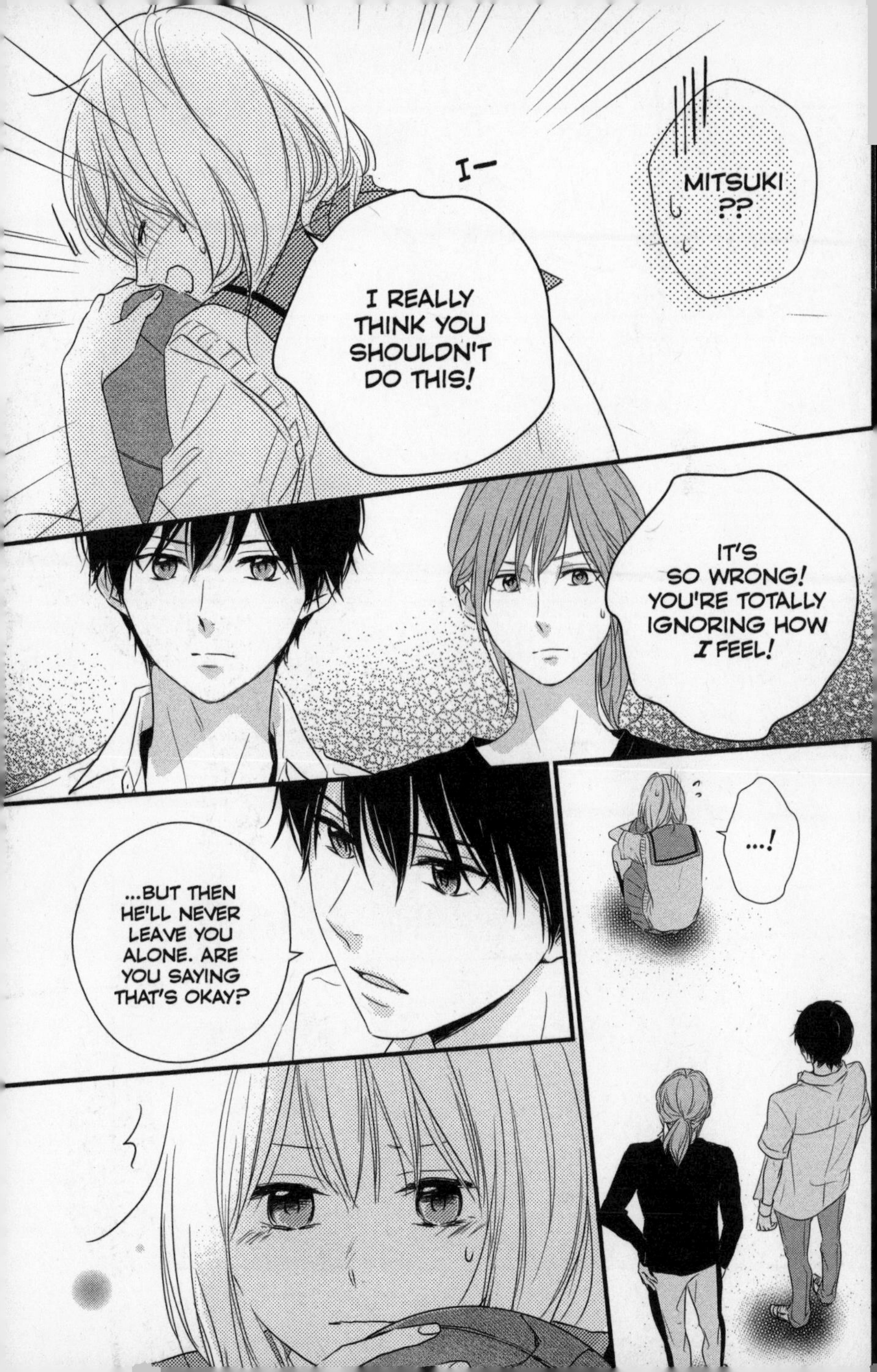
MITSUKI ??
I—
I REALLY THINK YOU SHOULDN'T DO THIS!
IT'S SO WRONG! YOU'RE TOTALLY IGNORING HOW *I* FEEL!
...!
...BUT THEN HE'LL NEVER LEAVE YOU ALONE. ARE YOU SAYING THAT'S OKAY?

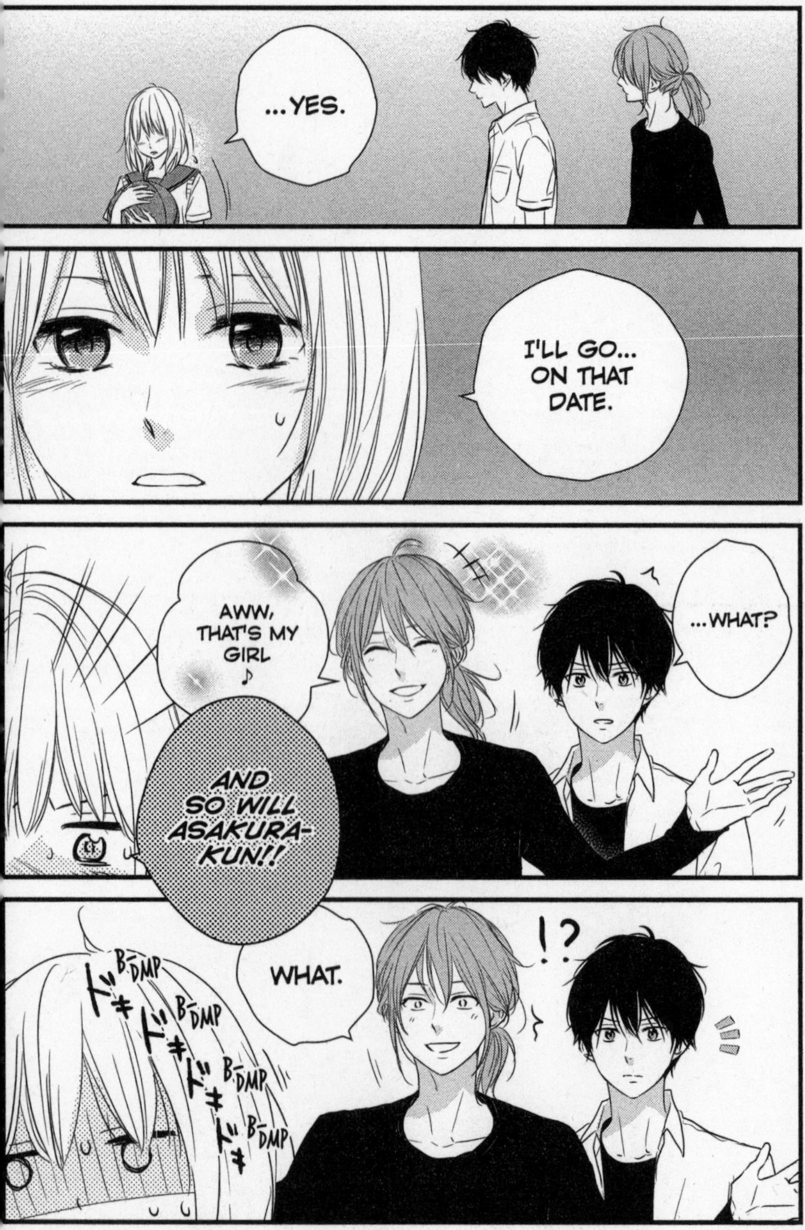
...YES.
I'LL GO... ON THAT DATE.
...WHAT?
AWW, THAT'S MY GIRL ♪
AND SO WILL ASAKURA-KUN!!
!?
WHAT.
B-DMP
B-DMP
B-DMP
B-DMP

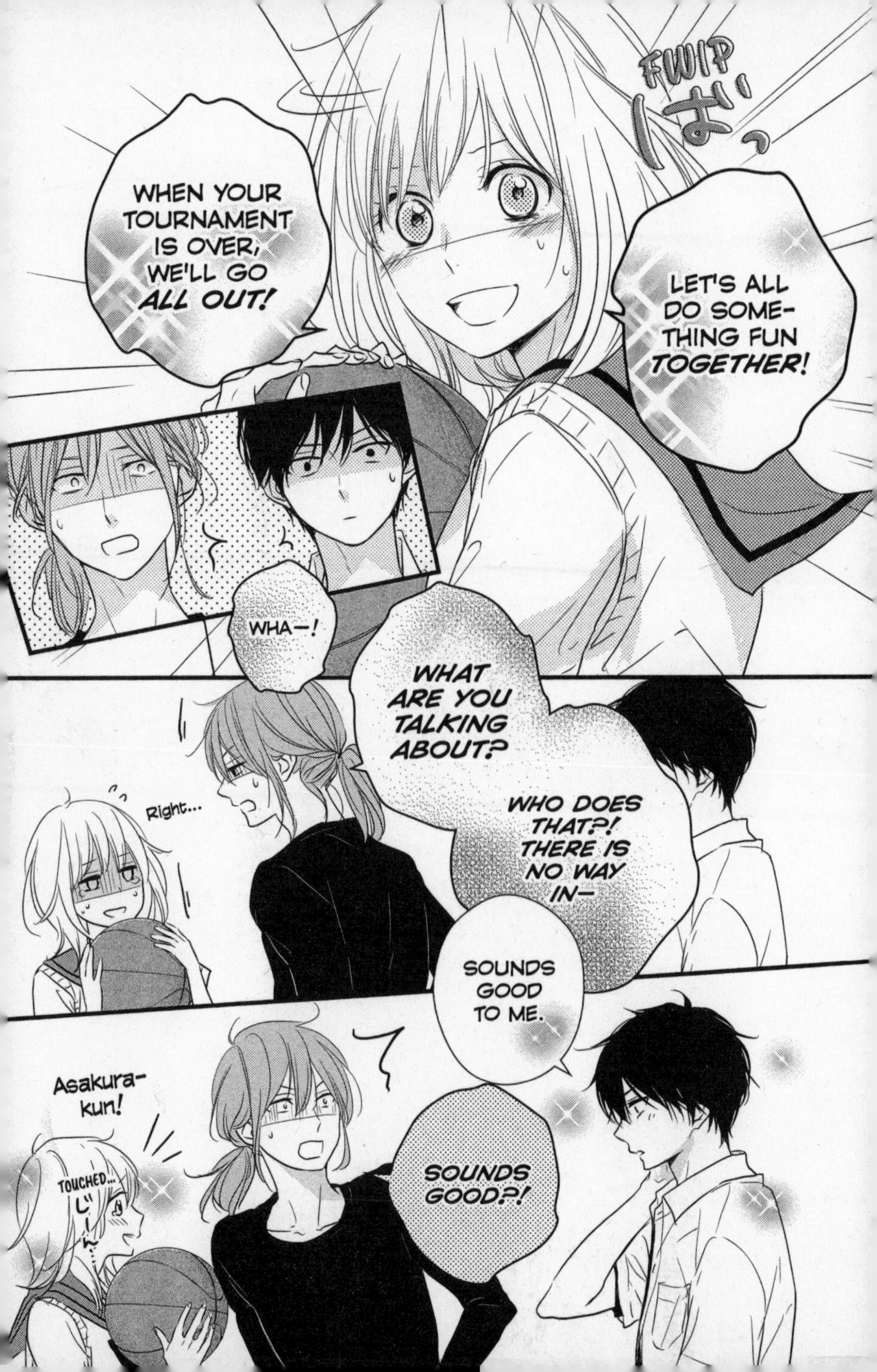

FWIP
ぱっ
LET'S ALL DO SOME-THING FUN TOGETHER!
WHEN YOUR TOURNAMENT IS OVER, WE'LL GO ALL OUT!
WHA—!
WHAT ARE YOU TALKING ABOUT?
WHO DOES THAT?! THERE IS NO WAY IN—
Right...
SOUNDS GOOD TO ME.
SOUNDS GOOD?!
Asakura-kun!
TOUCHED...
じーん

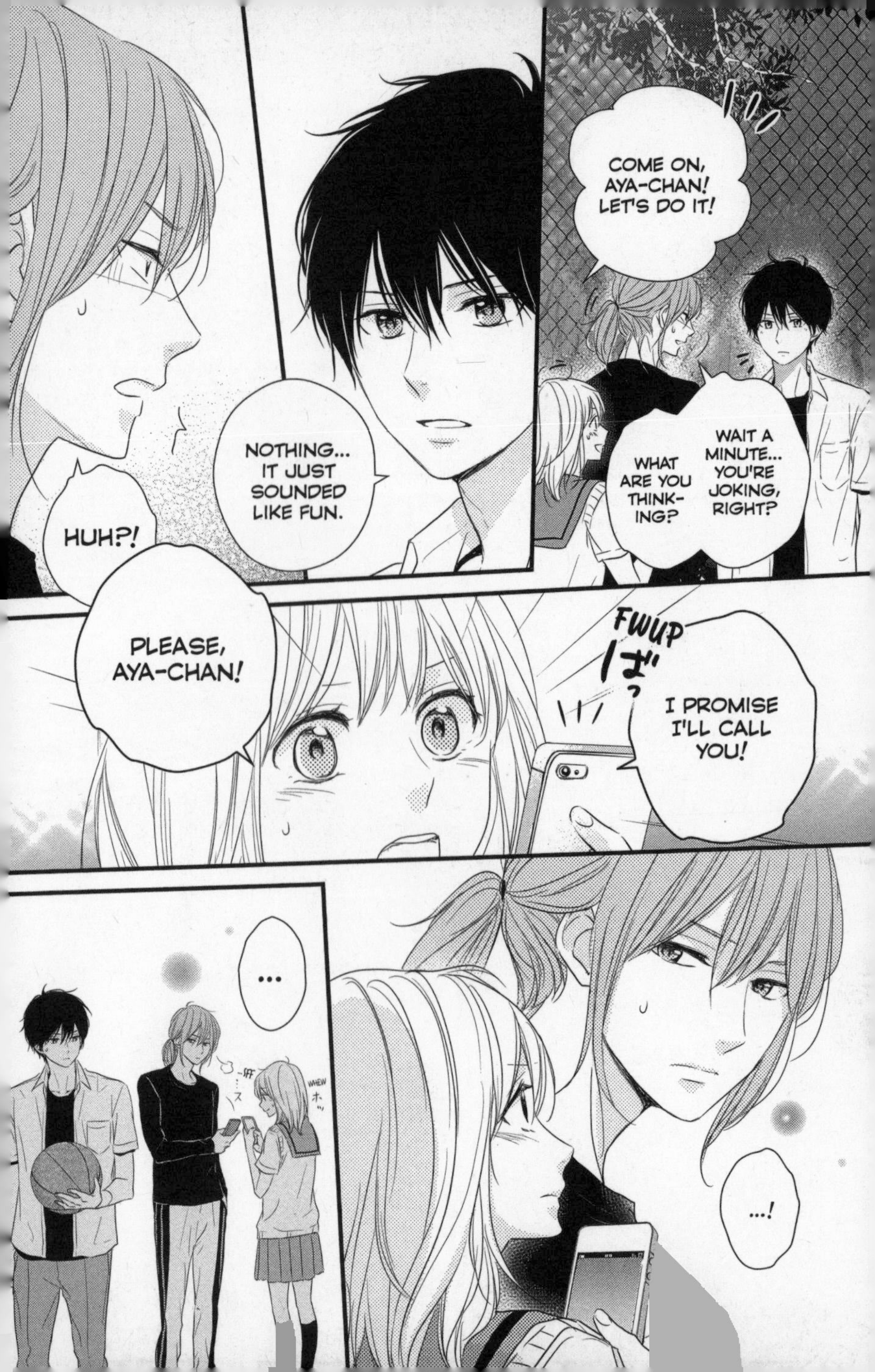
COME ON, AYA-CHAN! LET'S DO IT!
WAIT A MINUTE... YOU'RE JOKING, RIGHT?
WHAT ARE YOU THINK-ING?
NOTHING... IT JUST SOUNDED LIKE FUN.
HUH?!
FWUP
ばっ
I PROMISE I'LL CALL YOU!
PLEASE, AYA-CHAN!
...!
...
SFF
WHEW

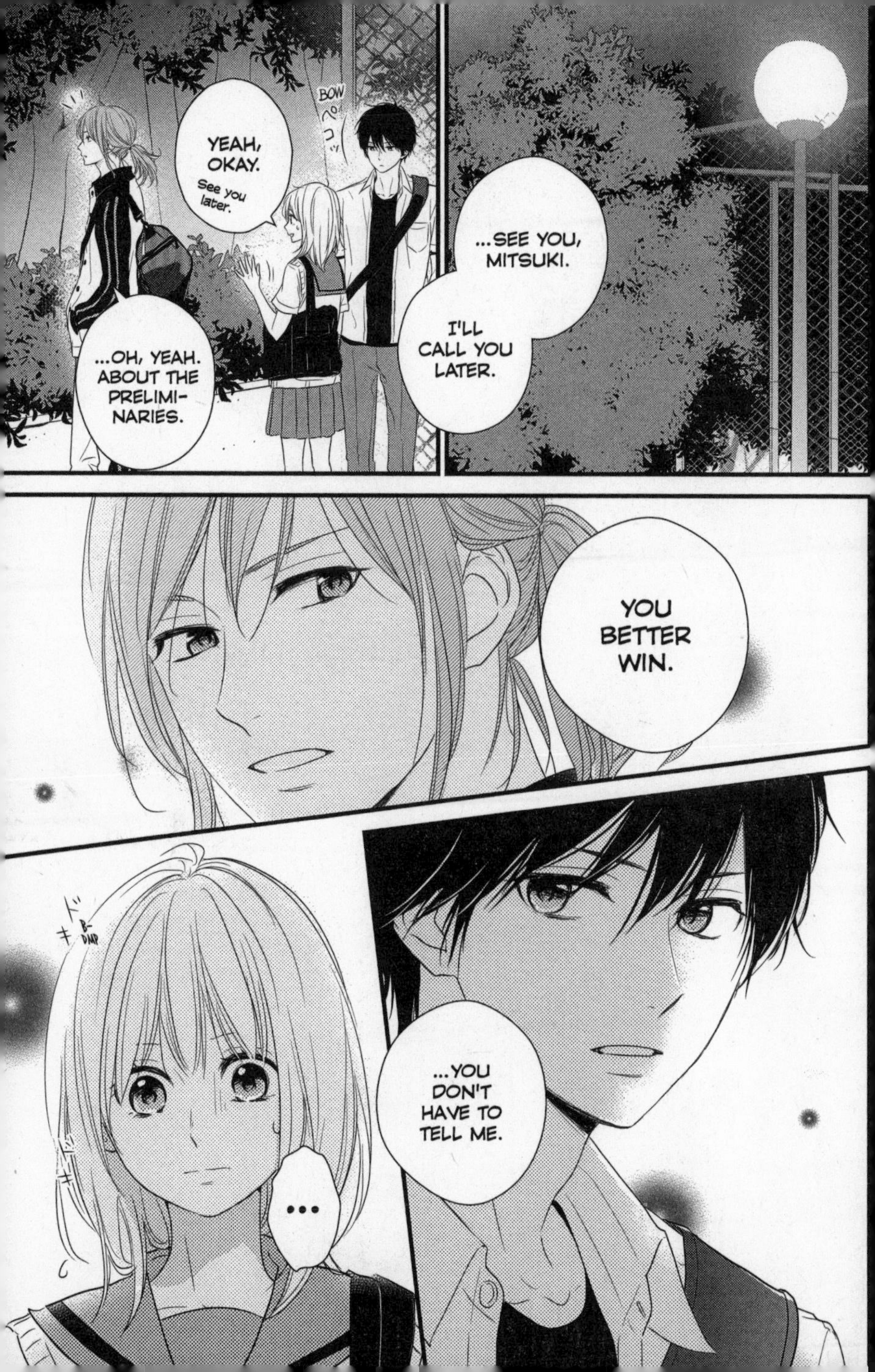
...SEE YOU, MITSUKI.
I'LL CALL YOU LATER.
BOW
YEAH, OKAY.
See you later.
...OH, YEAH. ABOUT THE PRELIMI-NARIES.
YOU BETTER WIN.
...YOU DON'T HAVE TO TELL ME.
B-DMP
...

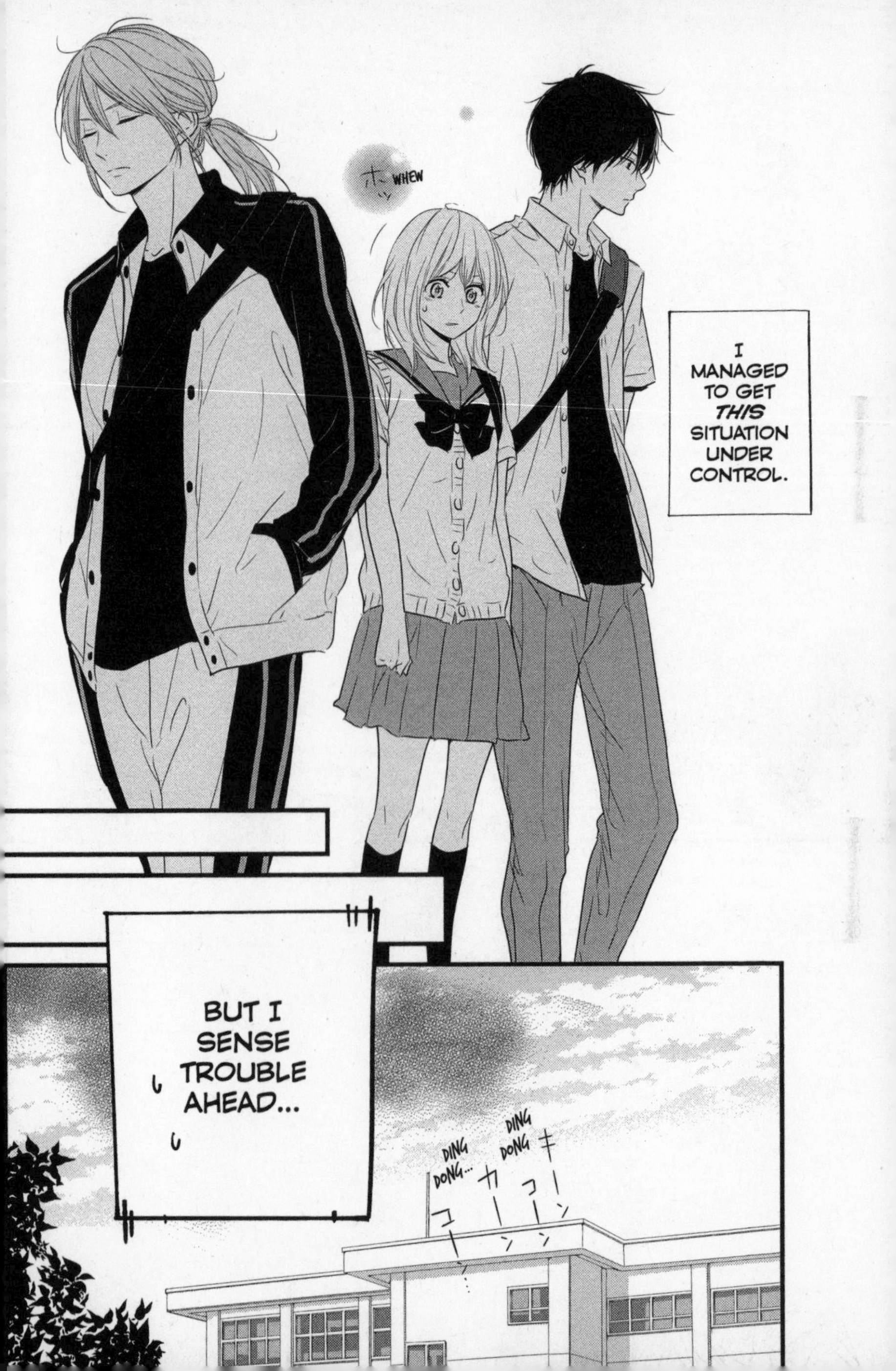
WHEW
I MANAGED TO GET *THIS* SITUATION UNDER CONTROL.
BUT I SENSE TROUBLE AHEAD...
DING DONG
DING DONG...

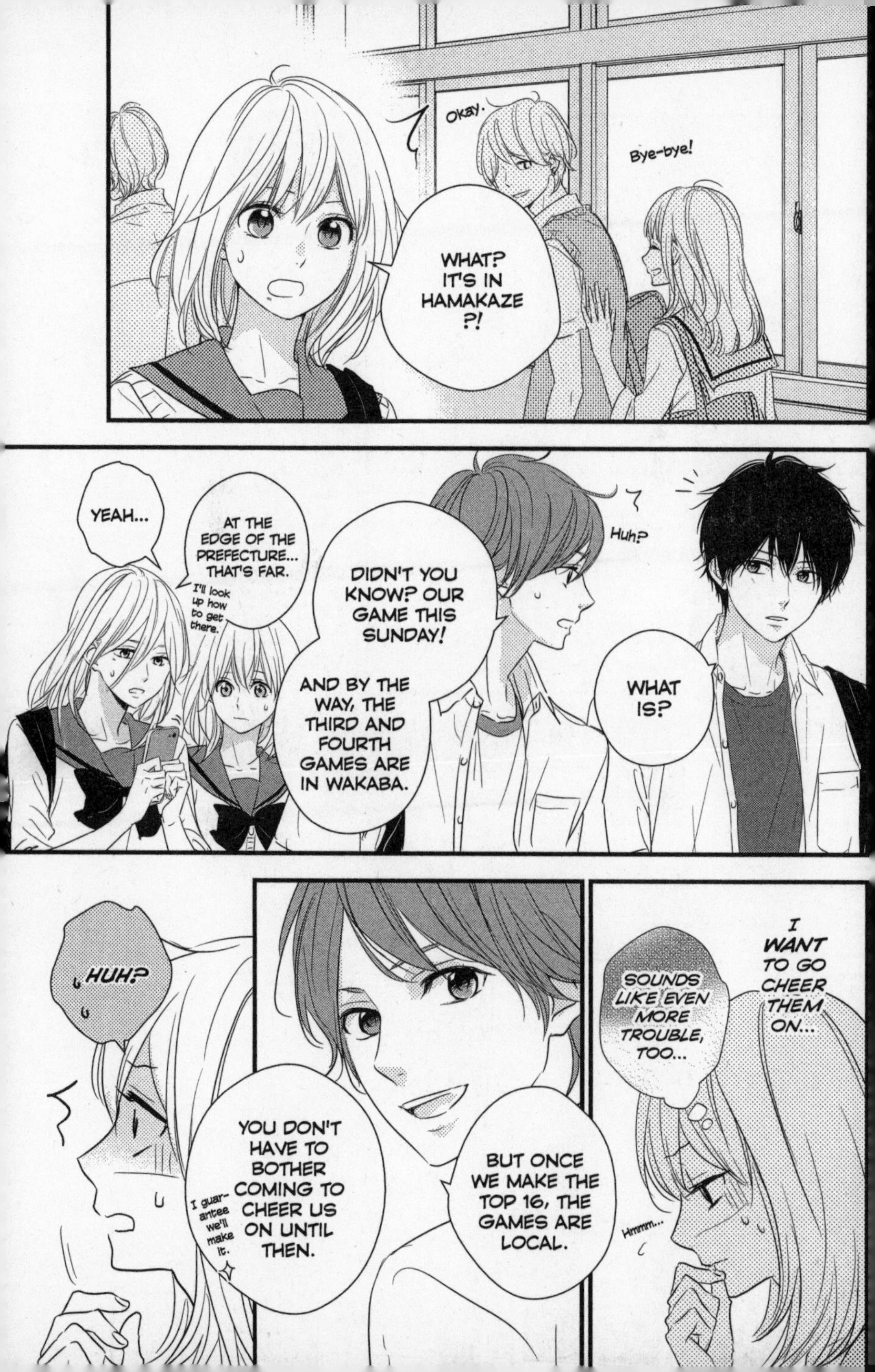
Bye-bye!
Okay.
WHAT? IT'S IN HAMAKAZE ?!
Huh?
WHAT IS?
DIDN'T YOU KNOW? OUR GAME THIS SUNDAY!
AND BY THE WAY, THE THIRD AND FOURTH GAMES ARE IN WAKABA.
AT THE EDGE OF THE PREFECTURE... THAT'S FAR.
I'll look up how to get there.
YEAH...
I WANT TO GO CHEER THEM ON...
SOUNDS LIKE EVEN MORE TROUBLE, TOO...
Hmmm...
BUT ONCE WE MAKE THE TOP 16, THE GAMES ARE LOCAL.
YOU DON'T HAVE TO BOTHER COMING TO CHEER US ON UNTIL THEN.
I guar-antee we'll make it.
HUH?

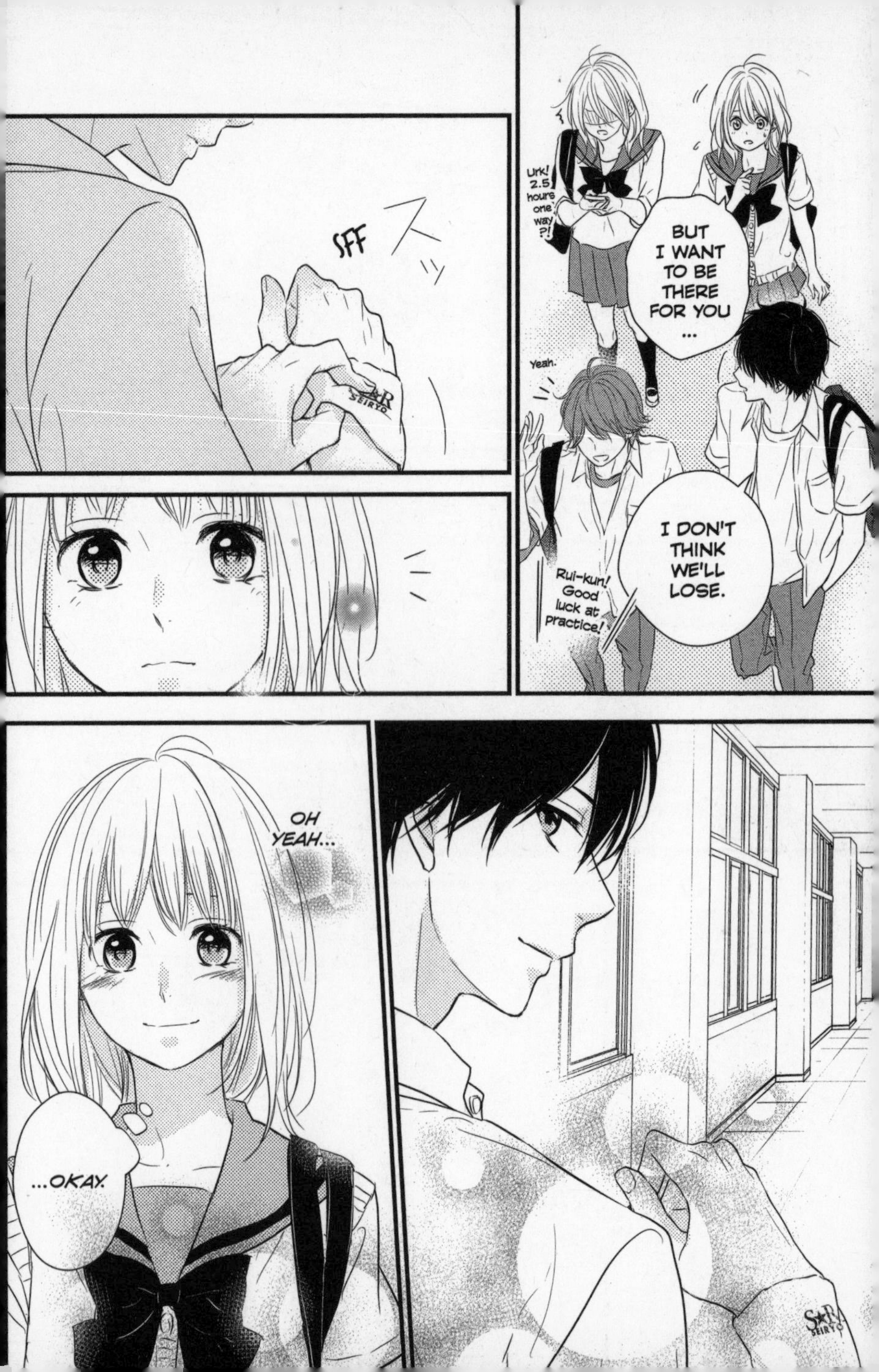

BUT I WANT TO BE THERE FOR YOU ...
Urk! 2.5 hours one way?!
Yeah.
I DON'T THINK WE'LL LOSE.
Rui-kun! Good luck at practice!
SFF
OH YEAH...
...OKAY.

NO! I CAN'T!

I'm sorry!

WHAT? YOU'RE NOT COMING?!

AWW, YOU'RE NOT GONNA COME WATCH?

I'M SORRY! I JUST REMEMBERED I HAVE SOMETHING TO DO TODAY!

I'M GONNA HEAD HOME, REINA-CHAN!

THIS IS NO TIME TO LET MY FEAR OF THE FUTURE GET ME DOWN!

Oh!

PRACTICE HARD, OKAY!

...YEAH.

YEAH!

WOW. SHE'S REALLY PUMPED ABOUT SOMETHING.

SNAP

FSH

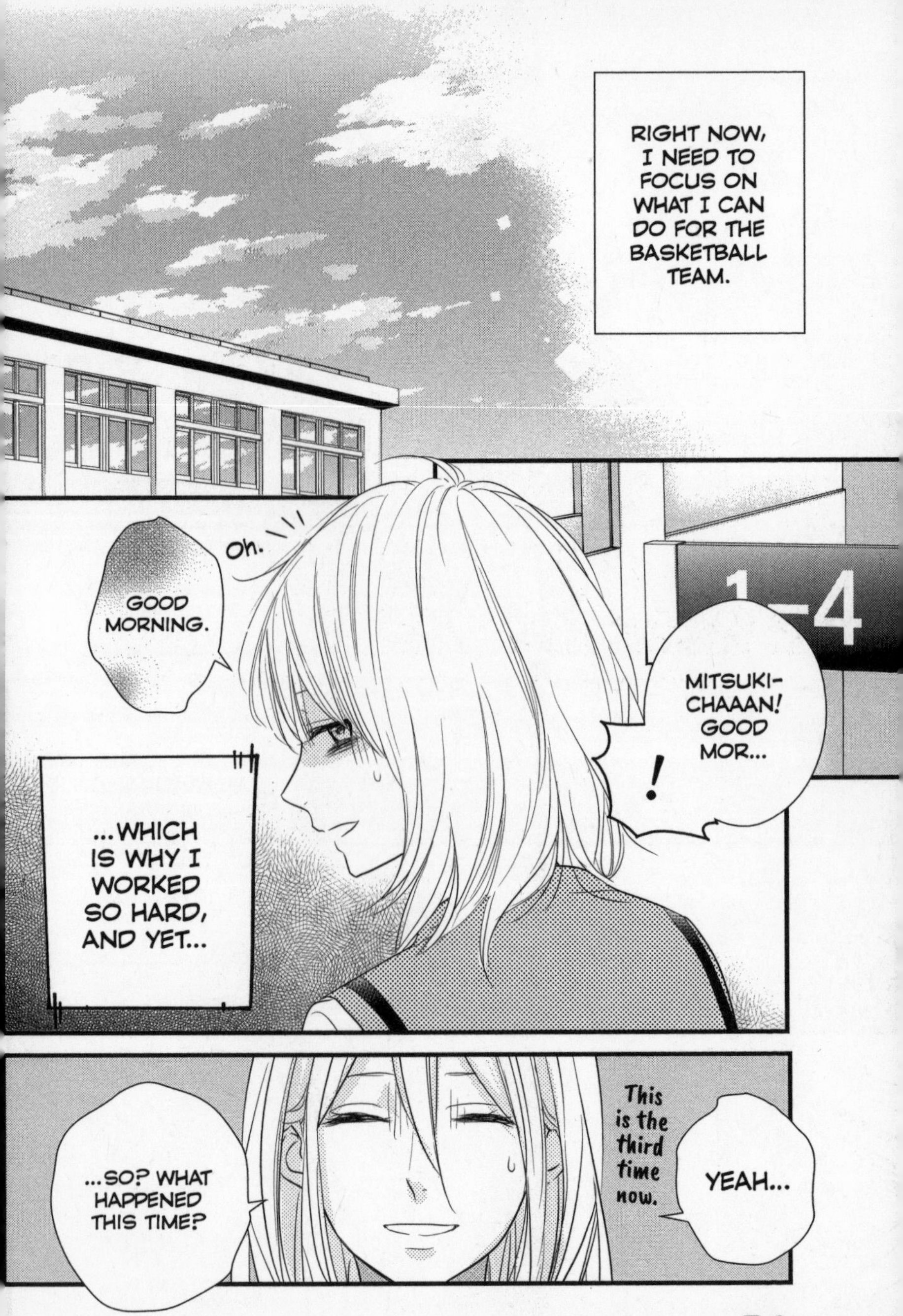

RIGHT NOW, I NEED TO FOCUS ON WHAT I CAN DO FOR THE BASKETBALL TEAM.
1-4
MITSUKI-CHAAAN! GOOD MOR...
!
Oh.
GOOD MORNING.
...WHICH IS WHY I WORKED SO HARD, AND YET...
YEAH...
This is the third time now.
...SO? WHAT HAPPENED THIS TIME?

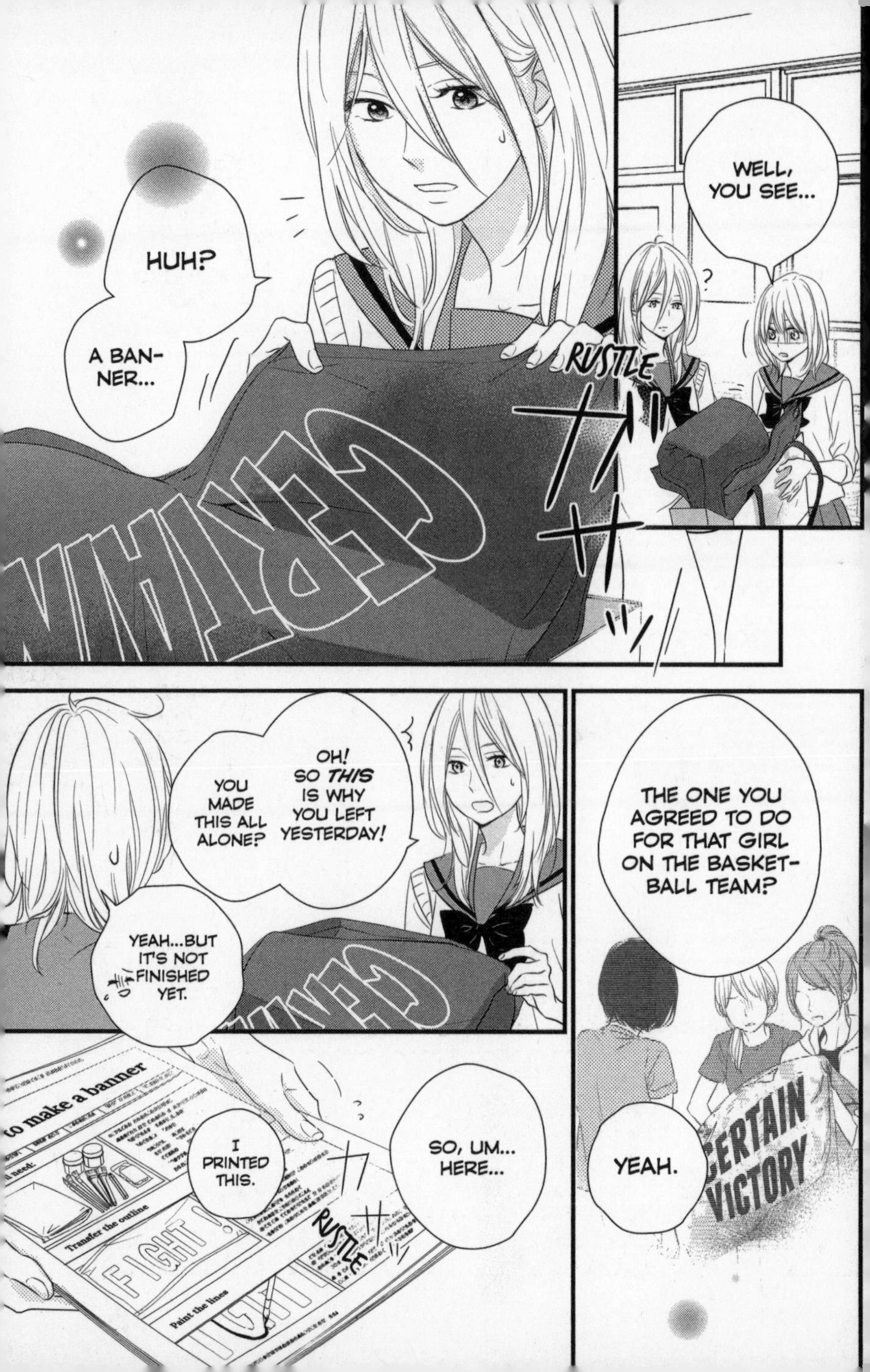
WELL, YOU SEE...
?
RUSTLE
HUH?
A BAN-NER...
THE ONE YOU AGREED TO DO FOR THAT GIRL ON THE BASKET-BALL TEAM?
YEAH.
CERTAIN VICTORY
OH! SO THIS IS WHY YOU LEFT YESTERDAY!
YOU MADE THIS ALL ALONE?
YEAH...BUT IT'S NOT FINISHED YET.
SO, UM... HERE...
I PRINTED THIS.
RUSTLE
to make a banner
Transfer the outline
FIGHT!
Paint the lines

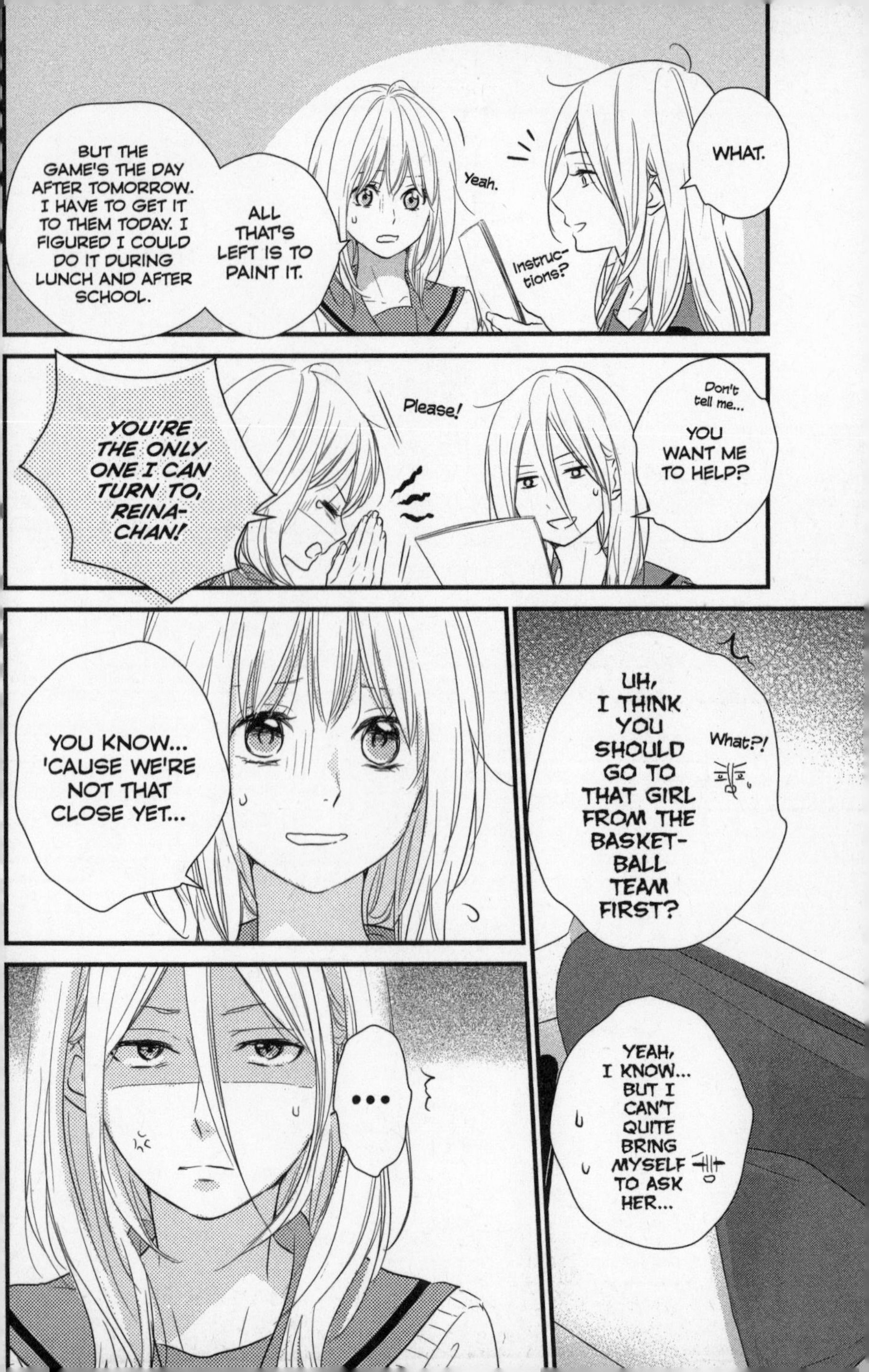
WHAT.
Instructions?
Yeah.
ALL THAT'S LEFT IS TO PAINT IT.
BUT THE GAME'S THE DAY AFTER TOMORROW. I HAVE TO GET IT TO THEM TODAY. I FIGURED I COULD DO IT DURING LUNCH AND AFTER SCHOOL.
Don't tell me...
YOU WANT ME TO HELP?
Please!
YOU'RE THE ONLY ONE I CAN TURN TO, REINA-CHAN!
UH, I THINK YOU SHOULD GO TO THAT GIRL FROM THE BASKETBALL TEAM FIRST?
What?!
YEAH, I KNOW... BUT I CAN'T QUITE BRING MYSELF TO ASK HER...
YOU KNOW... 'CAUSE WE'RE NOT THAT CLOSE YET...
...

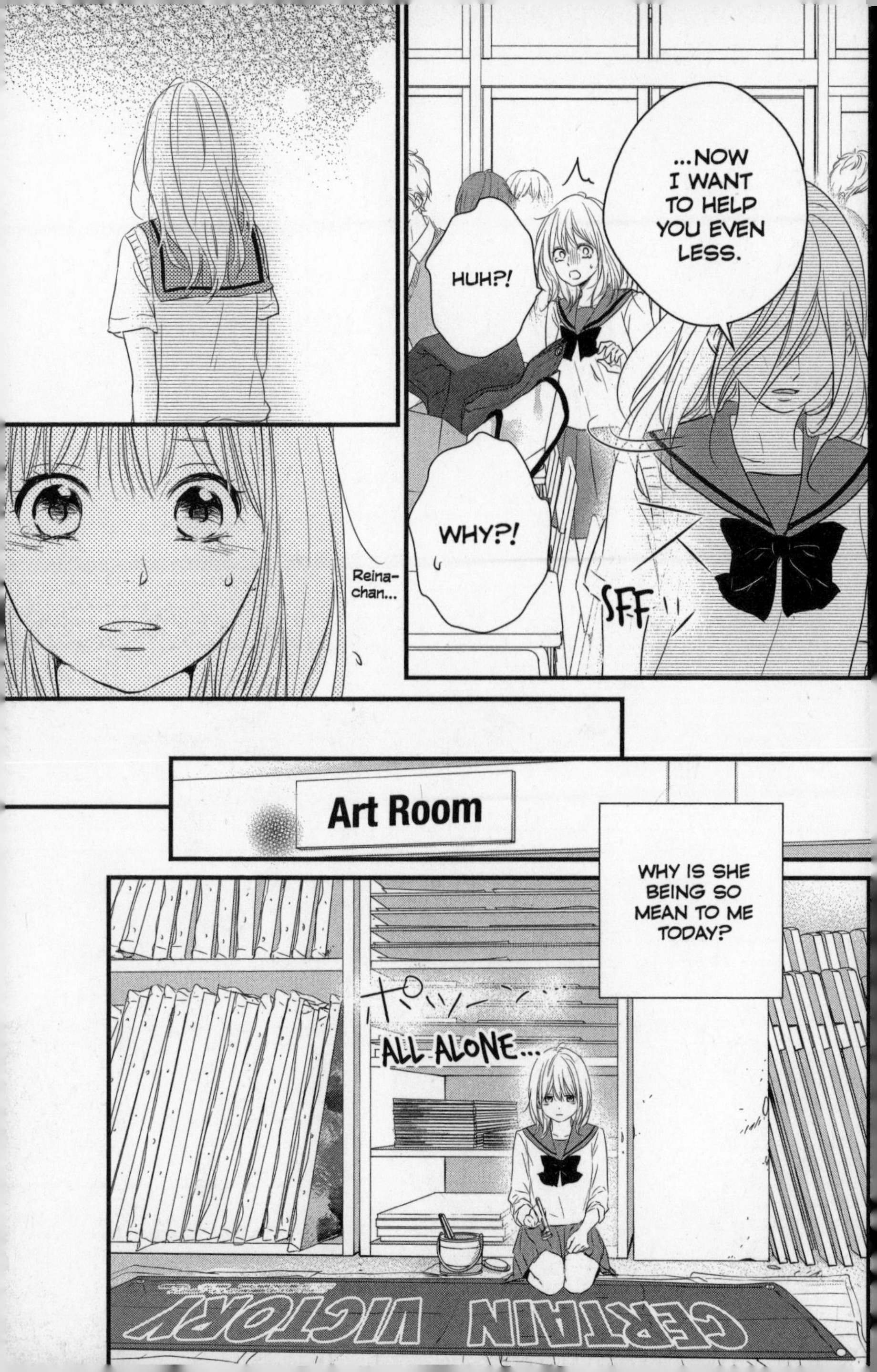
...NOW I WANT TO HELP YOU EVEN LESS.
HUH?!
SFF
WHY?!
Reina-chan...
Art Room
WHY IS SHE BEING SO MEAN TO ME TODAY?
ALL ALONE...
CERTAIN VICTORY

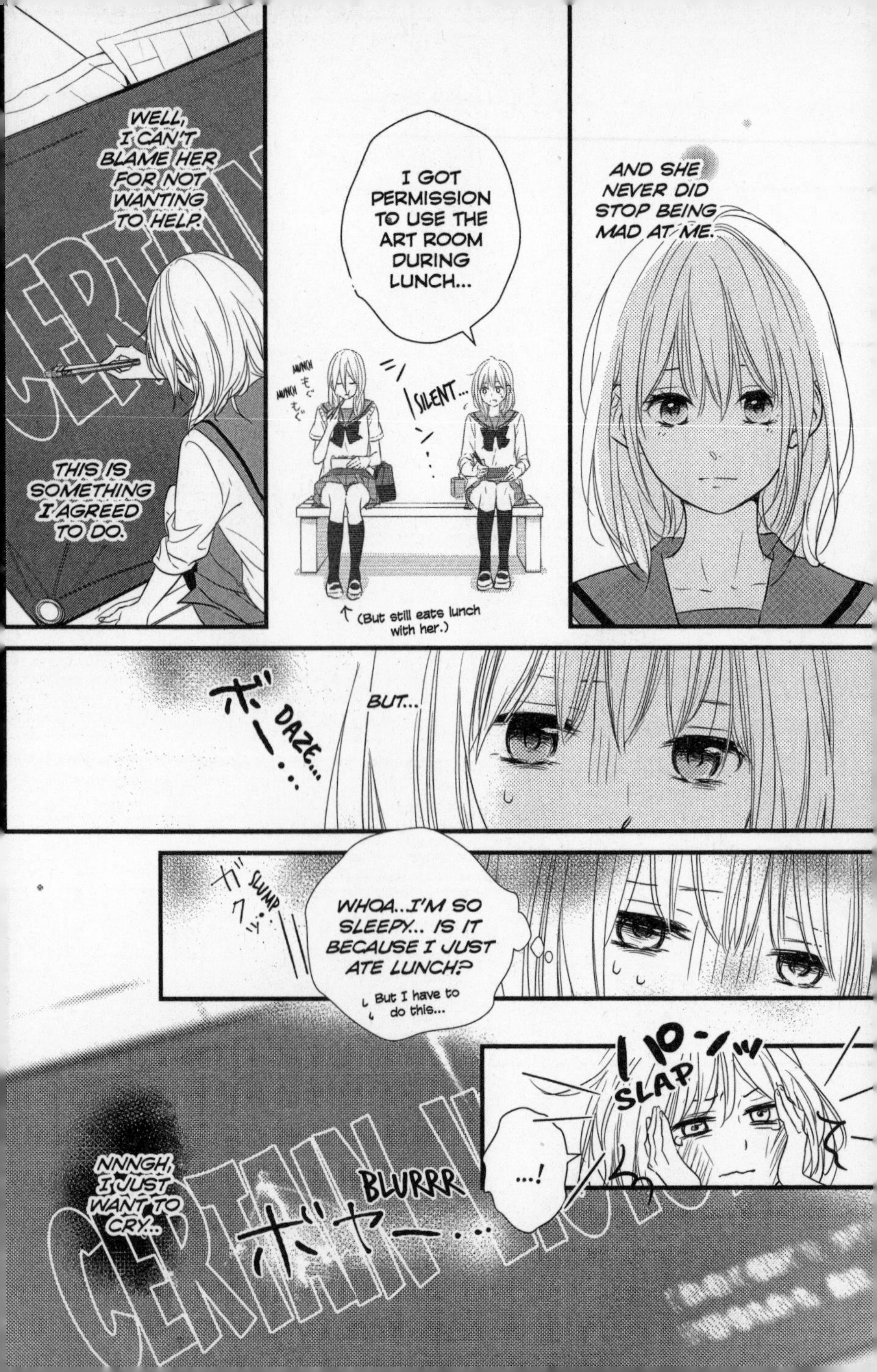
AND SHE NEVER DID STOP BEING MAD AT ME.
I GOT PERMISSION TO USE THE ART ROOM DURING LUNCH...
SILENT...
MUNCH もぐ
MUNCH もぐ
(But still eats lunch with her.)
WELL, I CAN'T BLAME HER FOR NOT WANTING TO HELP.
THIS IS SOMETHING I AGREED TO DO.
BUT...
ボー…
DAZE...
ガクッ
SLUMP
WHOA...I'M SO SLEEPY... IS IT BECAUSE I JUST ATE LUNCH?
But I have to do this...
パーンッ
SLAP
...!
NNNGH, I JUST WANT TO CRY...
BLURRR
ボヤー…

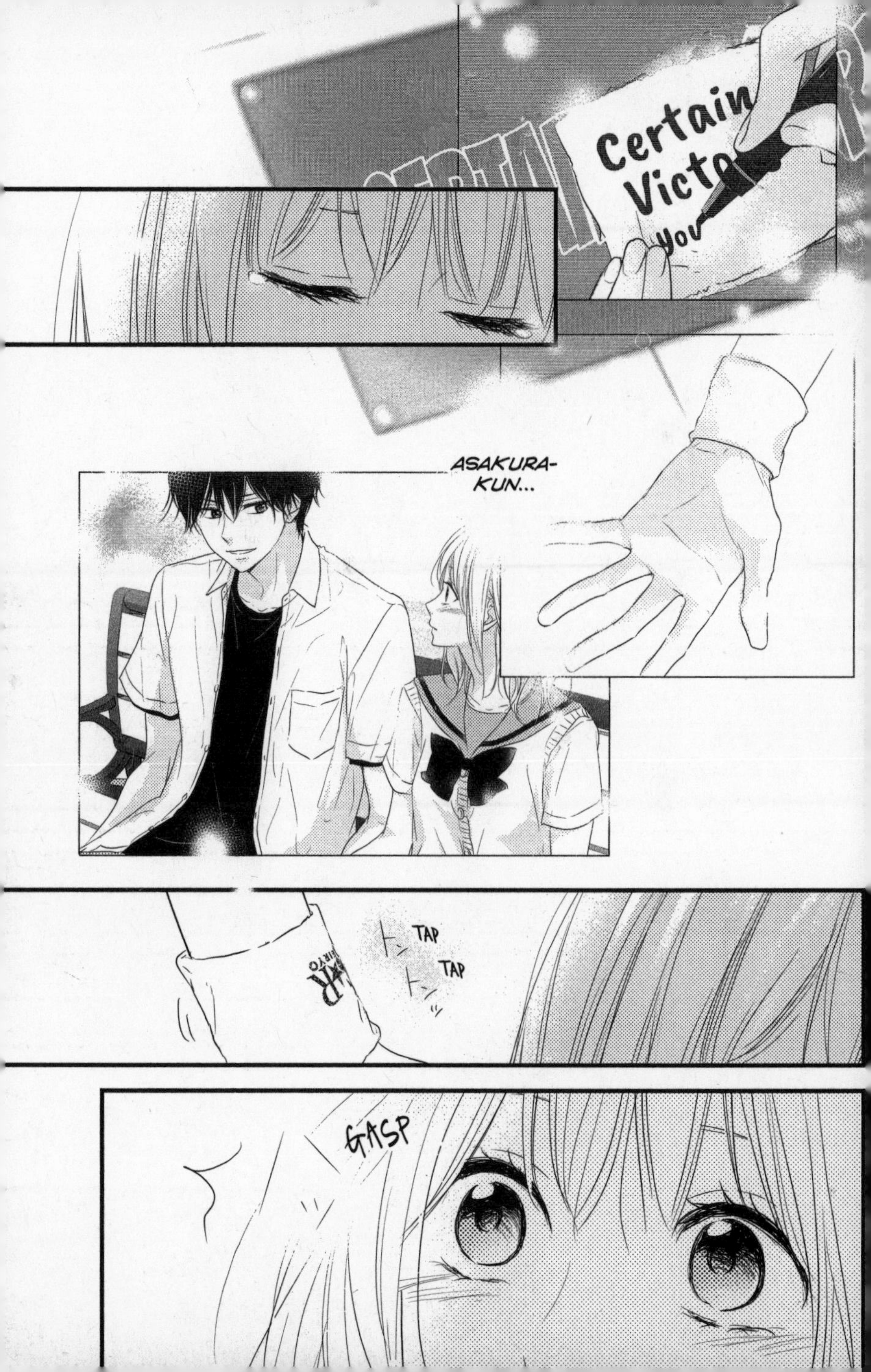
Certain Victo
you
ASAKURA-KUN...
TAP
TAP
GASP

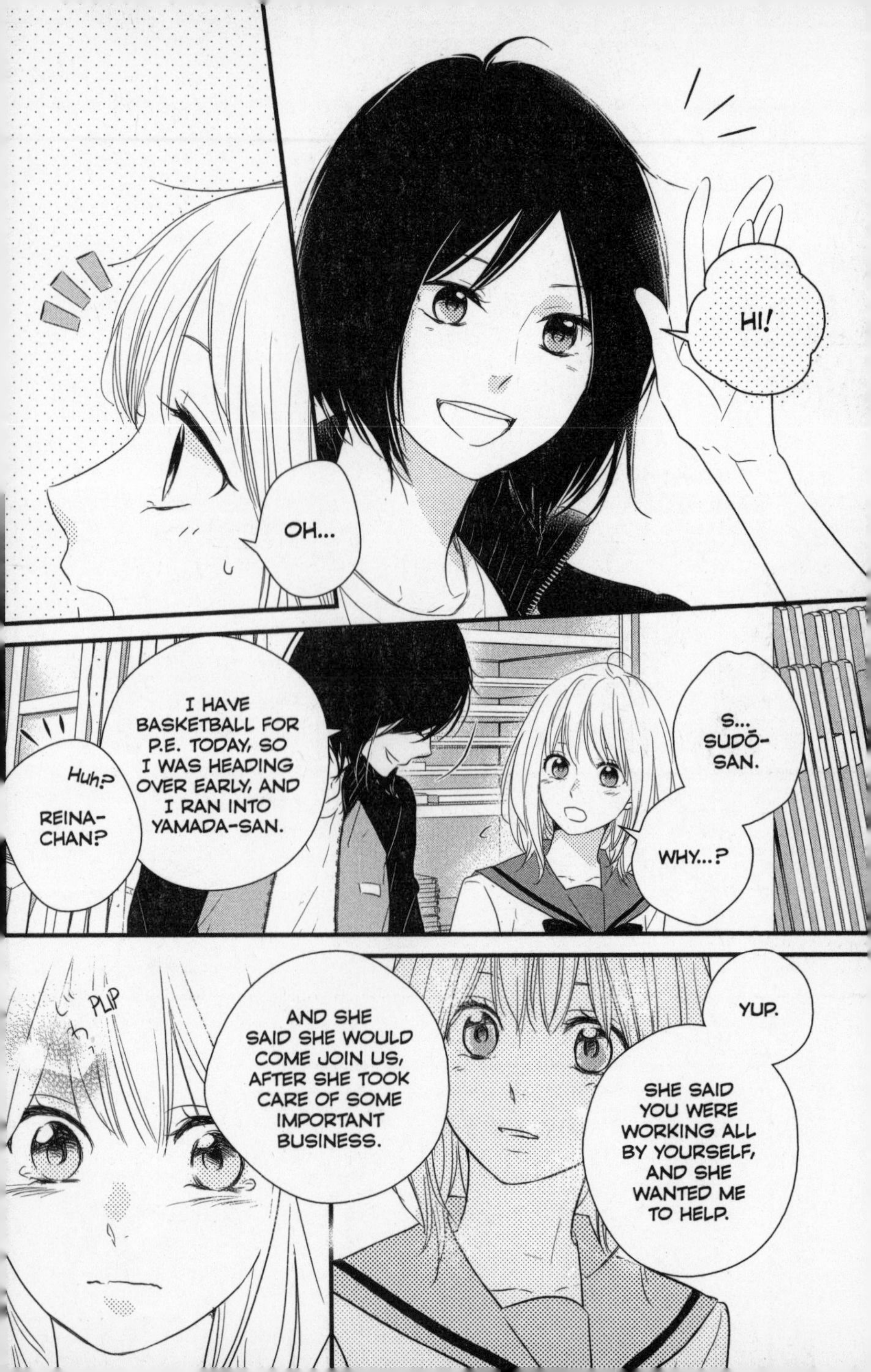
HI!
OH...
S... SUDŌ-SAN.
WHY...?
I HAVE BASKETBALL FOR P.E. TODAY, SO I WAS HEADING OVER EARLY, AND I RAN INTO YAMADA-SAN.
Huh?
REINA-CHAN?
YUP.
SHE SAID YOU WERE WORKING ALL BY YOURSELF, AND SHE WANTED ME TO HELP.
AND SHE SAID SHE WOULD COME JOIN US, AFTER SHE TOOK CARE OF SOME IMPORTANT BUSINESS.
PLIP

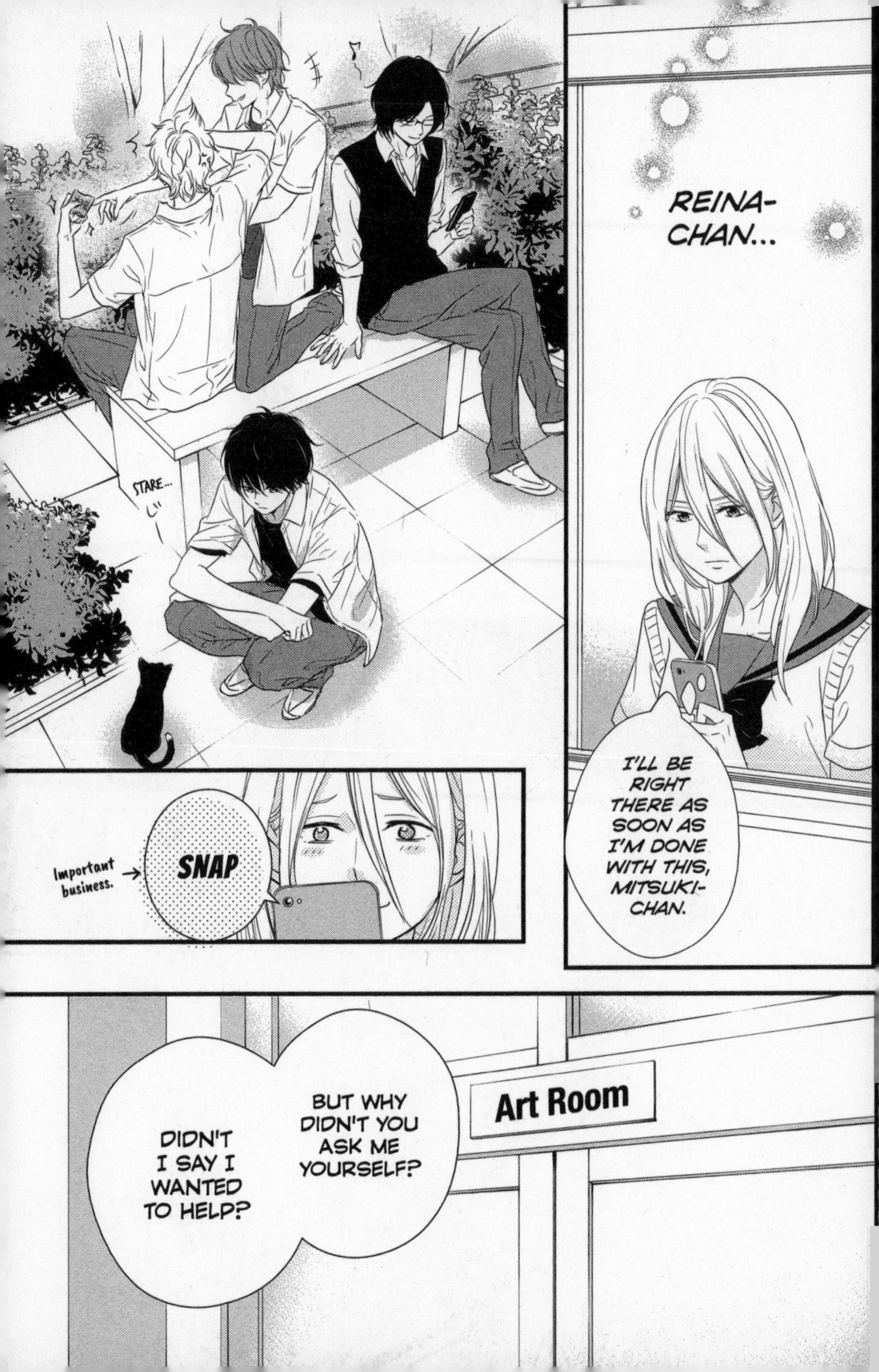
REINA-CHAN...
I'LL BE RIGHT THERE AS SOON AS I'M DONE WITH THIS, MITSUKI-CHAN.
STARE...
じー
Important business.
SNAP
Art Room
BUT WHY DIDN'T YOU ASK ME YOURSELF?
DIDN'T I SAY I WANTED TO HELP?

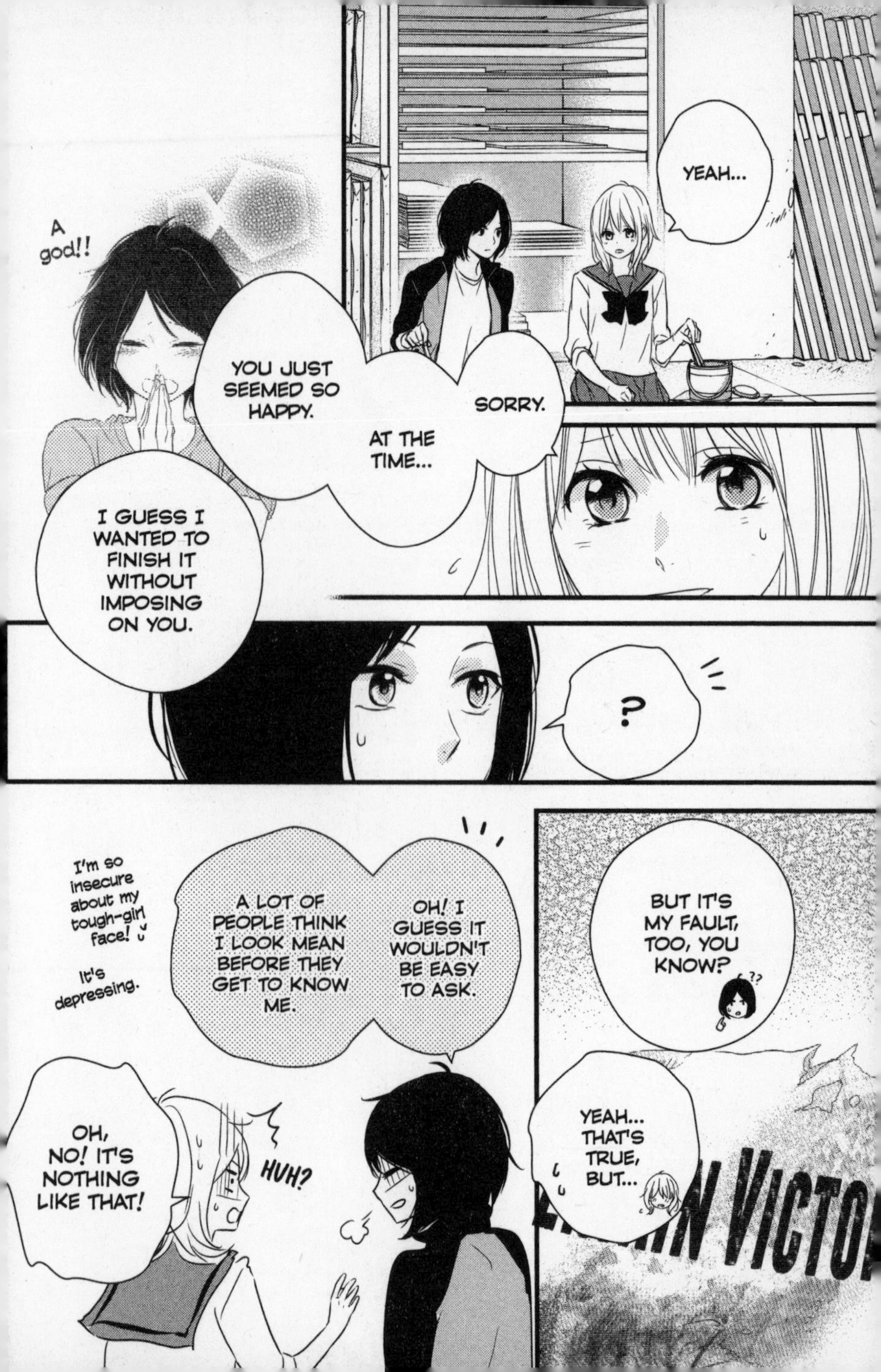
YEAH...
SORRY.
AT THE TIME...
YOU JUST SEEMED SO HAPPY.
I GUESS I WANTED TO FINISH IT WITHOUT IMPOSING ON YOU.
A god!!
?
BUT IT'S MY FAULT, TOO, YOU KNOW?
??
YEAH... THAT'S TRUE, BUT...
OH! I GUESS IT WOULDN'T BE EASY TO ASK.
A LOT OF PEOPLE THINK I LOOK MEAN BEFORE THEY GET TO KNOW ME.
HUH?
OH, NO! IT'S NOTHING LIKE THAT!
I'm so insecure about my tough-girl face!
It's depressing.

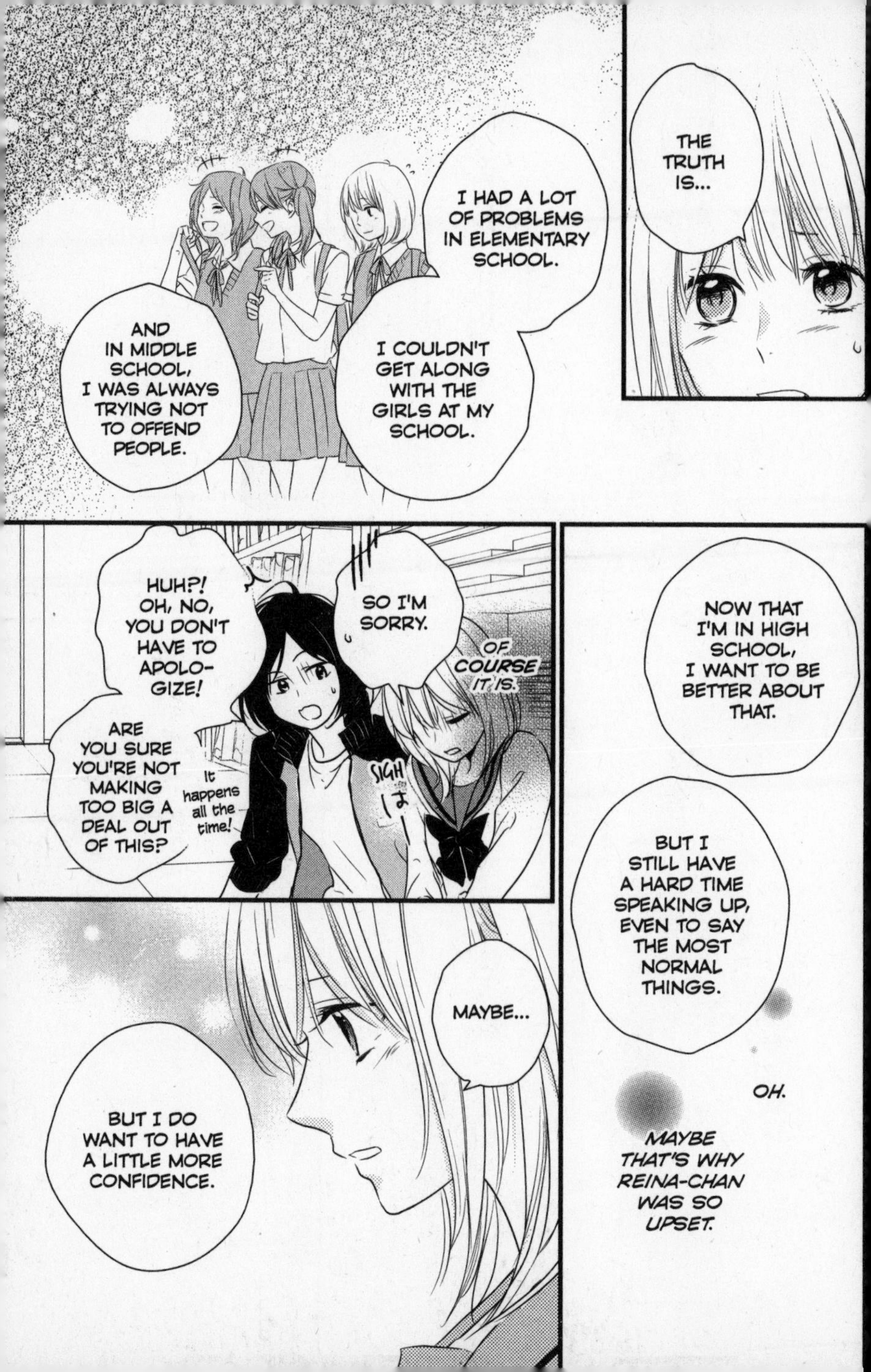
THE TRUTH IS...
I HAD A LOT OF PROBLEMS IN ELEMENTARY SCHOOL.
I COULDN'T GET ALONG WITH THE GIRLS AT MY SCHOOL.
AND IN MIDDLE SCHOOL, I WAS ALWAYS TRYING NOT TO OFFEND PEOPLE.
NOW THAT I'M IN HIGH SCHOOL, I WANT TO BE BETTER ABOUT THAT.
BUT I STILL HAVE A HARD TIME SPEAKING UP, EVEN TO SAY THE MOST NORMAL THINGS.
OH.
MAYBE THAT'S WHY REINA-CHAN WAS SO UPSET.
SO I'M SORRY.
OF COURSE IT IS.
HUH?! OH, NO, YOU DON'T HAVE TO APOLO-GIZE!
SIGH
は
ARE YOU SURE YOU'RE NOT MAKING TOO BIG A DEAL OUT OF THIS?
It happens all the time!
MAYBE...
BUT I DO WANT TO HAVE A LITTLE MORE CONFIDENCE.

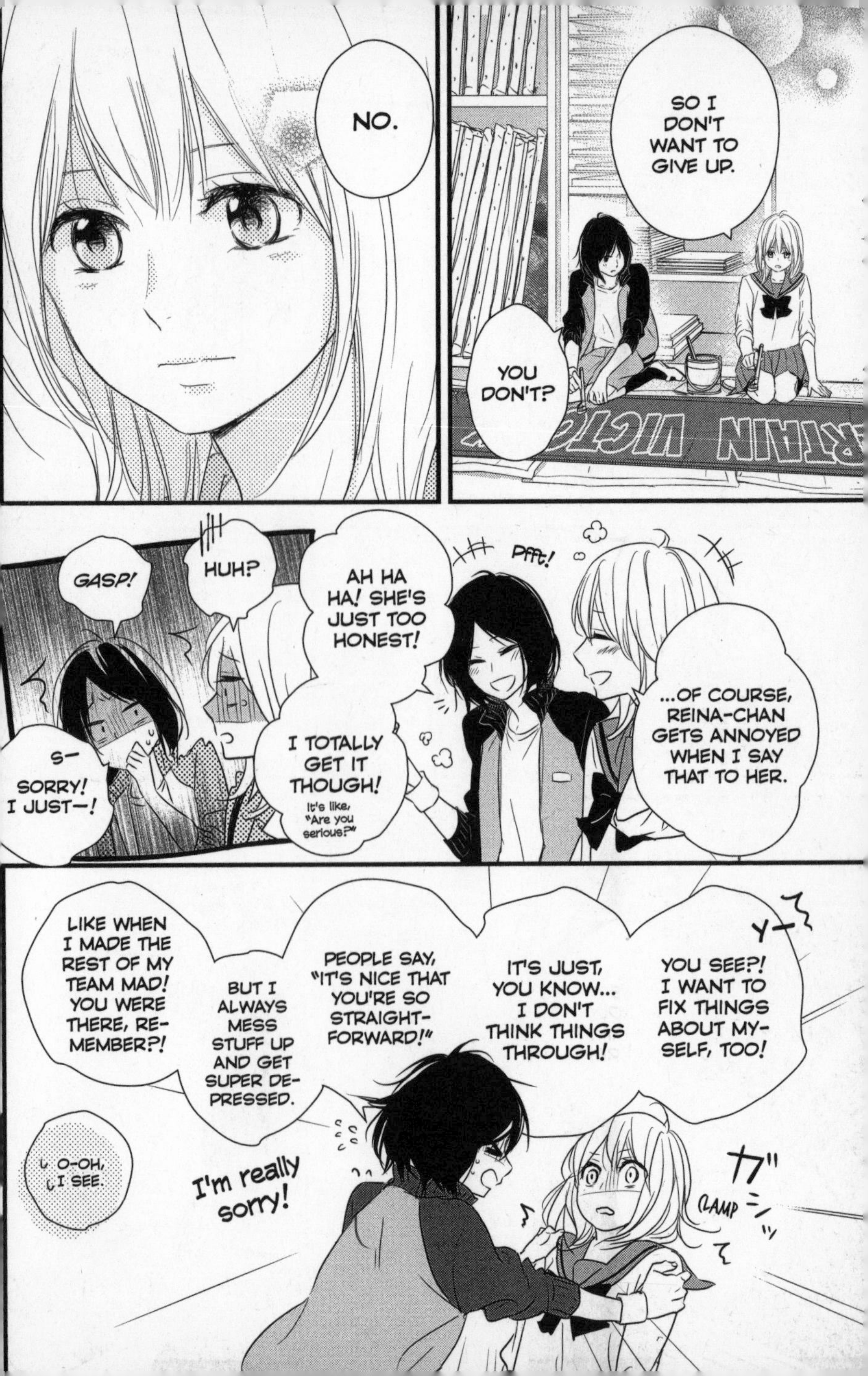
SO I DON'T WANT TO GIVE UP.
YOU DON'T?
NO.
...OF COURSE, REINA-CHAN GETS ANNOYED WHEN I SAY THAT TO HER.
Pfft!
AH HA HA! SHE'S JUST TOO HONEST!
I TOTALLY GET IT THOUGH!
It's like, "Are you serious?"
HUH?
GASP!
S— SORRY! I JUST—!
Y—
YOU SEE?! I WANT TO FIX THINGS ABOUT MY-SELF, TOO!
IT'S JUST, YOU KNOW... I DON'T THINK THINGS THROUGH!
PEOPLE SAY, "IT'S NICE THAT YOU'RE SO STRAIGHT-FORWARD!"
BUT I ALWAYS MESS STUFF UP AND GET SUPER DE-PRESSED.
LIKE WHEN I MADE THE REST OF MY TEAM MAD! YOU WERE THERE, RE-MEMBER?!
CLAMP
I'm really sorry!
O-OH, I SEE.

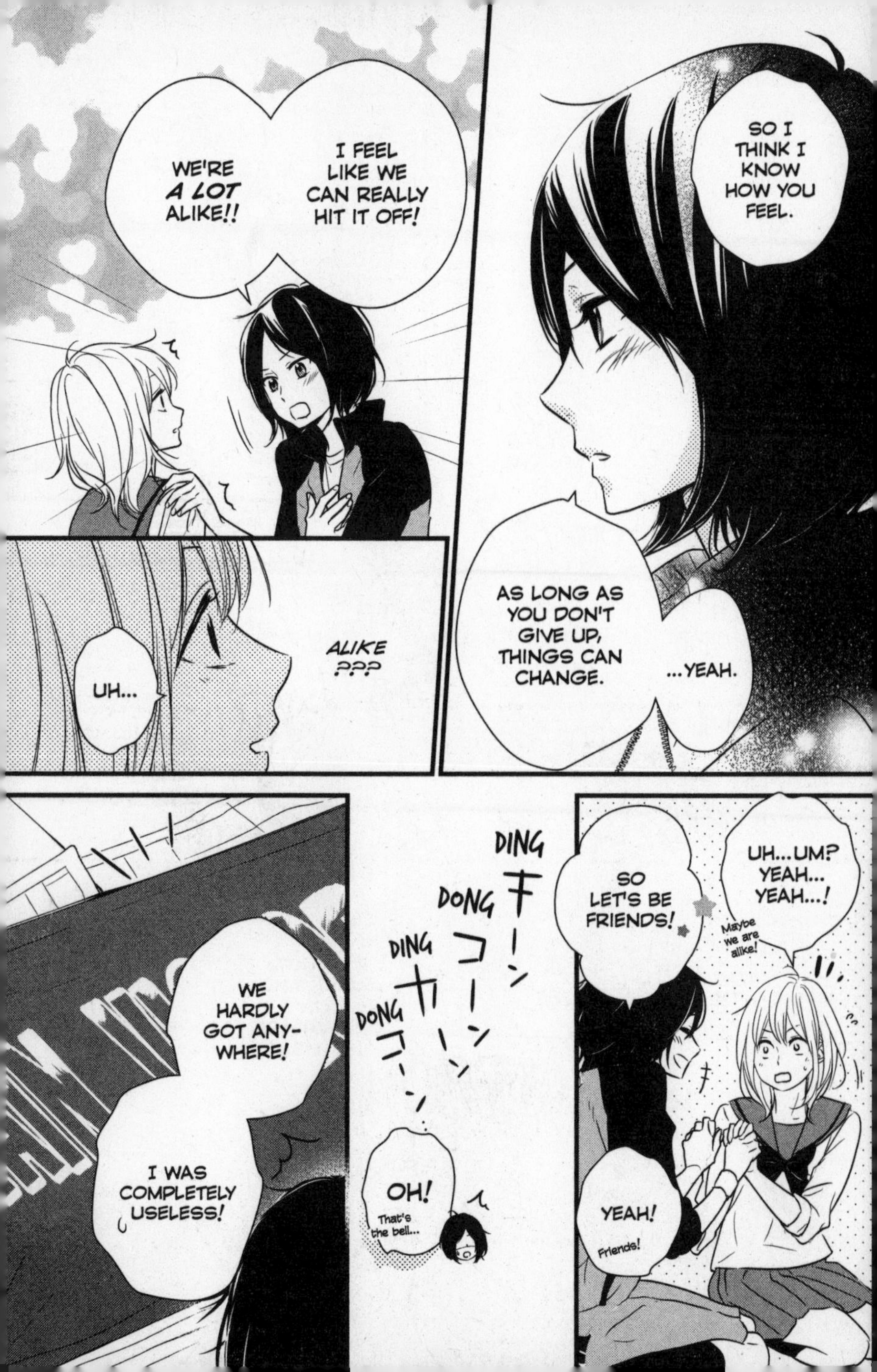
SO I THINK I KNOW HOW YOU FEEL.
AS LONG AS YOU DON'T GIVE UP, THINGS CAN CHANGE.
...YEAH.
I FEEL LIKE WE CAN REALLY HIT IT OFF!
WE'RE *A LOT* ALIKE!!
ALIKE ???
UH...
UH...UM? YEAH... YEAH...!
Maybe we are alike!
SO LET'S BE FRIENDS!
YEAH!
Friends!
DING
DONG
DING
DONG
OH!
That's the bell...
WE HARDLY GOT ANY-WHERE!
I WAS COMPLETELY USELESS!

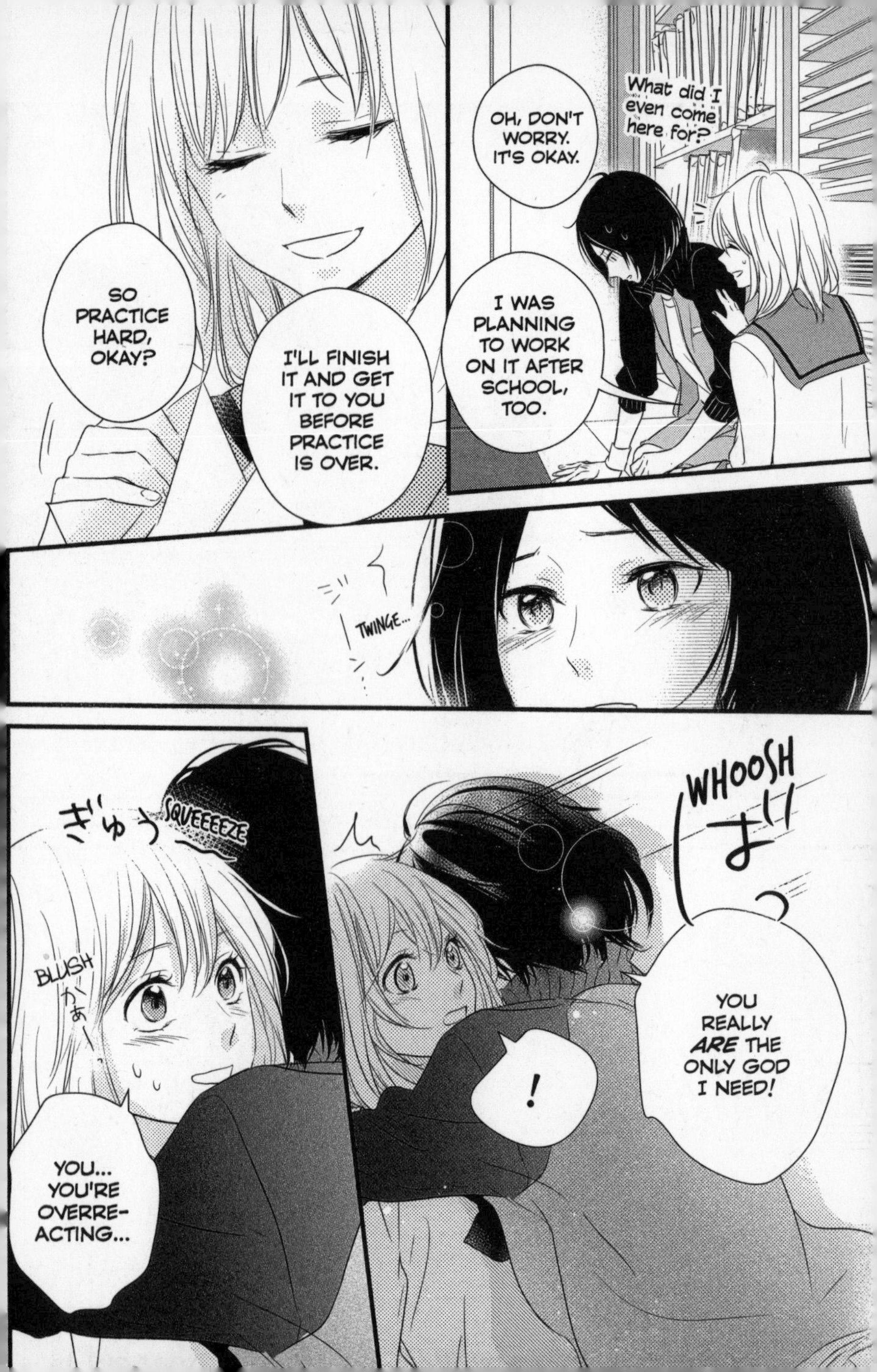
What did I even come here for?
OH, DON'T WORRY. IT'S OKAY.
I WAS PLANNING TO WORK ON IT AFTER SCHOOL, TOO.
I'LL FINISH IT AND GET IT TO YOU BEFORE PRACTICE IS OVER.
SO PRACTICE HARD, OKAY?
TWINGE...
WHOOSH
YOU REALLY *ARE* THE ONLY GOD I NEED!
!
ぎゅう
SQUEEEEEZE
BLUSH
YOU... YOU'RE OVERRE- ACTING...

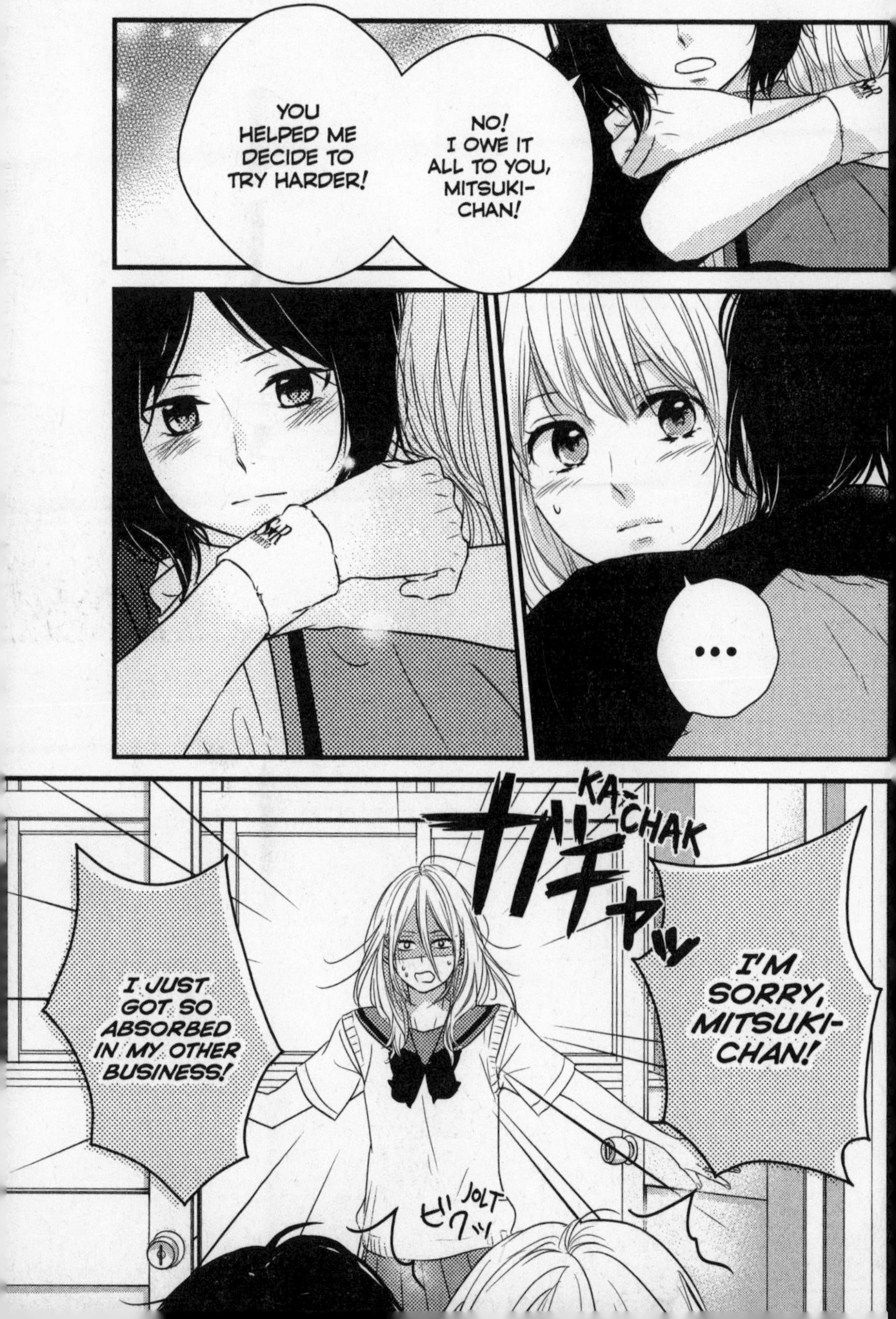
NO! I OWE IT ALL TO YOU, MITSUKI-CHAN!
YOU HELPED ME DECIDE TO TRY HARDER!
...
ガチャッ
KA-CHAK
I'M SORRY, MITSUKI-CHAN!
I JUST GOT SO ABSORBED IN MY OTHER BUSINESS!
ビクッ
JOLT

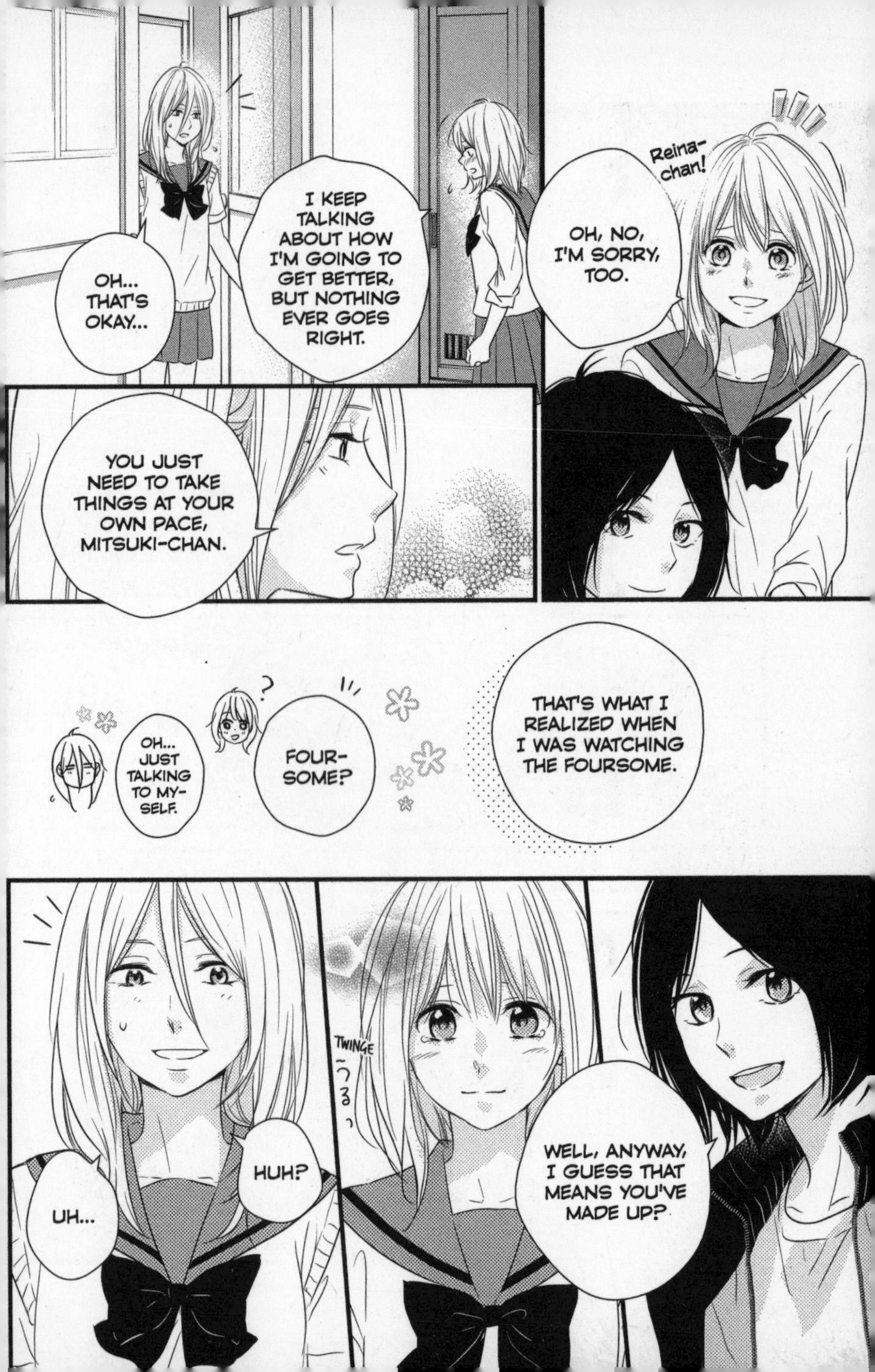
Reina-chan!
OH, NO, I'M SORRY, TOO.
I KEEP TALKING ABOUT HOW I'M GOING TO GET BETTER, BUT NOTHING EVER GOES RIGHT.
OH... THAT'S OKAY...
YOU JUST NEED TO TAKE THINGS AT YOUR OWN PACE, MITSUKI-CHAN.
THAT'S WHAT I REALIZED WHEN I WAS WATCHING THE FOURSOME.
FOUR-SOME?
OH... JUST TALKING TO MY-SELF.
WELL, ANYWAY, I GUESS THAT MEANS YOU'VE MADE UP?
TWINGE
HUH?
UH...

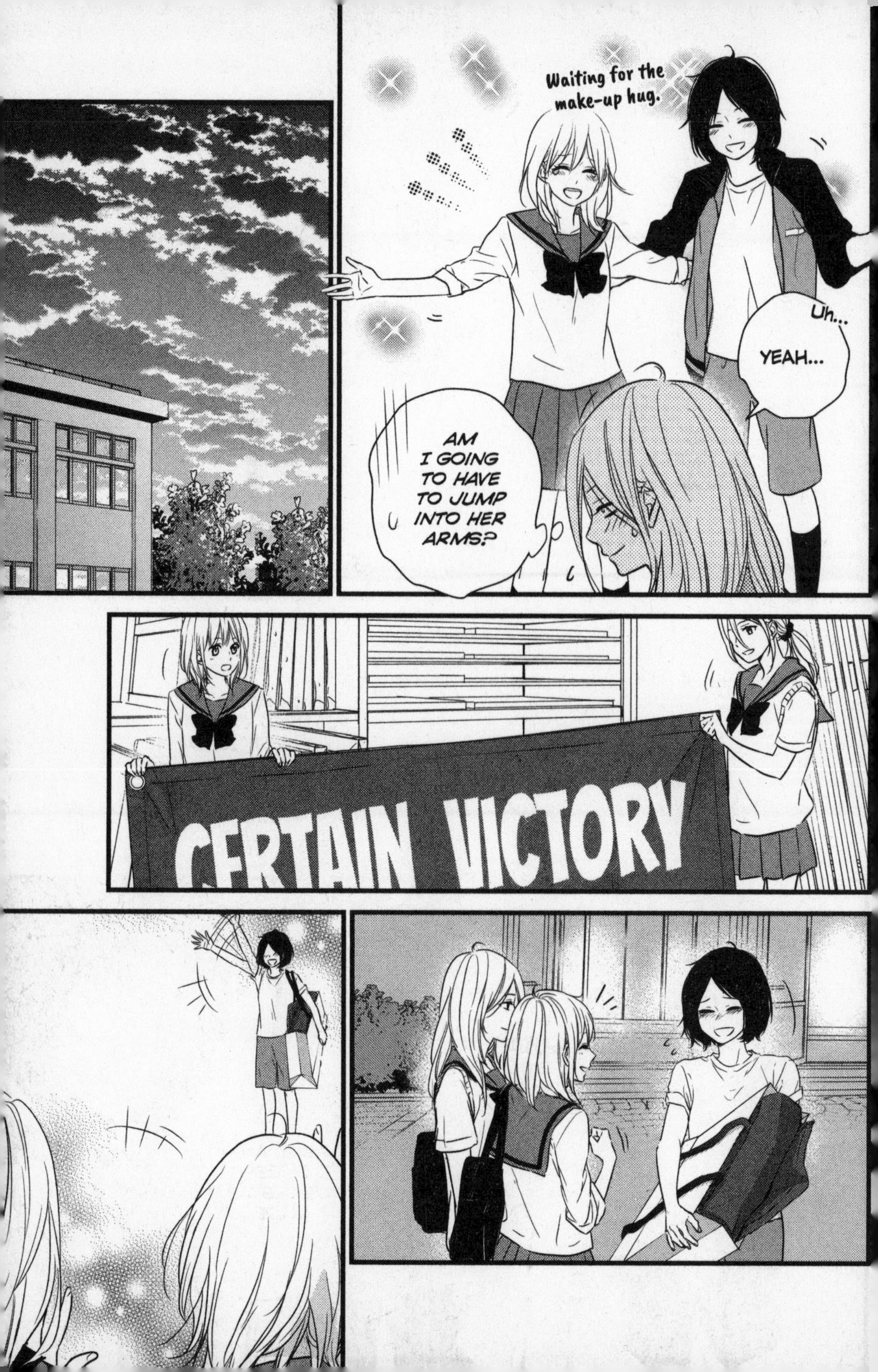
Waiting for the make-up hug.
Uh... YEAH...
AM I GOING TO HAVE TO JUMP INTO HER ARMS?
CERTAIN VICTORY

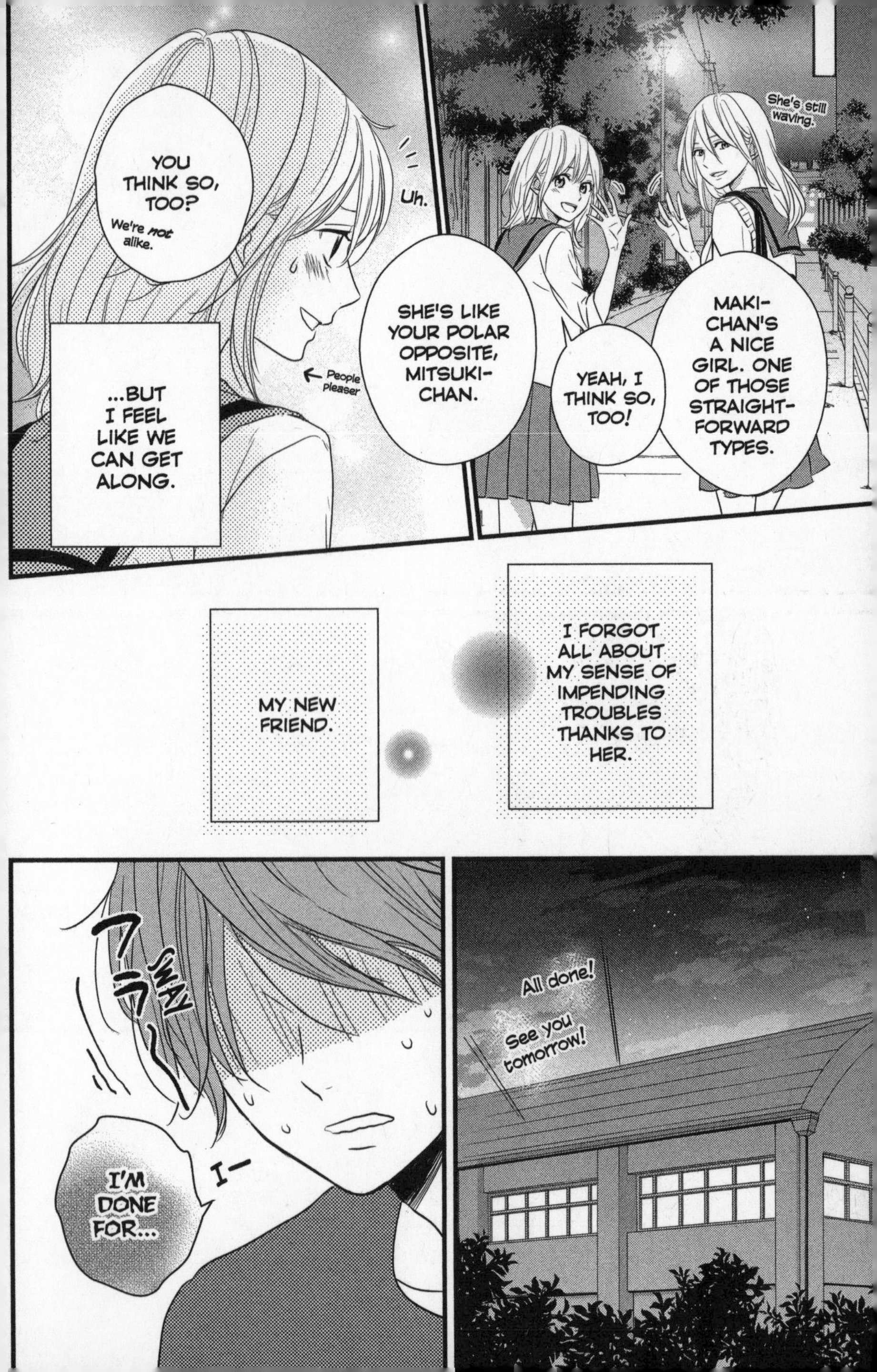
She's still waving.
MAKI-CHAN'S A NICE GIRL. ONE OF THOSE STRAIGHT-FORWARD TYPES.
YEAH, I THINK SO, TOO!
SHE'S LIKE YOUR POLAR OPPOSITE, MITSUKI-CHAN.
Uh.
YOU THINK SO, TOO?
We're *not* alike.
People pleaser
...BUT I FEEL LIKE WE CAN GET ALONG.
I FORGOT ALL ABOUT MY SENSE OF IMPENDING TROUBLES THANKS TO HER.
MY NEW FRIEND.
All done!
See you tomorrow!
SWAY
I—
I'M DONE FOR...

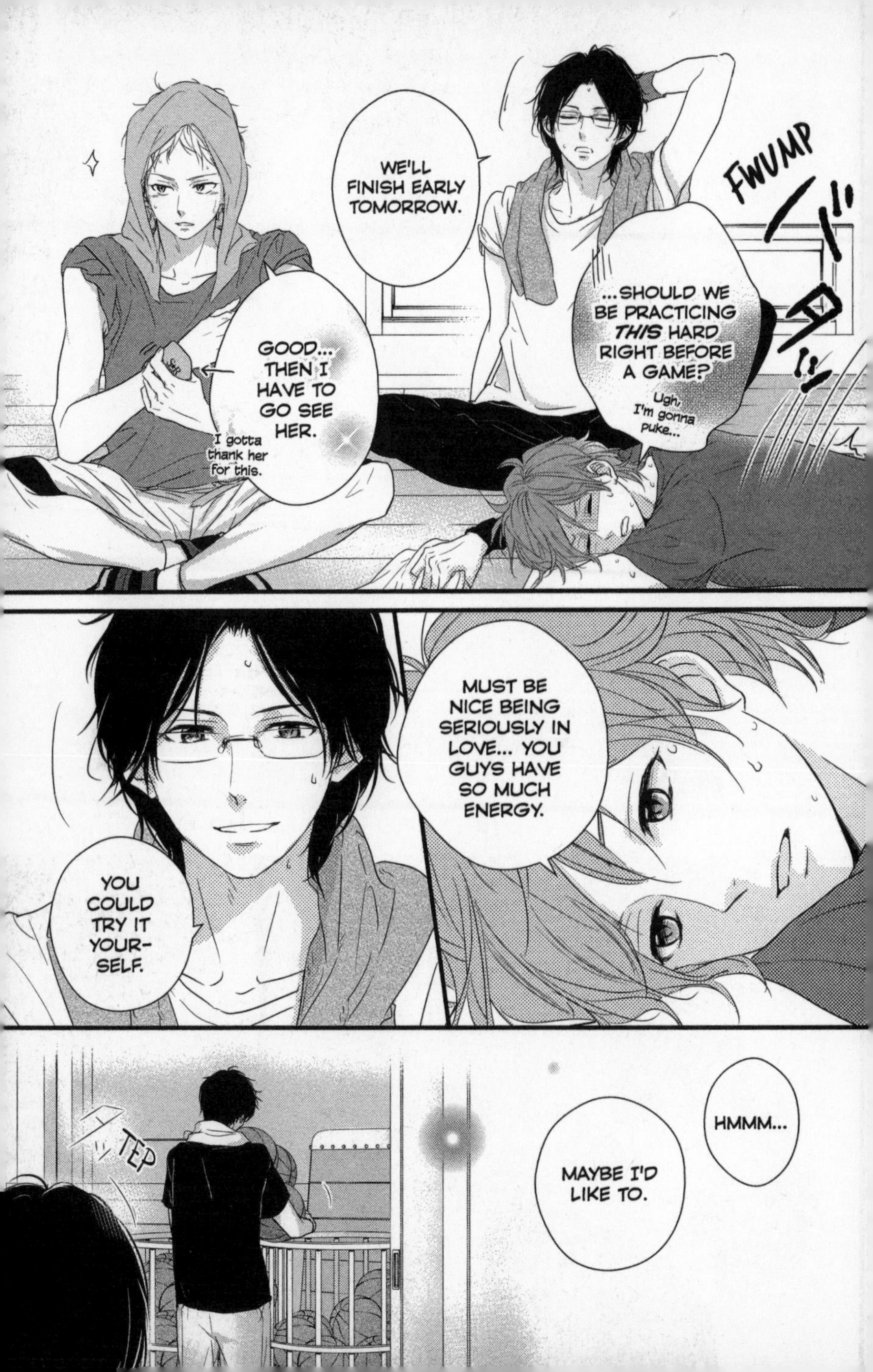
FWUMP
...SHOULD WE BE PRACTICING *THIS* HARD RIGHT BEFORE A GAME?
Ugh, I'm gonna puke...
WE'LL FINISH EARLY TOMORROW.
GOOD... THEN I HAVE TO GO SEE HER.
I gotta thank her for this.
MUST BE NICE BEING SERIOUSLY IN LOVE... YOU GUYS HAVE SO MUCH ENERGY.
YOU COULD TRY IT YOURSELF.
HMMM...
MAYBE I'D LIKE TO.
TEP

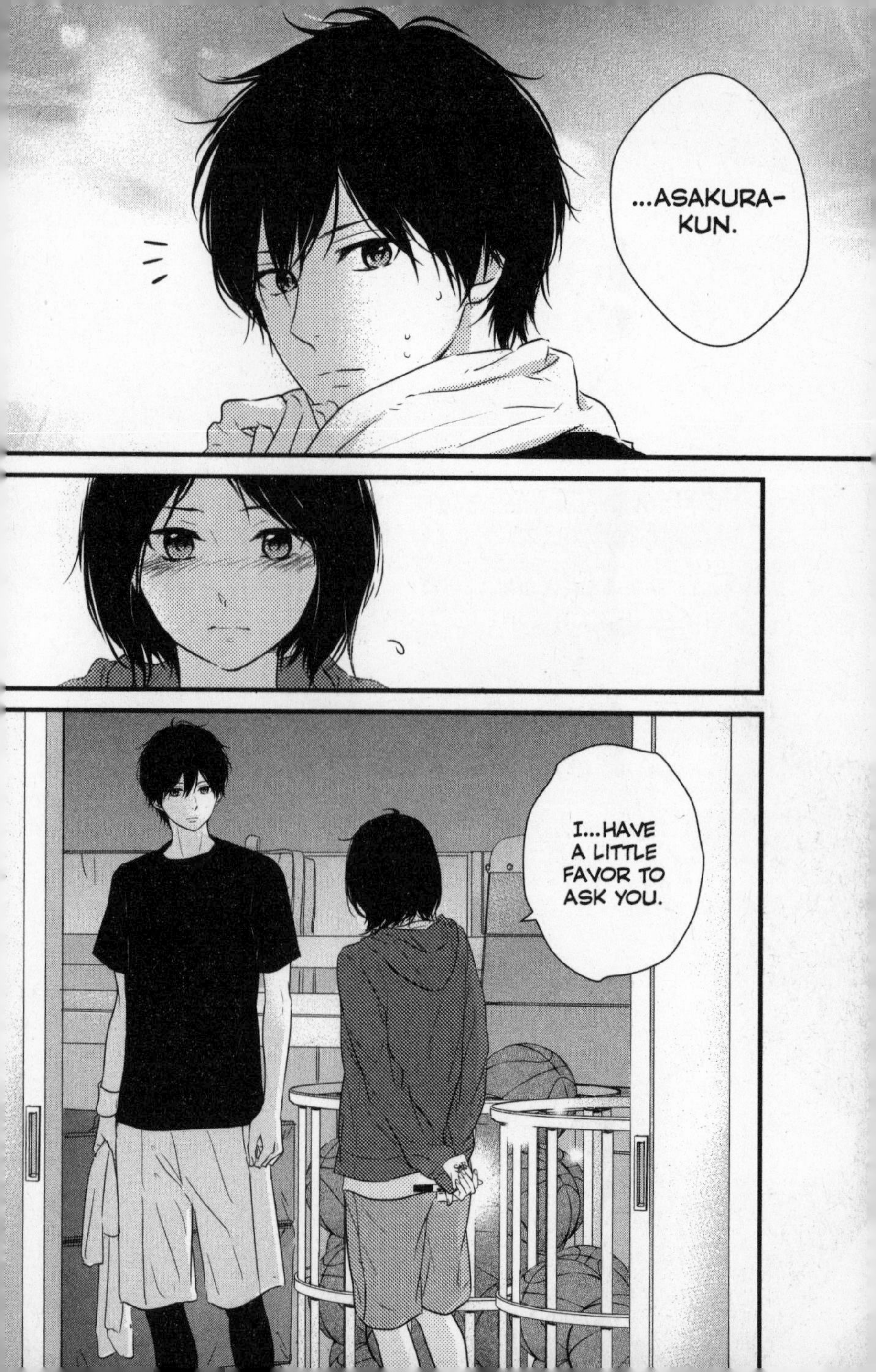
...ASAKURA-KUN.
I...HAVE A LITTLE FAVOR TO ASK YOU.

period 13: "Did This Love Become...Serious?"

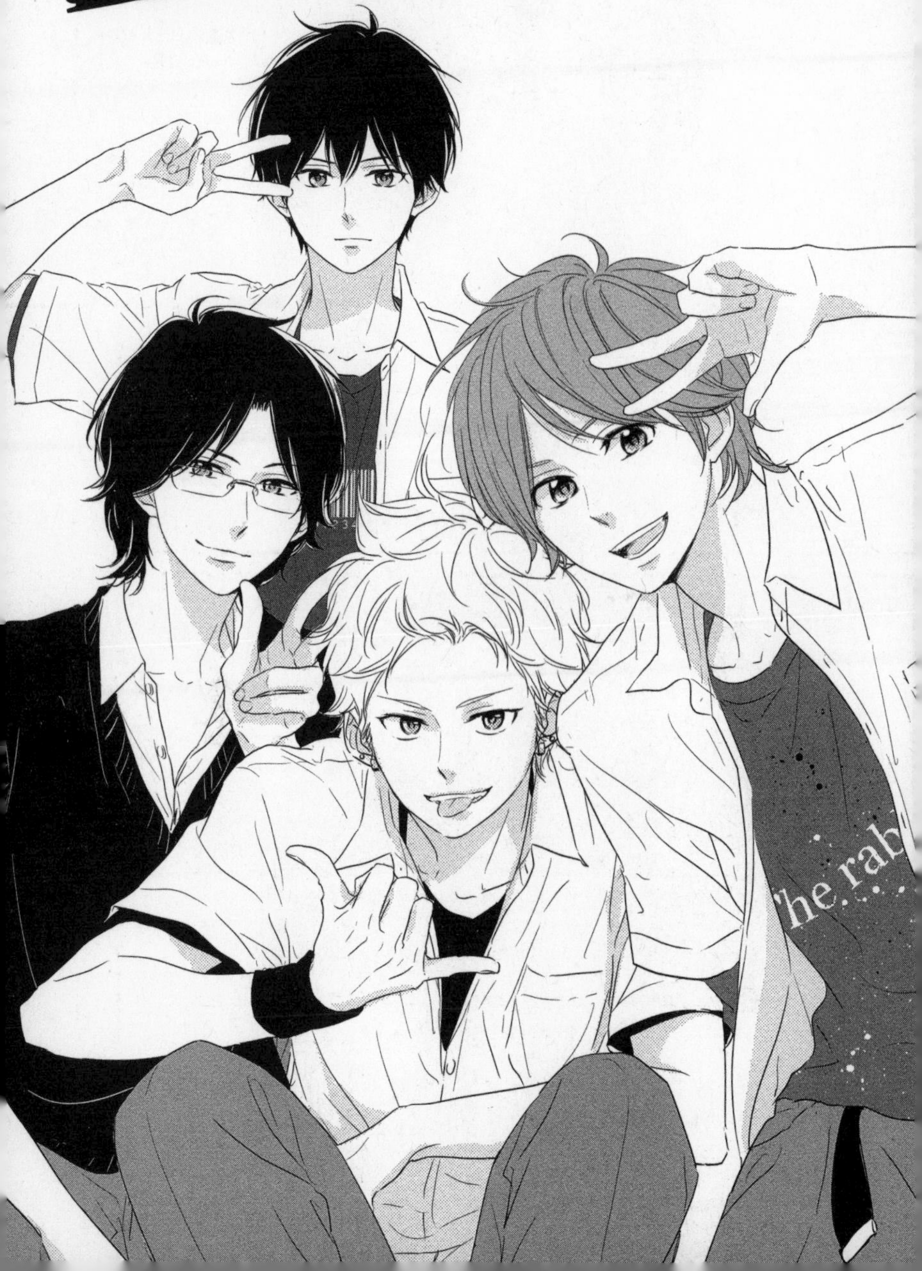

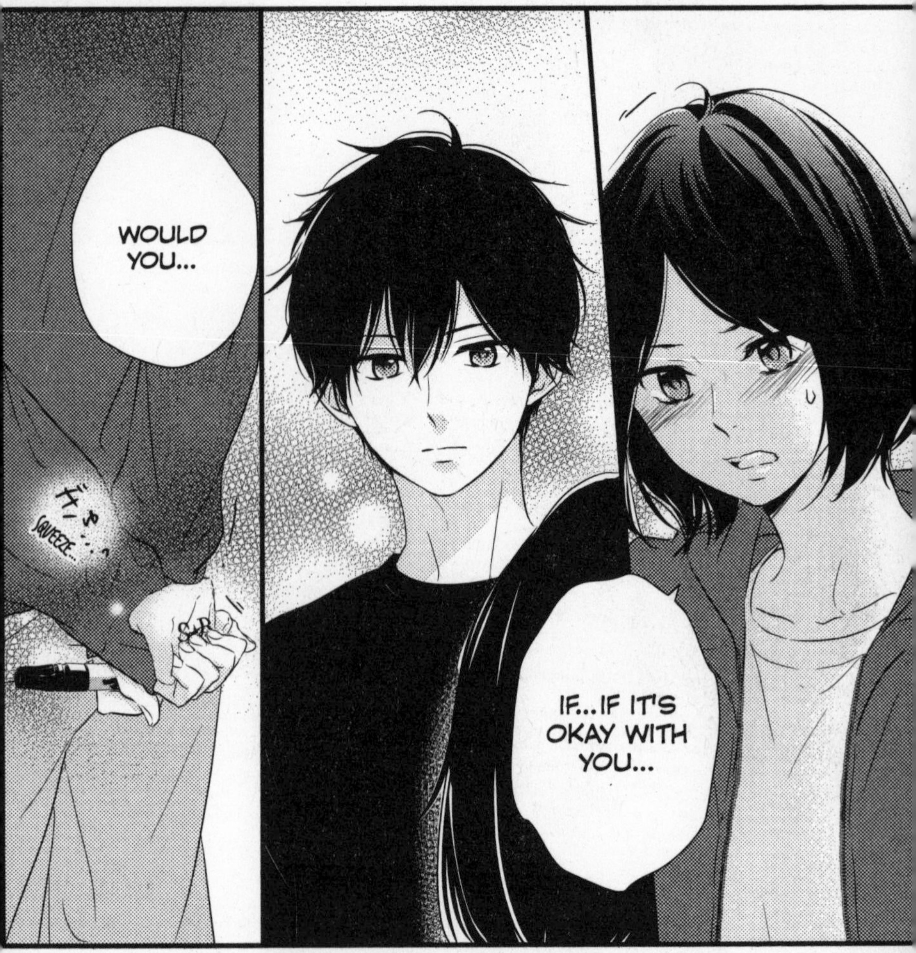
IF...IF IT'S OKAY WITH YOU...
WOULD YOU...
SQUEEZE...

Q. How did you decide on the characters' hair colors?

A. I chose them based on personality & how it would balance out when all the characters are together.

I thought it might work for Ryūji to have some color...but...

I just gotta go with white.

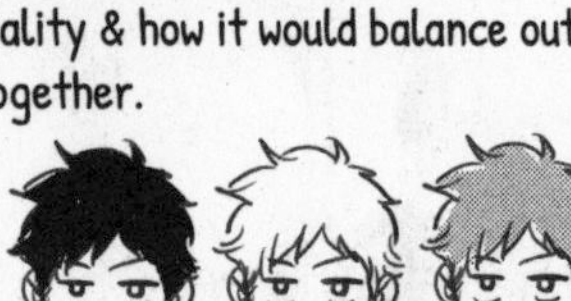

In color pictures, he's (ashy) blond.

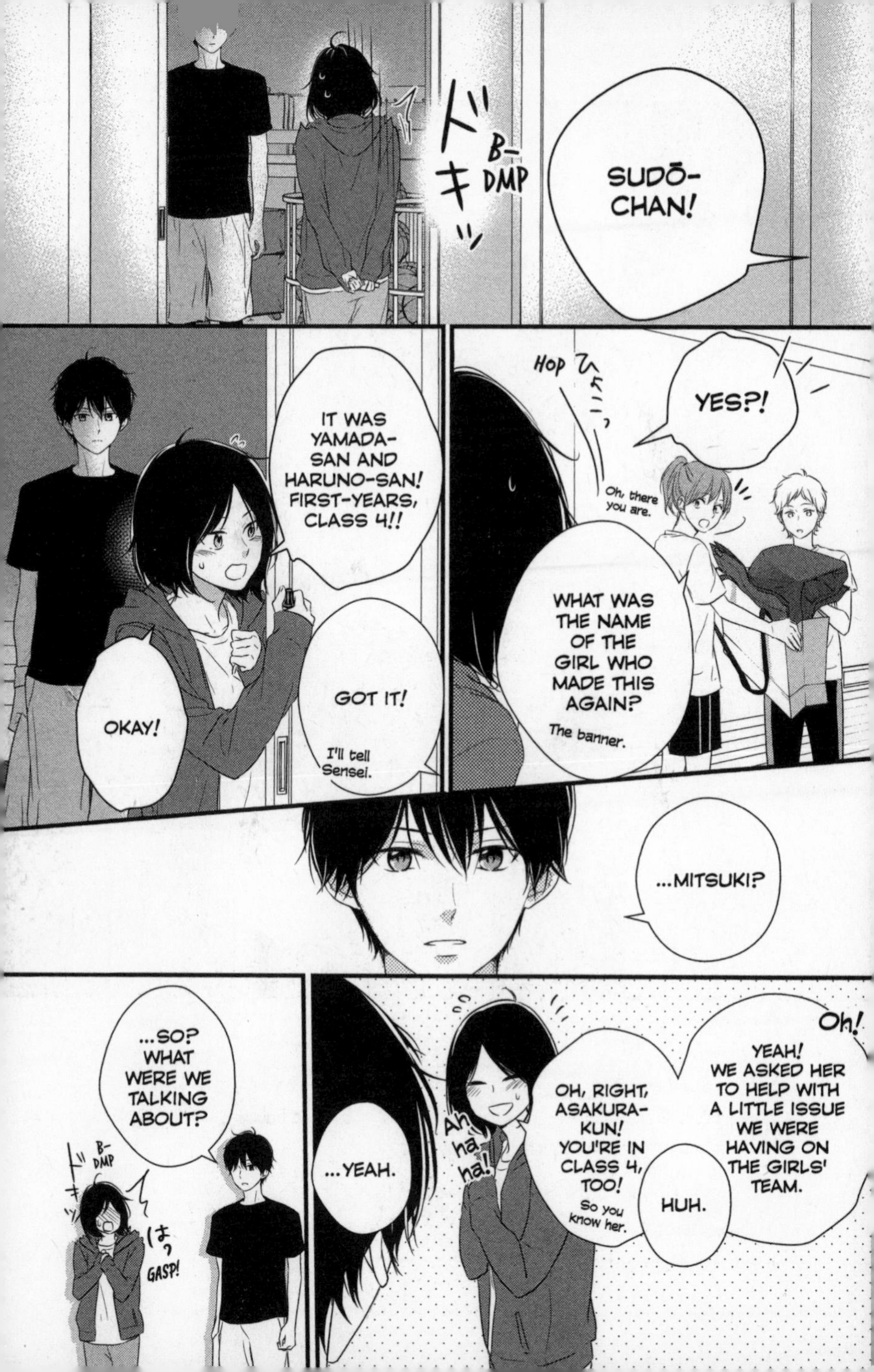
SUDŌ-CHAN!
ドキッ
B-DMP
HOP ひょこっ
YES?!
Oh, there you are.
WHAT WAS THE NAME OF THE GIRL WHO MADE THIS AGAIN?
The banner.
IT WAS YAMADA-SAN AND HARUNO-SAN! FIRST-YEARS, CLASS 4!!
GOT IT!
I'll tell Sensei.
OKAY!
...MITSUKI?
Oh!
YEAH! WE ASKED HER TO HELP WITH A LITTLE ISSUE WE WERE HAVING ON THE GIRLS' TEAM.
OH, RIGHT, ASAKURA-KUN! YOU'RE IN CLASS 4, TOO!
So you know her.
HUH.
Ah ha ha!
...YEAH.
...SO? WHAT WERE WE TALKING ABOUT?
ドキッ
B-DMP
はっ
GASP!

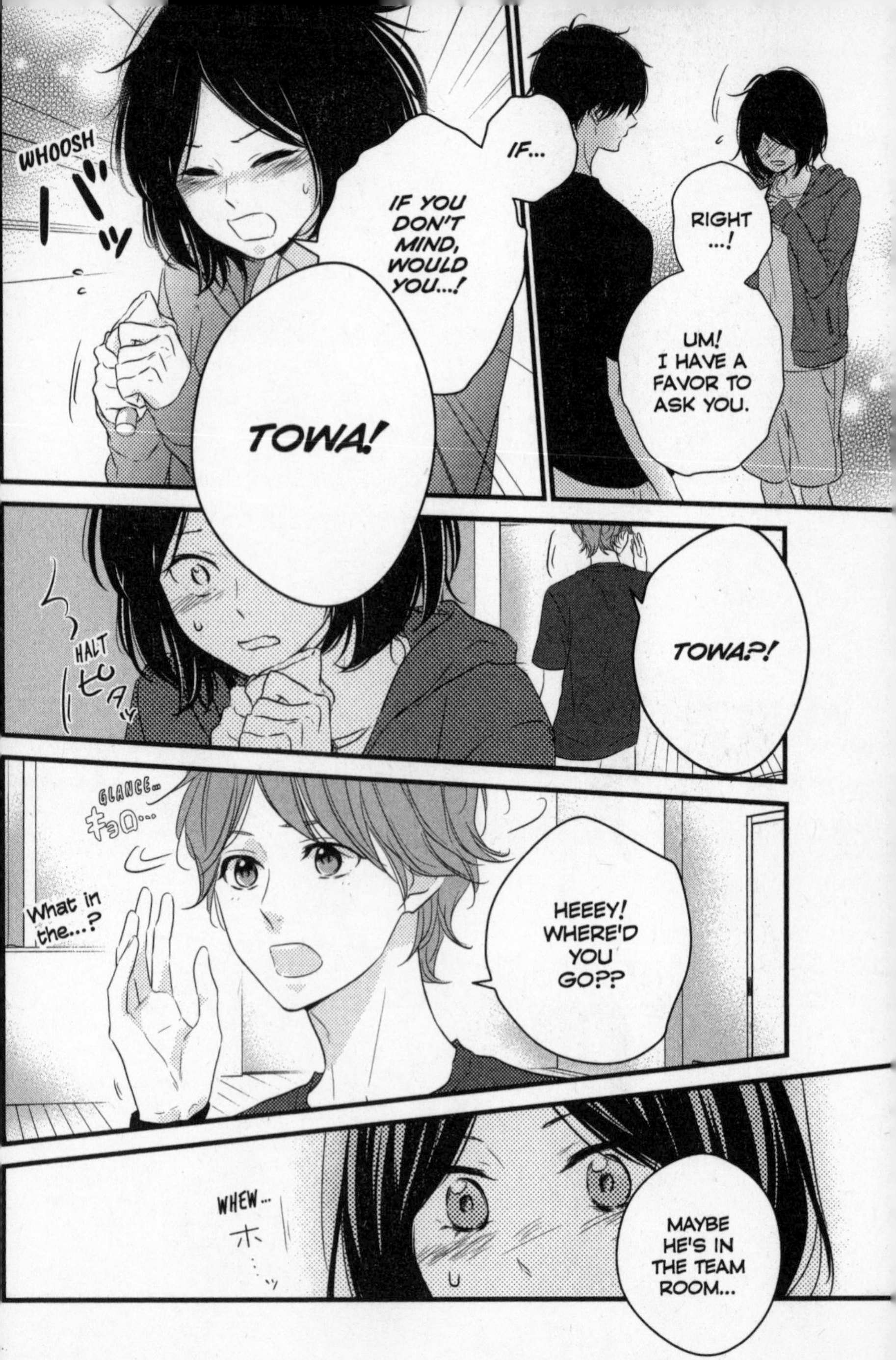
RIGHT ...!
UM! I HAVE A FAVOR TO ASK YOU.
IF...
IF YOU DON'T MIND, WOULD YOU...!
WHOOSH
TOWA!
TOWA?!
HALT
HEEEY! WHERE'D YOU GO??
GLANCE...
What in the...?
MAYBE HE'S IN THE TEAM ROOM...
WHEW...

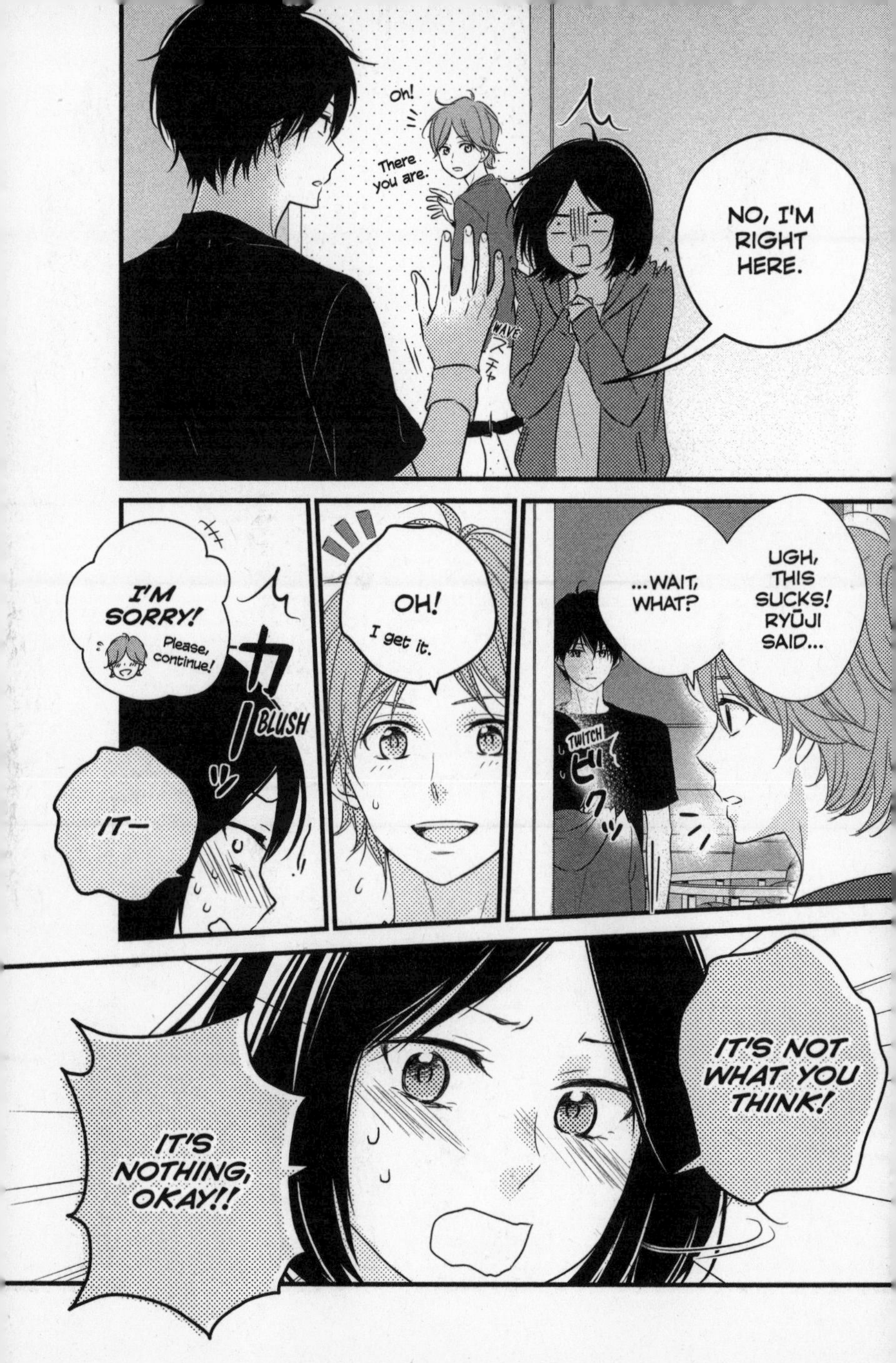
Oh!
There you are.
WAVE
NO, I'M RIGHT HERE.
UGH, THIS SUCKS! RYŪJI SAID...
...WAIT, WHAT?
TWITCH
OH!
I get it.
I'M SORRY!
Please, continue!
BLUSH
IT—
IT'S NOT WHAT YOU THINK!
IT'S NOTHING, OKAY!!

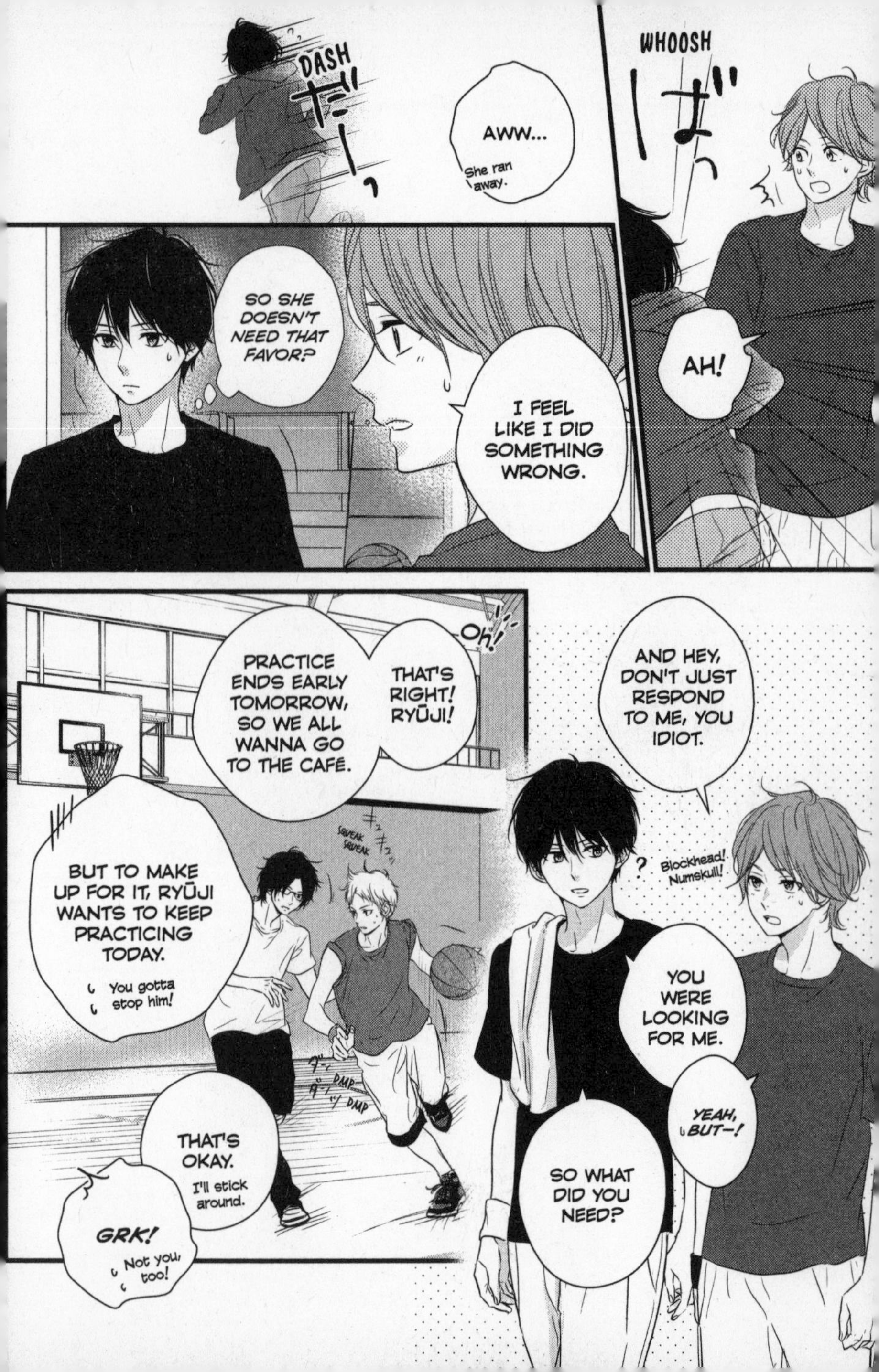
WHOOSH
AH!
DASH
AWW...
She ran away.
SO SHE DOESN'T NEED THAT FAVOR?
I FEEL LIKE I DID SOMETHING WRONG.
AND HEY, DON'T JUST RESPOND TO ME, YOU IDIOT.
Blockhead! Numskull!
?
YOU WERE LOOKING FOR ME.
YEAH, BUT—!
SO WHAT DID YOU NEED?
Oh!
THAT'S RIGHT! RYŪJI!
PRACTICE ENDS EARLY TOMORROW, SO WE ALL WANNA GO TO THE CAFÉ.
BUT TO MAKE UP FOR IT, RYŪJI WANTS TO KEEP PRACTICING TODAY.
You gotta stop him!
SQUEAK SQUEAK
DMP DMP
THAT'S OKAY.
I'll stick around.
GRK!
Not you, too!

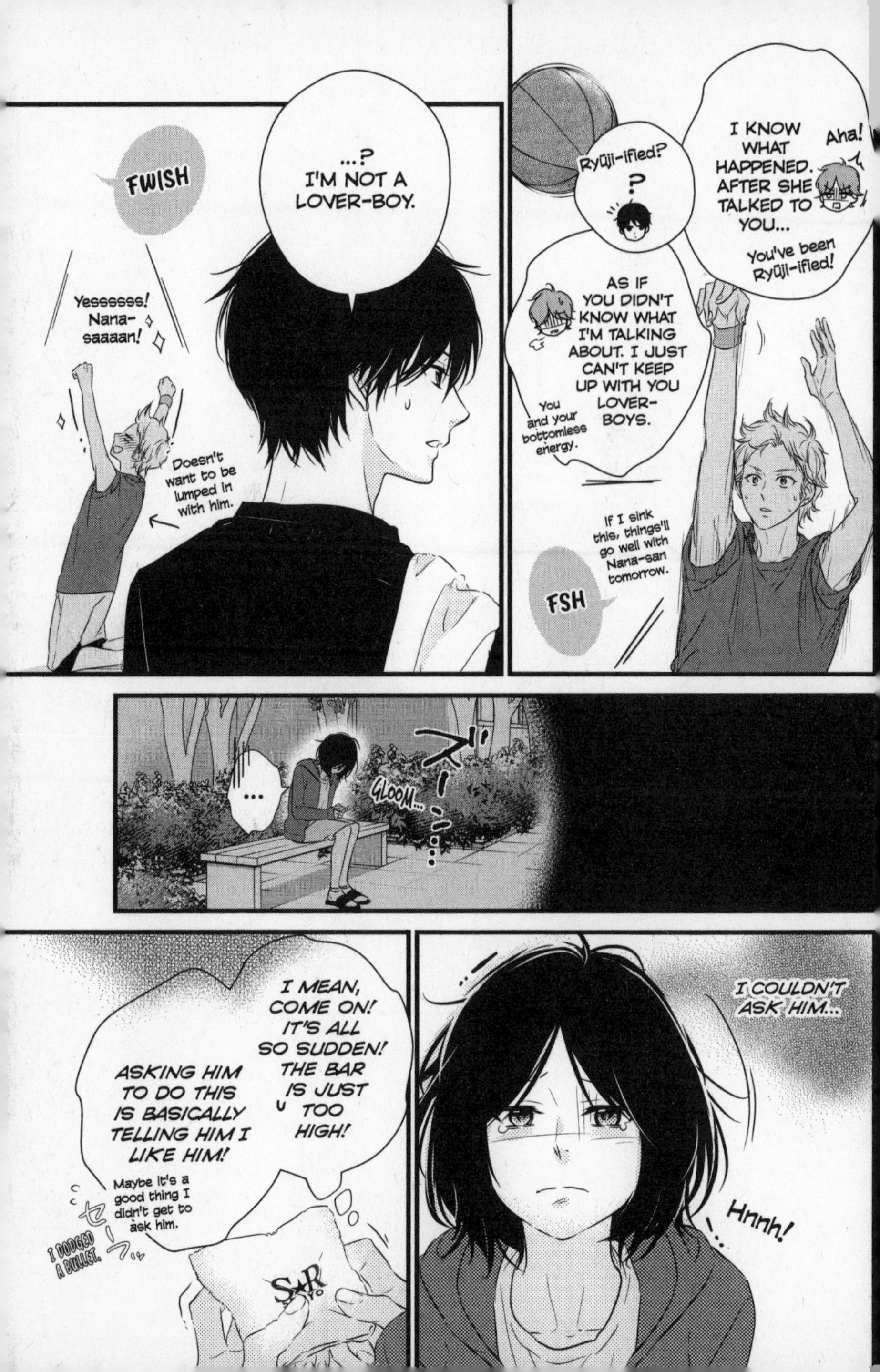
I KNOW WHAT HAPPENED. AFTER SHE TALKED TO YOU...
Aha!
You've been Ryūji-ified!
Ryūji-ified?
AS IF YOU DIDN'T KNOW WHAT I'M TALKING ABOUT. I JUST CAN'T KEEP UP WITH YOU LOVER-BOYS.
You and your bottomless energy.
If I sink this, things'll go well with Nana-san tomorrow.
FSH
...? I'M NOT A LOVER-BOY.
FWISH
Yessssss! Nana-saaaan!
Doesn't want to be lumped in with him.
GLOOM...
I COULDN'T ASK HIM...
Hnnh!
I MEAN, COME ON! IT'S ALL SO SUDDEN! THE BAR IS JUST TOO HIGH!
ASKING HIM TO DO THIS IS BASICALLY TELLING HIM I LIKE HIM!
Maybe it's a good thing I didn't get to ask him.
I DODGED A BULLET.

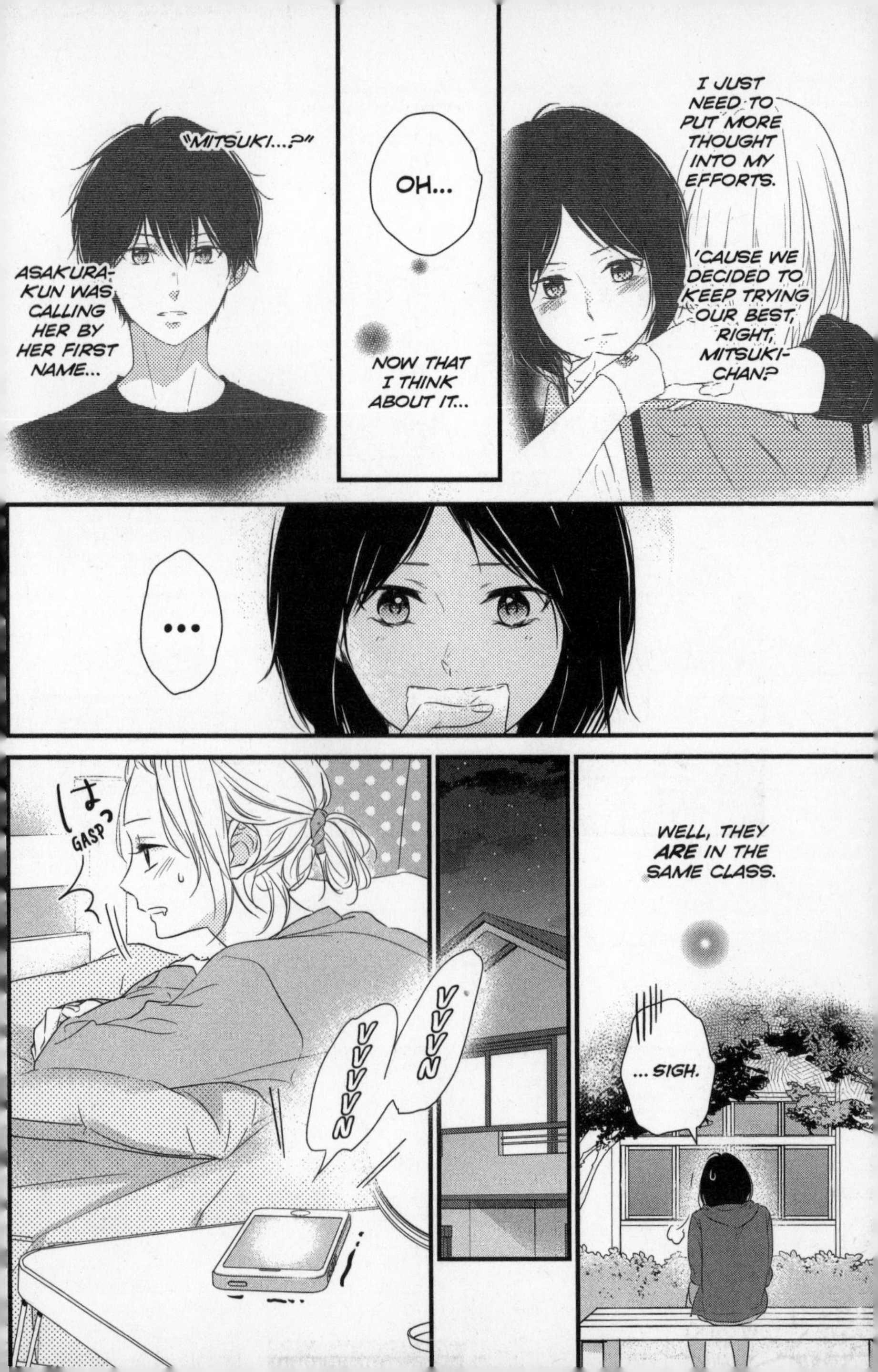
I JUST NEED TO PUT MORE THOUGHT INTO MY EFFORTS.
'CAUSE WE DECIDED TO KEEP TRYING OUR BEST, RIGHT, MITSUKI-CHAN?
OH...
NOW THAT I THINK ABOUT IT...
"MITSUKI...?"
ASAKURA-KUN WAS CALLING HER BY HER FIRST NAME...
...
WELL, THEY ARE IN THE SAME CLASS.
...SIGH.
VVVVN
VVVVN
はっ
GASP

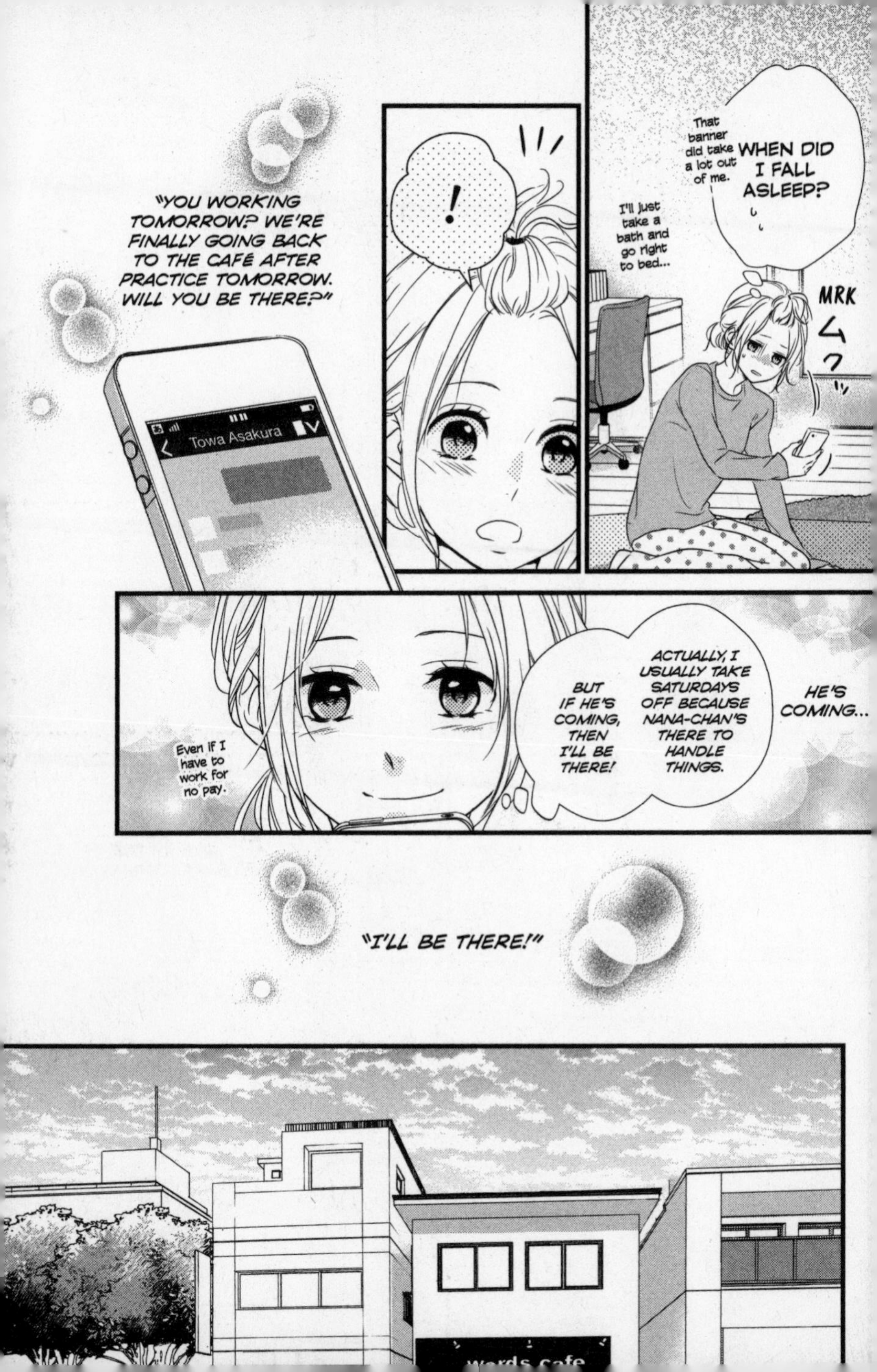
WHEN DID I FALL ASLEEP?
That banner did take a lot out of me.
I'll just take a bath and go right to bed...
MRK
!
"YOU WORKING TOMORROW? WE'RE FINALLY GOING BACK TO THE CAFÉ AFTER PRACTICE TOMORROW. WILL YOU BE THERE?"
Towa Asakura
HE'S COMING...
ACTUALLY, I USUALLY TAKE SATURDAYS OFF BECAUSE NANA-CHAN'S THERE TO HANDLE THINGS.
BUT IF HE'S COMING, THEN I'LL BE THERE!
Even if I have to work for no pay.
"I'LL BE THERE!"

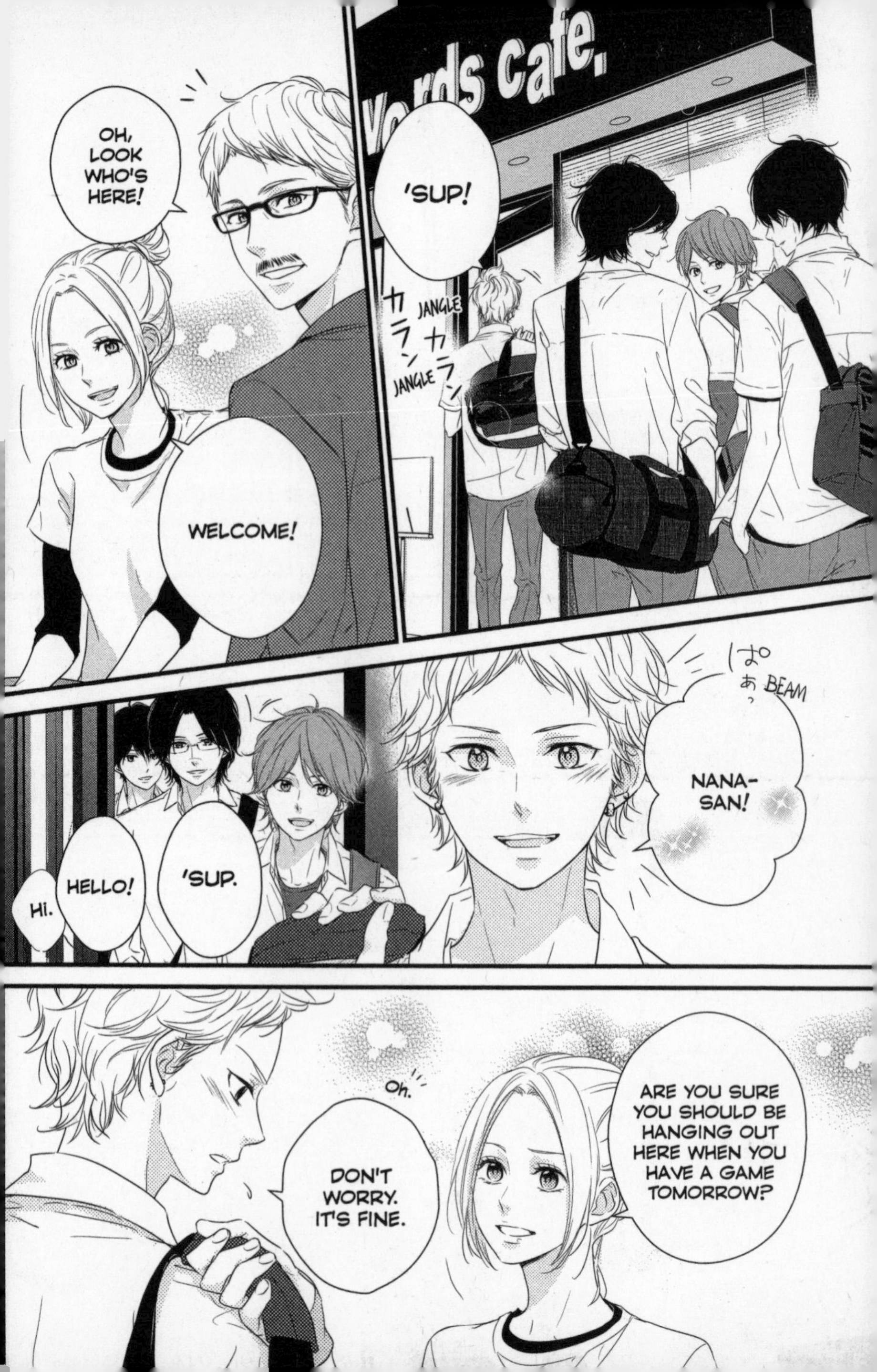
'SUP!
カラン JANGLE
カラン JANGLE
OH, LOOK WHO'S HERE!
WELCOME!
ぱぁっ BEAM
NANA-SAN!
'SUP.
HELLO!
Hi.
ARE YOU SURE YOU SHOULD BE HANGING OUT HERE WHEN YOU HAVE A GAME TOMORROW?
Oh.
DON'T WORRY. IT'S FINE.

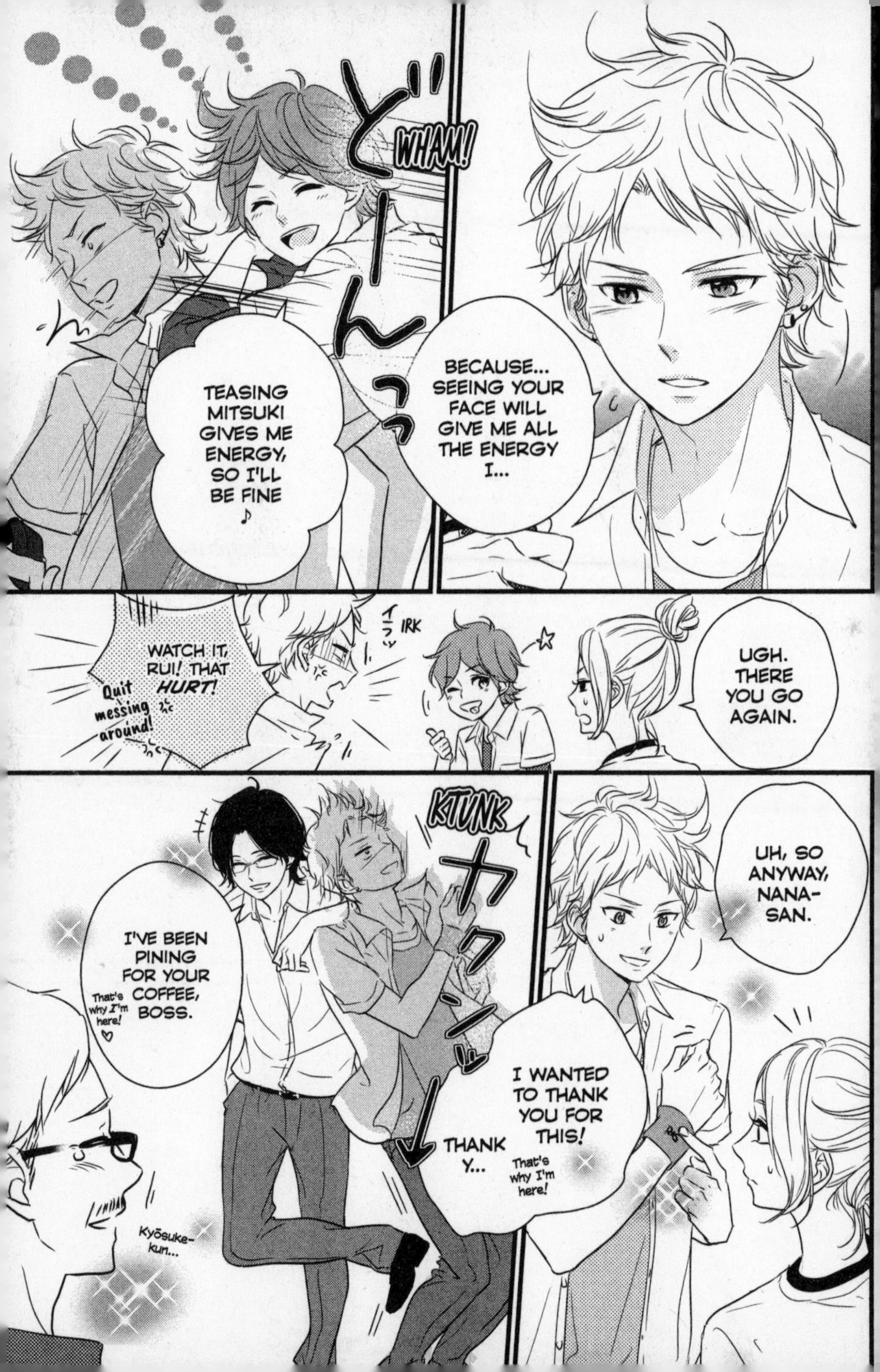
BECAUSE... SEEING YOUR FACE WILL GIVE ME ALL THE ENERGY I...
WHAM!
TEASING MITSUKI GIVES ME ENERGY, SO I'LL BE FINE ♪
UGH. THERE YOU GO AGAIN.
IRK
WATCH IT, RUI! THAT HURT!
Quit messing around!
UH, SO ANYWAY, NANA-SAN.
I WANTED TO THANK YOU FOR THIS!
That's why I'm here!
KTUNK
THANK Y...
I'VE BEEN PINING FOR YOUR COFFEE, BOSS.
That's why I'm here! ♡
Kyōsuke-kun...

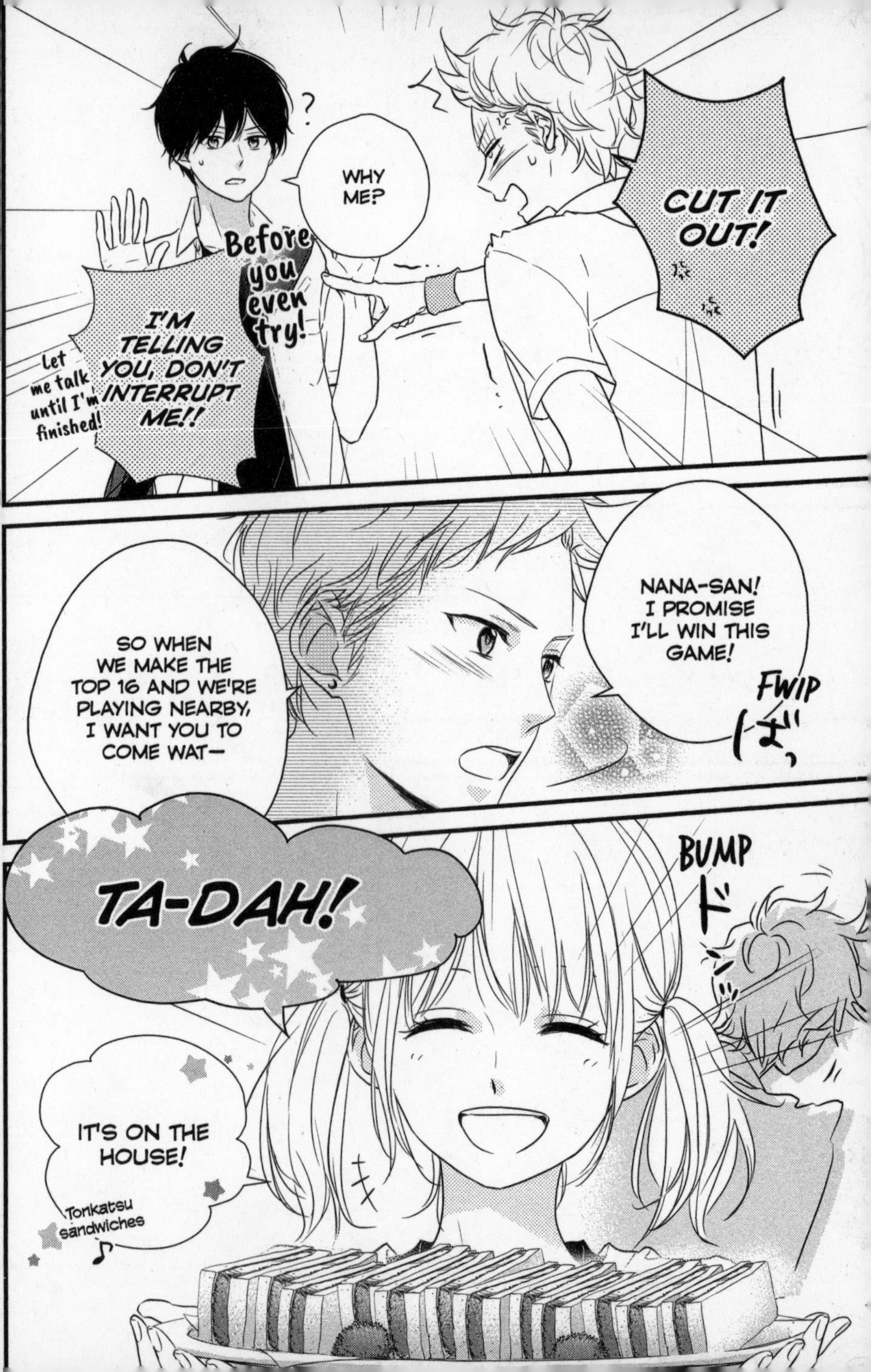
CUT IT OUT!
WHY ME?
Before you even try!
I'M TELLING YOU, DON'T INTERRUPT ME!!
Let me talk until I'm finished!
NANA-SAN! I PROMISE I'LL WIN THIS GAME!
FWIP
ぱ
SO WHEN WE MAKE THE TOP 16 AND WE'RE PLAYING NEARBY, I WANT YOU TO COME WAT—
BUMP
ド
TA-DAH!
IT'S ON THE HOUSE!
Tonkatsu sandwiches

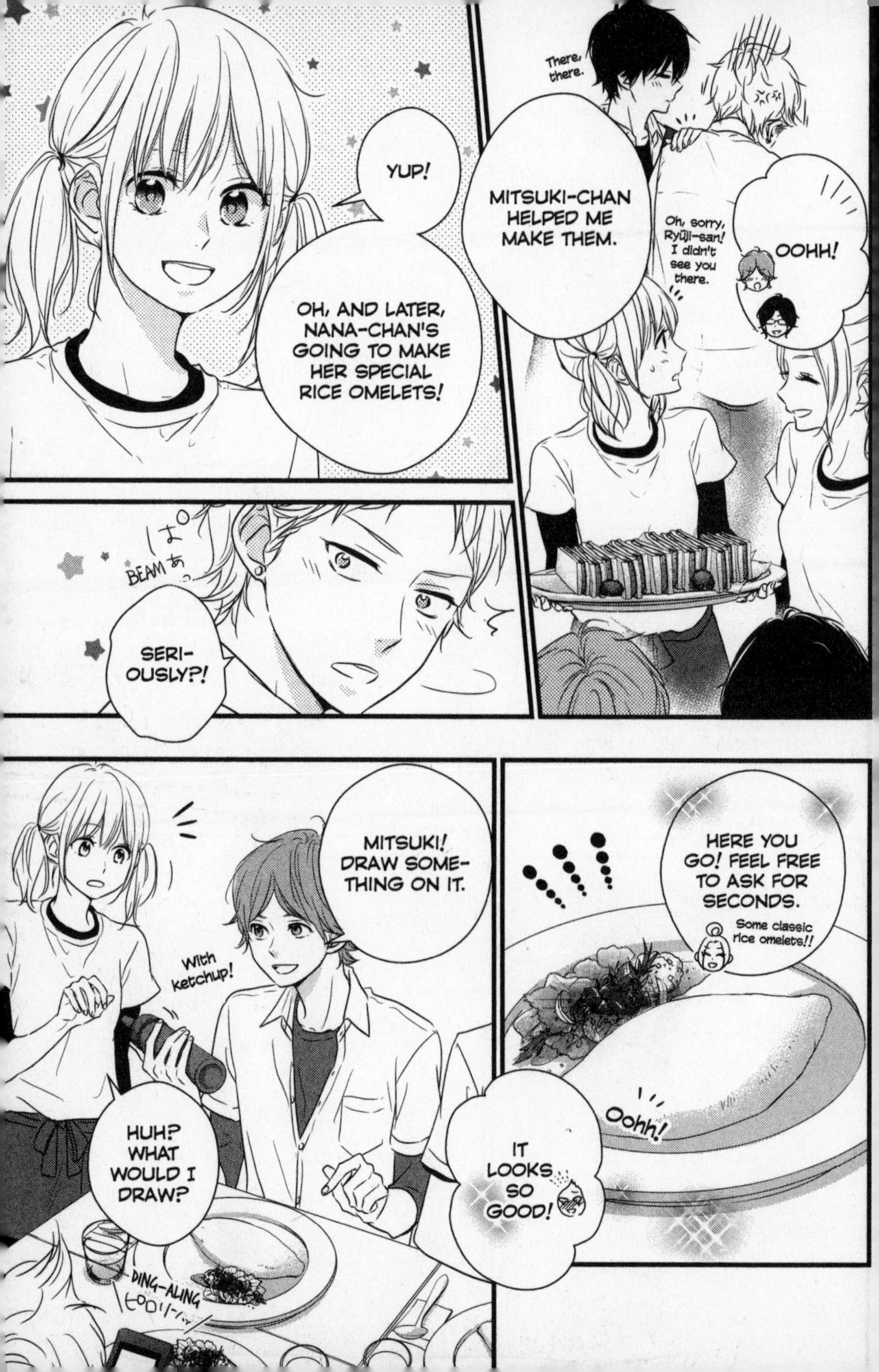
There, there.
MITSUKI-CHAN HELPED ME MAKE THEM.
Oh, sorry, Ryūji-san! I didn't see you there.
OOHH!
YUP!
OH, AND LATER, NANA-CHAN'S GOING TO MAKE HER SPECIAL RICE OMELETS!
BEAM
SERI-OUSLY?!
HERE YOU GO! FEEL FREE TO ASK FOR SECONDS.
Some classic rice omelets!!
Oohh!
IT LOOKS SO GOOD!
MITSUKI! DRAW SOME-THING ON IT.
With ketchup!
HUH? WHAT WOULD I DRAW?
DING-ALING

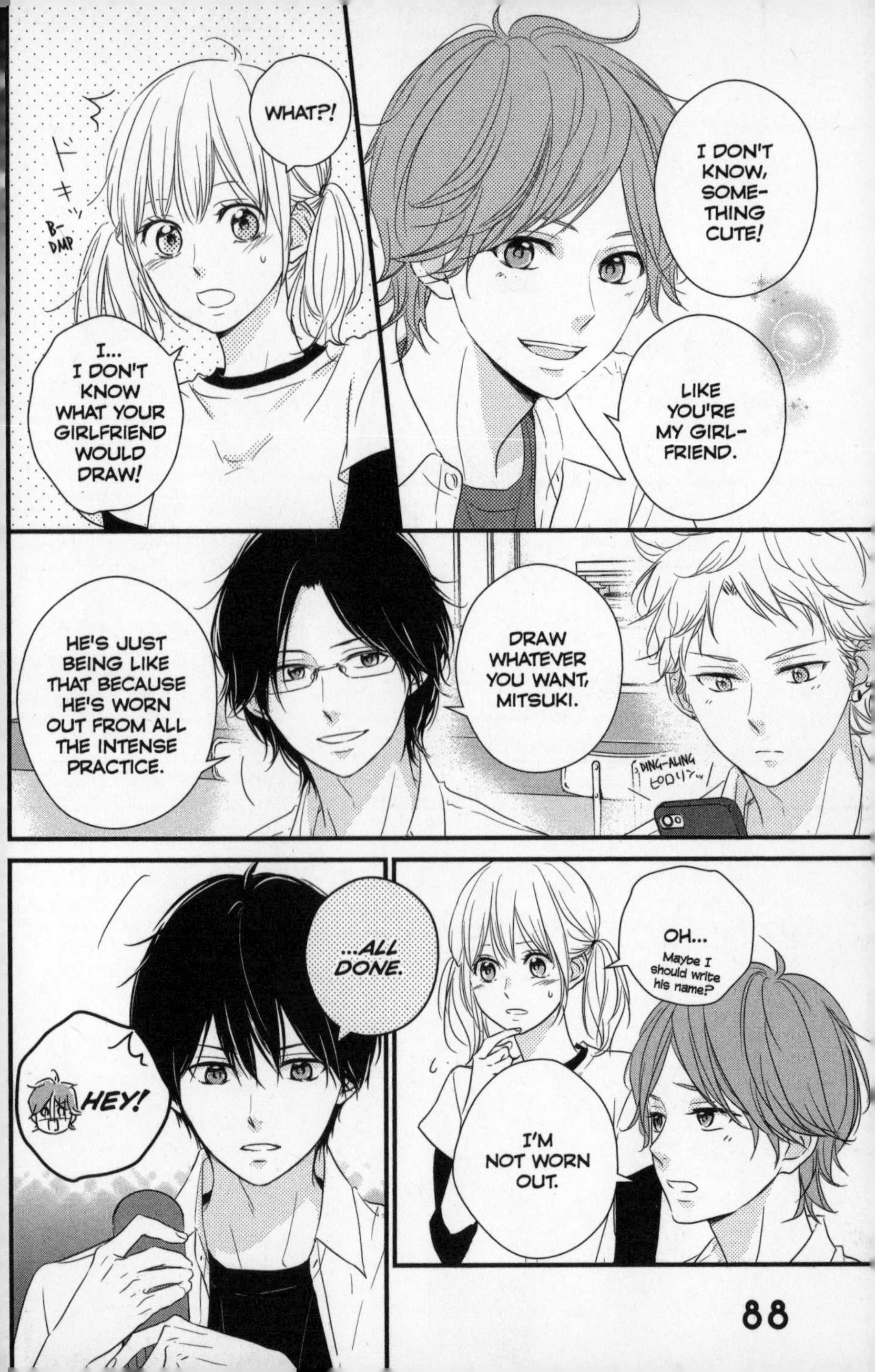
I DON'T KNOW, SOMETHING CUTE!
LIKE YOU'RE MY GIRLFRIEND.
WHAT?!
B-DMP
ドキッ
I... I DON'T KNOW WHAT YOUR GIRLFRIEND WOULD DRAW!
DING-ALING
ピロリ~
DRAW WHATEVER YOU WANT, MITSUKI.
HE'S JUST BEING LIKE THAT BECAUSE HE'S WORN OUT FROM ALL THE INTENSE PRACTICE.
OH... Maybe I should write his name?
I'M NOT WORN OUT.
...ALL DONE.
HEY!

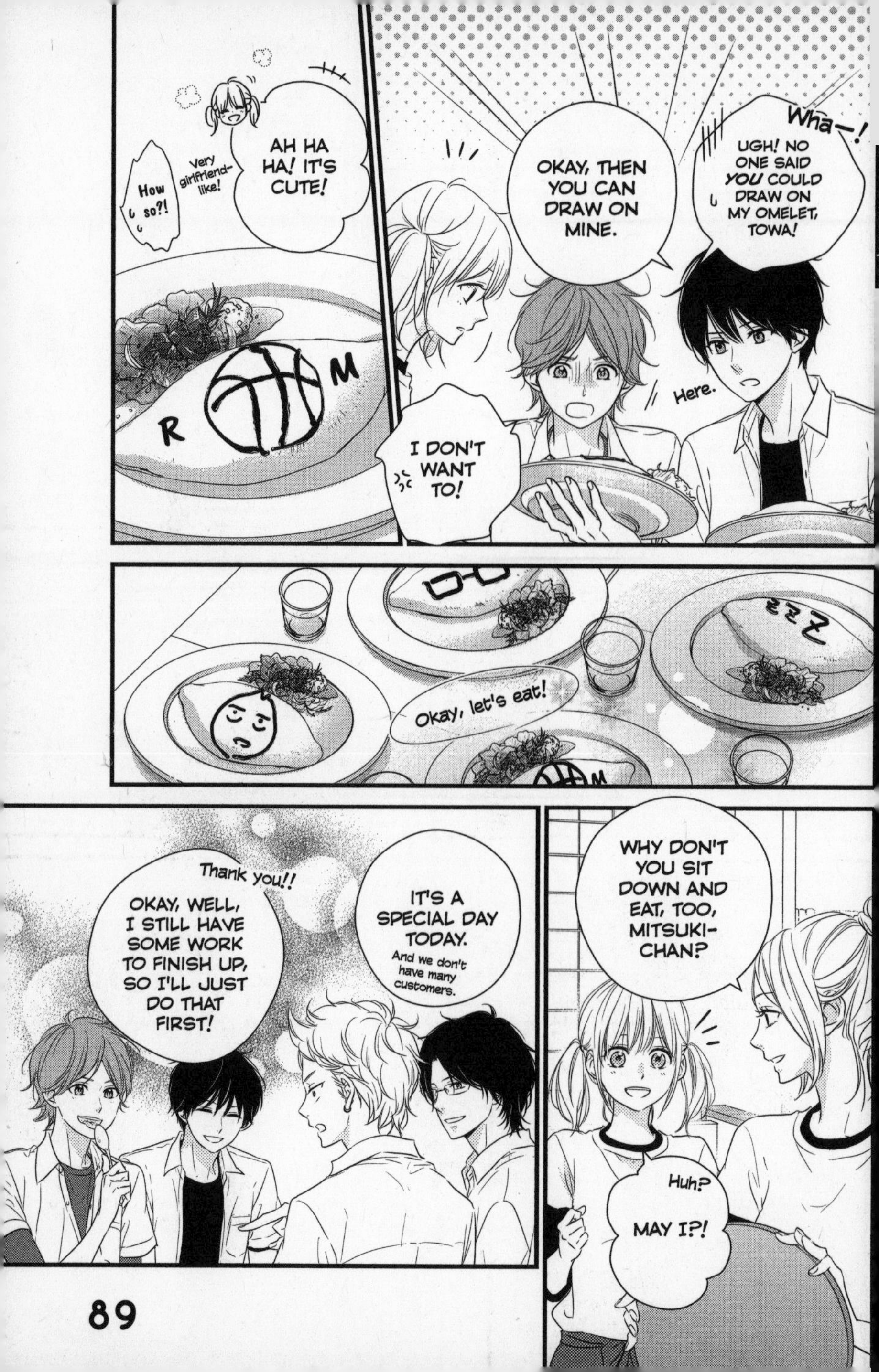
Wha—!
UGH! NO ONE SAID YOU COULD DRAW ON MY OMELET, TOWA!
OKAY, THEN YOU CAN DRAW ON MINE.
Here.
I DON'T WANT TO!
AH HA HA! IT'S CUTE!
Very girlfriend-like!
How so?!
R M
Okay, let's eat!
WHY DON'T YOU SIT DOWN AND EAT, TOO, MITSUKI-CHAN?
Huh?
MAY I?!
IT'S A SPECIAL DAY TODAY.
And we don't have many customers.
Thank you!!
OKAY, WELL, I STILL HAVE SOME WORK TO FINISH UP, SO I'LL JUST DO THAT FIRST!

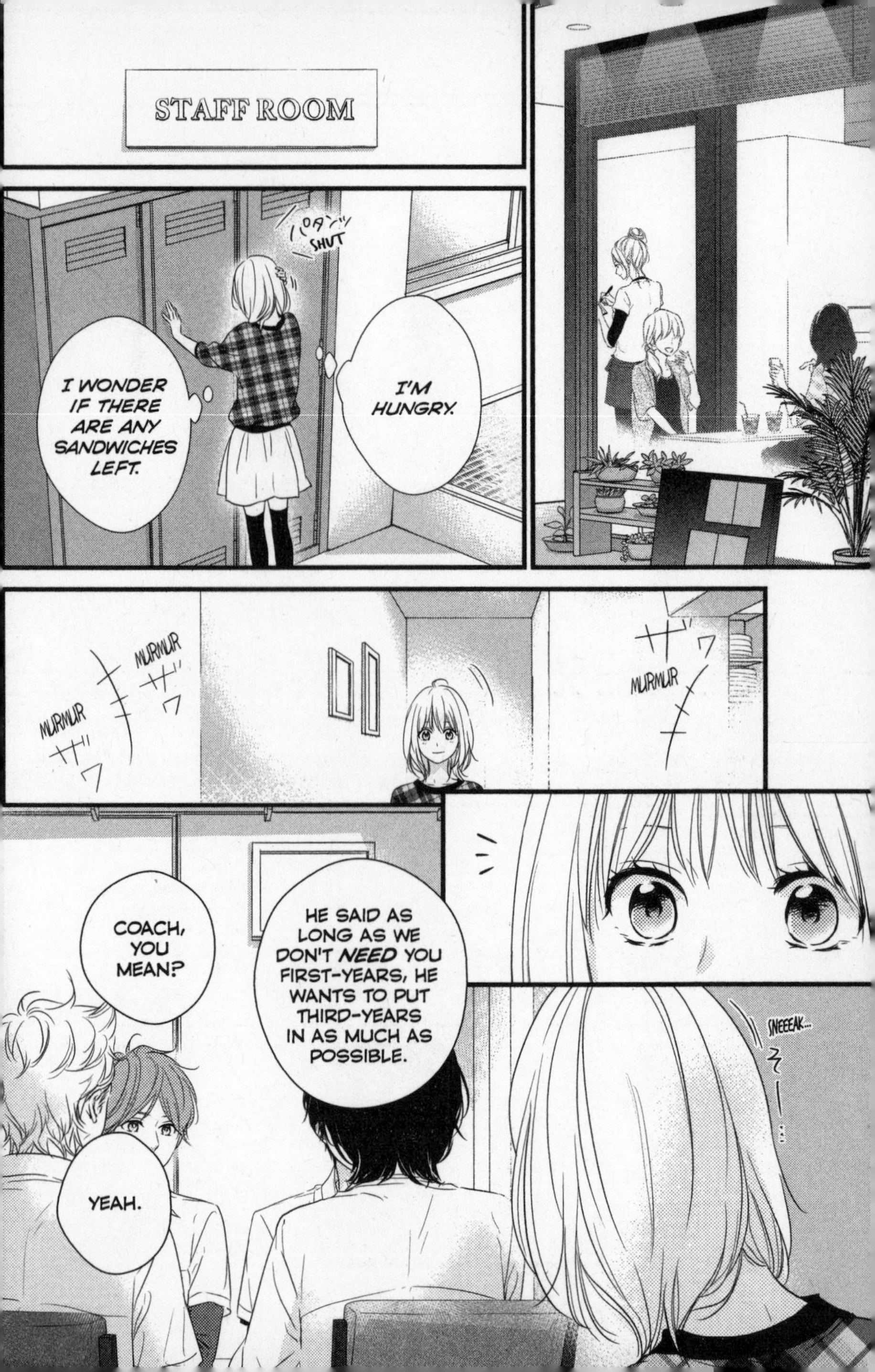
STAFF ROOM
SHUT
I'M HUNGRY.
I WONDER IF THERE ARE ANY SANDWICHES LEFT.
MURMUR
MURMUR
MURMUR
SNEEEAK...
HE SAID AS LONG AS WE DON'T NEED YOU FIRST-YEARS, HE WANTS TO PUT THIRD-YEARS IN AS MUCH AS POSSIBLE.
COACH, YOU MEAN?
YEAH.

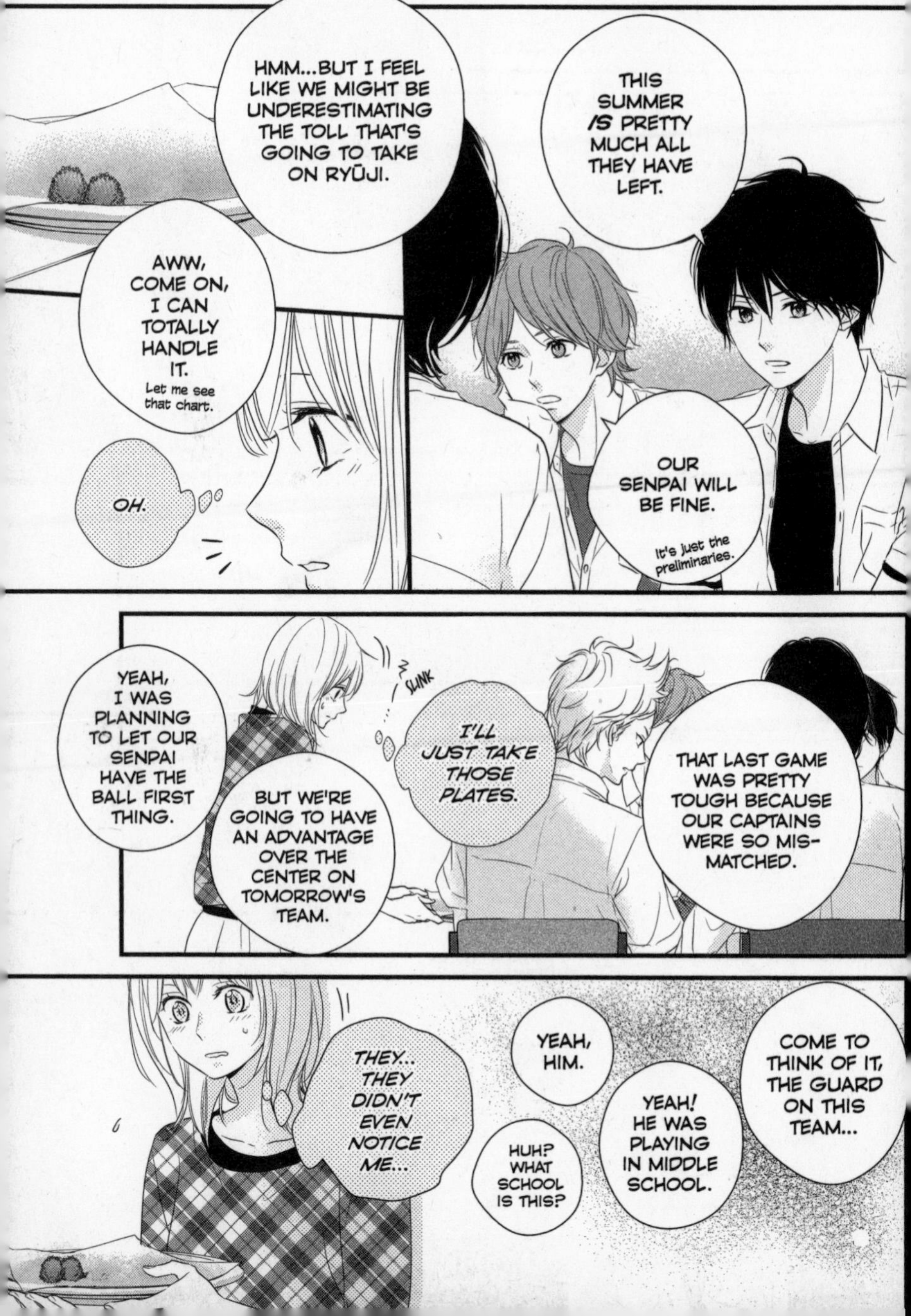
THIS SUMMER IS PRETTY MUCH ALL THEY HAVE LEFT.
HMM...BUT I FEEL LIKE WE MIGHT BE UNDERESTIMATING THE TOLL THAT'S GOING TO TAKE ON RYŪJI.
OUR SENPAI WILL BE FINE.
It's just the preliminaries.
AWW, COME ON, I CAN TOTALLY HANDLE IT.
Let me see that chart.
OH.
THAT LAST GAME WAS PRETTY TOUGH BECAUSE OUR CAPTAINS WERE SO MIS-MATCHED.
I'LL JUST TAKE THOSE PLATES.
SLINK
YEAH, I WAS PLANNING TO LET OUR SENPAI HAVE THE BALL FIRST THING.
BUT WE'RE GOING TO HAVE AN ADVANTAGE OVER THE CENTER ON TOMORROW'S TEAM.
COME TO THINK OF IT, THE GUARD ON THIS TEAM...
YEAH, HIM.
YEAH! HE WAS PLAYING IN MIDDLE SCHOOL.
HUH? WHAT SCHOOL IS THIS?
THEY... THEY DIDN'T EVEN NOTICE ME...

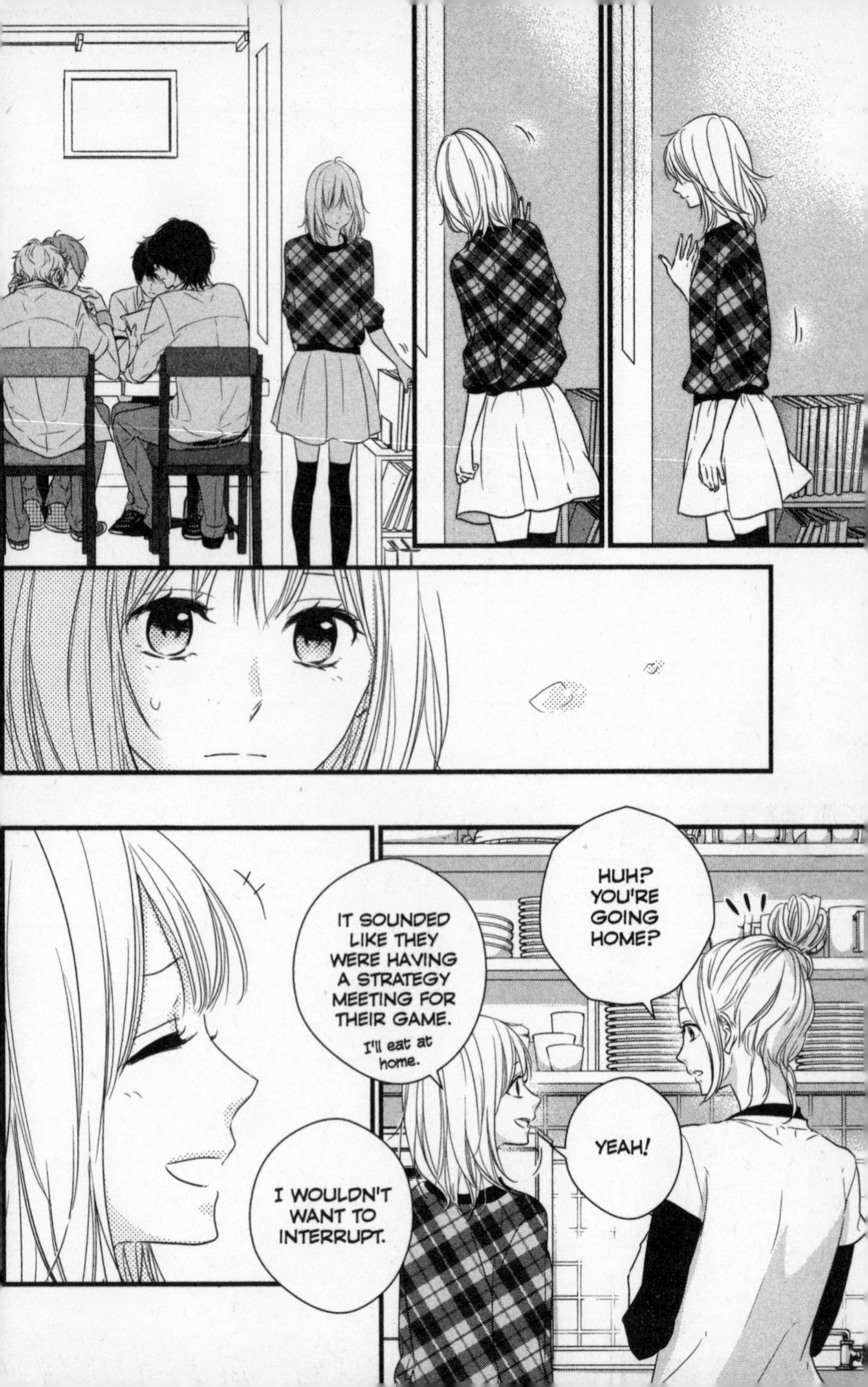
HUH? YOU'RE GOING HOME?
YEAH!
IT SOUNDED LIKE THEY WERE HAVING A STRATEGY MEETING FOR THEIR GAME.
I'll eat at home.
I WOULDN'T WANT TO INTERRUPT.

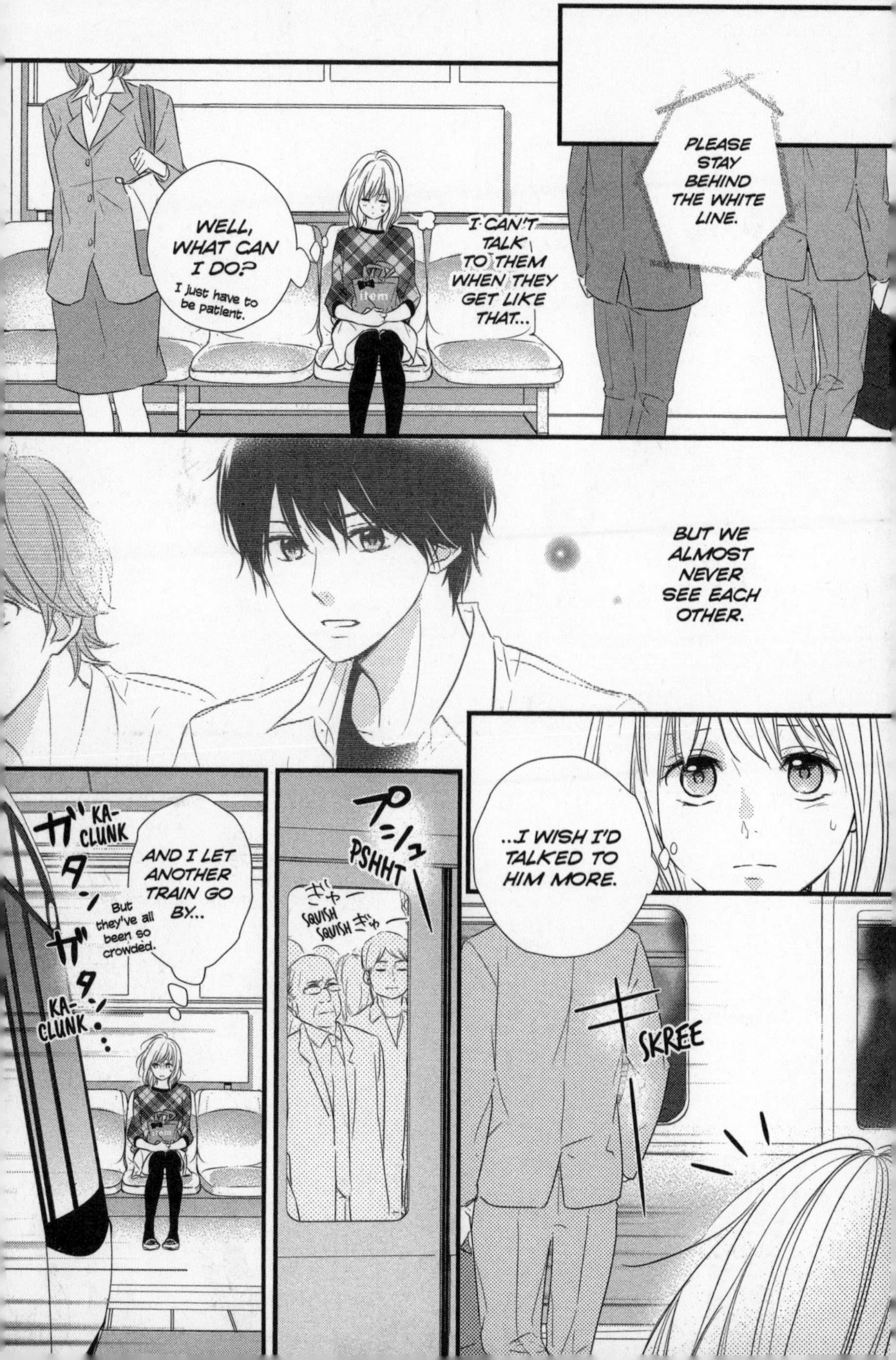
PLEASE STAY BEHIND THE WHITE LINE.
I CAN'T TALK TO THEM WHEN THEY GET LIKE THAT...
WELL, WHAT CAN I DO?
I just have to be patient.
BUT WE ALMOST NEVER SEE EACH OTHER.
...I WISH I'D TALKED TO HIM MORE.
SKREE
PSHHT
ぎゃー SQUISH SQUISH ぎゃー
KA-CLUNK
AND I LET ANOTHER TRAIN GO BY...
But they've all been so crowded.
KA-CLUNK

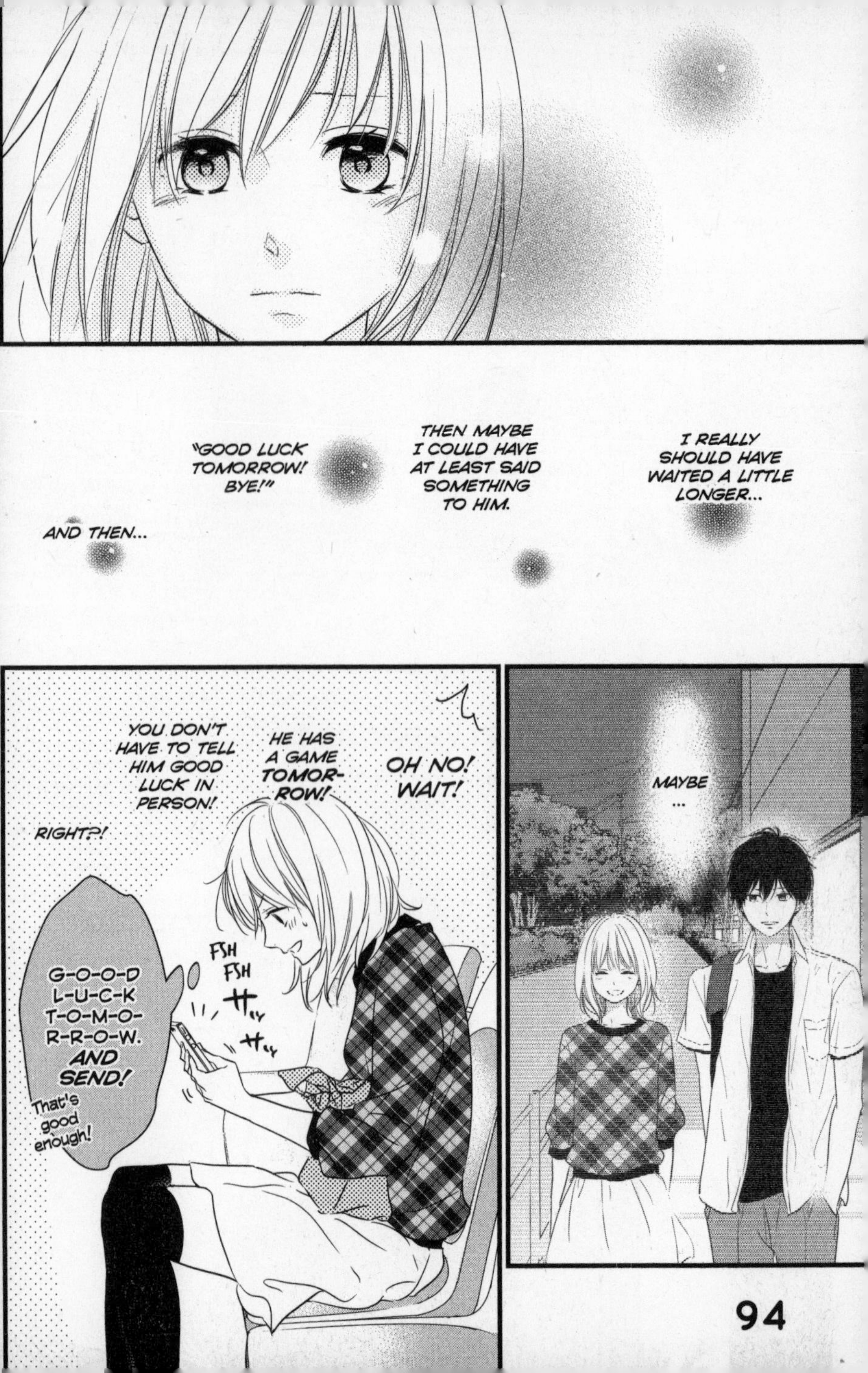
I REALLY SHOULD HAVE WAITED A LITTLE LONGER...
THEN MAYBE I COULD HAVE AT LEAST SAID SOMETHING TO HIM.
"GOOD LUCK TOMORROW! BYE!"
AND THEN...
MAYBE ...
OH NO! WAIT!
HE HAS A GAME TOMOR-ROW!
YOU DON'T HAVE TO TELL HIM GOOD LUCK IN PERSON!
RIGHT?!
FSH FSH
G-O-O-D L-U-C-K T-O-M-O-R-R-O-W. AND SEND!
That's good enough!

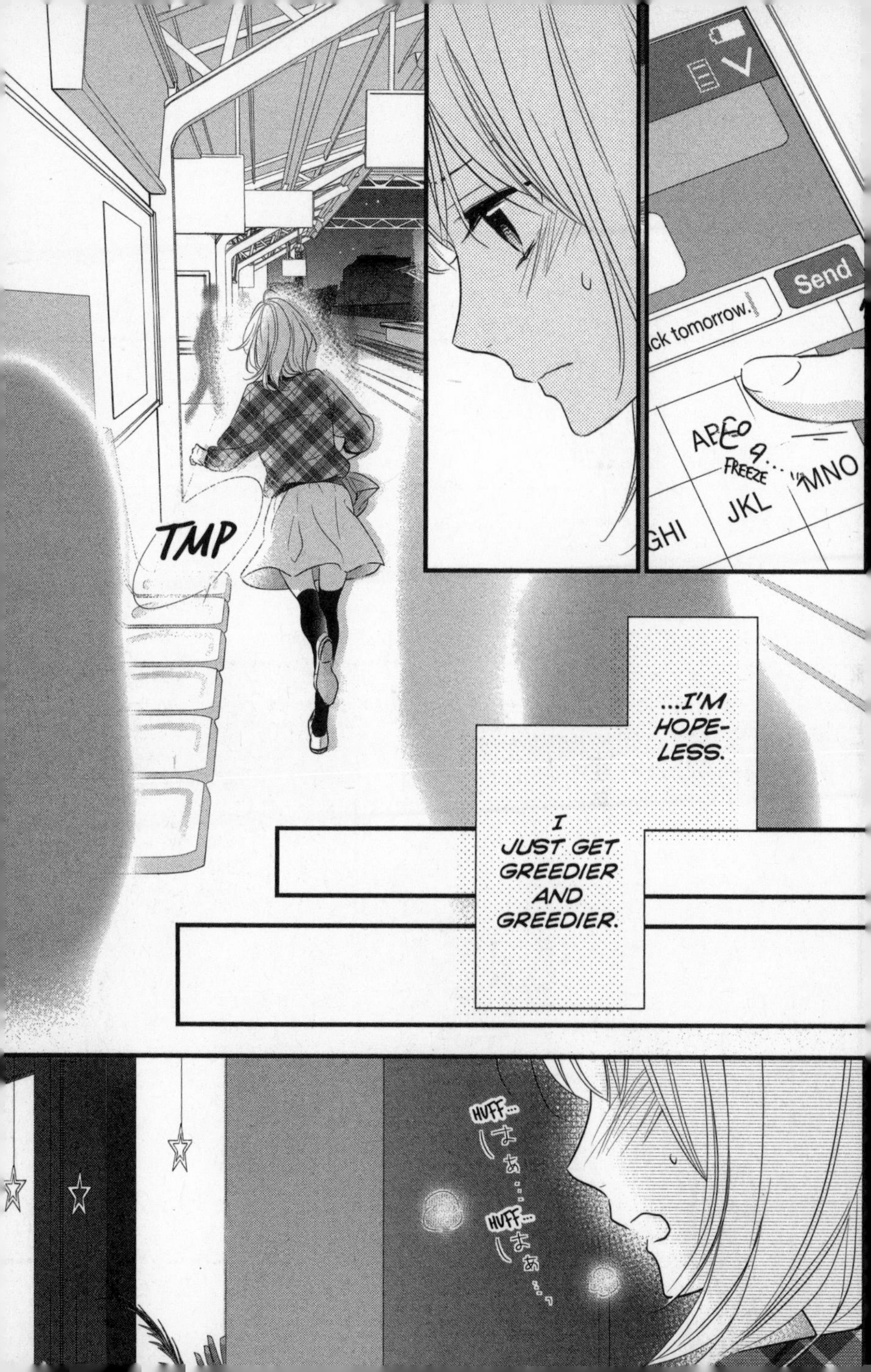
ck tomorrow.
Send
ABC
FREEZE
MNO
JKL
GHI
TMP
...I'M HOPE-LESS.
I JUST GET GREEDIER AND GREEDIER.
HUFF... はぁ…
HUFF... はぁ…

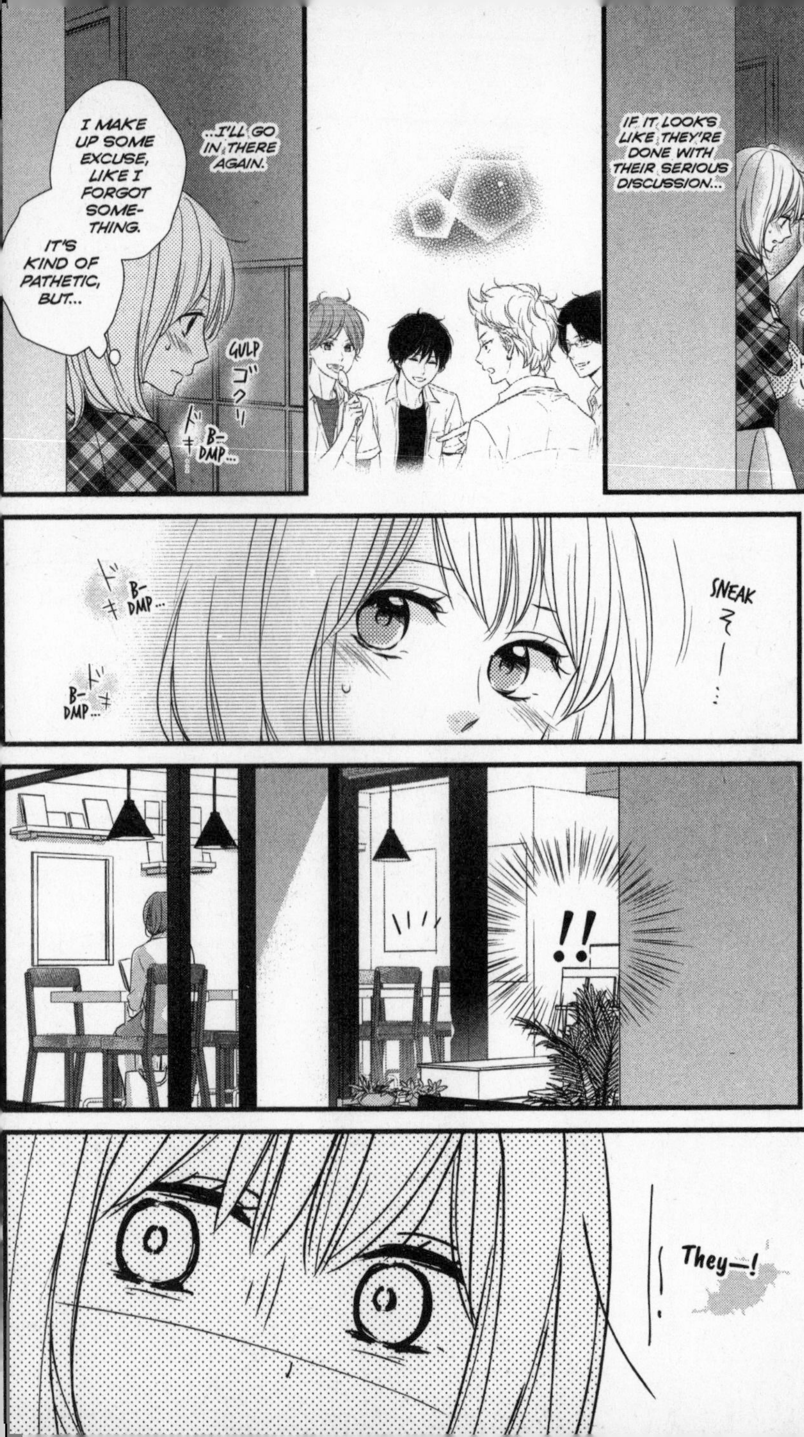
IF IT LOOKS LIKE THEY'RE DONE WITH THEIR SERIOUS DISCUSSION...
HUFF はぁ
HUFF はぁ
...I'LL GO IN THERE AGAIN.
I MAKE UP SOME EXCUSE, LIKE I FORGOT SOME-THING.
IT'S KIND OF PATHETIC, BUT...
GULP ゴクリ
B-DMP... ドキ
SNEAK そー...
B-DMP... ドキ
B-DMP... ドキ
!!
They—!

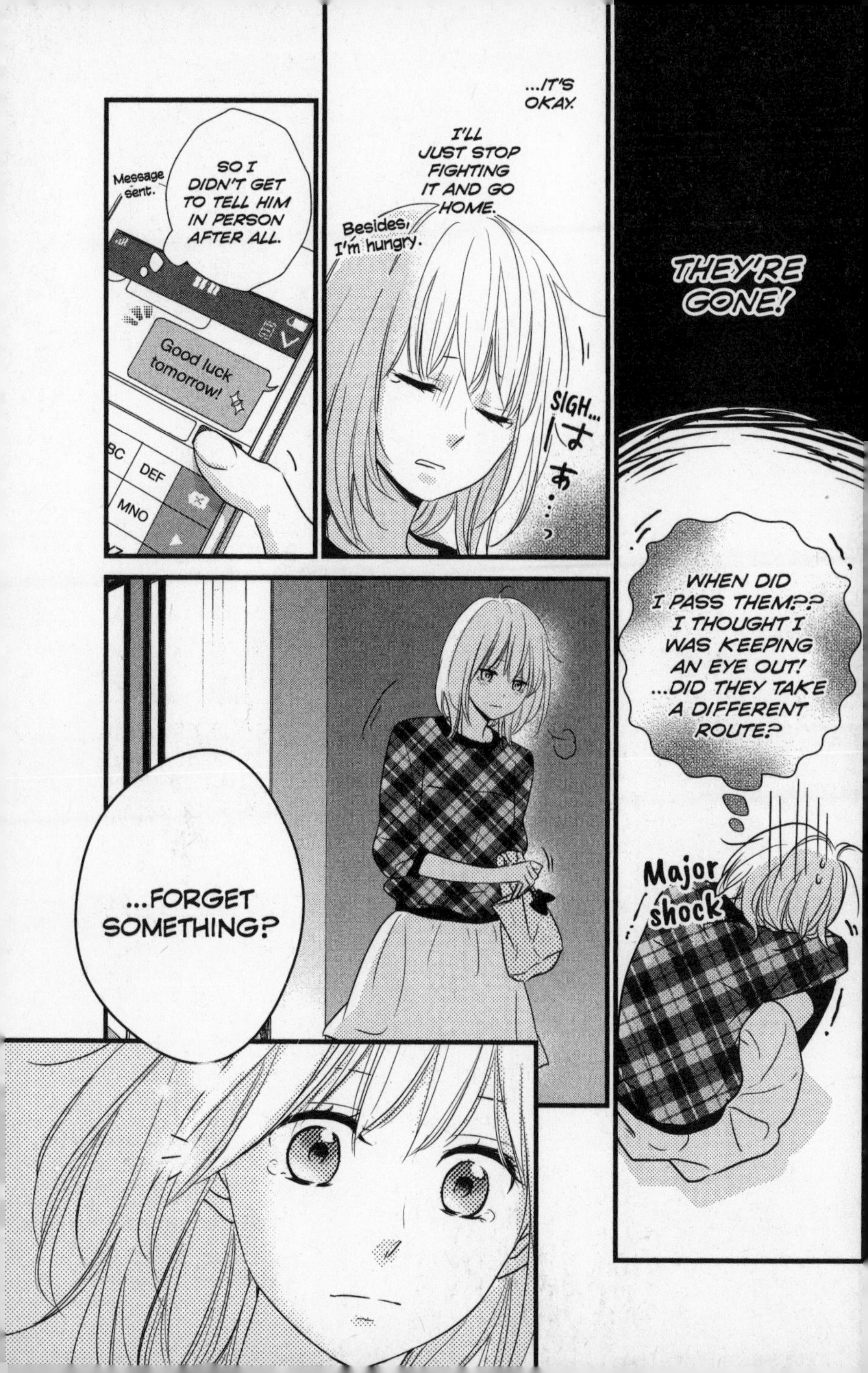
THEY'RE GONE!
WHEN DID I PASS THEM?? I THOUGHT I WAS KEEPING AN EYE OUT! ...DID THEY TAKE A DIFFERENT ROUTE?
Major shock
...IT'S OKAY.
I'LL JUST STOP FIGHTING IT AND GO HOME.
Besides, I'm hungry.
SIGH...
はぁ...っ
SO I DIDN'T GET TO TELL HIM IN PERSON AFTER ALL.
Message sent.
Good luck tomorrow!
DEF
MNO
...FORGET SOMETHING?

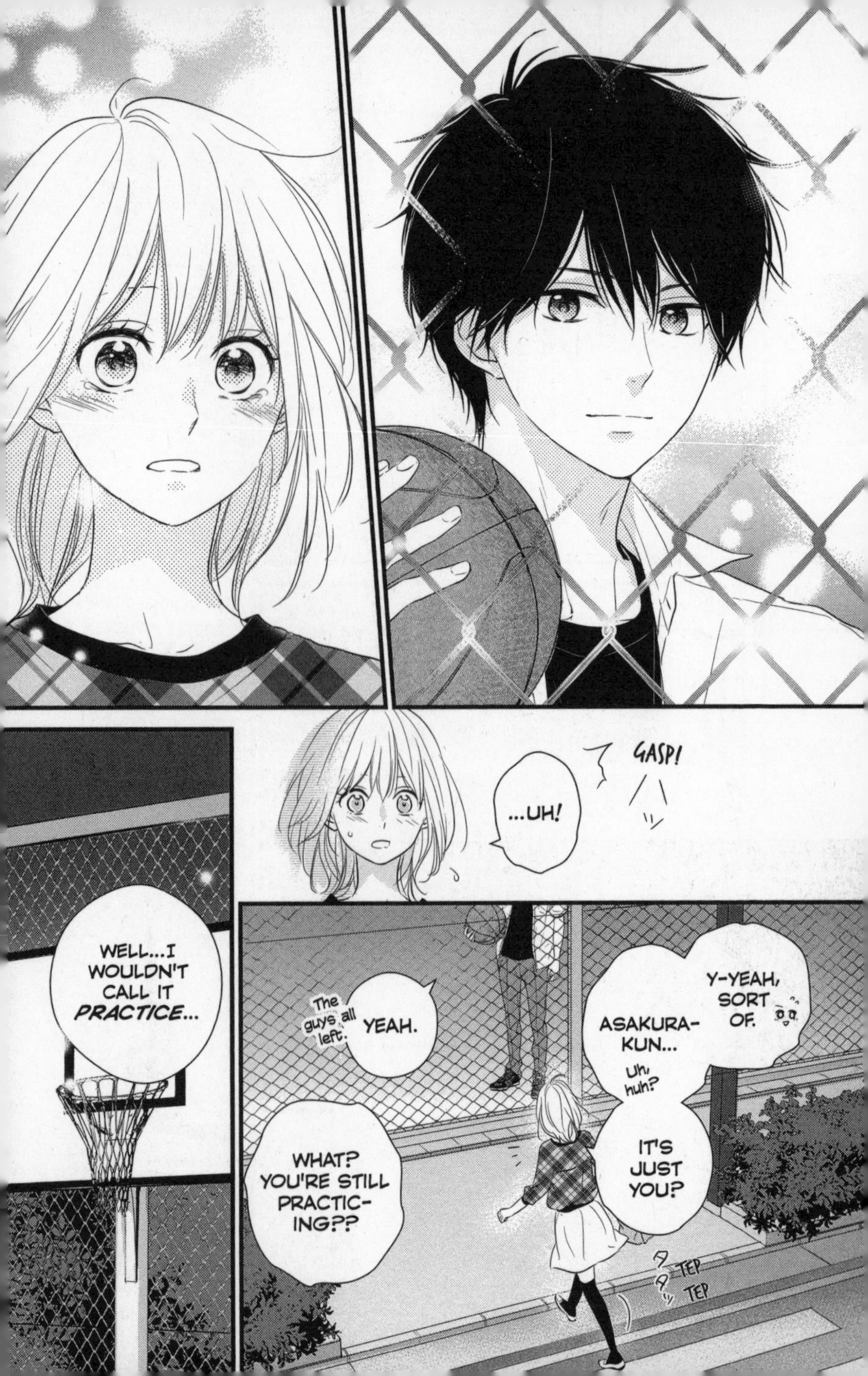
GASP!
...UH!
ASAKURA-KUN...
Y-YEAH, SORT OF.
Uh, huh?
IT'S JUST YOU?
YEAH.
The guys all left.
WHAT? YOU'RE STILL PRACTIC-ING??
TEP TEP
WELL...I WOULDN'T CALL IT PRACTICE...

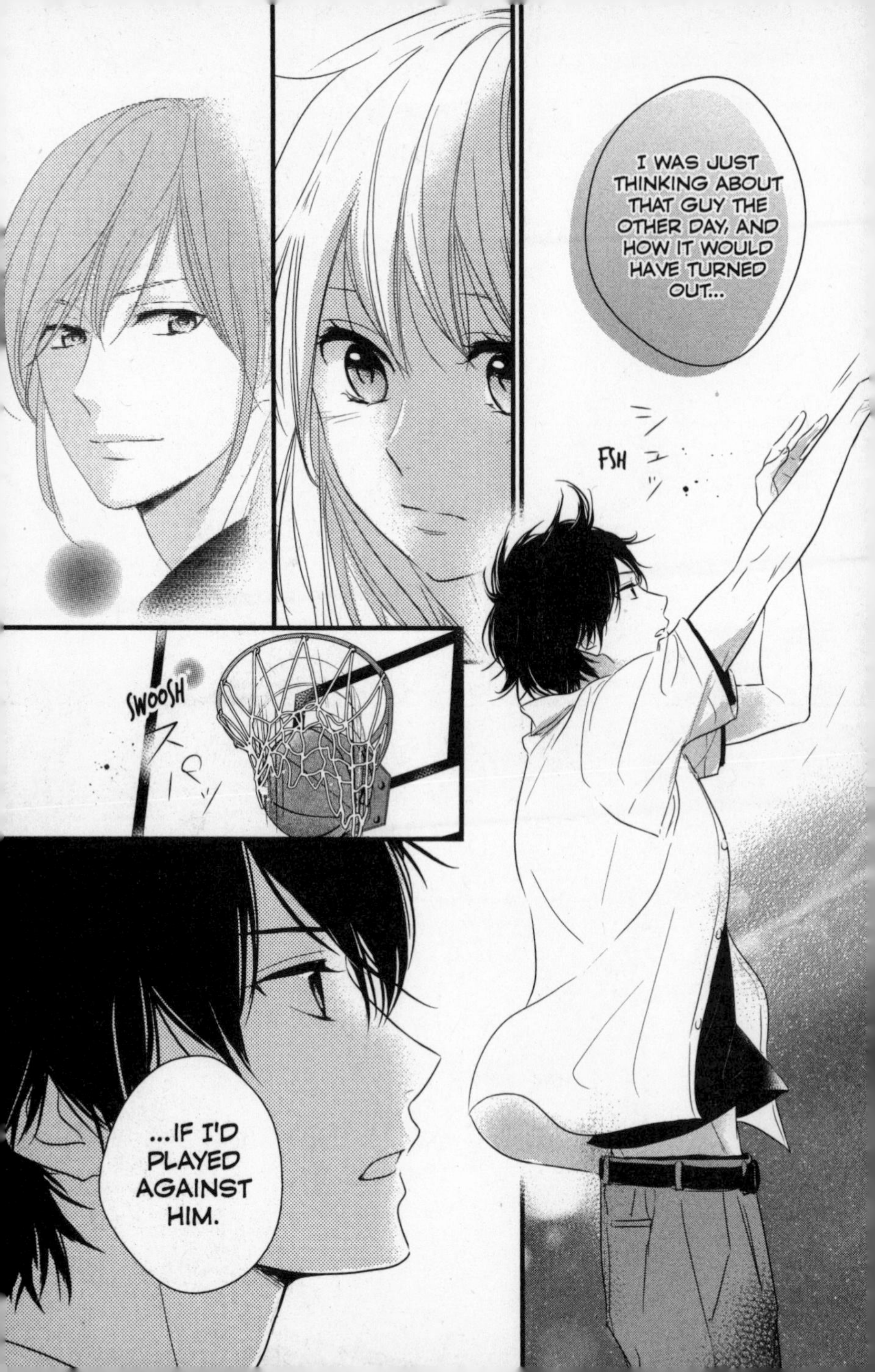
I WAS JUST THINKING ABOUT THAT GUY THE OTHER DAY, AND HOW IT WOULD HAVE TURNED OUT...
FSH
SWOOSH
...IF I'D PLAYED AGAINST HIM.

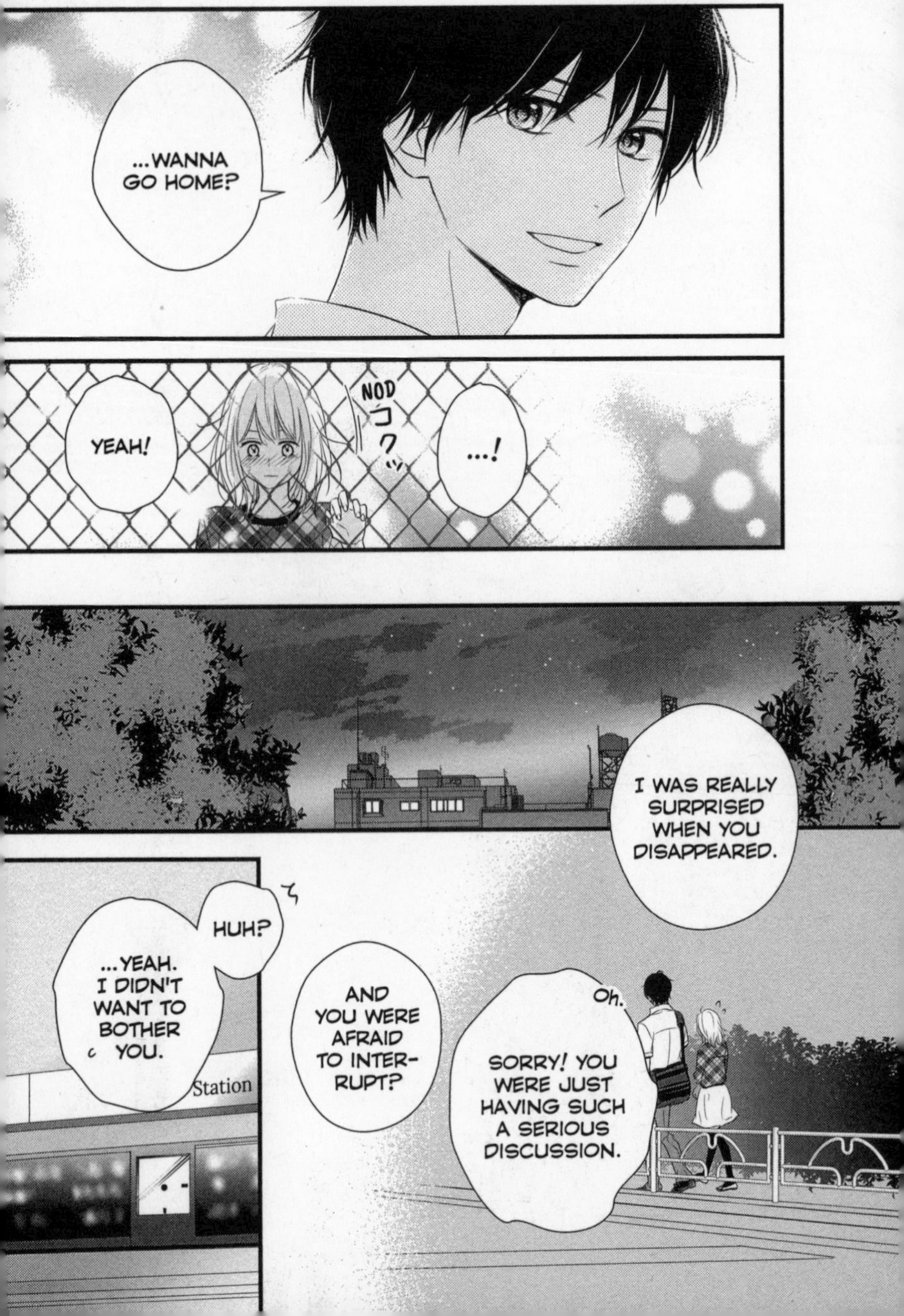
...WANNA GO HOME?
...!
NOD
コクッ
YEAH!
I WAS REALLY SURPRISED WHEN YOU DISAPPEARED.
Oh.
SORRY! YOU WERE JUST HAVING SUCH A SERIOUS DISCUSSION.
AND YOU WERE AFRAID TO INTER-RUPT?
HUH?
...YEAH. I DIDN'T WANT TO BOTHER YOU.
Station

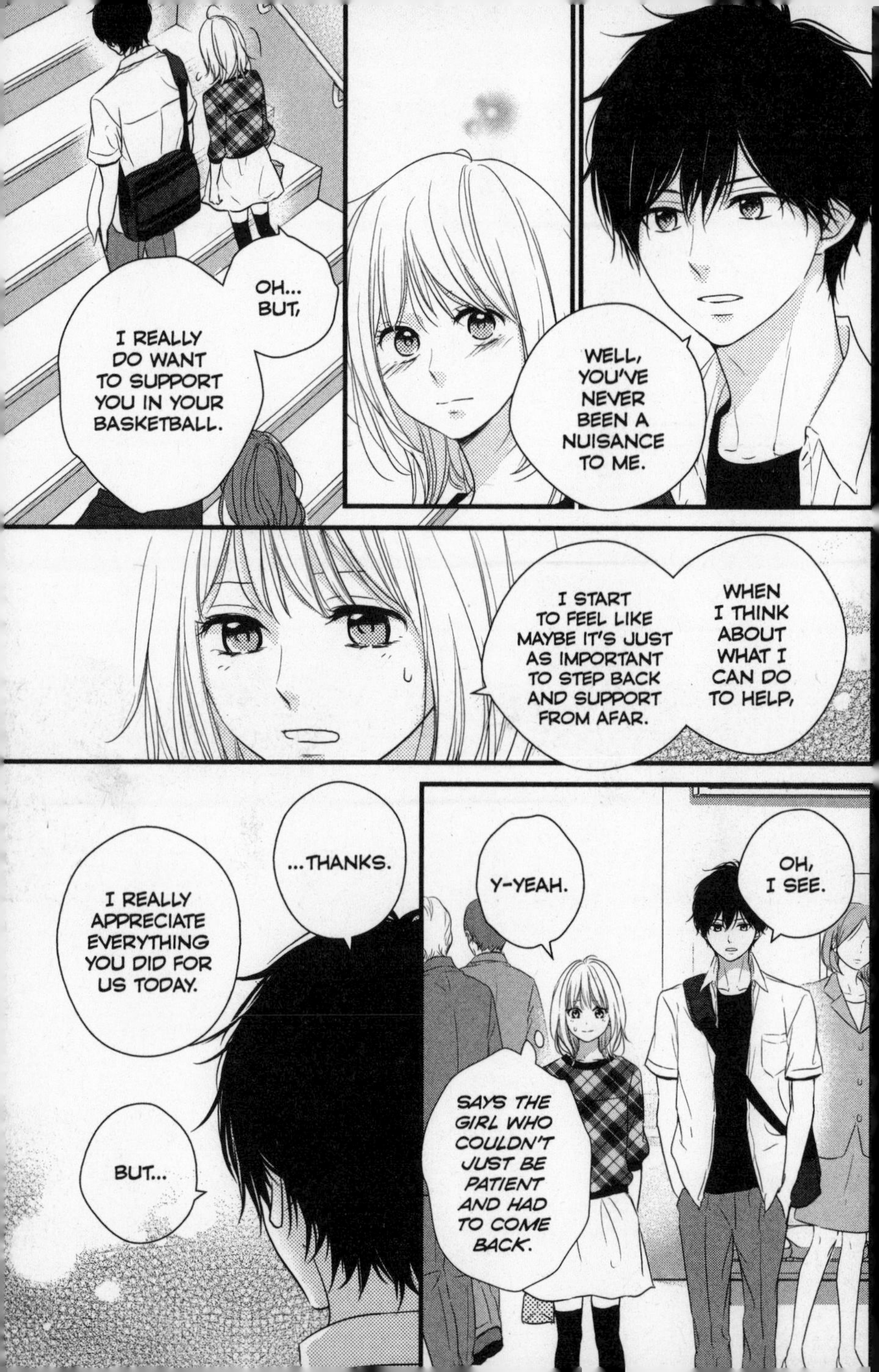
WELL, YOU'VE NEVER BEEN A NUISANCE TO ME.
OH... BUT,
I REALLY DO WANT TO SUPPORT YOU IN YOUR BASKETBALL.
WHEN I THINK ABOUT WHAT I CAN DO TO HELP,
I START TO FEEL LIKE MAYBE IT'S JUST AS IMPORTANT TO STEP BACK AND SUPPORT FROM AFAR.
OH, I SEE.
Y-YEAH.
SAYS THE GIRL WHO COULDN'T JUST BE PATIENT AND HAD TO COME BACK.
...THANKS.
I REALLY APPRECIATE EVERYTHING YOU DID FOR US TODAY.
BUT...

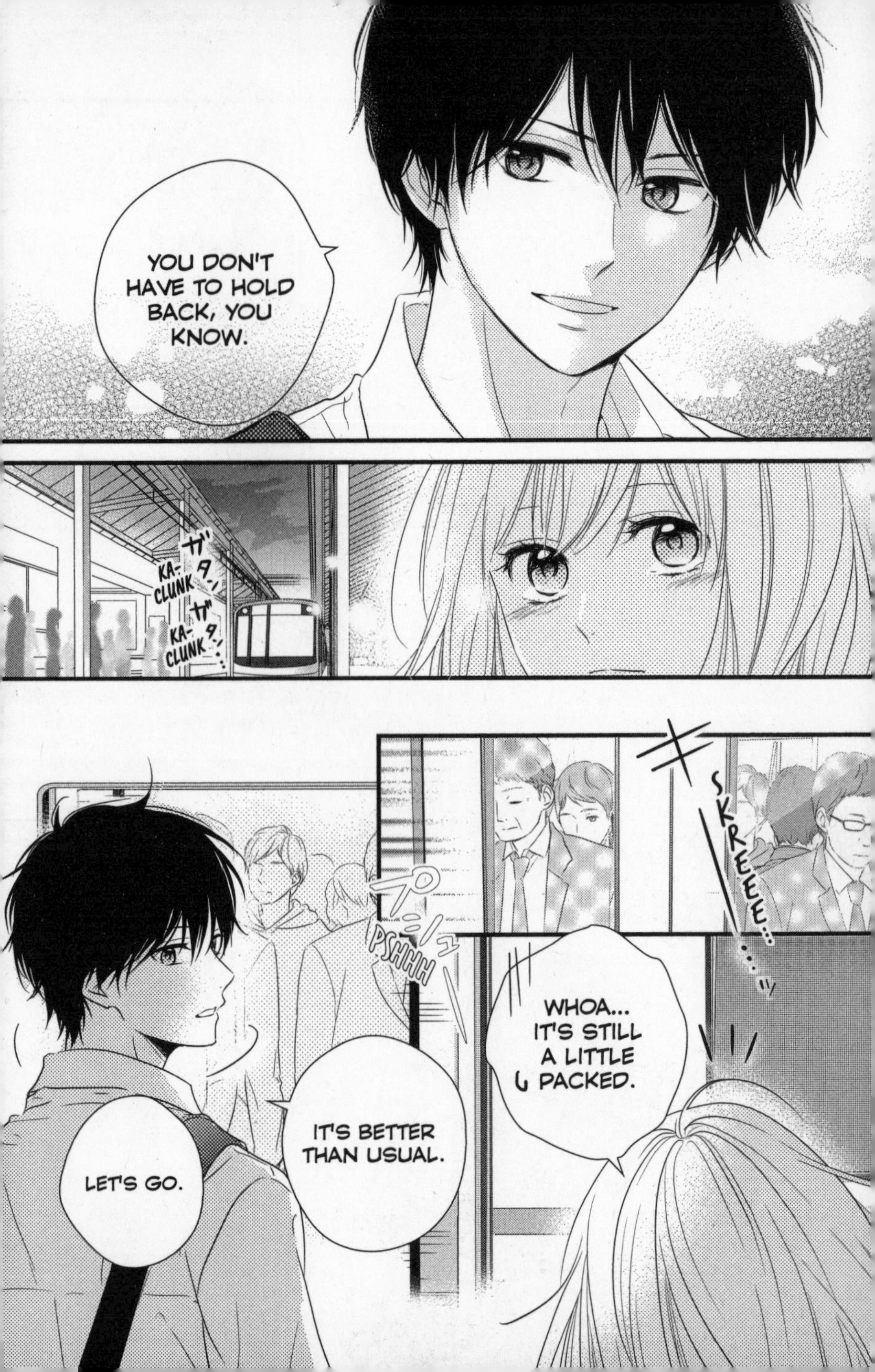
YOU DON'T HAVE TO HOLD BACK, YOU KNOW.
KA-CLUNK
KA-CLUNK
SKREEEE...
WHOA... IT'S STILL A LITTLE PACKED.
PSHHH
IT'S BETTER THAN USUAL.
LET'S GO.

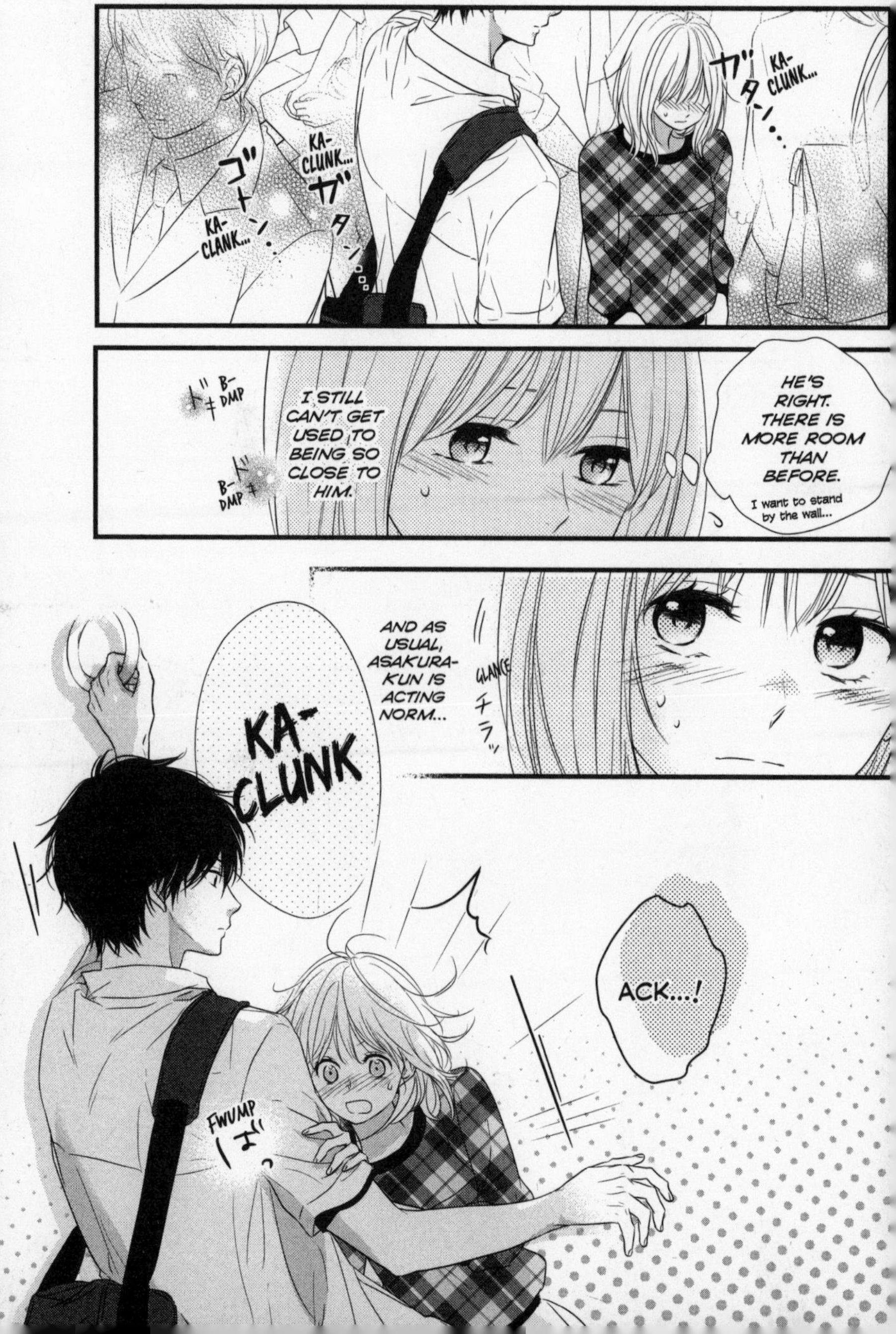
KA-CLUNK...
ガタン…
KA-CLUNK...
ガタン
KA-CLANK...
ゴトン…
HE'S RIGHT. THERE IS MORE ROOM THAN BEFORE.
I want to stand by the wall...
I STILL CAN'T GET USED TO BEING SO CLOSE TO HIM.
B-DMP
ドキ
B-DMP
ドキ
GLANCE
チラッ
AND AS USUAL, ASAKURA-KUN IS ACTING NORM...
KA-CLUNK
ACK...!
FWUMP
ぼふっ

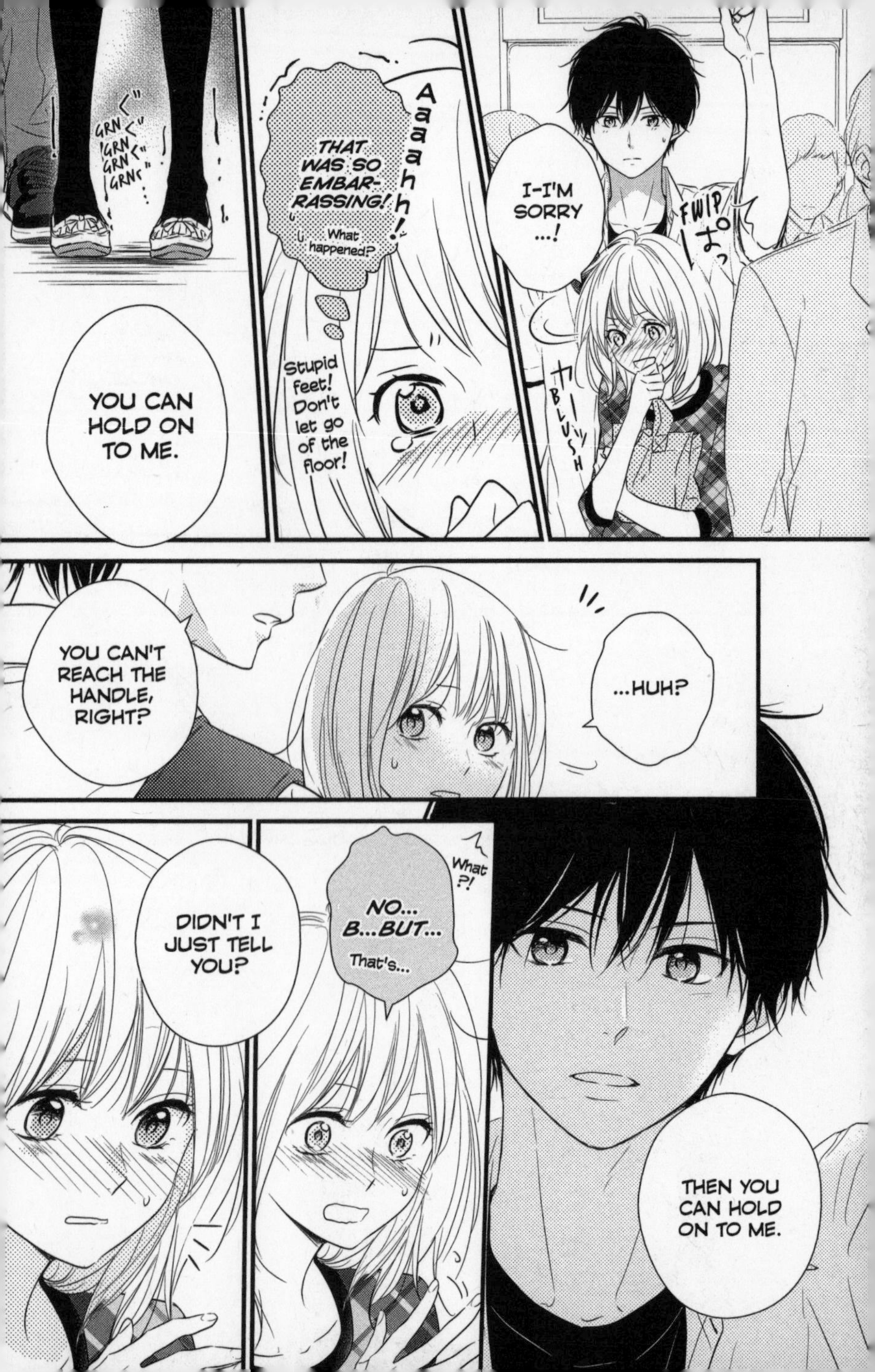
I-I'M SORRY ...!
FWIP
ぱっ
BLUSH
Aaaaahh!
THAT WAS SO EMBARRASSING!
What happened?
Stupid feet! Don't let go of the floor!
GRN GRN GRN GRN
YOU CAN HOLD ON TO ME.
...HUH?
YOU CAN'T REACH THE HANDLE, RIGHT?
THEN YOU CAN HOLD ON TO ME.
What?!
NO... B...BUT...
That's...
DIDN'T I JUST TELL YOU?

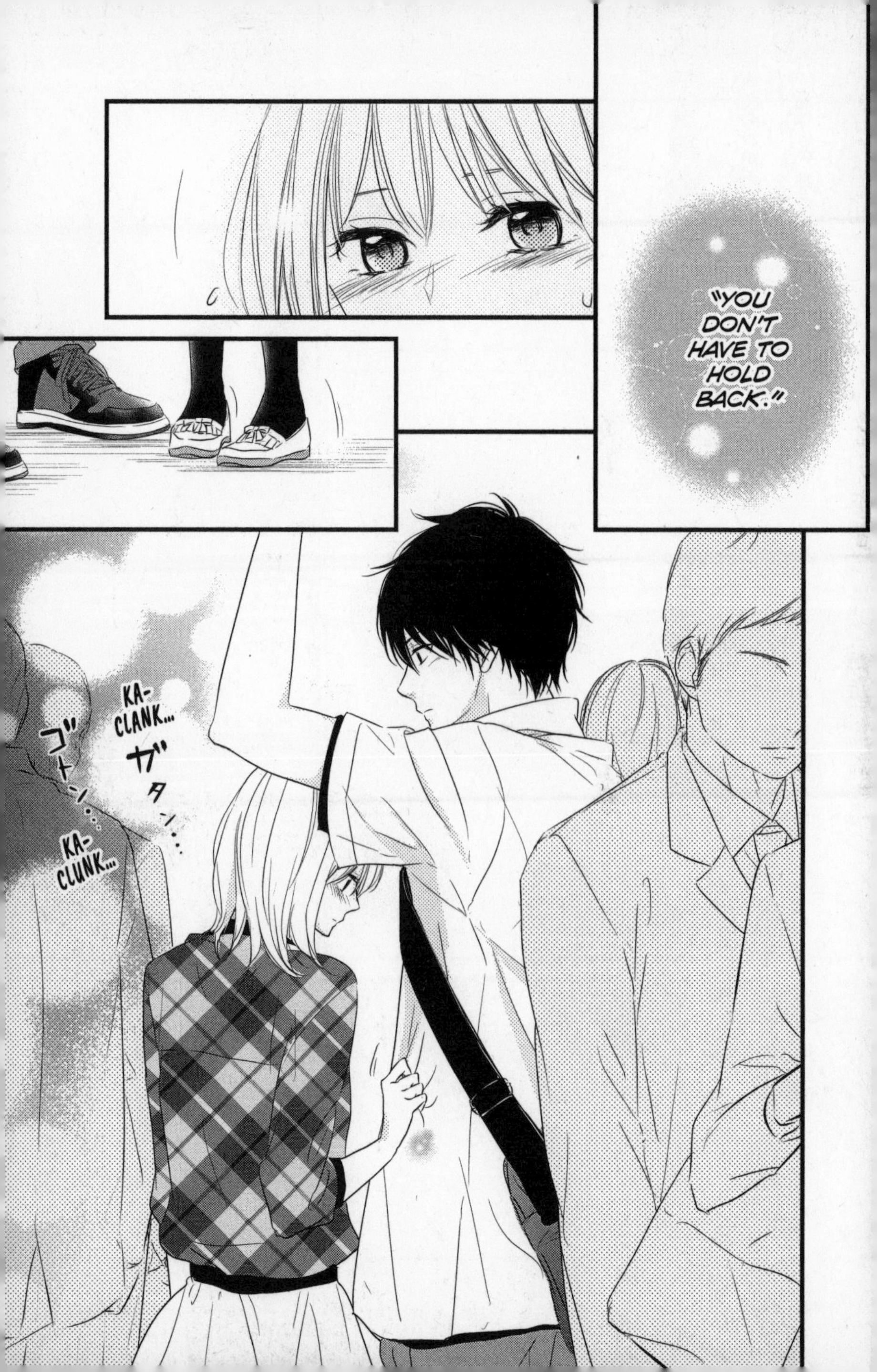
"YOU DON'T HAVE TO HOLD BACK."
KA-CLANK...
ガタン…
ゴトン…
KA-CLUNK...

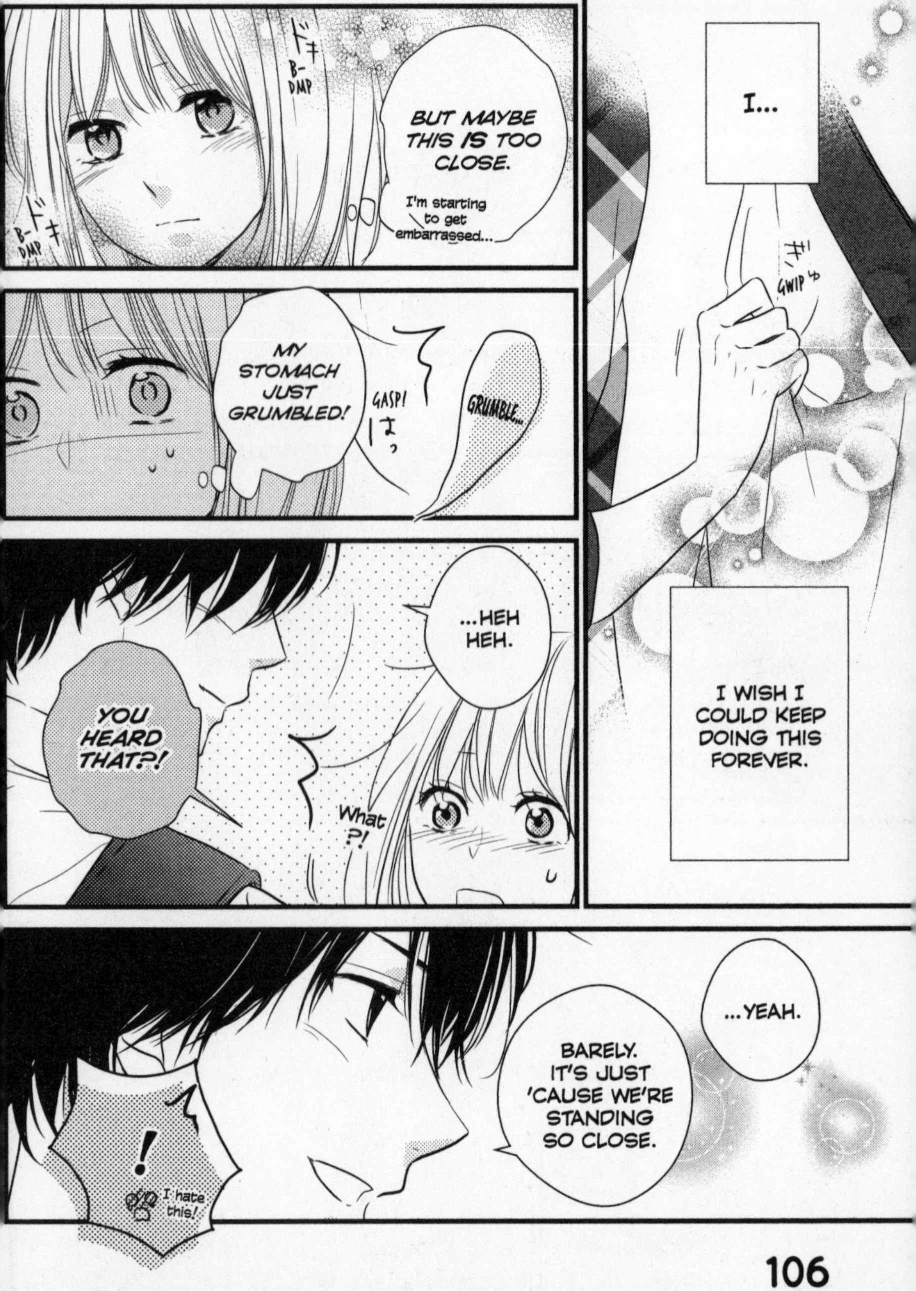
I...
GWIP
I WISH I COULD KEEP DOING THIS FOREVER.
ドキ B-DMP
BUT MAYBE THIS IS TOO CLOSE.
I'm starting to get embarrassed...
ドキ B-DMP
GRUMBLE...
はっ GASP!
MY STOMACH JUST GRUMBLED!
...HEH HEH.
What?!
YOU HEARD THAT?!
...YEAH.
BARELY. IT'S JUST 'CAUSE WE'RE STANDING SO CLOSE.
!
I hate this!

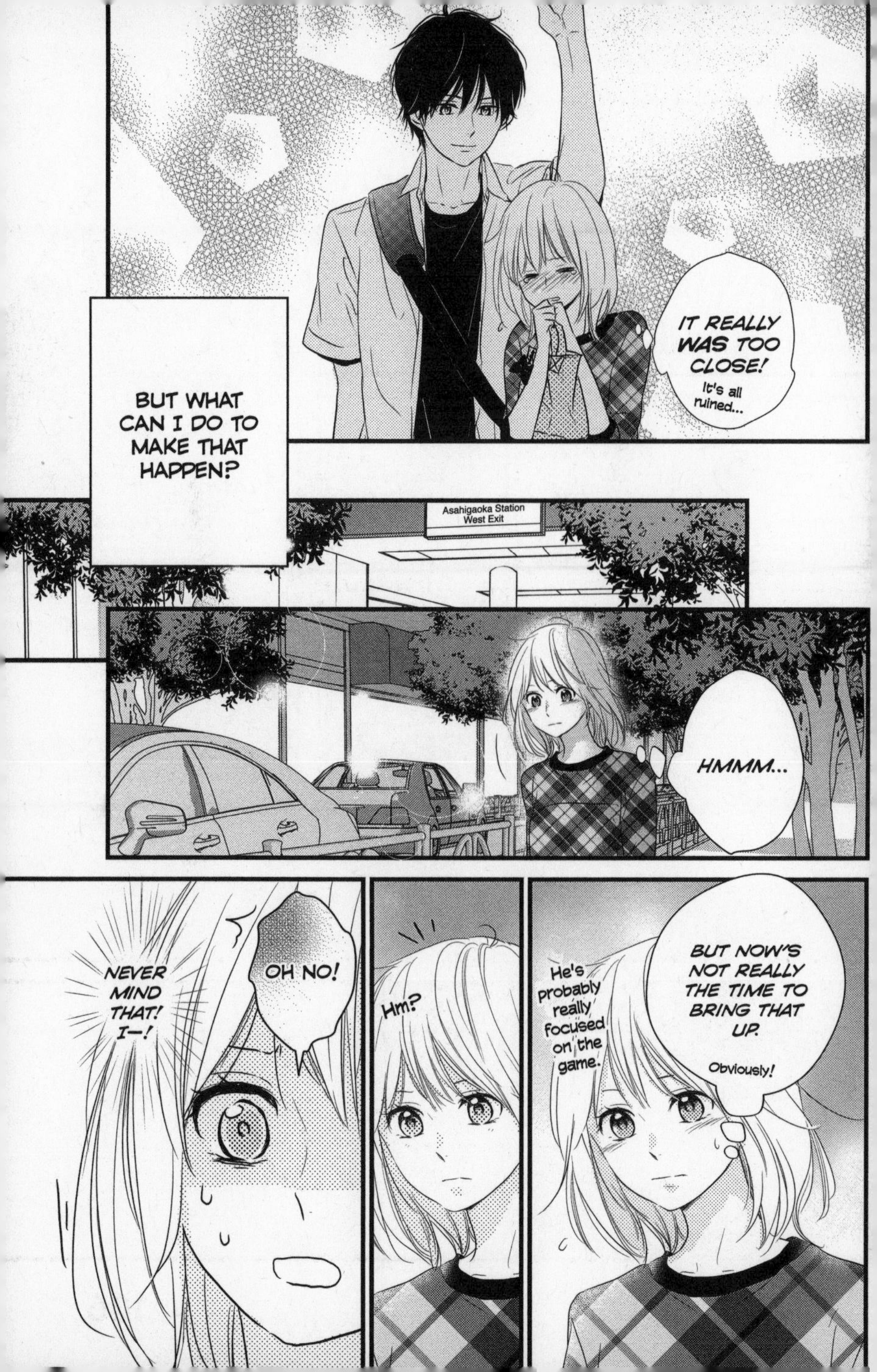
IT REALLY WAS TOO CLOSE!
It's all ruined...
BUT WHAT CAN I DO TO MAKE THAT HAPPEN?
Asahigaoka Station West Exit
HMMM...
BUT NOW'S NOT REALLY THE TIME TO BRING THAT UP.
Obviously!
He's probably really focused on the game.
Hm?
OH NO!
NEVER MIND THAT! I—!

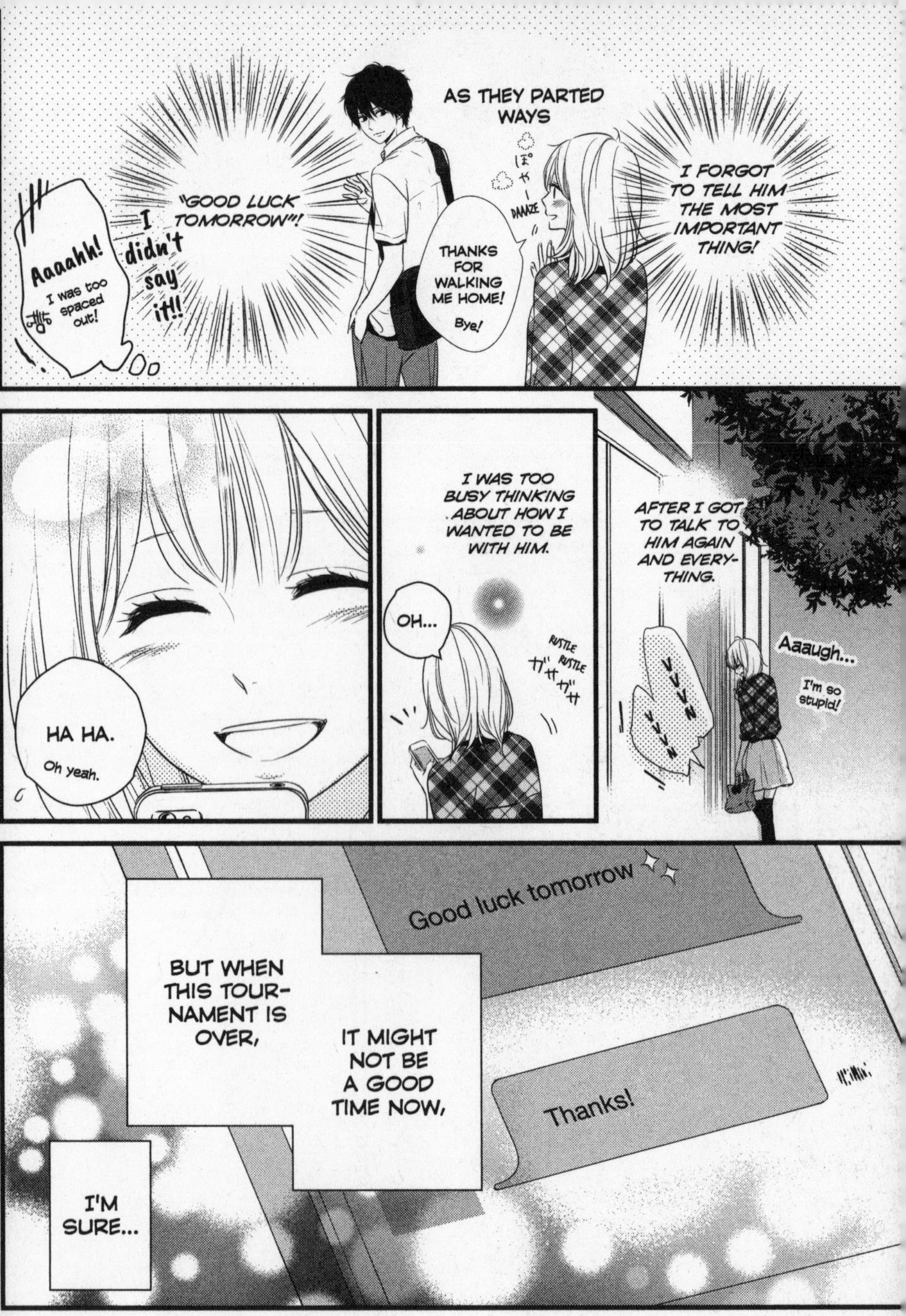
I FORGOT TO TELL HIM THE MOST IMPORTANT THING!
AS THEY PARTED WAYS
DAAAZE
THANKS FOR WALKING ME HOME!
Bye!
"GOOD LUCK TOMORROW"!
I didn't say it!!
Aaaahh!
I was too spaced out!
AFTER I GOT TO TALK TO HIM AGAIN AND EVERY-THING.
Aaaugh...
I'm so stupid!
I WAS TOO BUSY THINKING ABOUT HOW I WANTED TO BE WITH HIM.
RUSTLE RUSTLE
ガサガサ
OH...
HA HA.
Oh yeah.
Good luck tomorrow
Thanks!
IT MIGHT NOT BE A GOOD TIME NOW,
BUT WHEN THIS TOUR-NAMENT IS OVER,
I'M SURE...

period 14: "Doing 'That' with 'That Girl'?!"

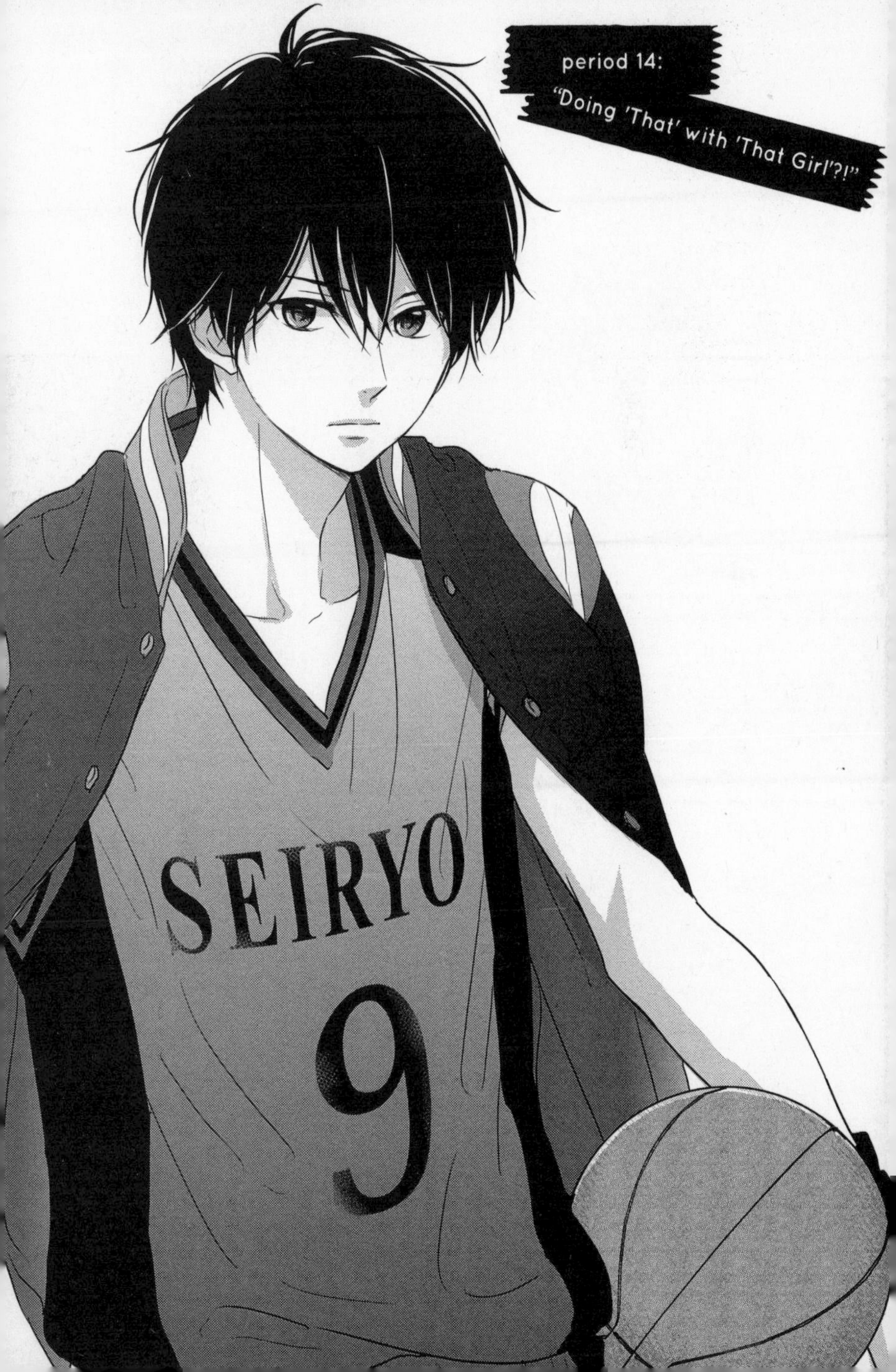
SEIRYO
9

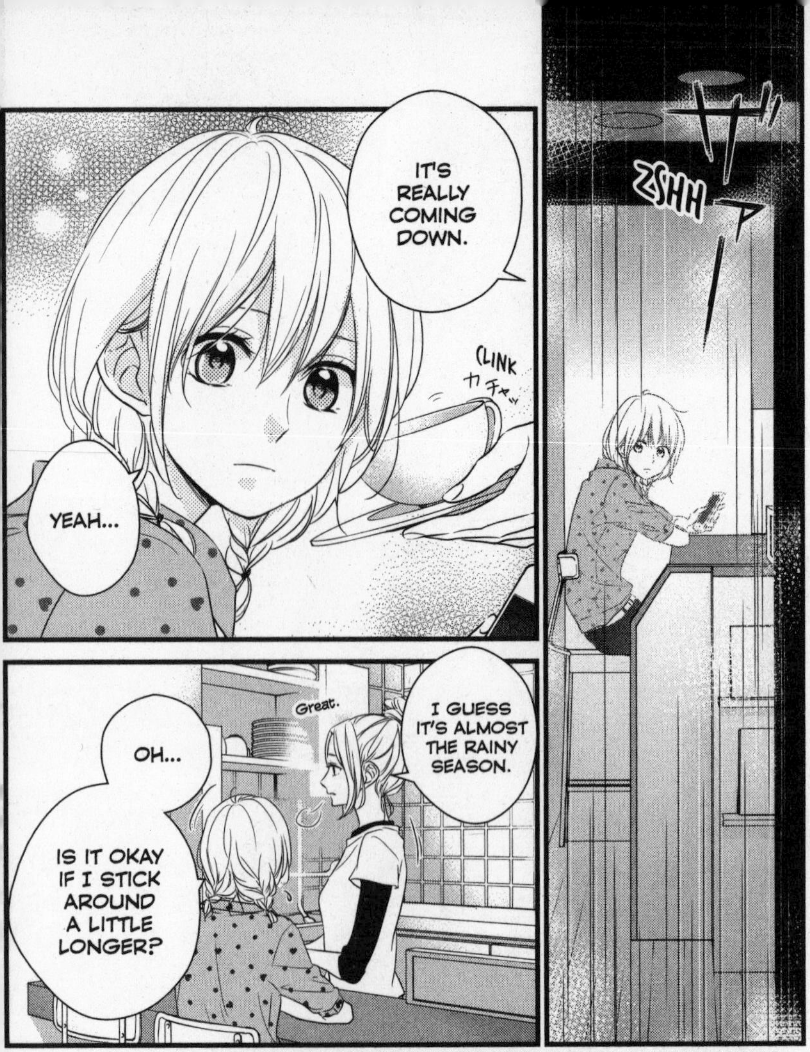
ZSHH
ザァー
IT'S REALLY COMING DOWN.
CLINK
カチャッ
YEAH...
I GUESS IT'S ALMOST THE RAINY SEASON.
Great.
OH...
IS IT OKAY IF I STICK AROUND A LITTLE LONGER?

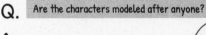

Q. Are the characters modeled after anyone?

A. No... But...

When I went to a game for research the other day, there were some athletes that I sort of associated with each of the characters, so I got really excited! They were all so radiant!!

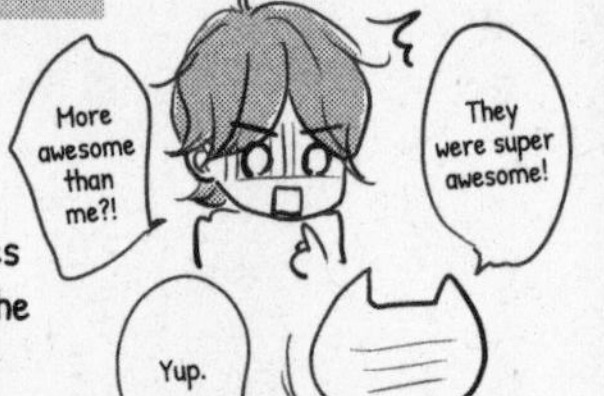
They were super awesome!
More awesome than me?!
Yup.
NOD
コクッ

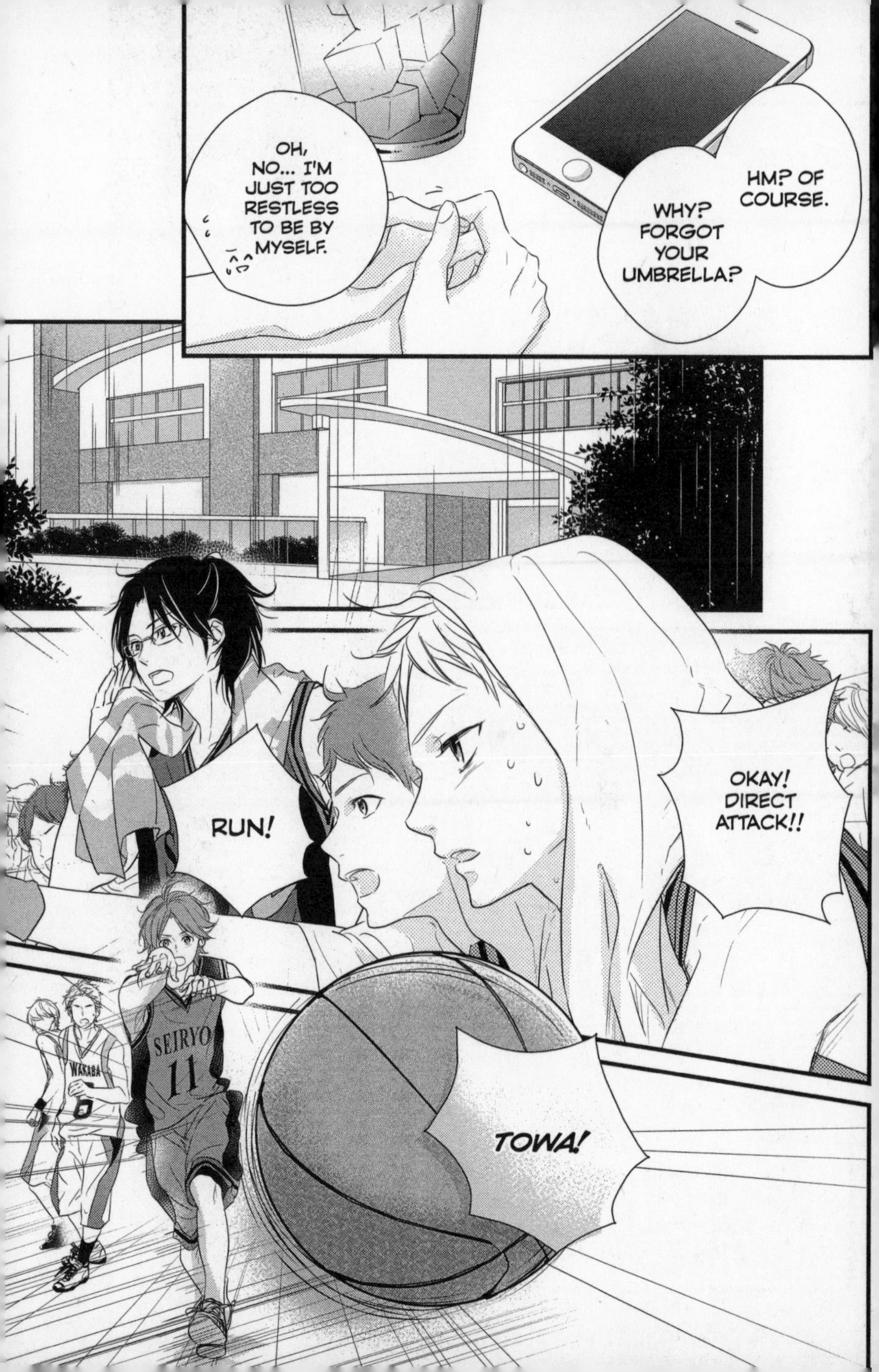
HM? OF COURSE.
WHY? FORGOT YOUR UMBRELLA?
OH, NO... I'M JUST TOO RESTLESS TO BE BY MYSELF.
OKAY! DIRECT ATTACK!!
RUN!
TOWA!

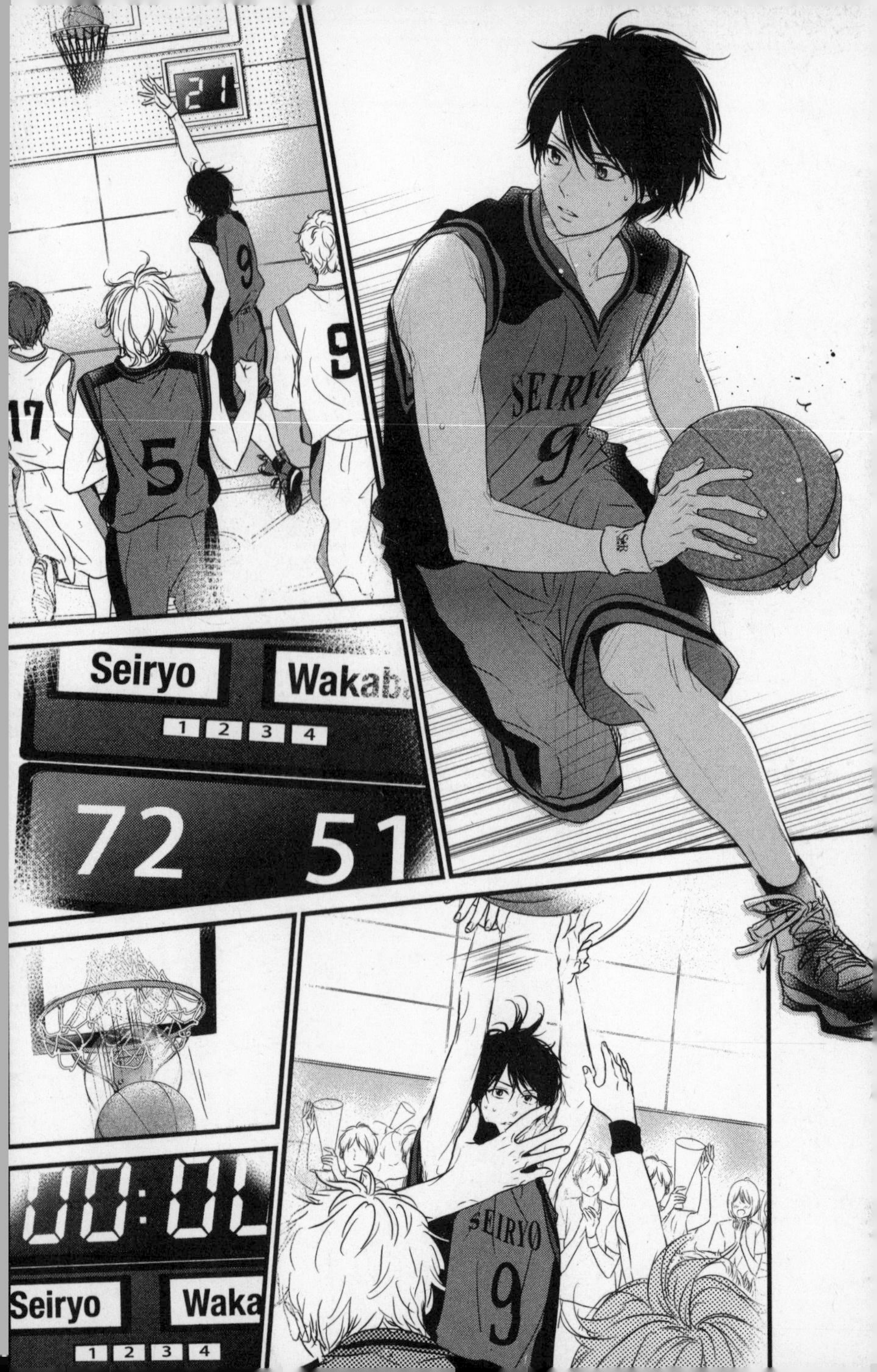
SEIRYO
9
21
9
9
17
5
Seiryo
Wakab.
1 2 3 4
72
51
SEIRYO
9
Seiryo
Waka
1 2 3 4

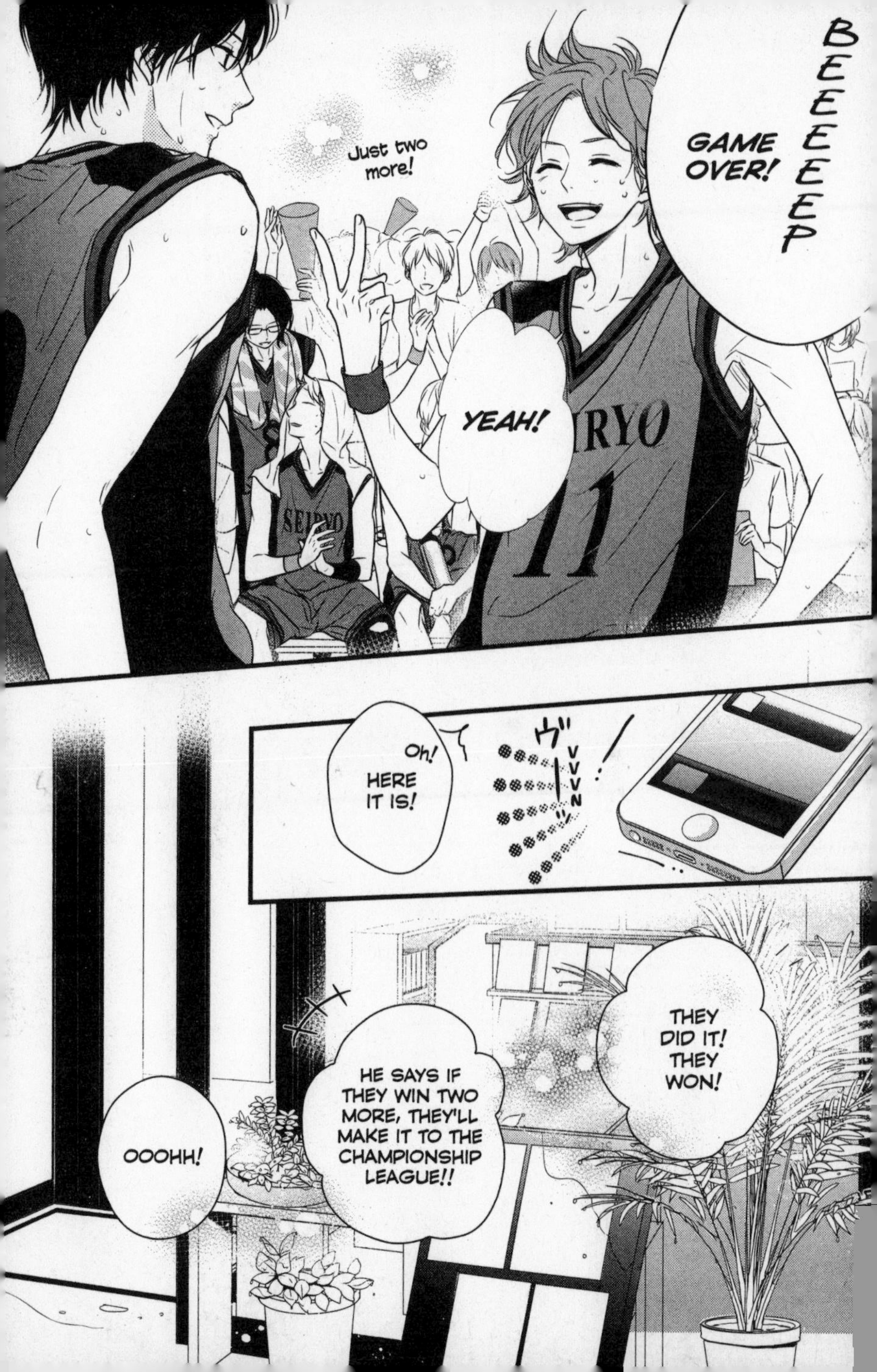
BEEEEEP
GAME OVER!
Just two more!
YEAH!
ヴ VVVN
Oh! HERE IT IS!
THEY DID IT! THEY WON!
HE SAYS IF THEY WIN TWO MORE, THEY'LL MAKE IT TO THE CHAMPIONSHIP LEAGUE!!
OOOHH!

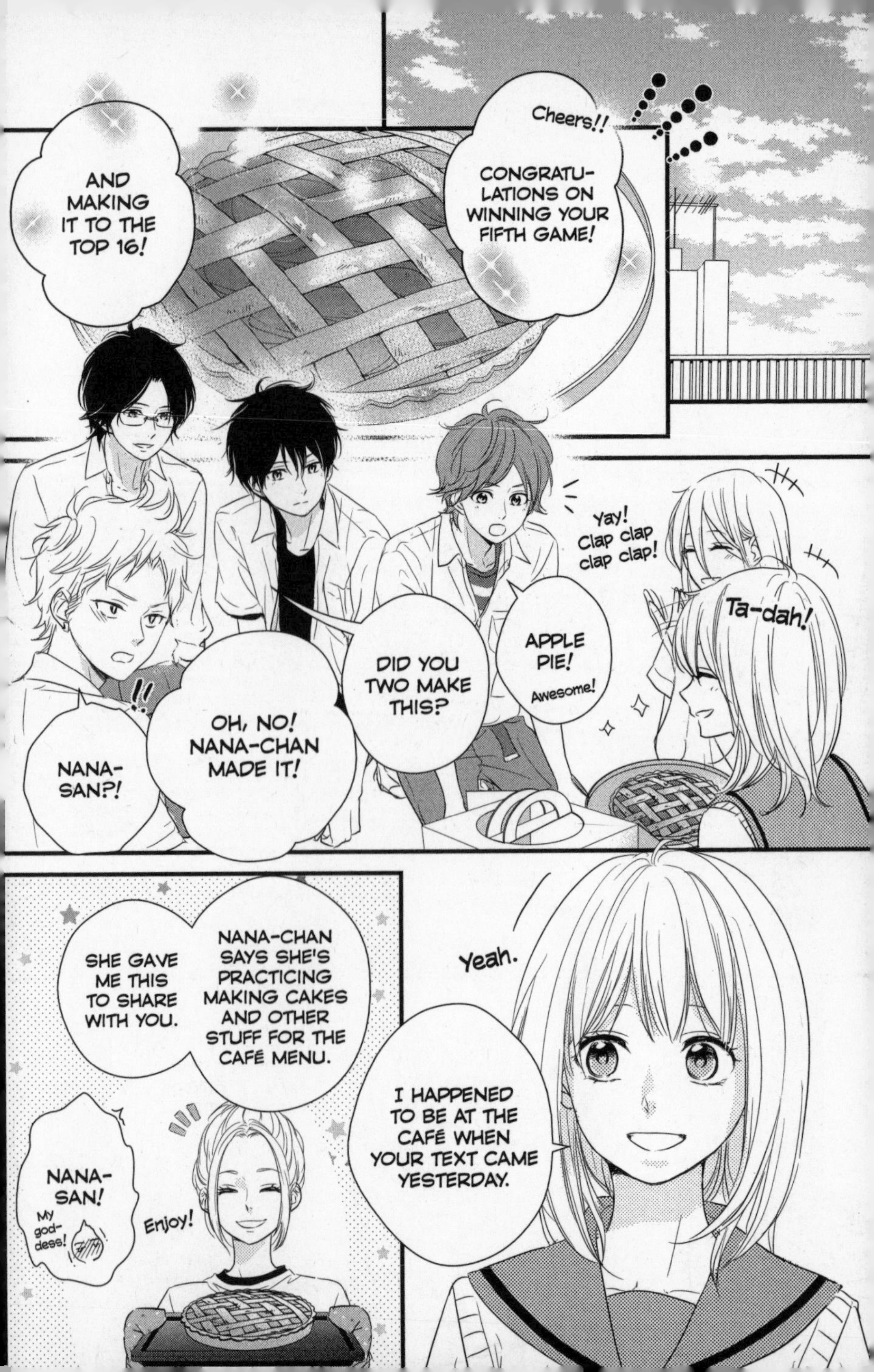
Cheers!!
CONGRATULATIONS ON WINNING YOUR FIFTH GAME!
AND MAKING IT TO THE TOP 16!
Yay! Clap clap clap clap!
Ta-dah!
APPLE PIE! Awesome!
DID YOU TWO MAKE THIS?
OH, NO! NANA-CHAN MADE IT!
NANA-SAN?!
Yeah.
I HAPPENED TO BE AT THE CAFÉ WHEN YOUR TEXT CAME YESTERDAY.
NANA-CHAN SAYS SHE'S PRACTICING MAKING CAKES AND OTHER STUFF FOR THE CAFÉ MENU.
SHE GAVE ME THIS TO SHARE WITH YOU.
NANA-SAN!
My goddess!
Enjoy!

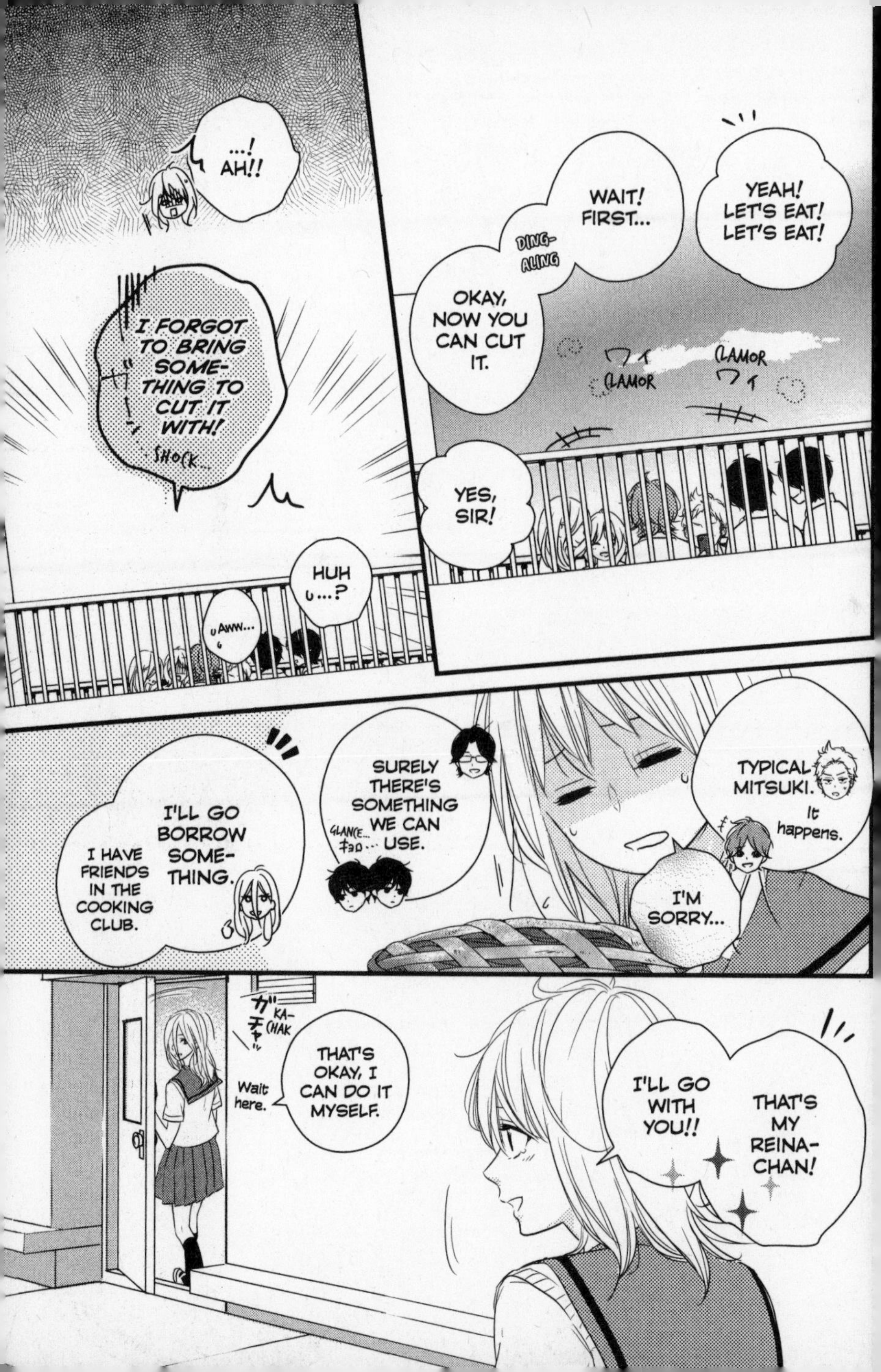

YEAH! LET'S EAT! LET'S EAT!
WAIT! FIRST...
DING-ALING
OKAY, NOW YOU CAN CUT IT.
CLAMOR
CLAMOR
YES, SIR!
...! AH!!
I FORGOT TO BRING SOME-THING TO CUT IT WITH!
SHOCK...
HUH...?
AWW...
TYPICAL MITSUKI.
It happens.
I'M SORRY...
SURELY THERE'S SOMETHING WE CAN USE.
GLANCE...
I'LL GO BORROW SOME-THING.
I HAVE FRIENDS IN THE COOKING CLUB.
THAT'S MY REINA-CHAN!
I'LL GO WITH YOU!!
THAT'S OKAY, I CAN DO IT MYSELF.
Wait here.
KA-CHAK

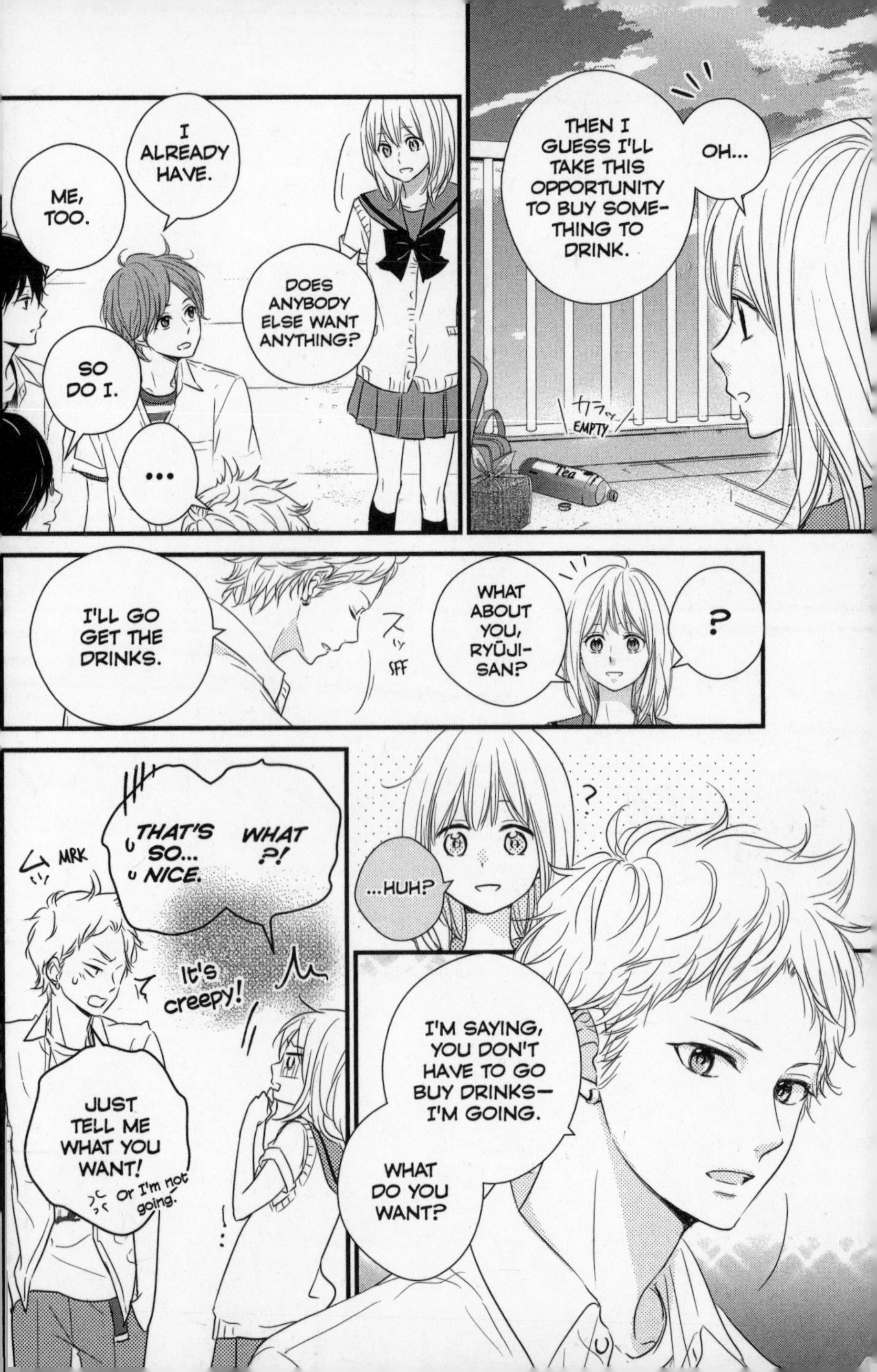
OH...
THEN I GUESS I'LL TAKE THIS OPPORTUNITY TO BUY SOME-THING TO DRINK.
EMPTY
Tea
DOES ANYBODY ELSE WANT ANYTHING?
I ALREADY HAVE.
ME, TOO.
SO DO I.
...
?
WHAT ABOUT YOU, RYŪJI-SAN?
SFF
I'LL GO GET THE DRINKS.
?
...HUH?
I'M SAYING, YOU DON'T HAVE TO GO BUY DRINKS— I'M GOING.
WHAT DO YOU WANT?
WHAT?!
THAT'S SO... NICE.
It's creepy!
MRK
JUST TELL ME WHAT YOU WANT!
Or I'm not going.

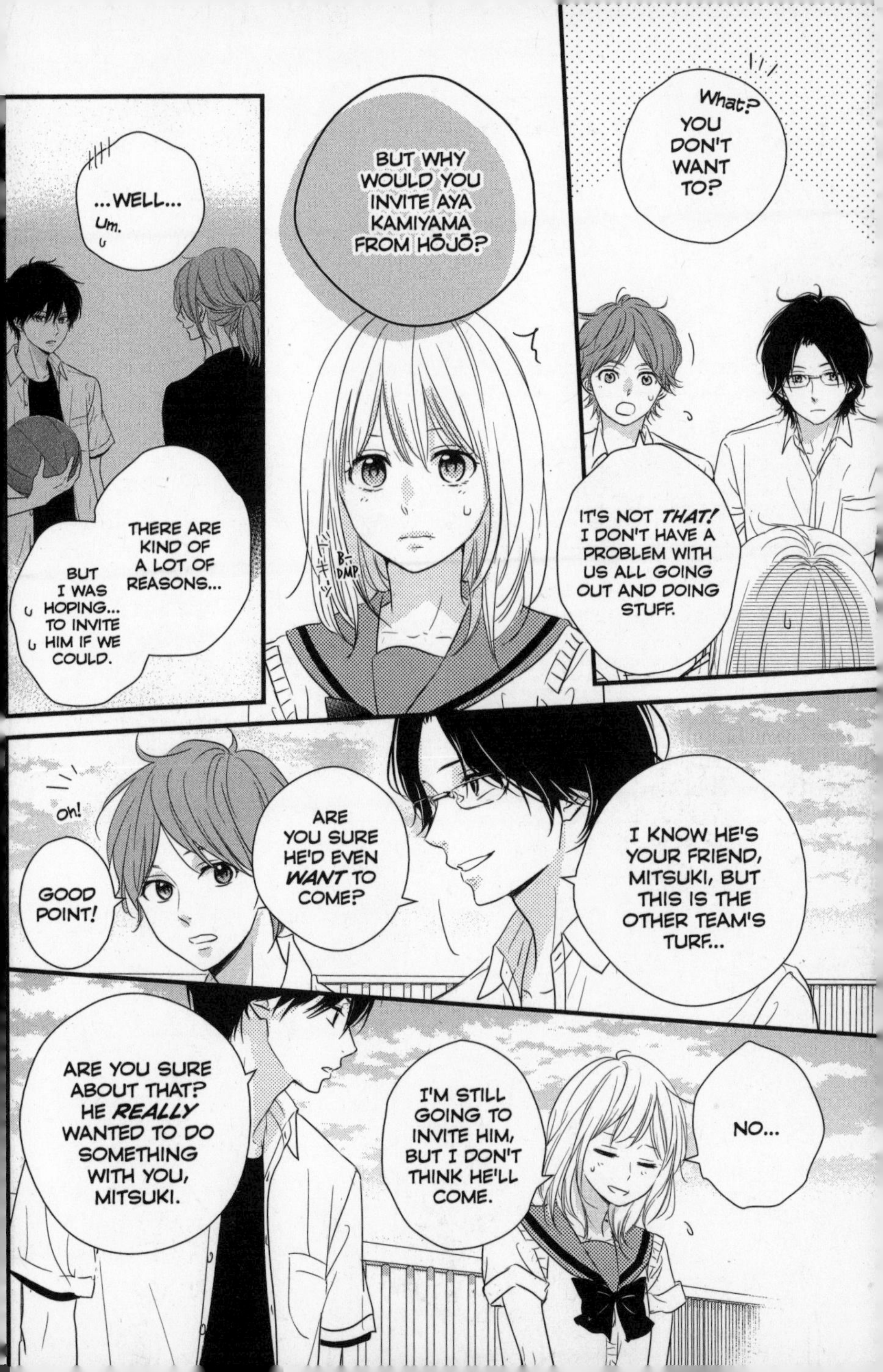
What? YOU DON'T WANT TO?
IT'S NOT *THAT!* I DON'T HAVE A PROBLEM WITH US ALL GOING OUT AND DOING STUFF.
BUT WHY WOULD YOU INVITE AYA KAMIYAMA FROM HŌJŌ?
B-DMP
...WELL...
Um.
THERE ARE KIND OF A LOT OF REASONS...
BUT I WAS HOPING... TO INVITE HIM IF WE COULD.
I KNOW HE'S YOUR FRIEND, MITSUKI, BUT THIS IS THE OTHER TEAM'S TURF...
ARE YOU SURE HE'D EVEN ***WANT*** TO COME?
Oh!
GOOD POINT!
NO...
I'M STILL GOING TO INVITE HIM, BUT I DON'T THINK HE'LL COME.
ARE YOU SURE ABOUT THAT? HE ***REALLY*** WANTED TO DO SOMETHING WITH YOU, MITSUKI.

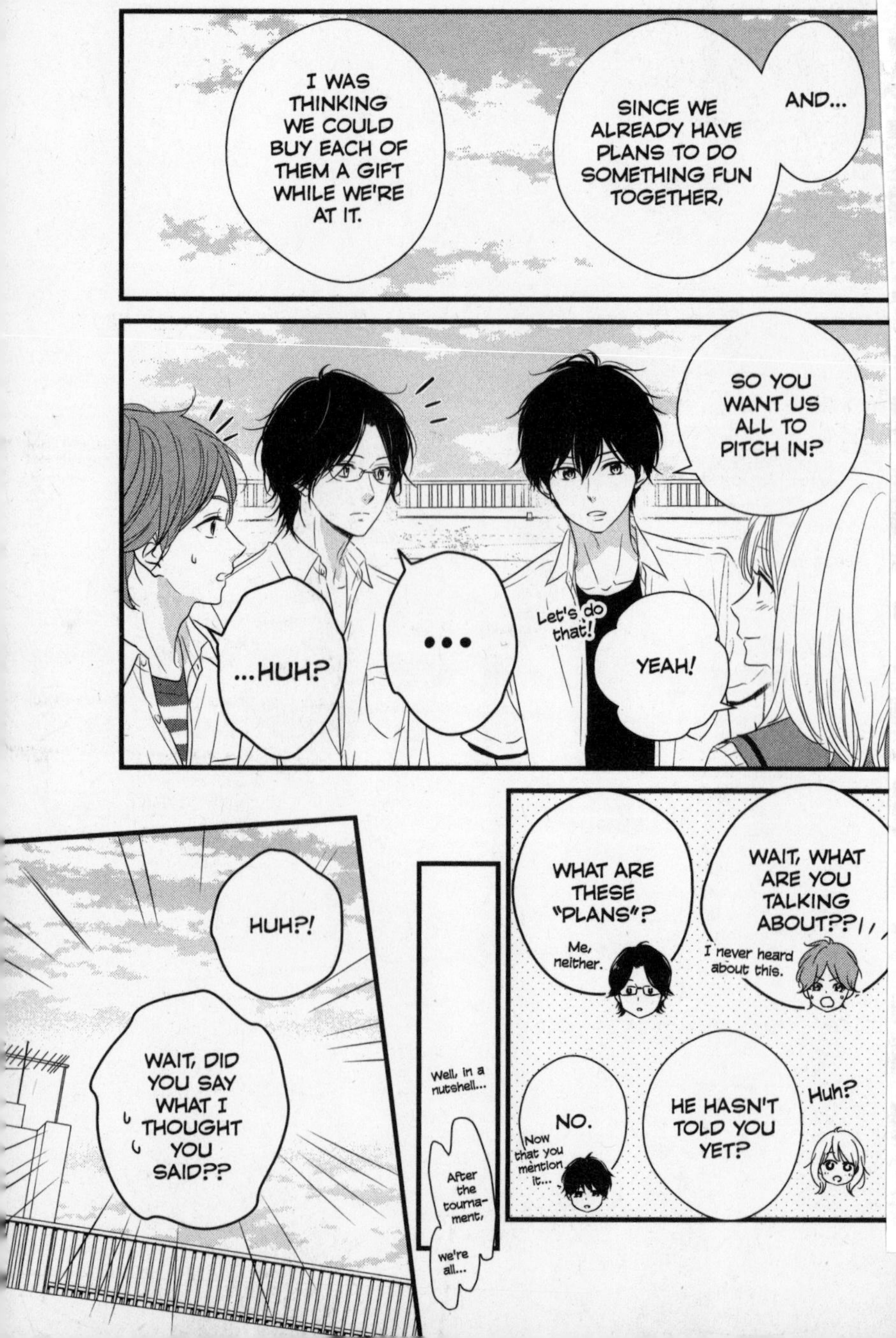
SINCE WE ALREADY HAVE PLANS TO DO SOMETHING FUN TOGETHER,
AND...
I WAS THINKING WE COULD BUY EACH OF THEM A GIFT WHILE WE'RE AT IT.
SO YOU WANT US ALL TO PITCH IN?
YEAH!
Let's do that!
...
...HUH?
WAIT, WHAT ARE YOU TALKING ABOUT??
I never heard about this.
WHAT ARE THESE "PLANS"?
Me, neither.
Huh?
HE HASN'T TOLD YOU YET?
NO.
Now that you mention it...
Well, in a nutshell...
After the tournament,
we're all...
HUH?!
WAIT, DID YOU SAY WHAT I THOUGHT YOU SAID??

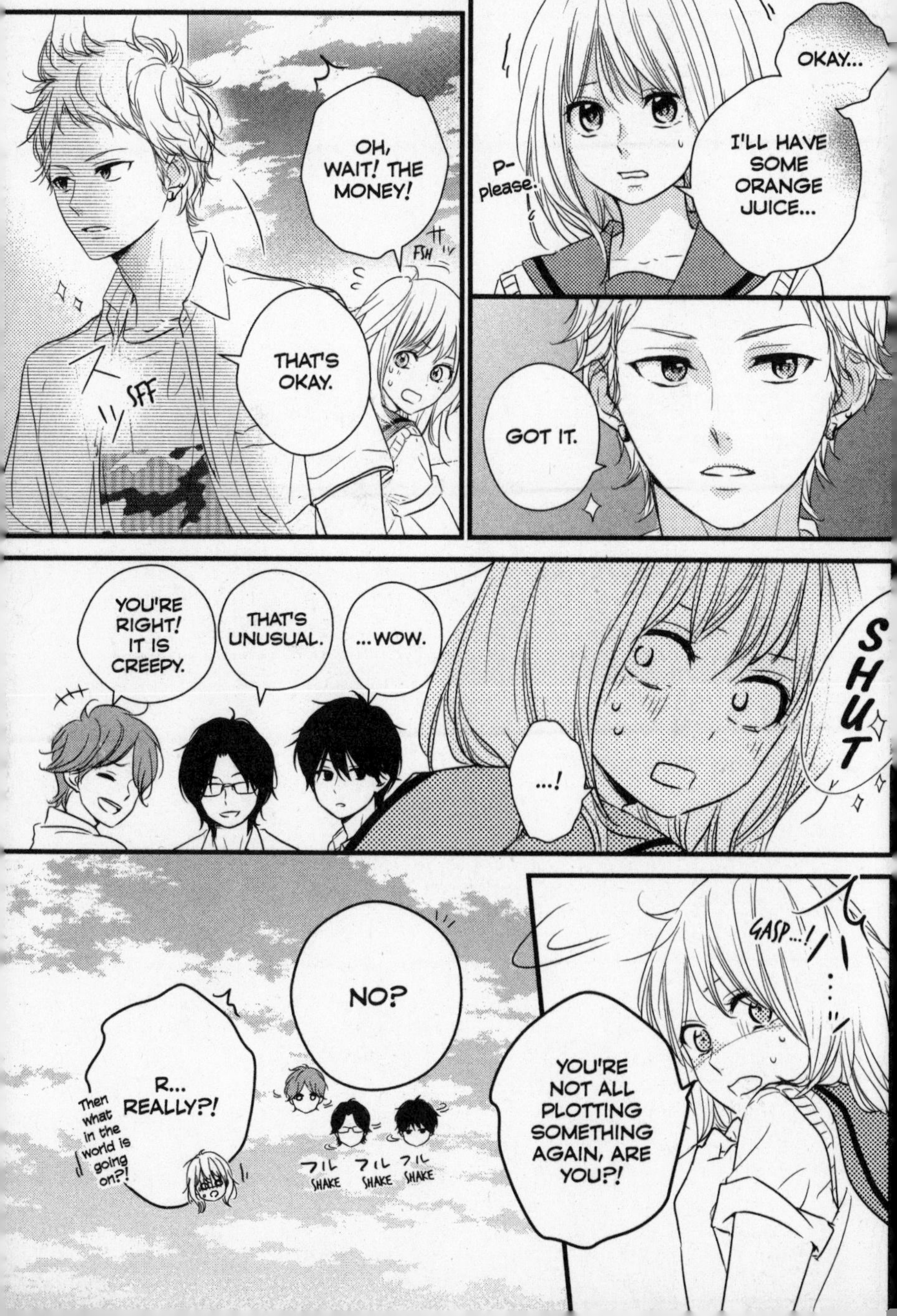
OKAY...
I'LL HAVE SOME ORANGE JUICE...
P-please.
GOT IT.
OH, WAIT! THE MONEY!
FSH
THAT'S OKAY.
SFF
SHUT
...!
...WOW.
THAT'S UNUSUAL.
YOU'RE RIGHT! IT IS CREEPY.
GASP...!
YOU'RE NOT ALL PLOTTING SOMETHING AGAIN, ARE YOU?!
NO?
R... REALLY?!
Then what in the world is going on?!
フル SHAKE
フル SHAKE
フル SHAKE

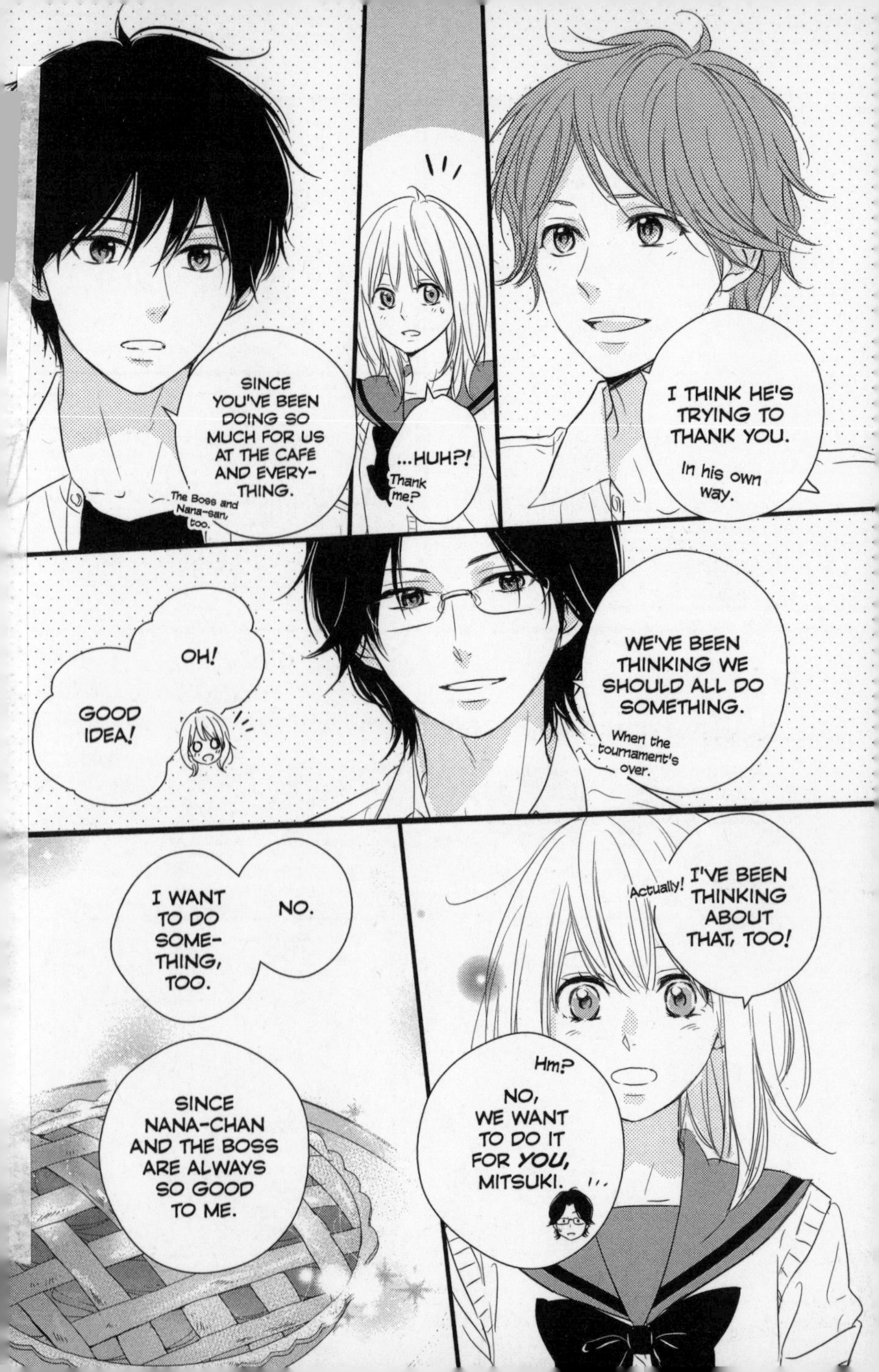
I THINK HE'S TRYING TO THANK YOU.
In his own way.
...HUH?!
Thank me?
SINCE YOU'VE BEEN DOING SO MUCH FOR US AT THE CAFÉ AND EVERY-THING.
The Boss and Nana-san, too.
WE'VE BEEN THINKING WE SHOULD ALL DO SOMETHING.
When the tournament's over.
OH!
GOOD IDEA!
Actually!
I'VE BEEN THINKING ABOUT THAT, TOO!
Hm?
NO, WE WANT TO DO IT FOR *YOU*, MITSUKI.
NO.
I WANT TO DO SOME-THING, TOO.
SINCE NANA-CHAN AND THE BOSS ARE ALWAYS SO GOOD TO ME.

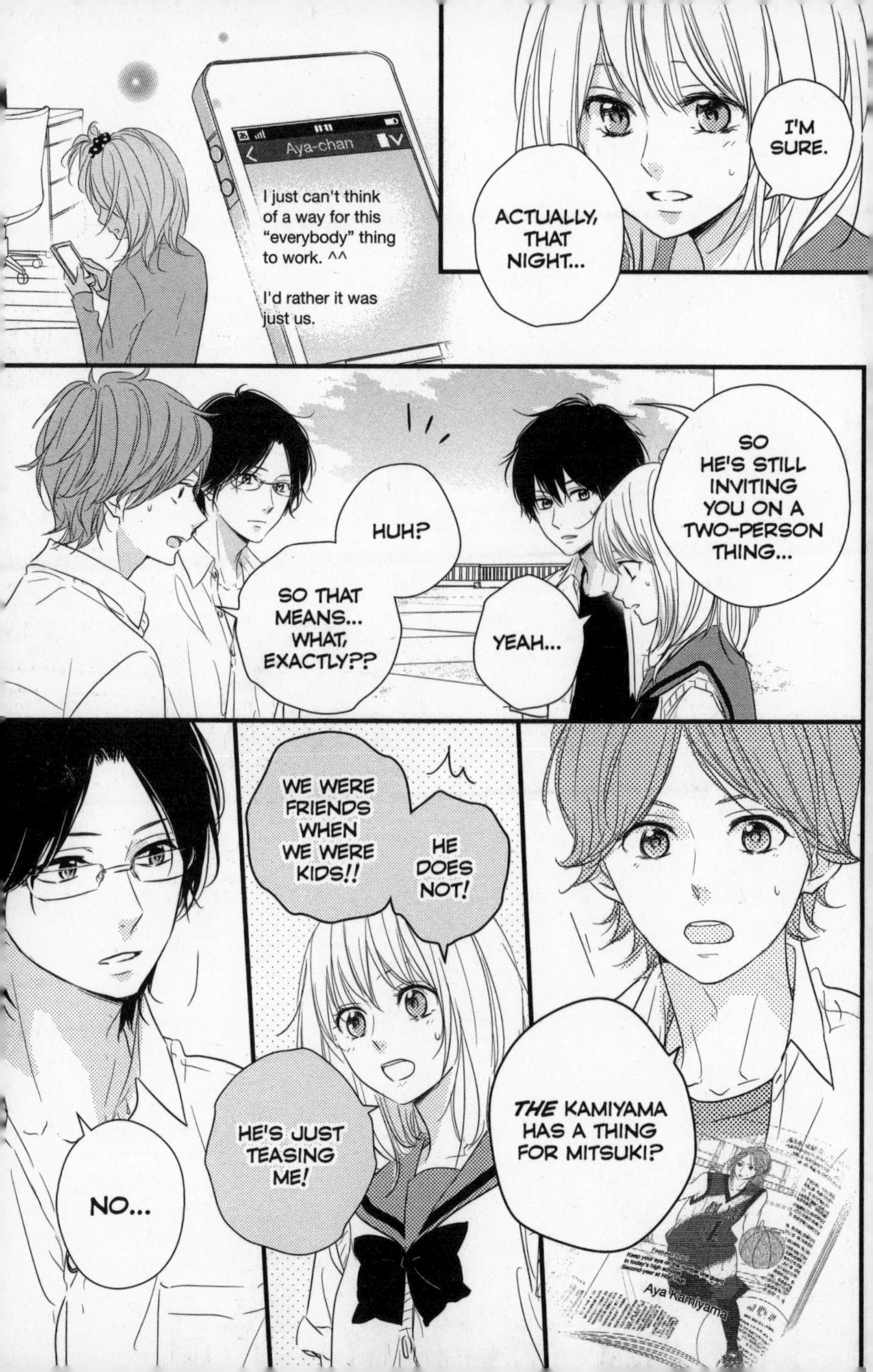
I'M SURE.
ACTUALLY, THAT NIGHT...
Aya-chan
I just can't think of a way for this "everybody" thing to work. ^^
I'd rather it was just us.
SO HE'S STILL INVITING YOU ON A TWO-PERSON THING...
YEAH...
HUH?
SO THAT MEANS... WHAT, EXACTLY??
THE KAMIYAMA HAS A THING FOR MITSUKI?
Aya Kamiyama
HE DOES NOT!
WE WERE FRIENDS WHEN WE WERE KIDS!!
HE'S JUST TEASING ME!
NO...

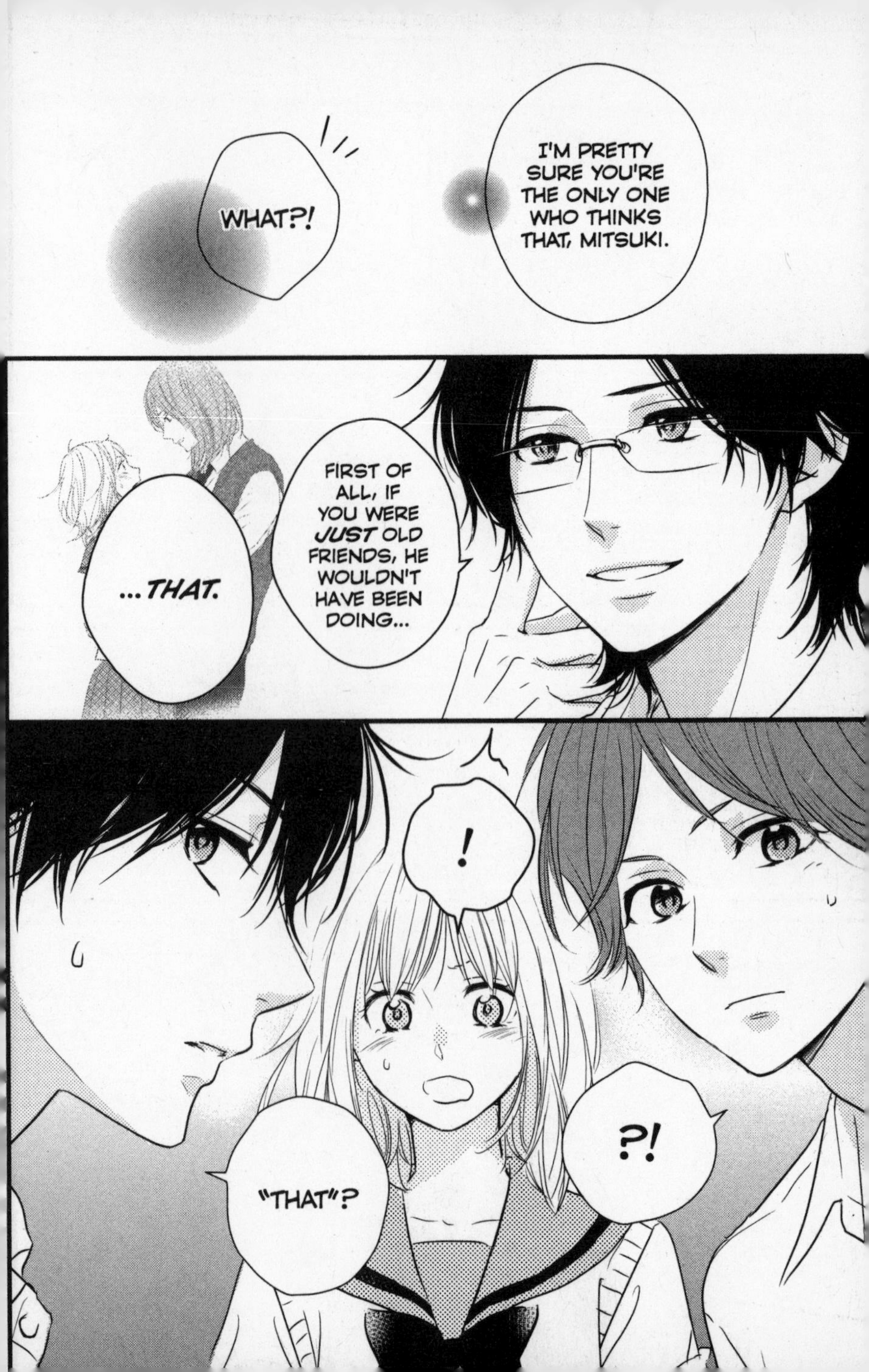
I'M PRETTY SURE YOU'RE THE ONLY ONE WHO THINKS THAT, MITSUKI.
WHAT?!
FIRST OF ALL, IF YOU WERE *JUST* OLD FRIENDS, HE WOULDN'T HAVE BEEN DOING...
...*THAT.*
!
?!
"THAT"?

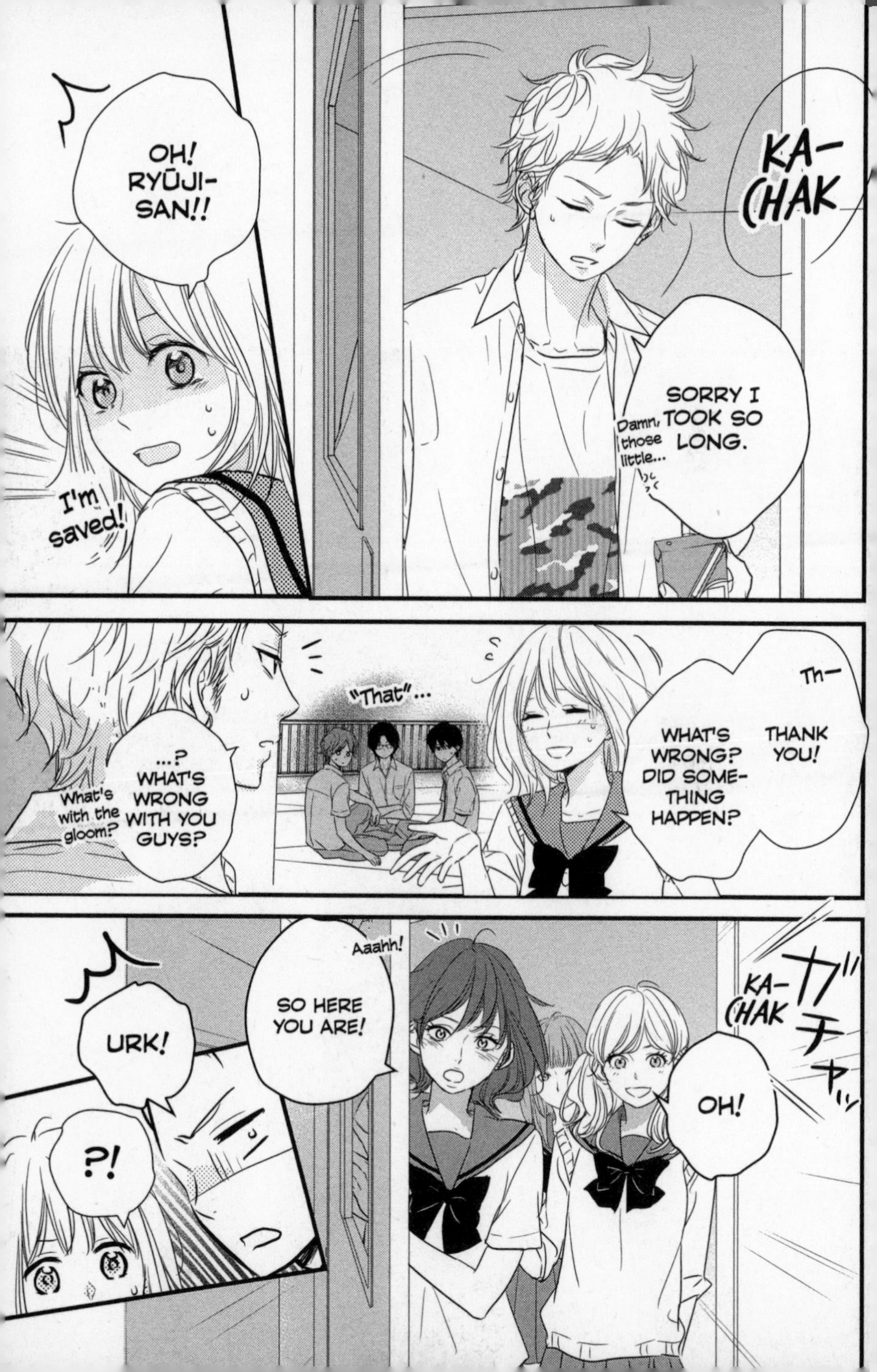
KA-CHAK
SORRY I TOOK SO LONG.
Damn, those little...
OH! RYŪJI-SAN!!
I'm saved!
Th-
THANK YOU!
WHAT'S WRONG? DID SOME-THING HAPPEN?
"That"...
...? WHAT'S WRONG WITH YOU GUYS?
What's with the gloom?
KA-CHAK
ガチャッ
OH!
Aaahh!
SO HERE YOU ARE!
URK!
?!

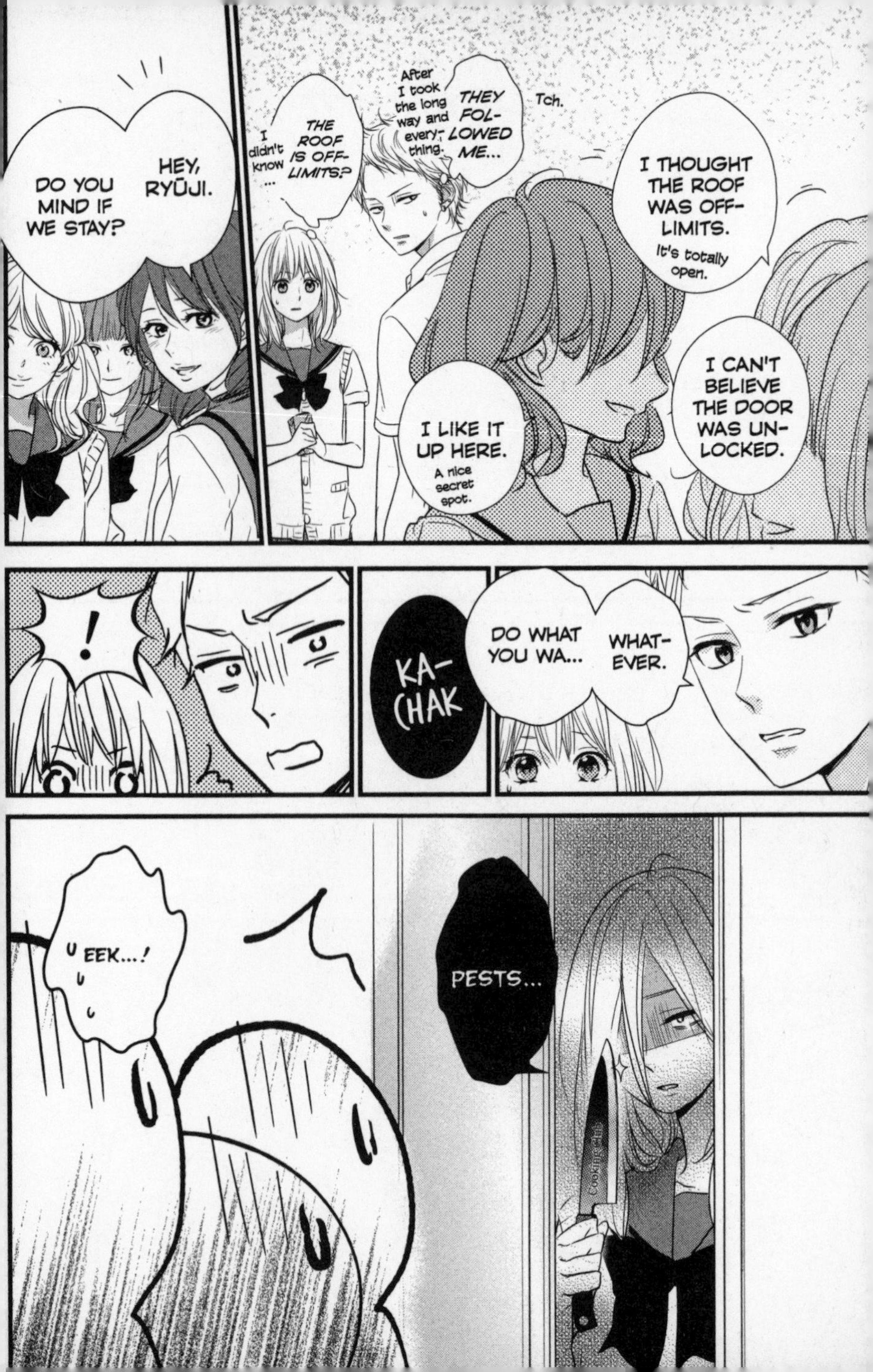
I THOUGHT THE ROOF WAS OFF-LIMITS.
It's totally open.
Tch.
THEY FOL-LOWED ME...
After I took the long way and every-thing.
THE ROOF IS OFF-LIMITS?
I didn't know ...
I CAN'T BELIEVE THE DOOR WAS UN-LOCKED.
I LIKE IT UP HERE.
A nice secret spot.
HEY, RYŪJI.
DO YOU MIND IF WE STAY?
WHAT-EVER.
DO WHAT YOU WA...
KA-CHAK
!
PESTS...
EEK...!

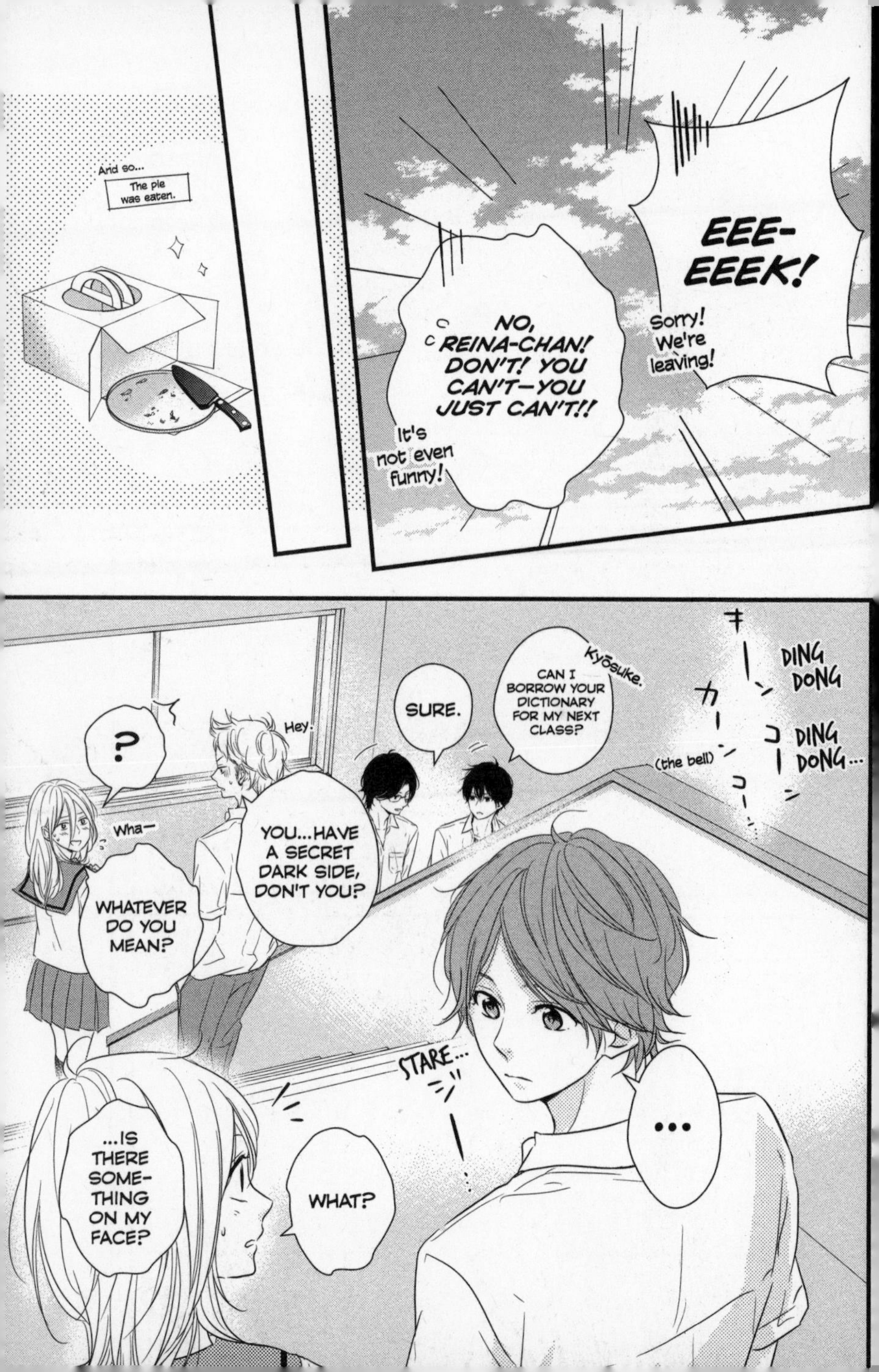
EEE-EEEK!
Sorry! We're leaving!
NO, REINA-CHAN! DON'T! YOU CAN'T—YOU JUST CAN'T!!
It's not even funny!
And so...
The pie was eaten.
DING DONG
DING DONG...
(the bell)
Kyōsuke.
CAN I BORROW YOUR DICTIONARY FOR MY NEXT CLASS?
SURE.
Hey.
?
YOU...HAVE A SECRET DARK SIDE, DON'T YOU?
Wha—
WHATEVER DO YOU MEAN?
...
STARE...
WHAT?
...IS THERE SOMETHING ON MY FACE?

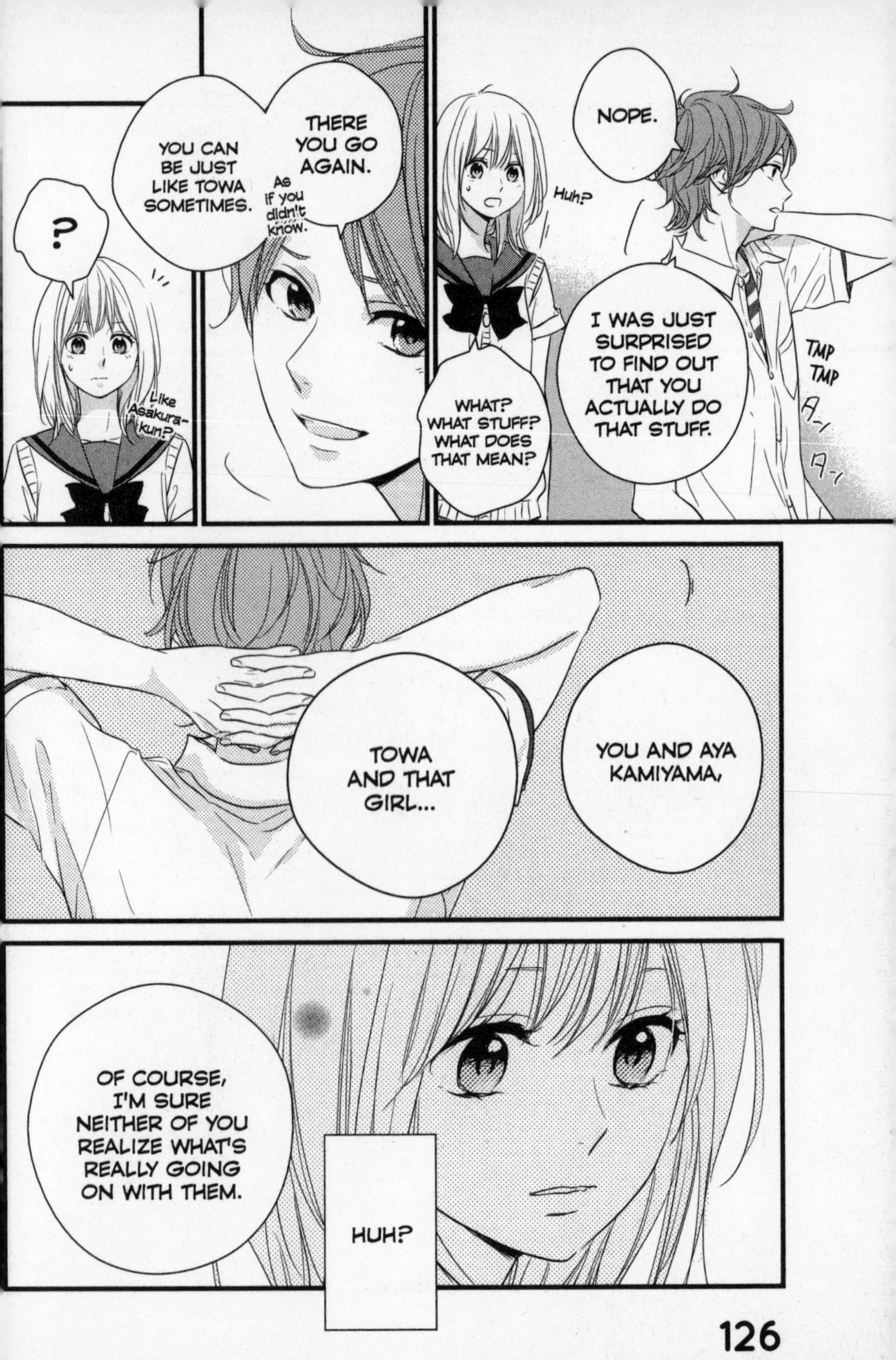
NOPE.
Huh?
I WAS JUST SURPRISED TO FIND OUT THAT YOU ACTUALLY DO THAT STUFF.
WHAT? WHAT STUFF? WHAT DOES THAT MEAN?
TMP TMP
THERE YOU GO AGAIN.
As if you didn't know.
YOU CAN BE JUST LIKE TOWA SOMETIMES.
?
Like Asakura-kun?
YOU AND AYA KAMIYAMA,
TOWA AND THAT GIRL...
OF COURSE, I'M SURE NEITHER OF YOU REALIZE WHAT'S REALLY GOING ON WITH THEM.
HUH?

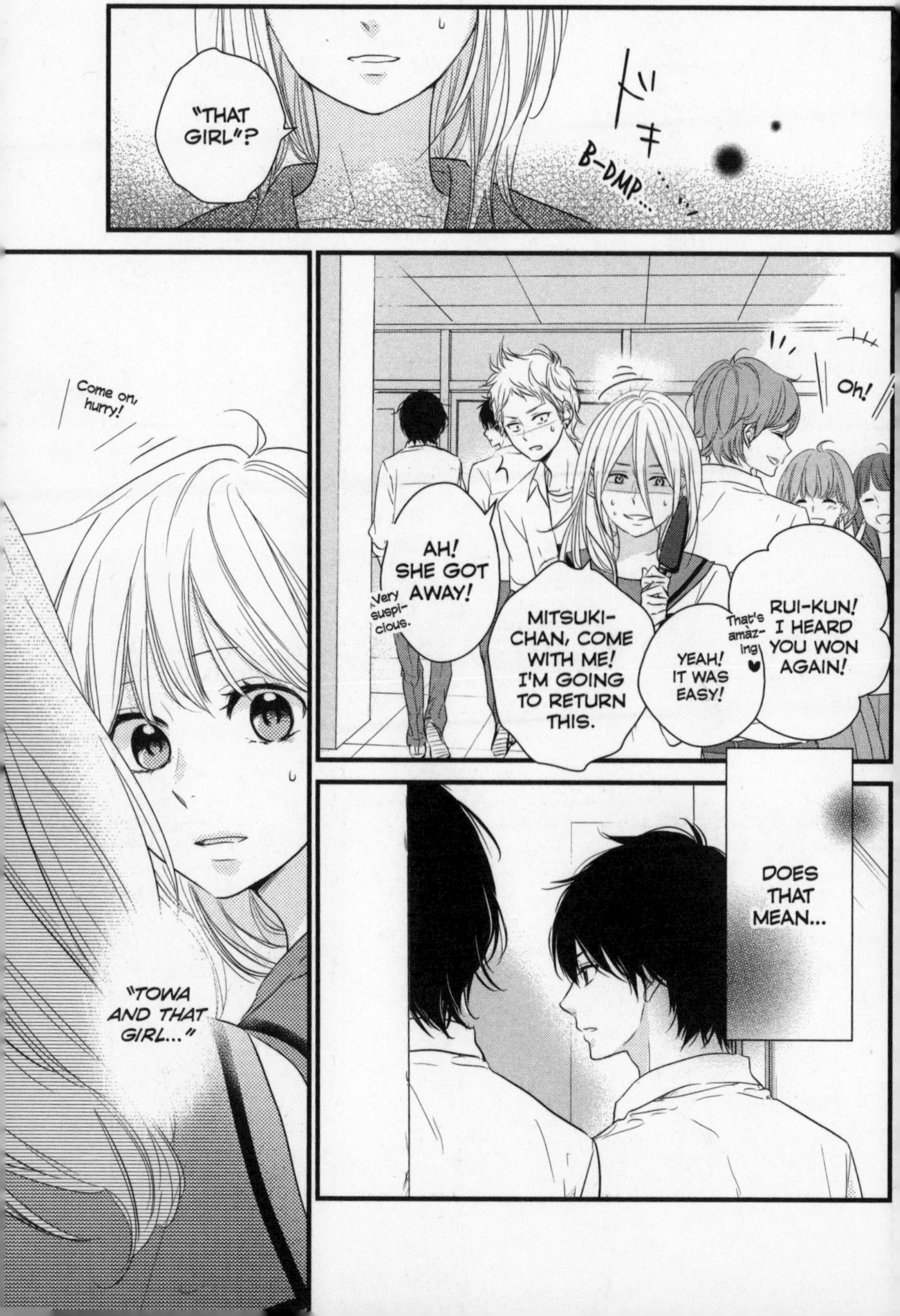
"THAT GIRL"?
ドキ
B-DMP...
Oh!
RUI-KUN! I HEARD YOU WON AGAIN!
That's amazing ♥
YEAH! IT WAS EASY!
MITSUKI-CHAN, COME WITH ME! I'M GOING TO RETURN THIS.
AH! SHE GOT AWAY!
Very suspicious.
DOES THAT MEAN...
Come on, hurry!
"TOWA AND THAT GIRL..."

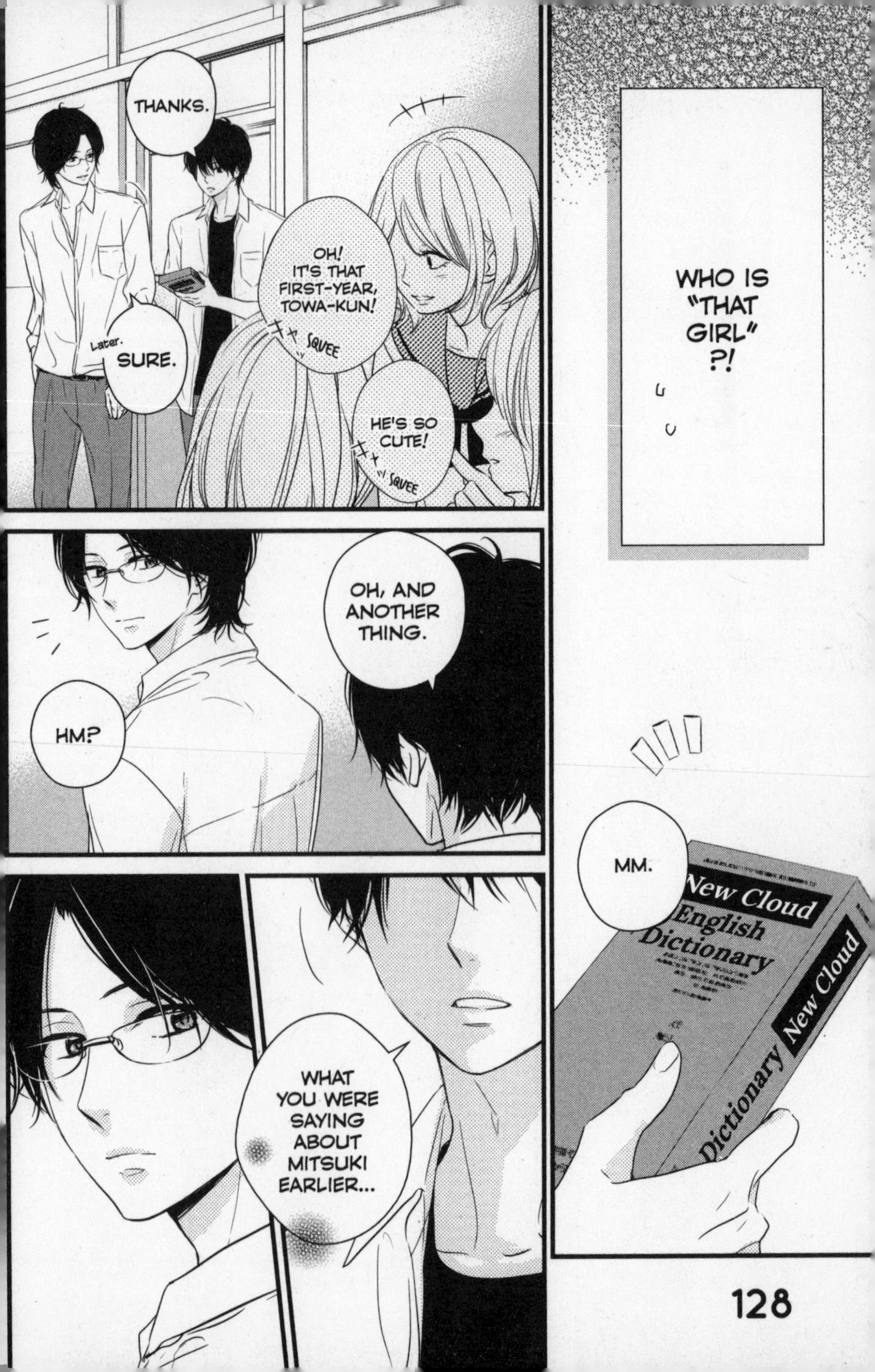
WHO IS "THAT GIRL"?!
MM.
New Cloud English Dictionary
New Cloud Dictionary
THANKS.
OH! IT'S THAT FIRST-YEAR, TOWA-KUN!
SQUEE
SURE.
Later.
HE'S SO CUTE!
SQUEE
OH, AND ANOTHER THING.
HM?
WHAT YOU WERE SAYING ABOUT MITSUKI EARLIER...

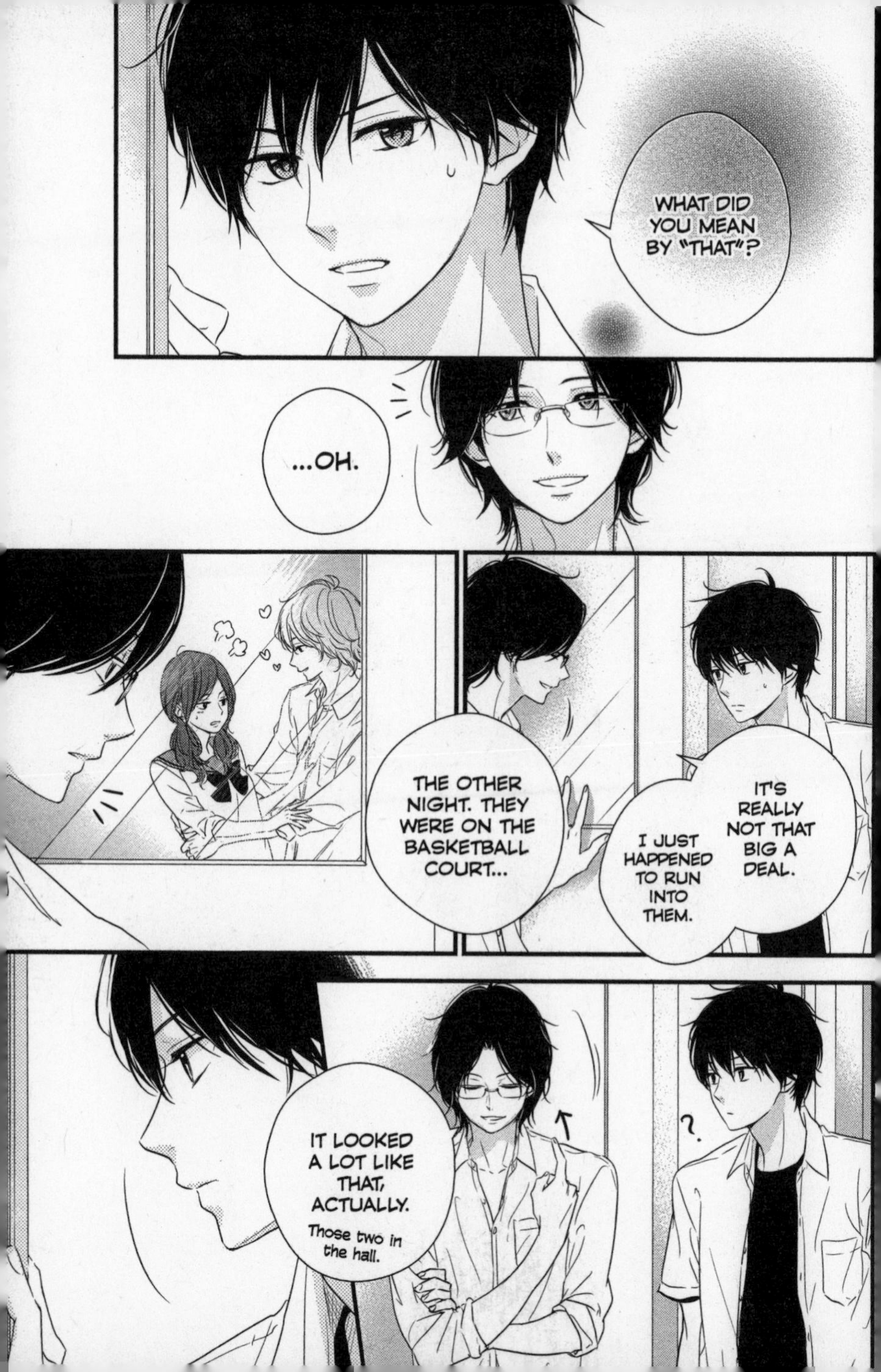
WHAT DID YOU MEAN BY "THAT"?
...OH.
IT'S REALLY NOT THAT BIG A DEAL.
I JUST HAPPENED TO RUN INTO THEM.
THE OTHER NIGHT. THEY WERE ON THE BASKETBALL COURT...
IT LOOKED A LOT LIKE THAT, ACTUALLY.
Those two in the hall.

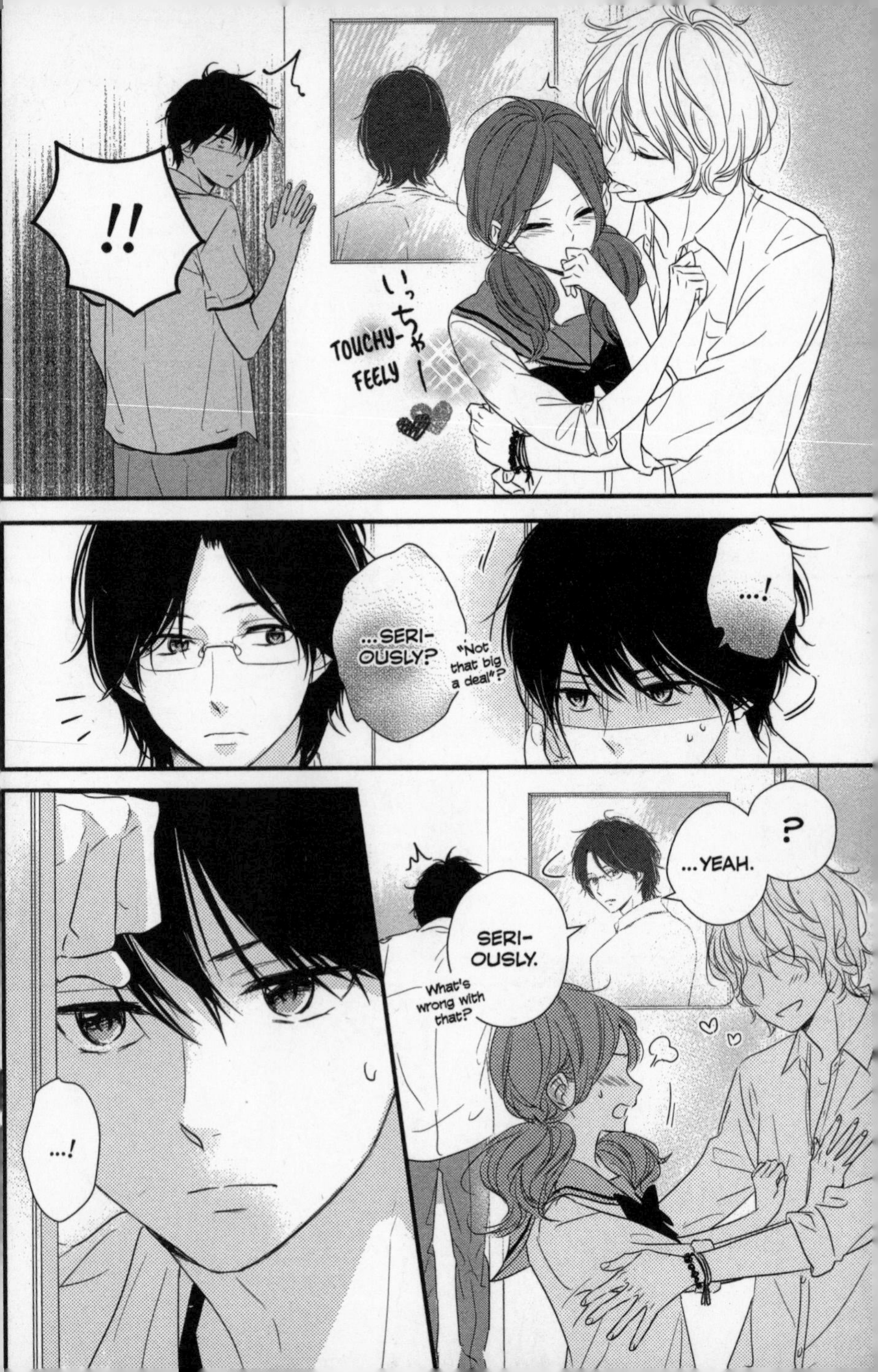
いっちゃー
TOUCHY-FEELY
!!
...!
"Not that big a deal"?
...SERI-OUSLY?
?
...YEAH.
SERI-OUSLY.
What's wrong with that?
...!

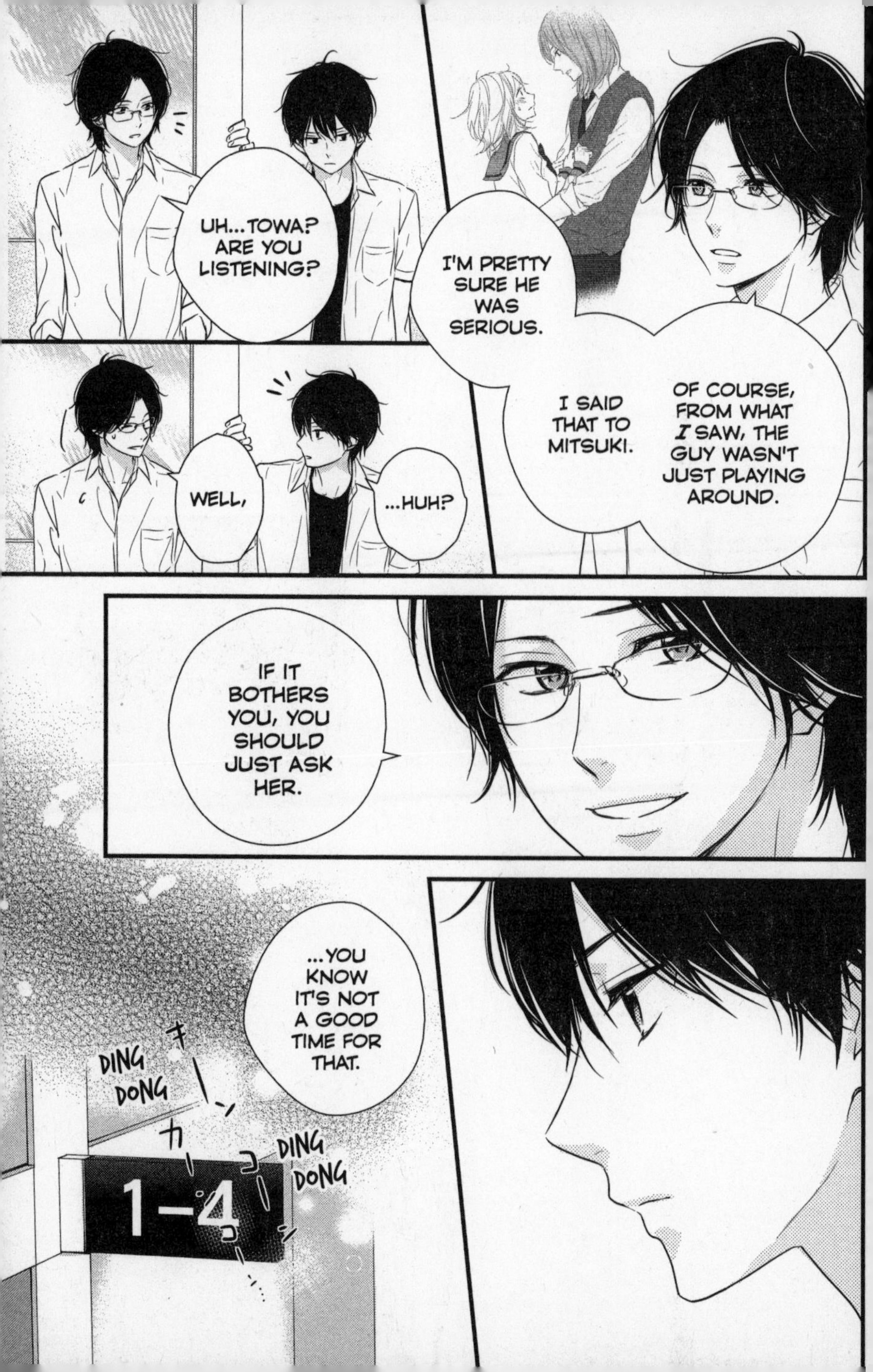
I'M PRETTY SURE HE WAS SERIOUS.
OF COURSE, FROM WHAT *I* SAW, THE GUY WASN'T JUST PLAYING AROUND.
I SAID THAT TO MITSUKI.
UH...TOWA? ARE YOU LISTENING?
...HUH?
WELL,
IF IT BOTHERS YOU, YOU SHOULD JUST ASK HER.
...YOU KNOW IT'S NOT A GOOD TIME FOR THAT.
DING DONG
DING DONG
1-4

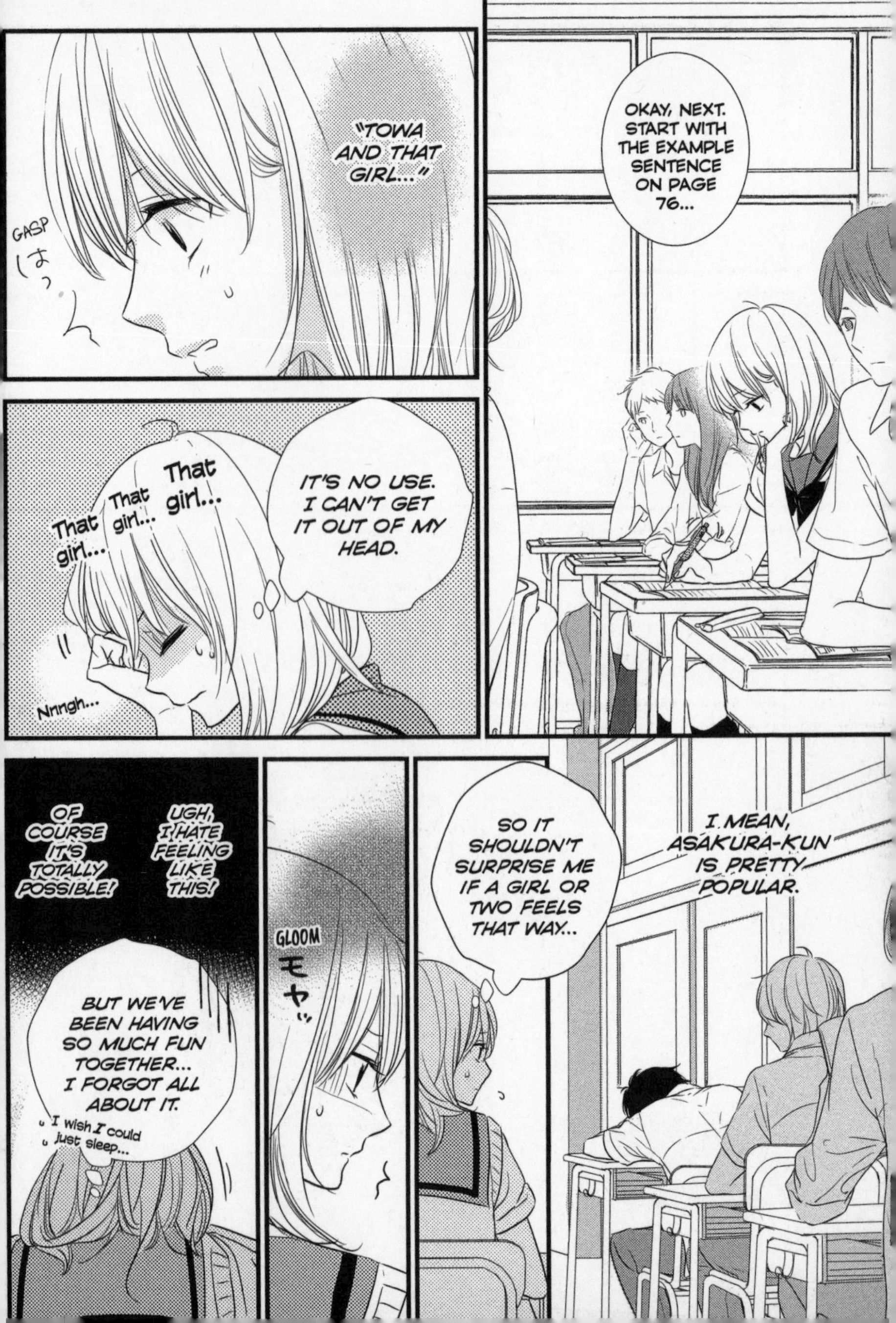
OKAY, NEXT. START WITH THE EXAMPLE SENTENCE ON PAGE 76...
"TOWA AND THAT GIRL..."
GASP
はっ
IT'S NO USE. I CAN'T GET IT OUT OF MY HEAD.
That girl...
That girl...
That girl...
Nnngh...
I MEAN, ASAKURA-KUN IS PRETTY POPULAR.
SO IT SHOULDN'T SURPRISE ME IF A GIRL OR TWO FEELS THAT WAY...
GLOOM
モヤッ
UGH, I HATE FEELING LIKE THIS!
OF COURSE IT'S TOTALLY POSSIBLE!
BUT WE'VE BEEN HAVING SO MUCH FUN TOGETHER... I FORGOT ALL ABOUT IT.
I wish I could just sleep...

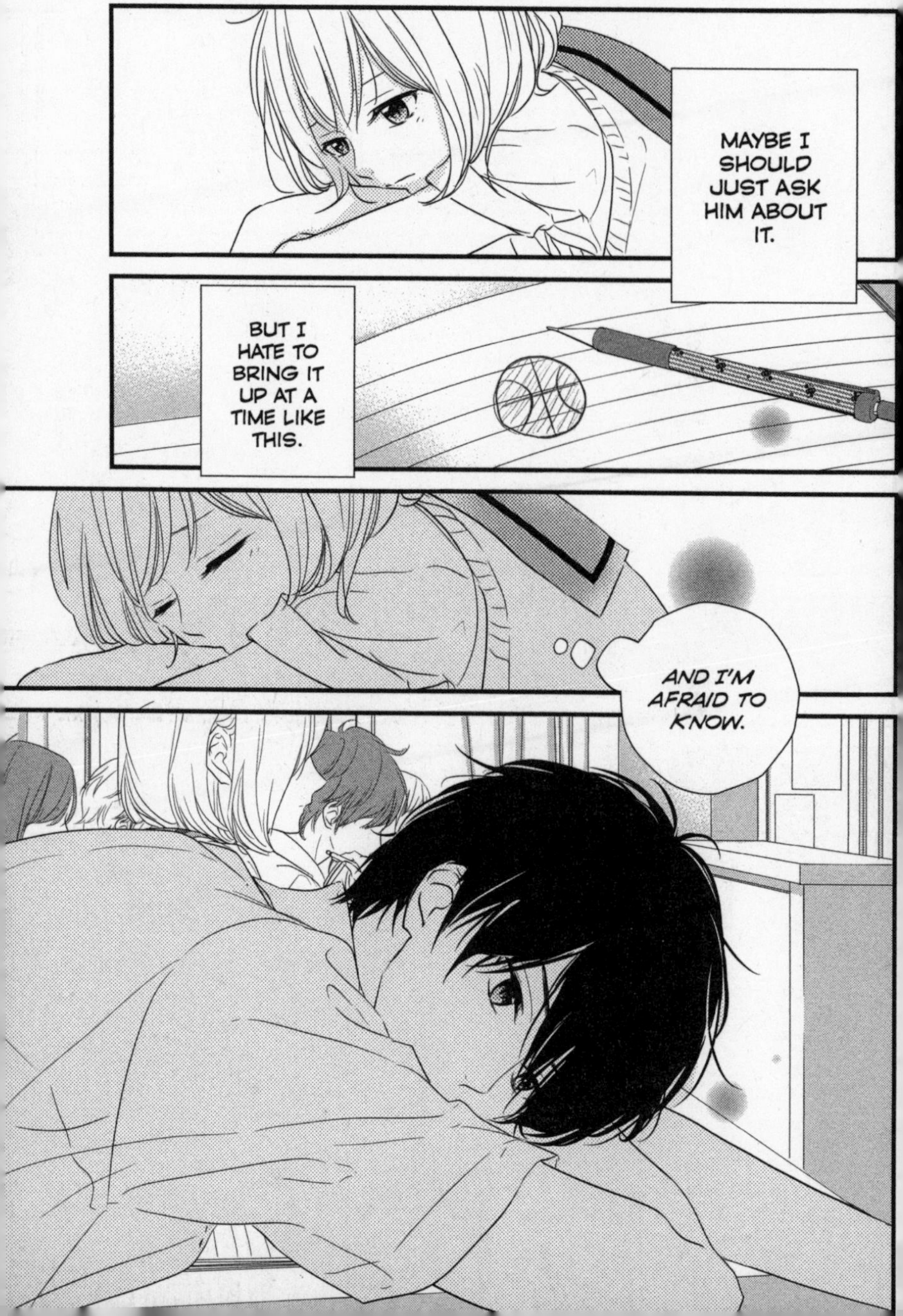
MAYBE I SHOULD JUST ASK HIM ABOUT IT.
BUT I HATE TO BRING IT UP AT A TIME LIKE THIS.
AND I'M AFRAID TO KNOW.

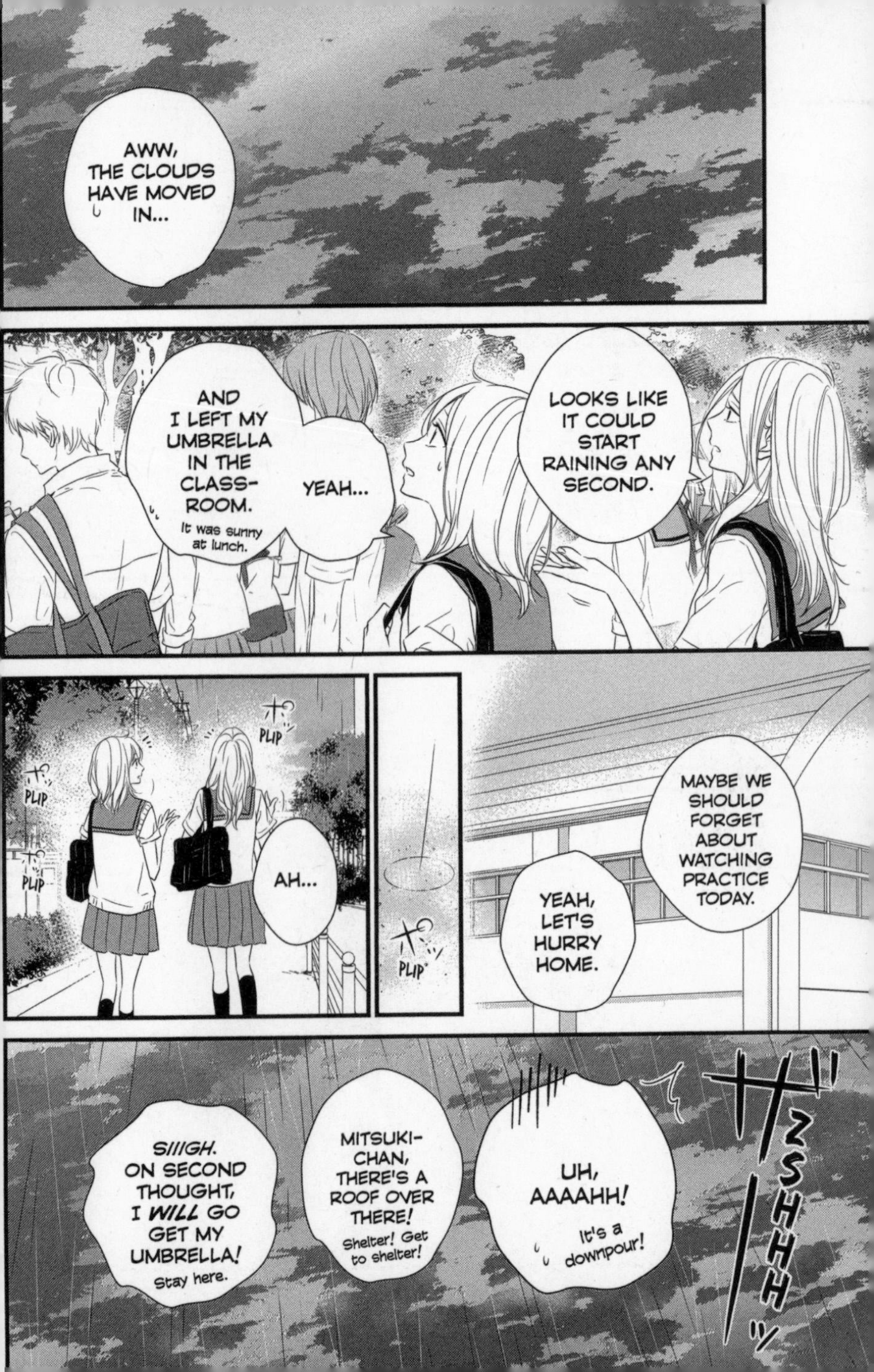
AWW, THE CLOUDS HAVE MOVED IN...
LOOKS LIKE IT COULD START RAINING ANY SECOND.
YEAH...
AND I LEFT MY UMBRELLA IN THE CLASSROOM.
It was sunny at lunch.
MAYBE WE SHOULD FORGET ABOUT WATCHING PRACTICE TODAY.
YEAH, LET'S HURRY HOME.
PLIP
PLIP
AH...
PLIP
PLIP
ZSHHHH
UH, AAAAHH!
It's a downpour!
MITSUKI-CHAN, THERE'S A ROOF OVER THERE!
Shelter! Get to shelter!
SIIIGH. ON SECOND THOUGHT, I WILL GO GET MY UMBRELLA!
Stay here.

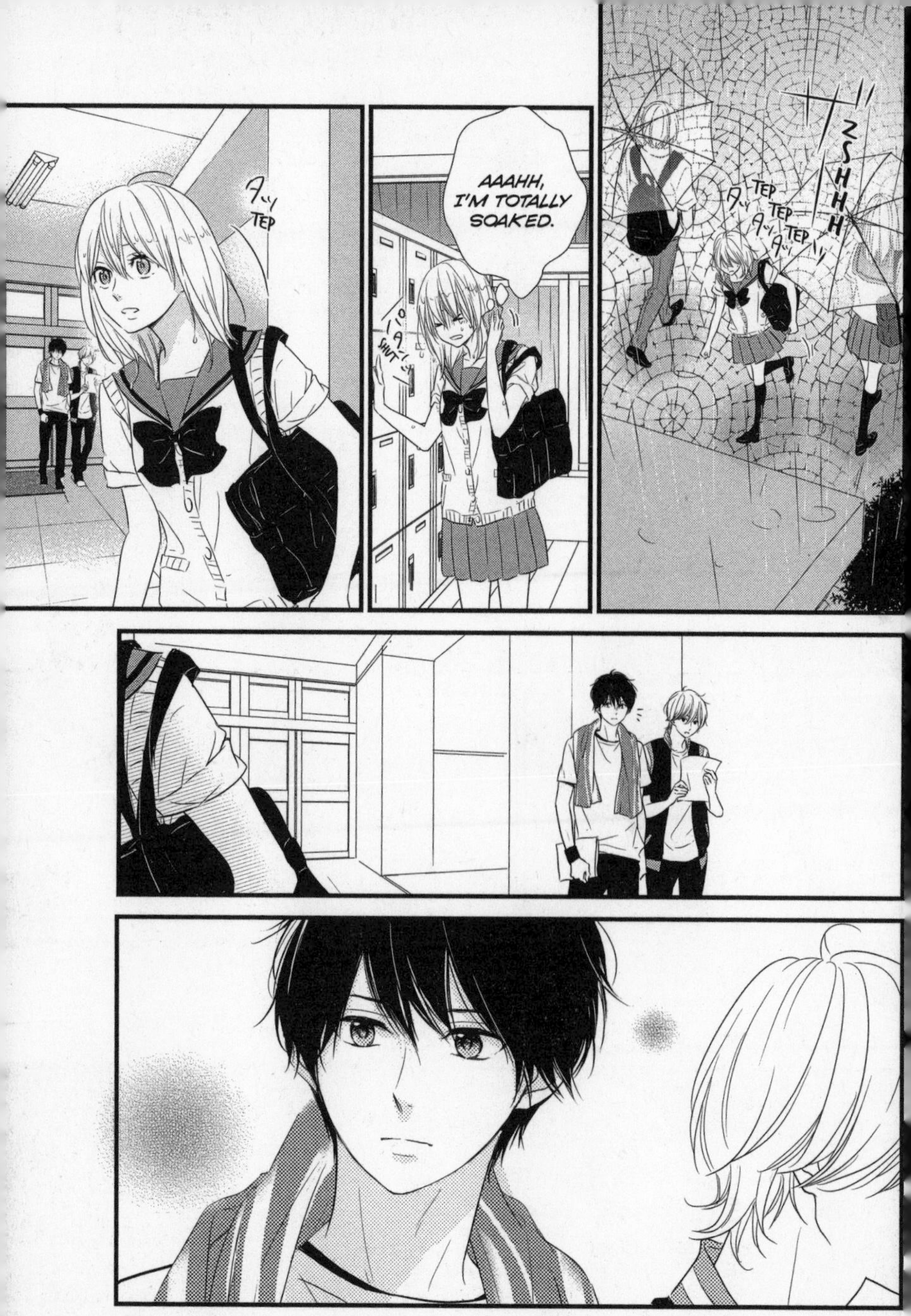
ZSHHH
TEP
TEP
TEP
AAAHH, I'M TOTALLY SOAKED.
SHUT
TEP

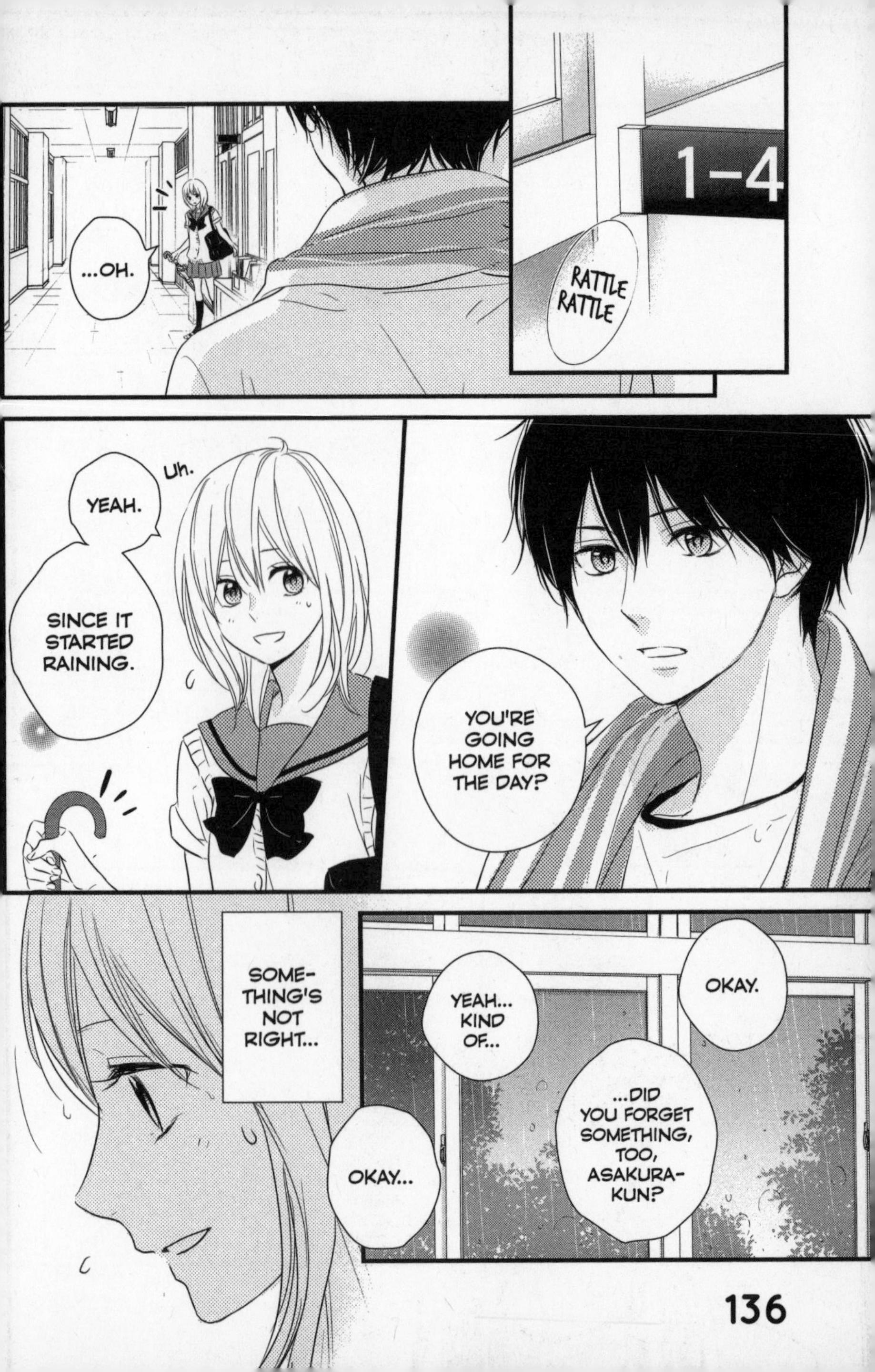
1-4
RATTLE RATTLE
...OH.
YOU'RE GOING HOME FOR THE DAY?
Uh.
YEAH.
SINCE IT STARTED RAINING.
OKAY.
...DID YOU FORGET SOMETHING, TOO, ASAKURA-KUN?
YEAH... KIND OF...
OKAY...
SOME-THING'S NOT RIGHT...

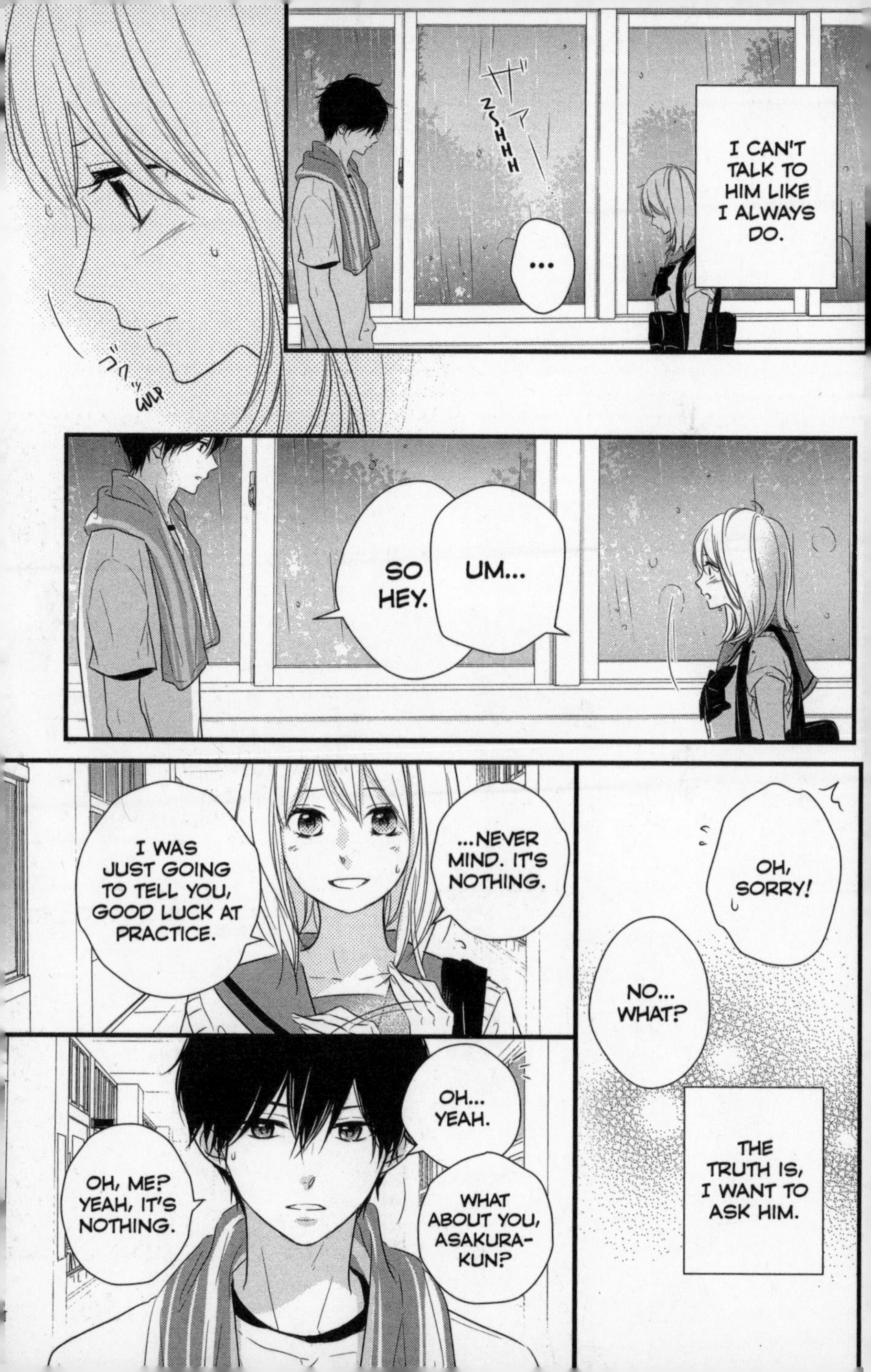
I CAN'T TALK TO HIM LIKE I ALWAYS DO.
ザァー
ZSHHH
...
ゴクッ
GULP
UM...
SO HEY.
OH, SORRY!
NO... WHAT?
THE TRUTH IS, I WANT TO ASK HIM.
...NEVER MIND. IT'S NOTHING.
I WAS JUST GOING TO TELL YOU, GOOD LUCK AT PRACTICE.
OH... YEAH.
WHAT ABOUT YOU, ASAKURA-KUN?
OH, ME? YEAH, IT'S NOTHING.

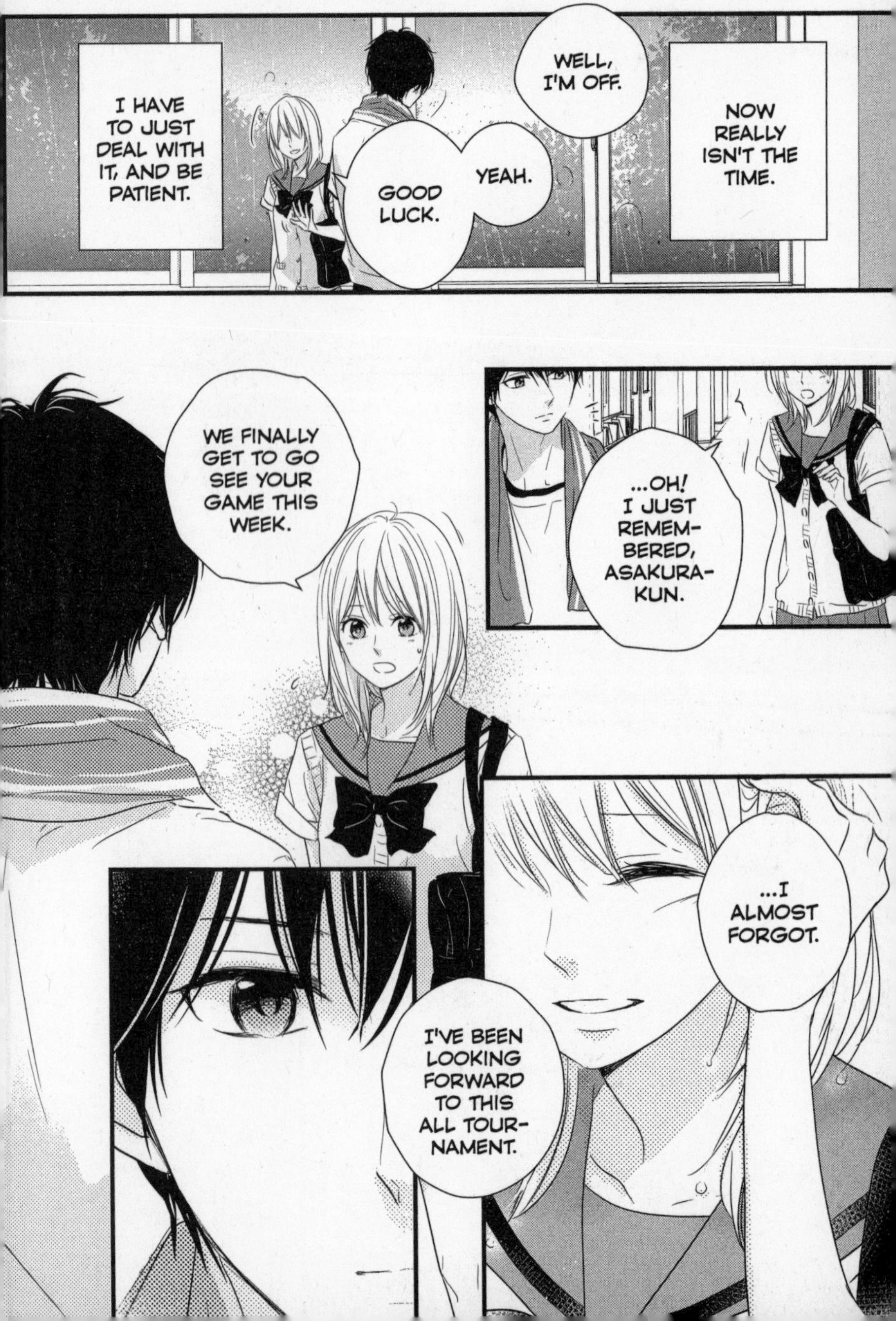
NOW REALLY ISN'T THE TIME.
WELL, I'M OFF.
YEAH.
GOOD LUCK.
I HAVE TO JUST DEAL WITH IT, AND BE PATIENT.
...OH! I JUST REMEMBERED, ASAKURA-KUN.
WE FINALLY GET TO GO SEE YOUR GAME THIS WEEK.
...I ALMOST FORGOT.
I'VE BEEN LOOKING FORWARD TO THIS ALL TOURNAMENT.

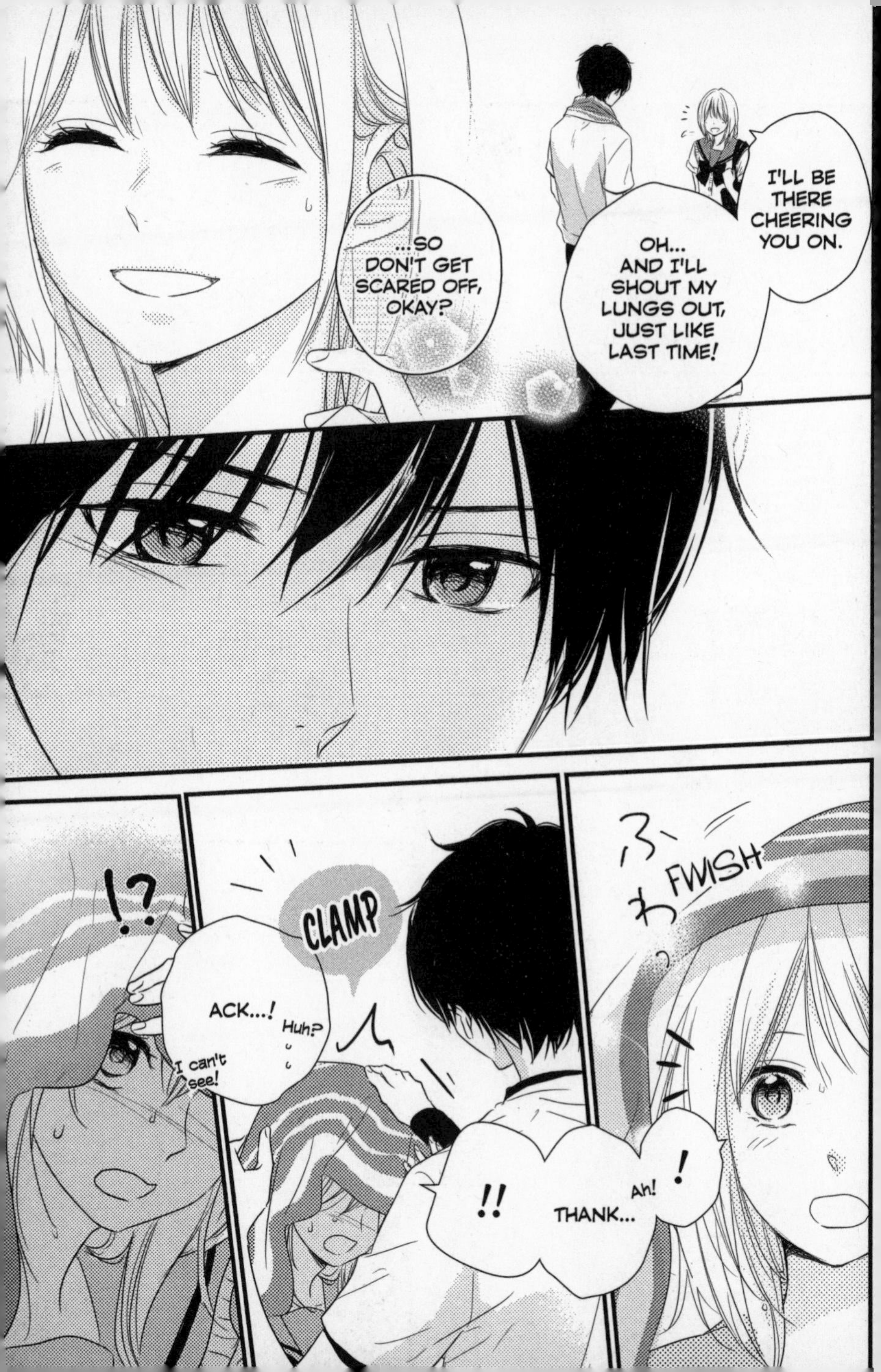
I'LL BE THERE CHEERING YOU ON.
OH... AND I'LL SHOUT MY LUNGS OUT, JUST LIKE LAST TIME!
...SO DON'T GET SCARED OFF, OKAY?
ふわ
FWISH
!
Ah!
THANK...
!!
CLAMP
!?
ACK...!
Huh?
I can't see!

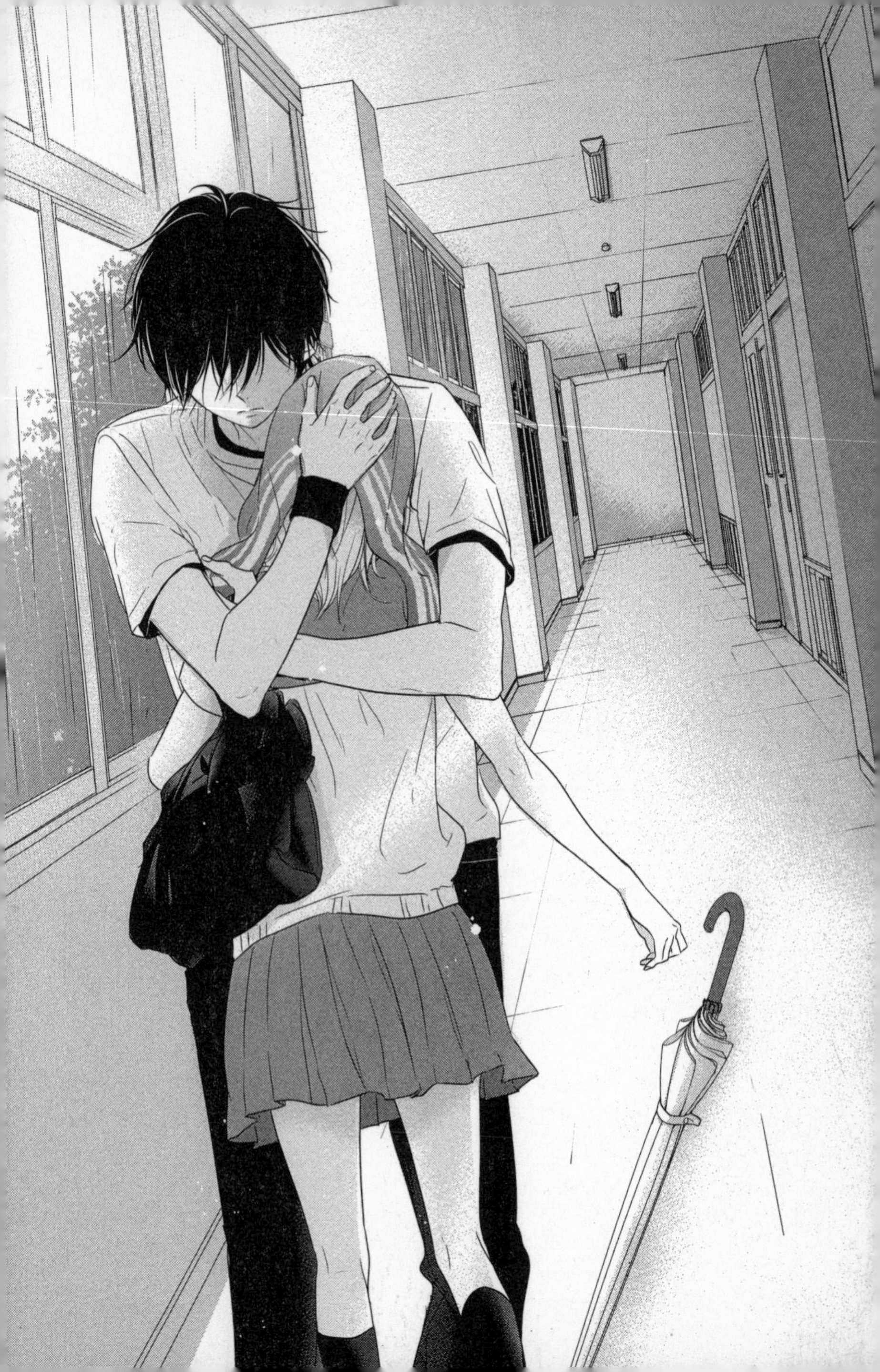

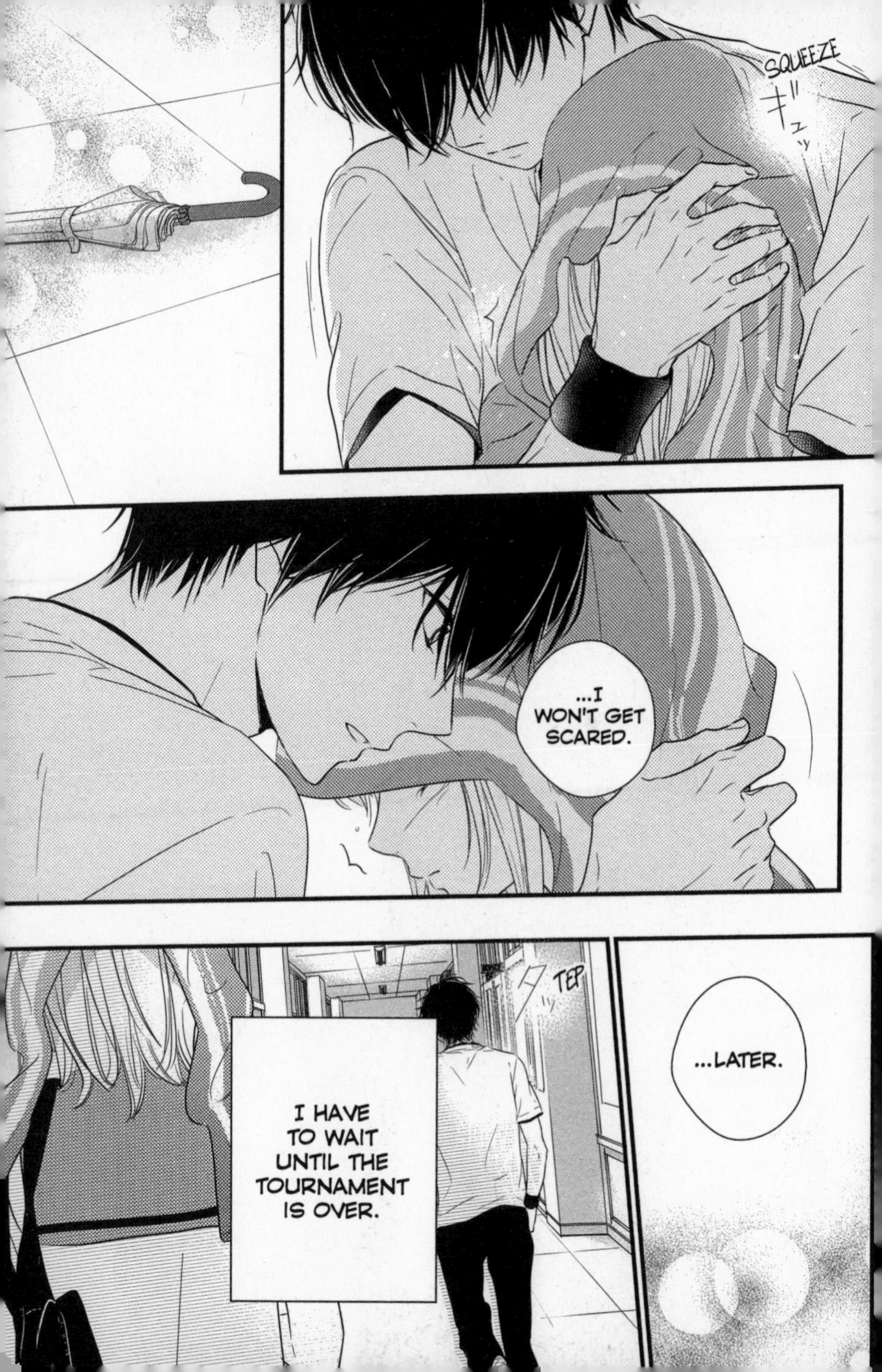
SQUEEZE
ギュッ
...I WON'T GET SCARED.
...LATER.
TEP
タッ
I HAVE TO WAIT UNTIL THE TOURNAMENT IS OVER.

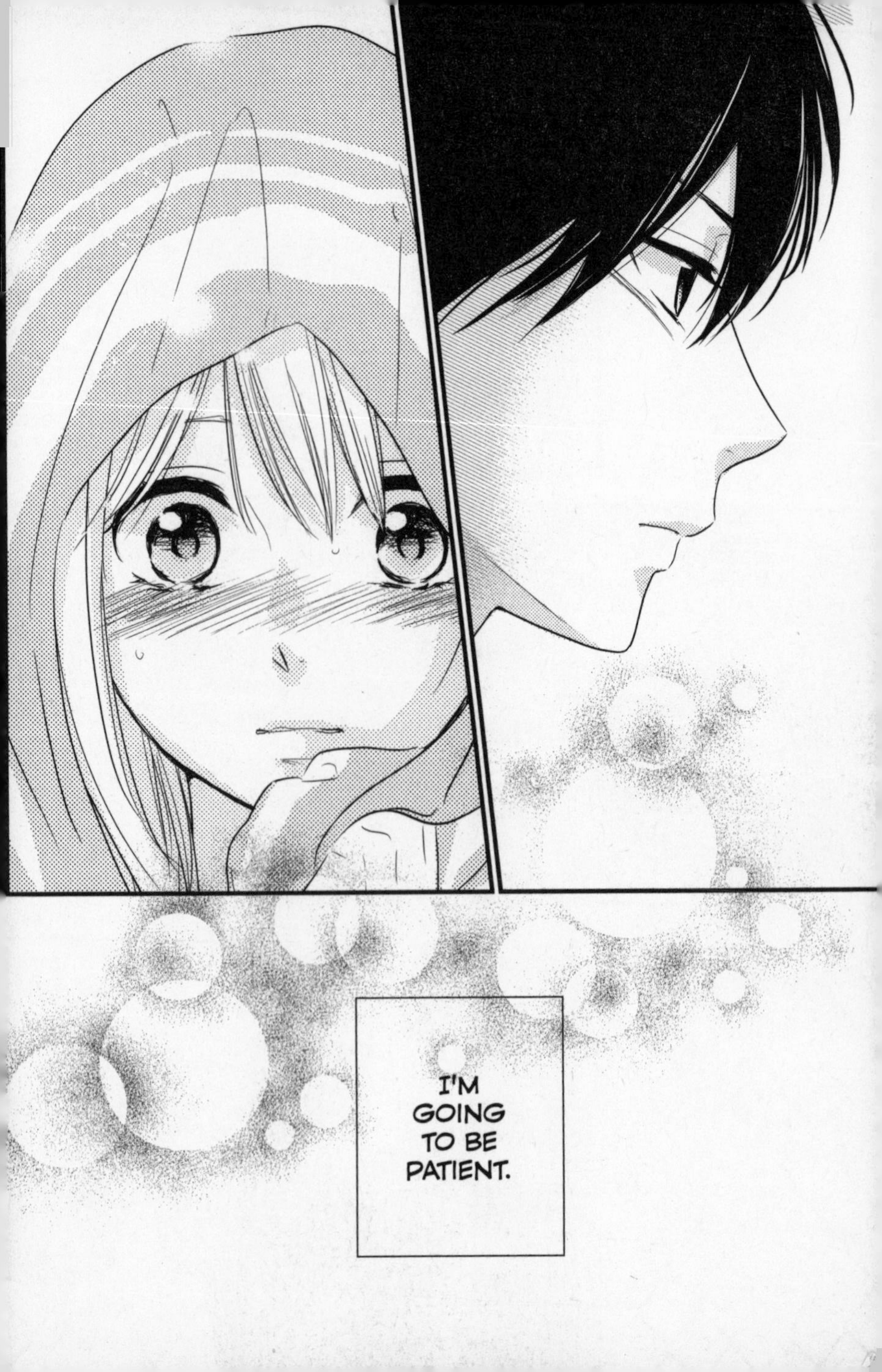
I'M GOING TO BE PATIENT.

period 15: "Where Does Seriousness Lead?!"

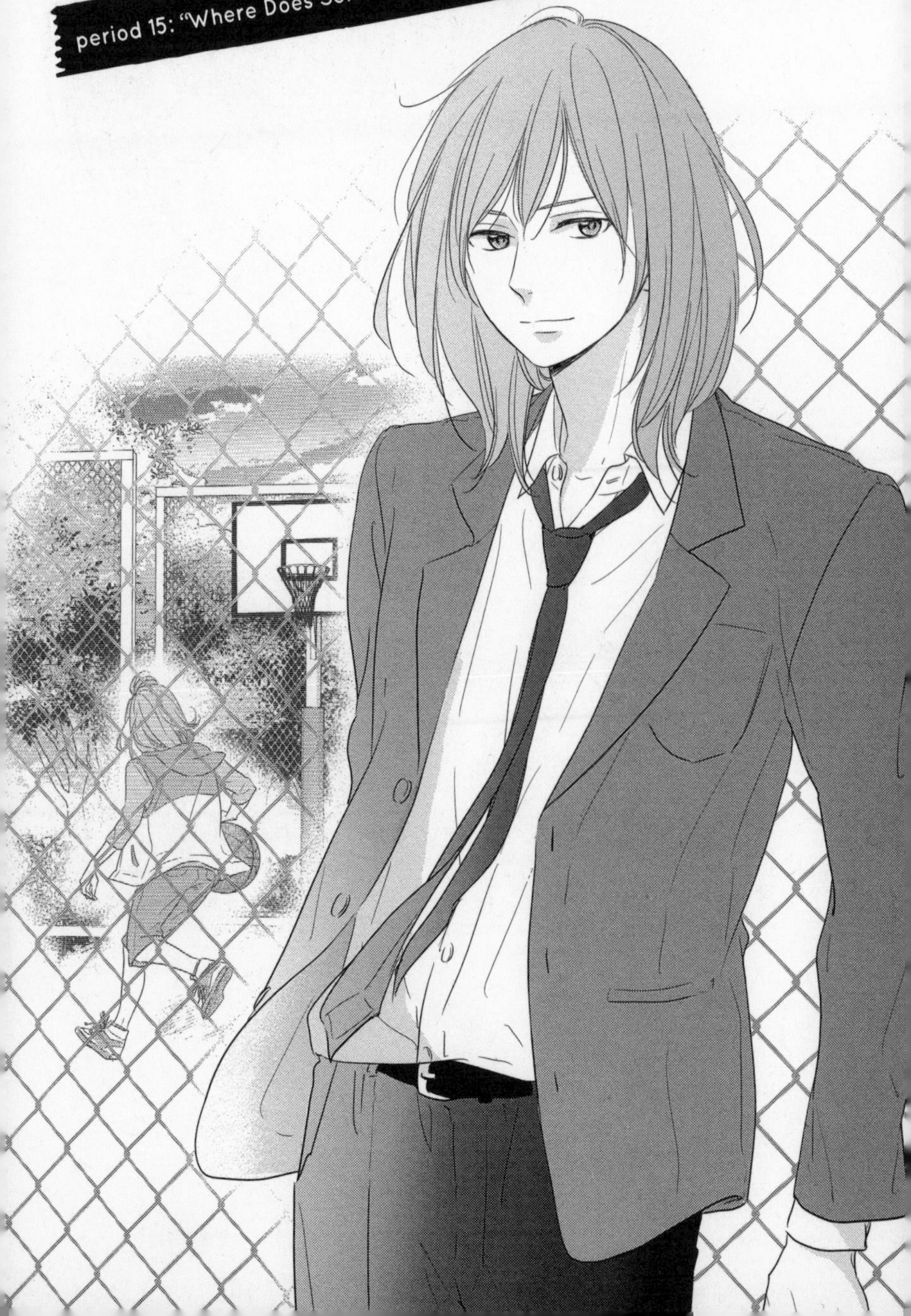

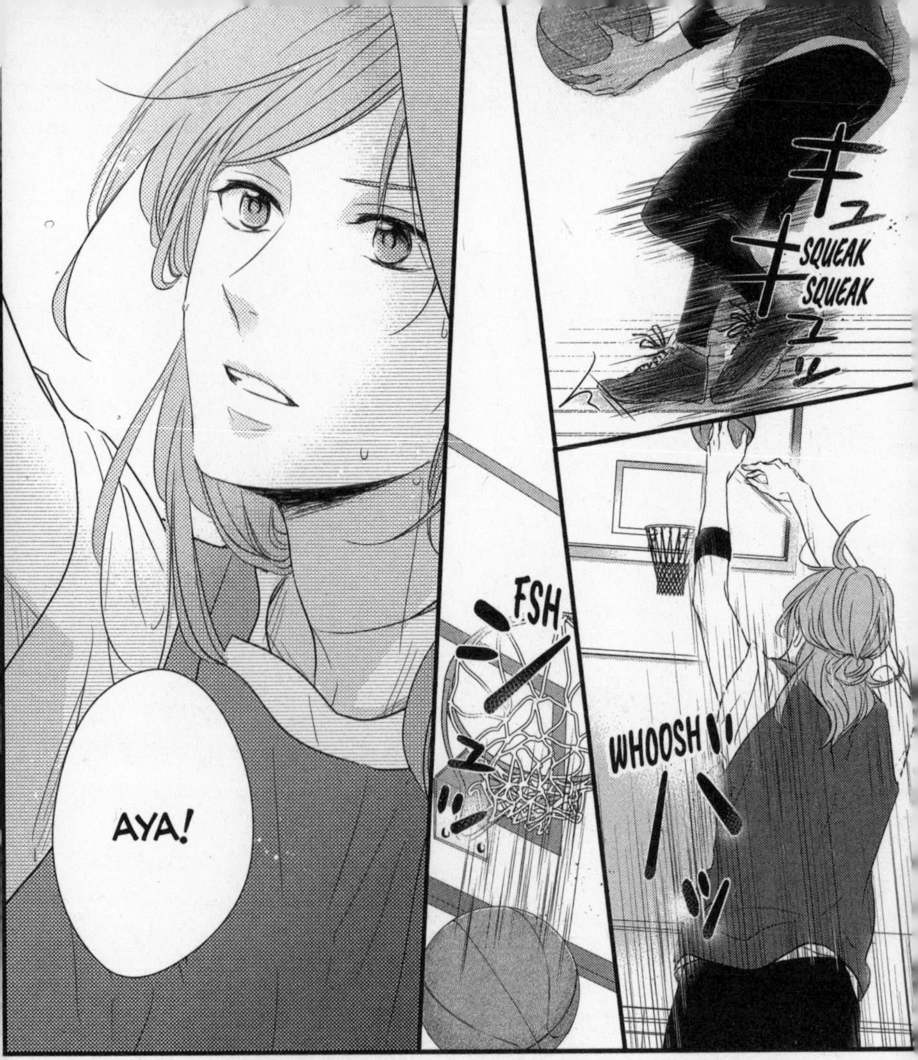
SQUEAK
SQUEAK
WHOOSH
FSH
AYA!

Q. About your work process.

A. I do it all digitally.

From outlining, to storyboarding, to final drafts—I'm having a staring contest with my computer. Color drawings, too.

(The programs I use are Manga Studio and SAI.)

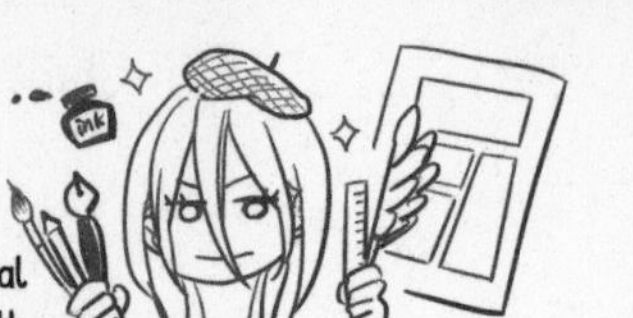

Reina-chan can draw manga.

...And so, this Q&A corner comes to an end. Let's meet again in Volume 4!

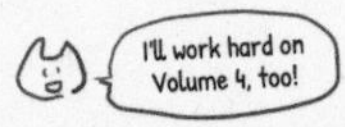
I'll work hard on Volume 4, too!

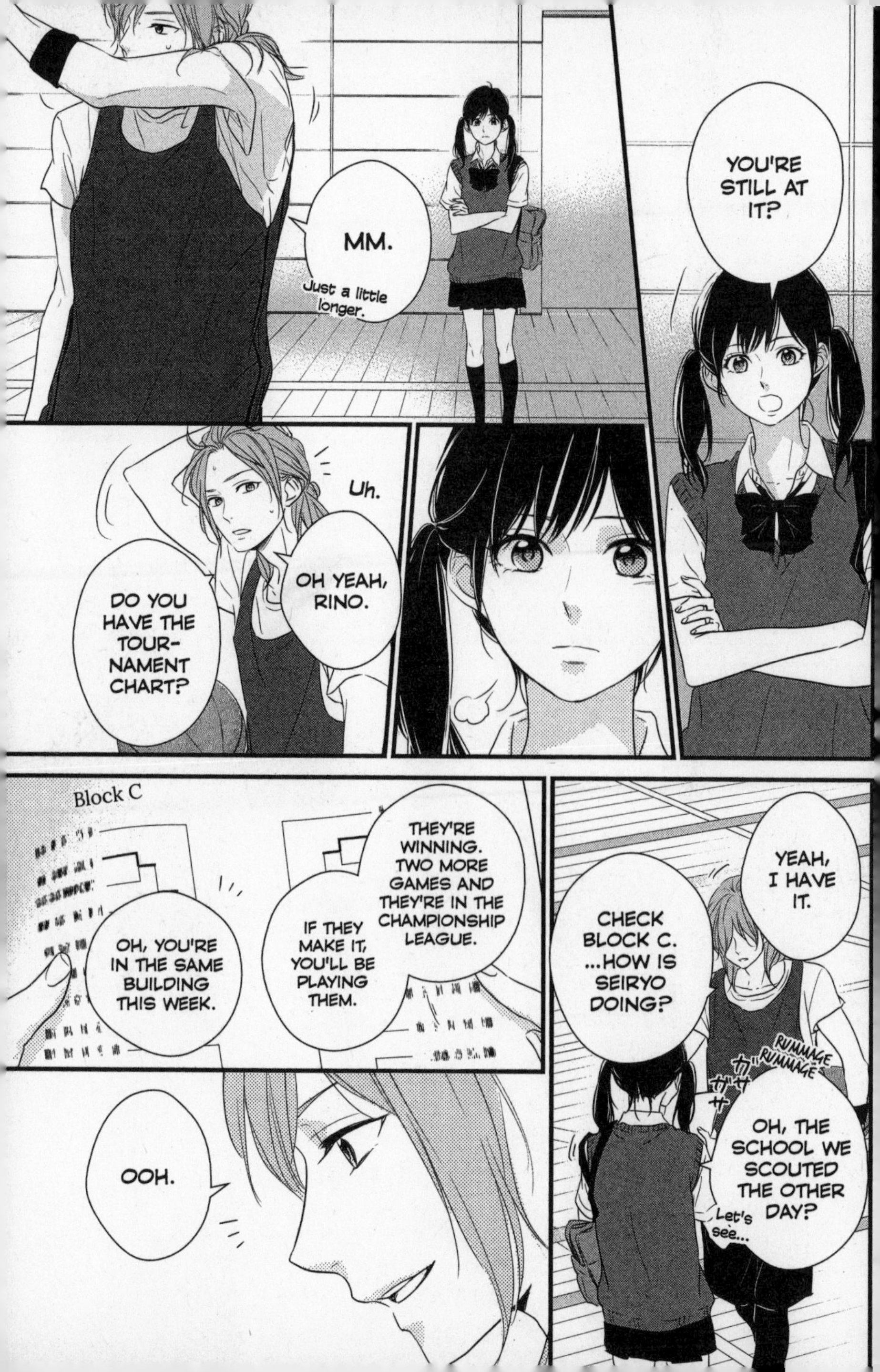
YOU'RE STILL AT IT?
MM.
Just a little longer.
Uh.
OH YEAH, RINO.
DO YOU HAVE THE TOUR-NAMENT CHART?
YEAH, I HAVE IT.
CHECK BLOCK C. ...HOW IS SEIRYO DOING?
RUMMAGE RUMMAGE
OH, THE SCHOOL WE SCOUTED THE OTHER DAY?
Let's see...
Block C
THEY'RE WINNING. TWO MORE GAMES AND THEY'RE IN THE CHAMPIONSHIP LEAGUE.
IF THEY MAKE IT, YOU'LL BE PLAYING THEM.
OH, YOU'RE IN THE SAME BUILDING THIS WEEK.
OOH.

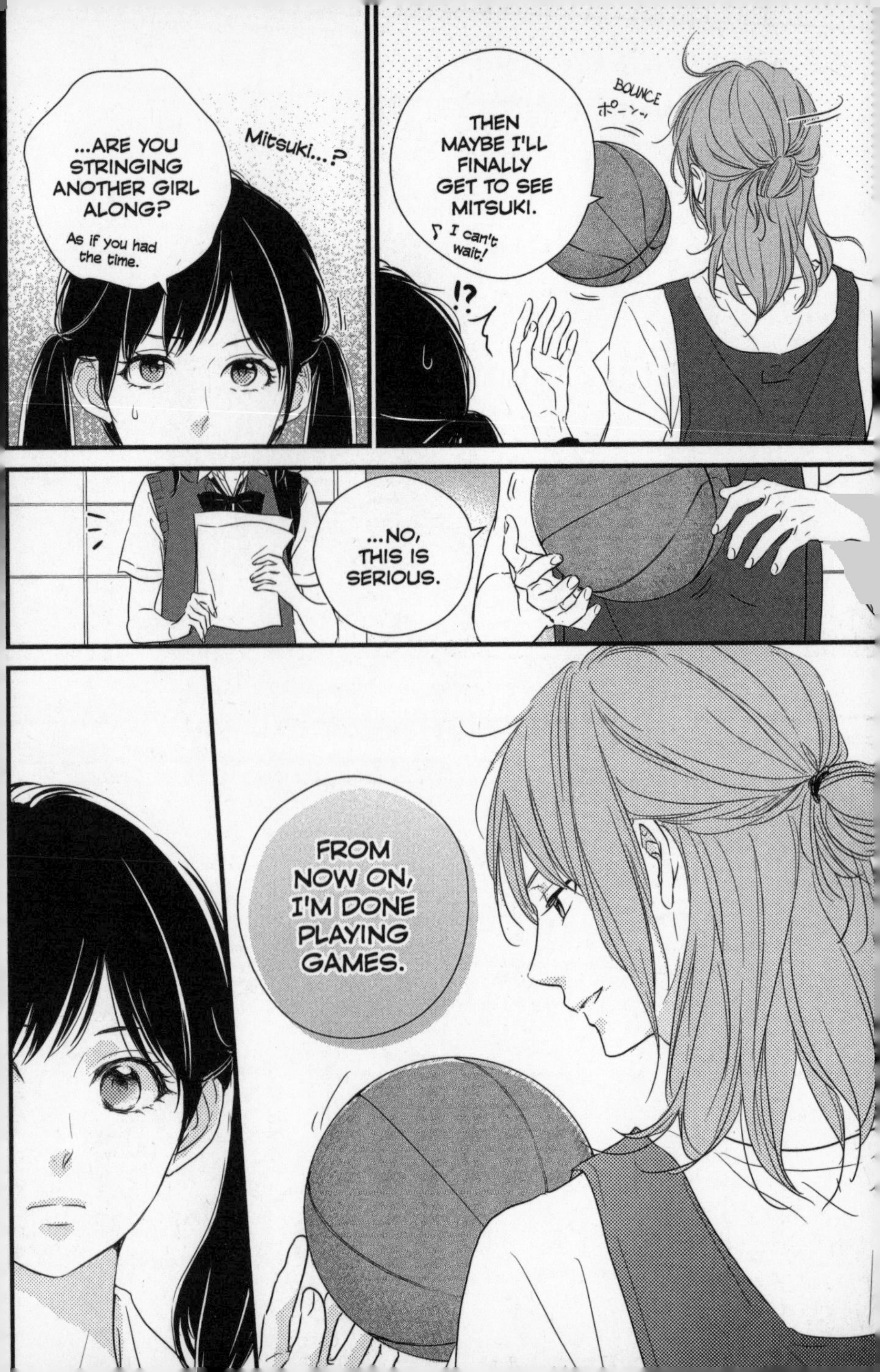
BOUNCE
ポーンッ
THEN MAYBE I'LL FINALLY GET TO SEE MITSUKI.
I can't wait!
!?
Mitsuki...?
...ARE YOU STRINGING ANOTHER GIRL ALONG?
As if you had the time.
...NO, THIS IS SERIOUS.
FROM NOW ON, I'M DONE PLAYING GAMES.

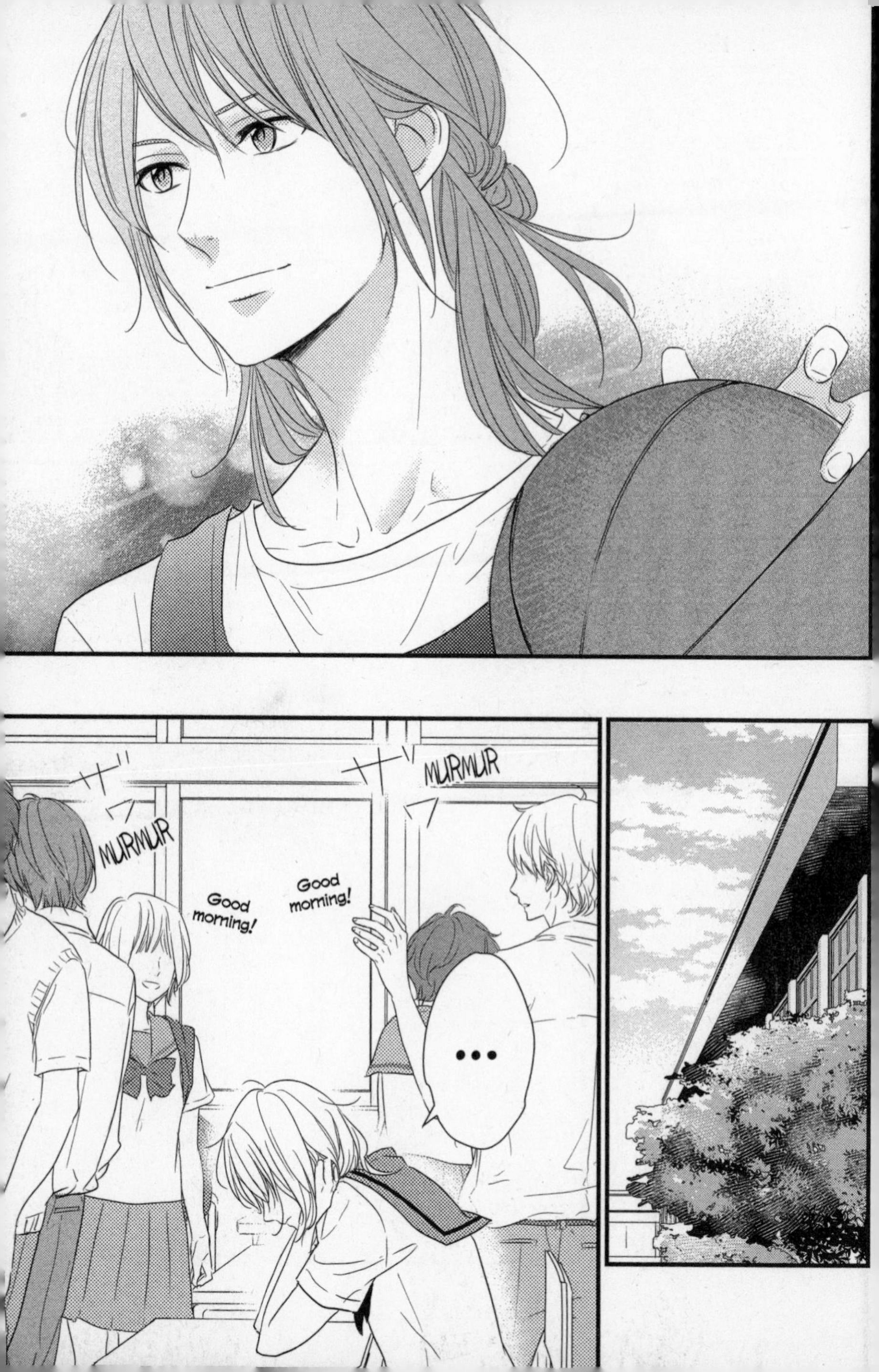
ザワ
MURMUR
ザワ
MURMUR
Good morning!
Good morning!
...

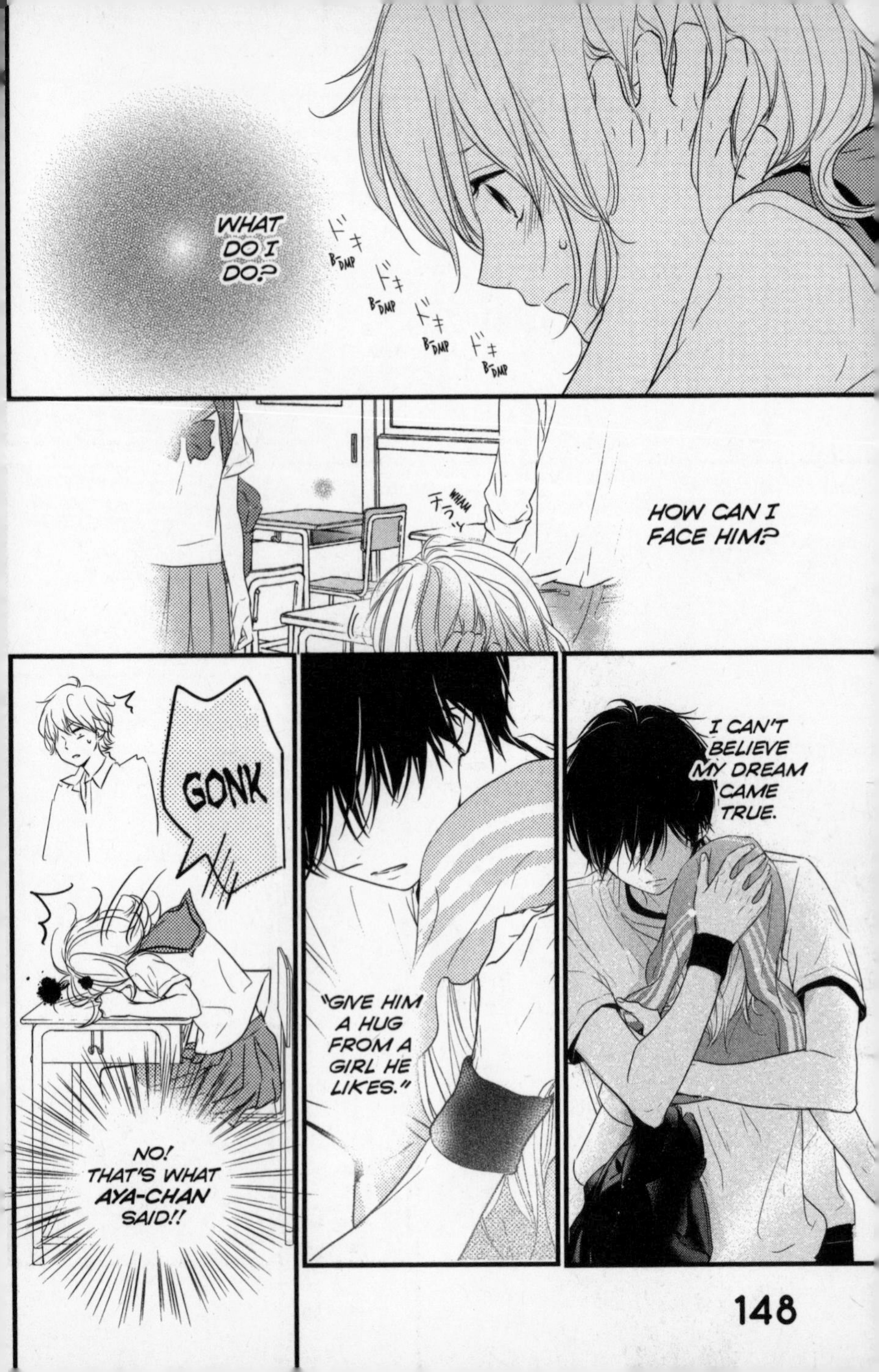
WHAT DO I DO?
ドキ B-DMP
ドキ B-DMP
ドキ B-DMP
ドキ B-DMP
HOW CAN I FACE HIM?
I CAN'T BELIEVE MY DREAM CAME TRUE.
"GIVE HIM A HUG FROM A GIRL HE LIKES."
GONK
NO! THAT'S WHAT AYA-CHAN SAID!!

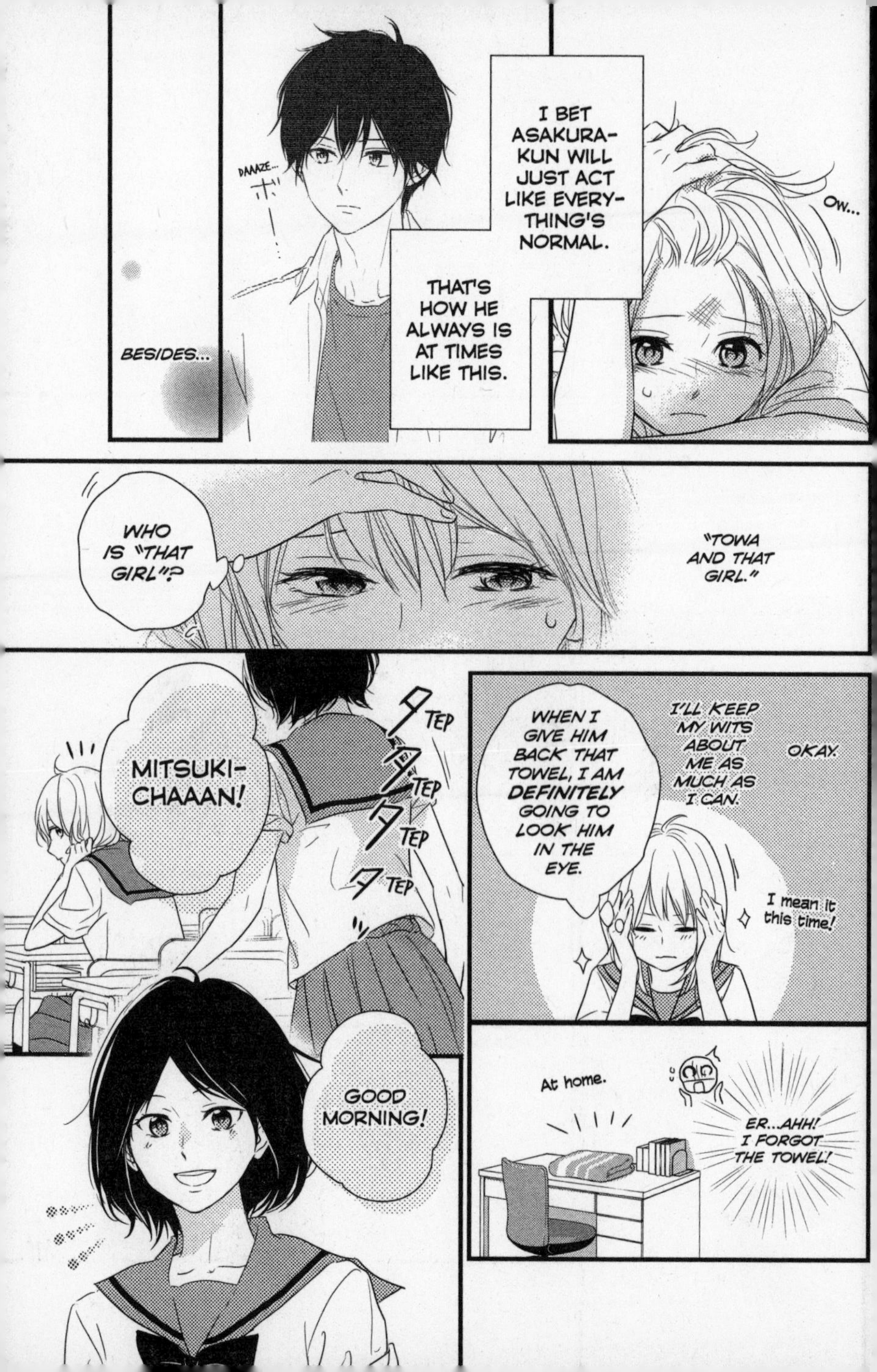
OW...
I BET ASAKURA-KUN WILL JUST ACT LIKE EVERYTHING'S NORMAL.
THAT'S HOW HE ALWAYS IS AT TIMES LIKE THIS.
DAAAZE...
BESIDES...
"TOWA AND THAT GIRL."
WHO IS "THAT GIRL"?
OKAY.
I'LL KEEP MY WITS ABOUT ME AS MUCH AS I CAN.
WHEN I GIVE HIM BACK THAT TOWEL, I AM DEFINITELY GOING TO LOOK HIM IN THE EYE.
I mean it this time!
At home.
ER...AHH! I FORGOT THE TOWEL!
TEP
TEP
TEP
TEP
MITSUKI-CHAAAN!
GOOD MORNING!

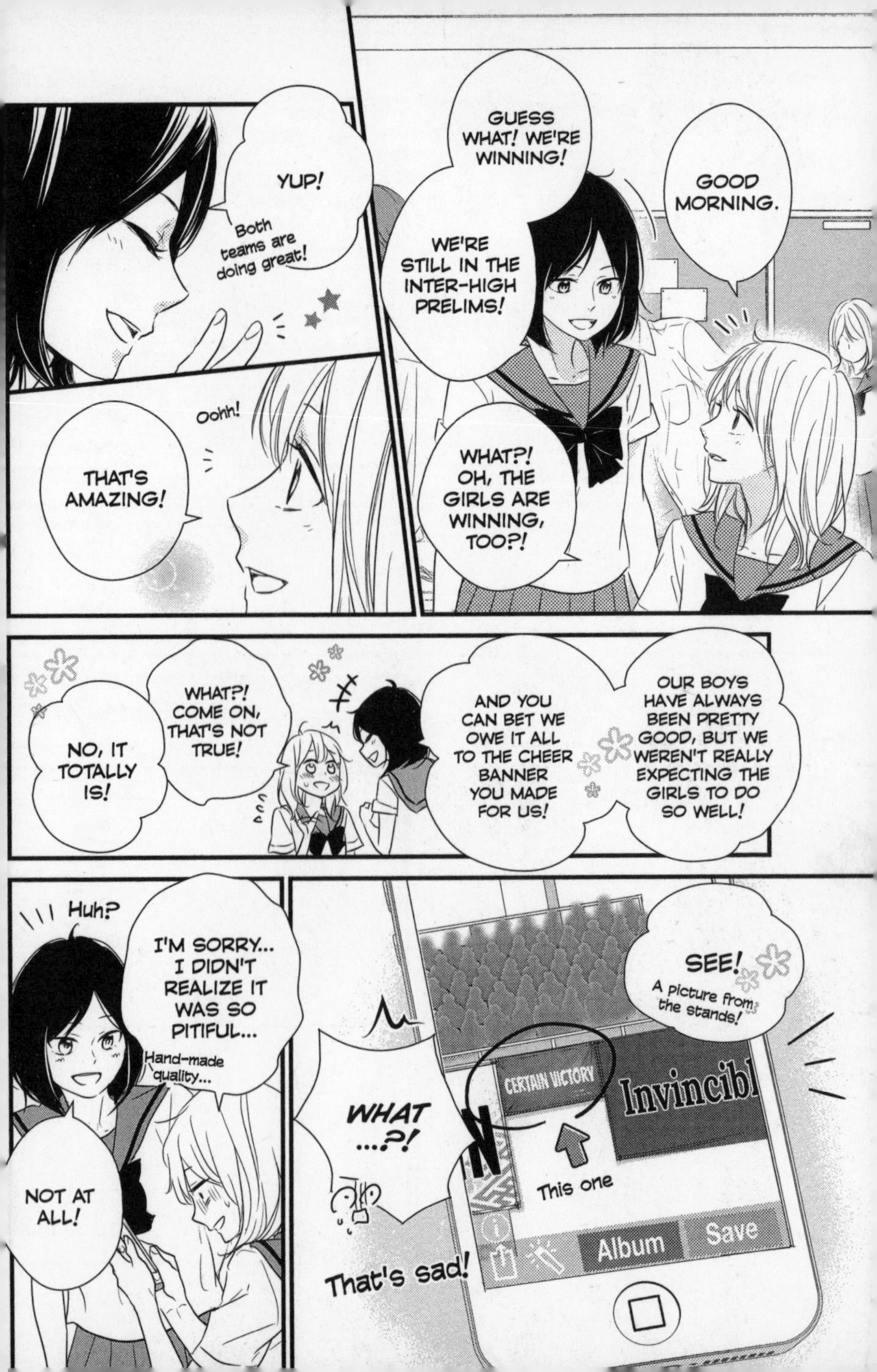
GOOD MORNING.
GUESS WHAT! WE'RE WINNING!
WE'RE STILL IN THE INTER-HIGH PRELIMS!
WHAT?! OH, THE GIRLS ARE WINNING, TOO?!
YUP!
Both teams are doing great!
Oohh!
THAT'S AMAZING!
OUR BOYS HAVE ALWAYS BEEN PRETTY GOOD, BUT WE WEREN'T REALLY EXPECTING THE GIRLS TO DO SO WELL!
AND YOU CAN BET WE OWE IT ALL TO THE CHEER BANNER YOU MADE FOR US!
WHAT?! COME ON, THAT'S NOT TRUE!
NO, IT TOTALLY IS!
SEE!
A picture from the stands!
CERTAIN VICTORY
Invincibl
This one
Album
Save
WHAT ...?!
That's sad!
Huh?
I'M SORRY... I DIDN'T REALIZE IT WAS SO PITIFUL...
Hand-made quality...
NOT AT ALL!

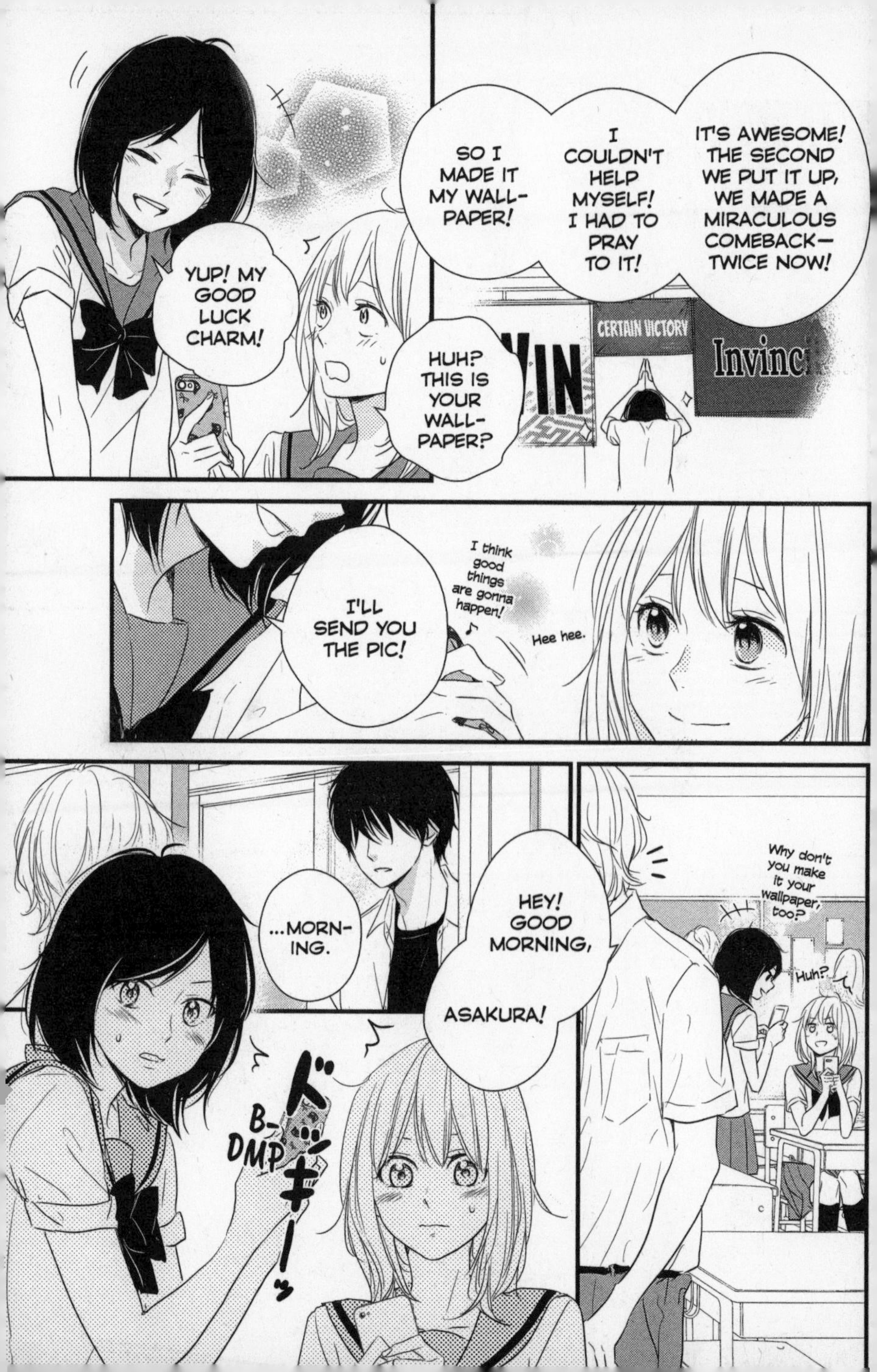
IT'S AWESOME! THE SECOND WE PUT IT UP, WE MADE A MIRACULOUS COMEBACK—TWICE NOW!
I COULDN'T HELP MYSELF! I HAD TO PRAY TO IT!
SO I MADE IT MY WALL-PAPER!
Invinc
CERTAIN VICTORY
IN
HUH? THIS IS YOUR WALL-PAPER?
YUP! MY GOOD LUCK CHARM!
Hee hee.
I think good things are gonna happen! ♪
I'LL SEND YOU THE PIC!
Why don't you make it your wallpaper, too?
Huh?
HEY! GOOD MORNING,
ASAKURA!
...MORN-ING.
ドキーッ
B-DMP

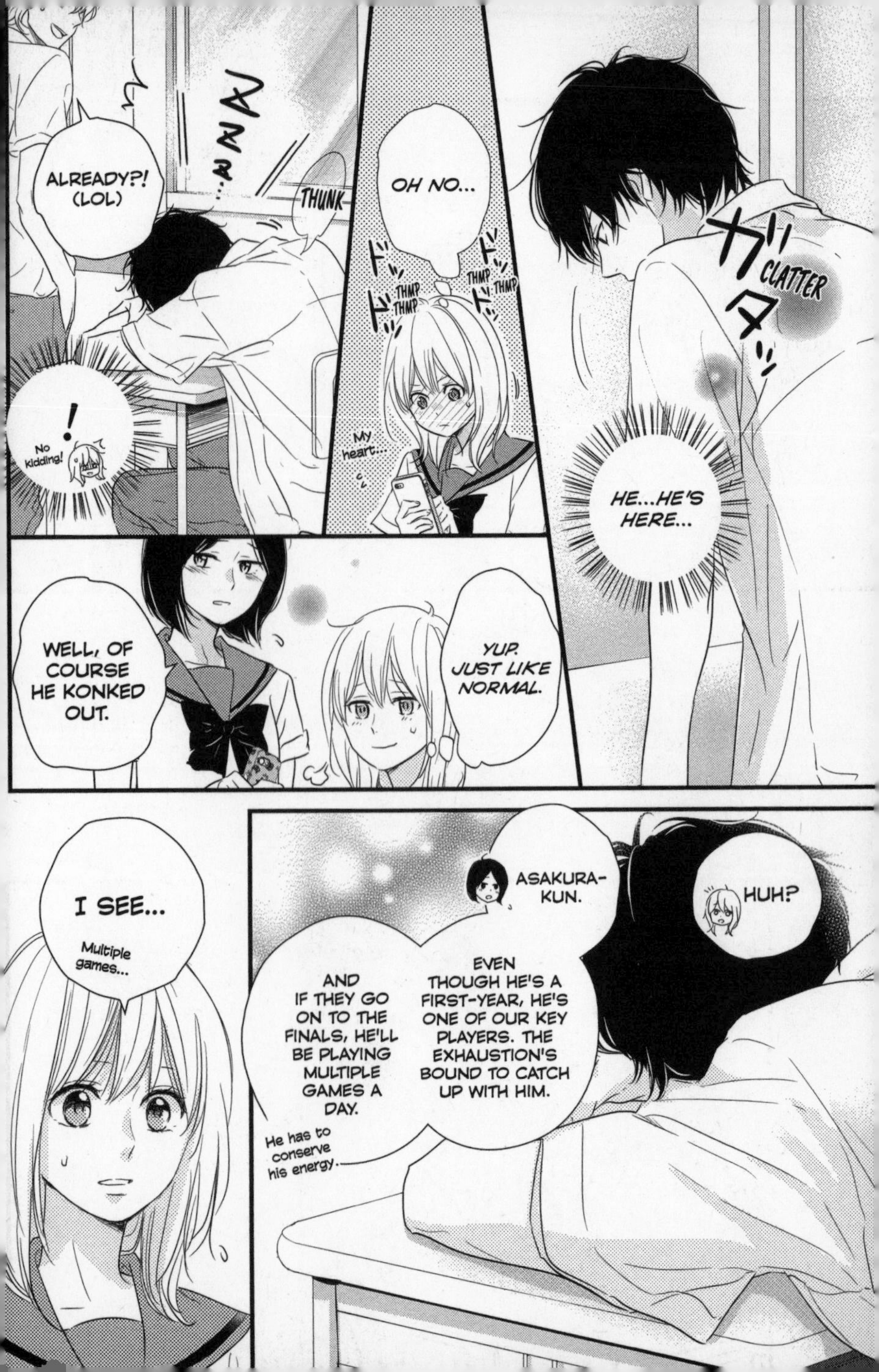
CLATTER
HE...HE'S HERE...
OH NO...
THMP THMP THMP THMP
My heart...
ZZZ...
THUNK
ALREADY?! (LOL)
!
No kidding!
YUP. JUST LIKE NORMAL.
WELL, OF COURSE HE KONKED OUT.
HUH?
ASAKURA-KUN.
EVEN THOUGH HE'S A FIRST-YEAR, HE'S ONE OF OUR KEY PLAYERS. THE EXHAUSTION'S BOUND TO CATCH UP WITH HIM.
AND IF THEY GO ON TO THE FINALS, HE'LL BE PLAYING MULTIPLE GAMES A DAY.
He has to conserve his energy.
I SEE...
Multiple games...

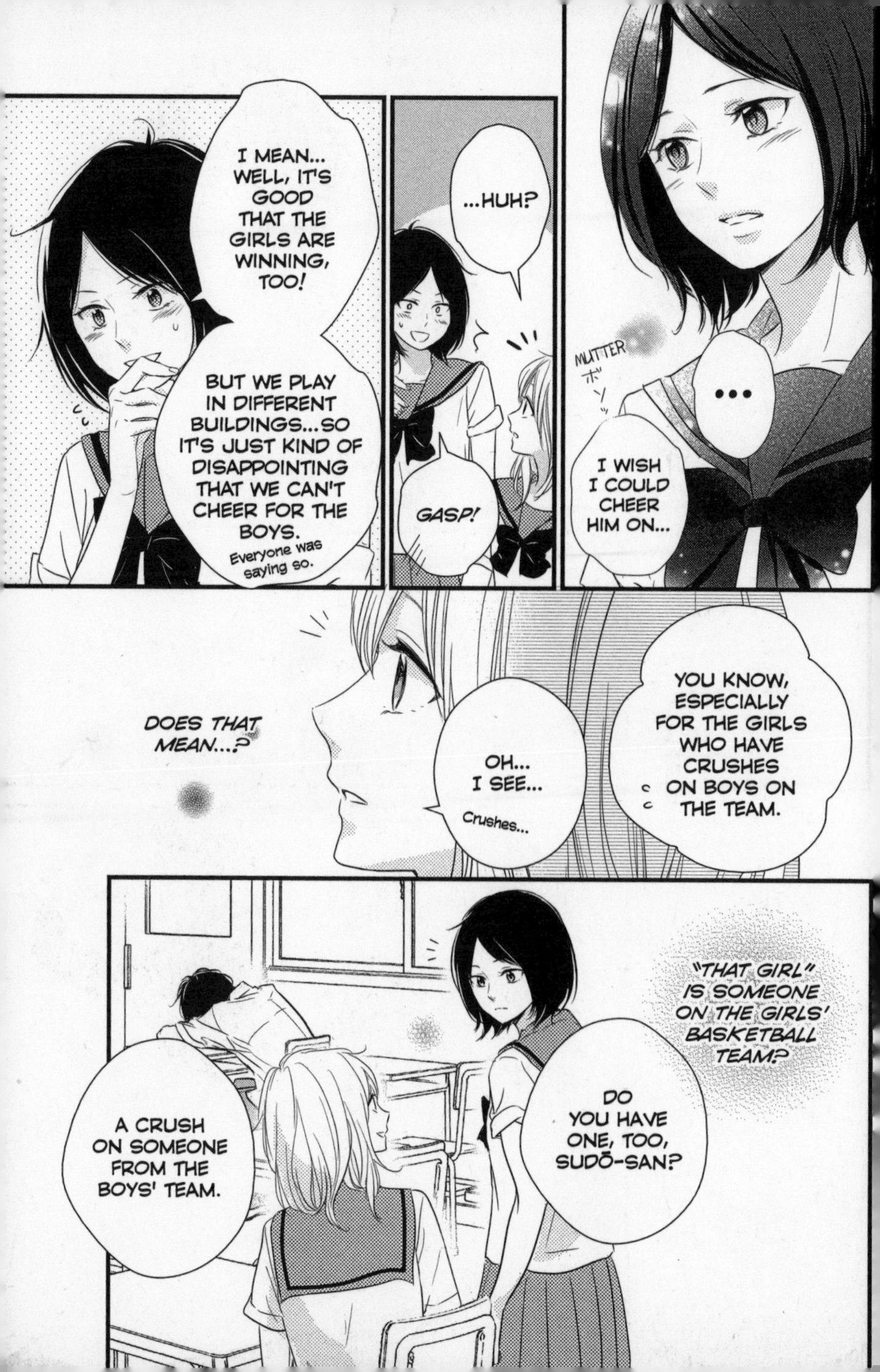
...
MUTTER
ボソッ
I WISH I COULD CHEER HIM ON...
...HUH?
GASP!
I MEAN... WELL, IT'S GOOD THAT THE GIRLS ARE WINNING, TOO!
BUT WE PLAY IN DIFFERENT BUILDINGS...SO IT'S JUST KIND OF DISAPPOINTING THAT WE CAN'T CHEER FOR THE BOYS.
Everyone was saying so.
YOU KNOW, ESPECIALLY FOR THE GIRLS WHO HAVE CRUSHES ON BOYS ON THE TEAM.
OH... I SEE...
Crushes...
DOES THAT MEAN...?
"THAT GIRL" IS SOMEONE ON THE GIRLS' BASKETBALL TEAM?
DO YOU HAVE ONE, TOO, SUDŌ-SAN?
A CRUSH ON SOMEONE FROM THE BOYS' TEAM.

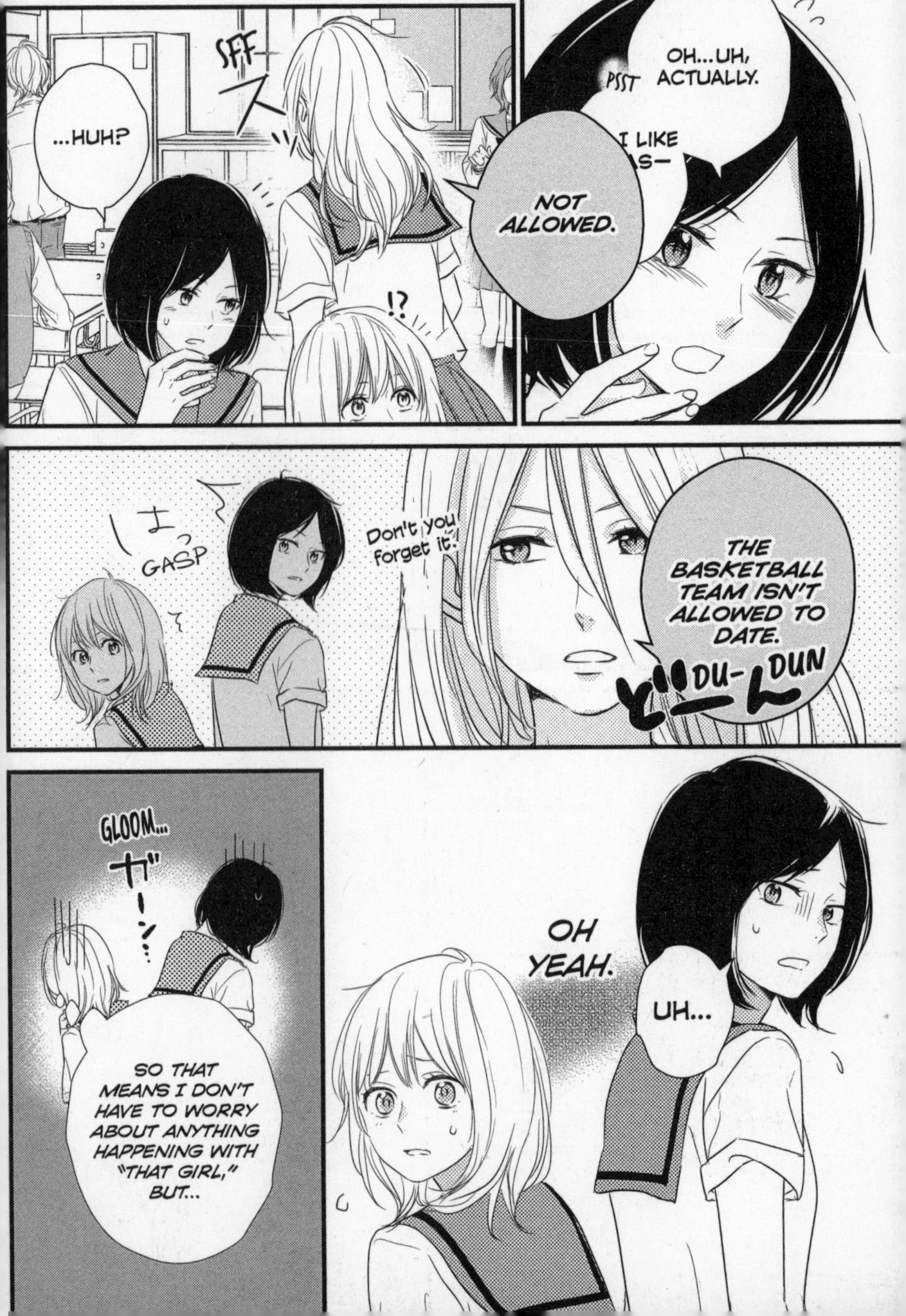
OH...UH, ACTUALLY.
PSST
I LIKE AS—
NOT ALLOWED.
SFF
...HUH?
!?
THE BASKETBALL TEAM ISN'T ALLOWED TO DATE.
DU-DUN
Don't you forget it!
GASP
UH...
OH YEAH.
GLOOM...
SO THAT MEANS I DON'T HAVE TO WORRY ABOUT ANYTHING HAPPENING WITH "THAT GIRL," BUT...

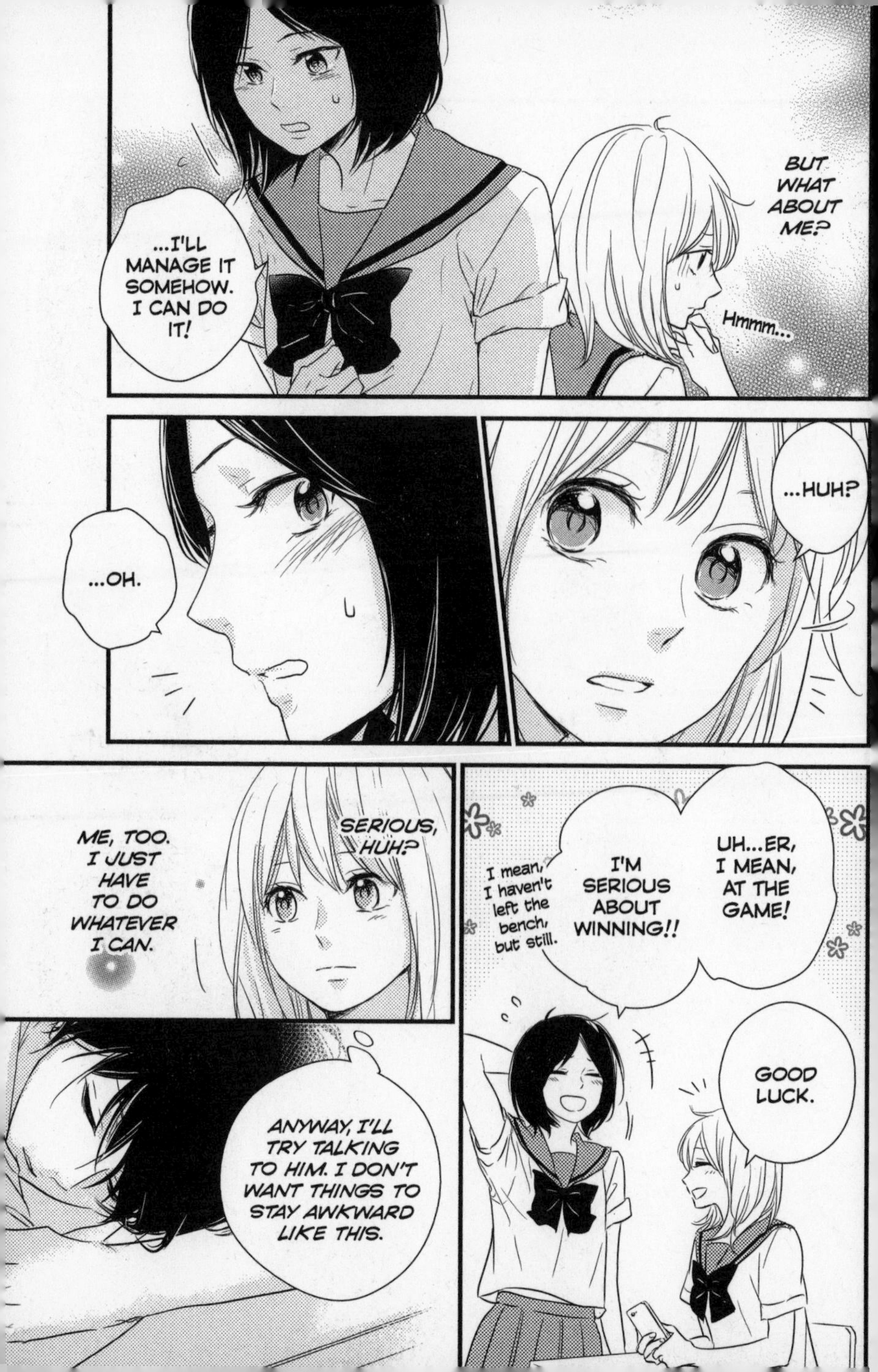
BUT WHAT ABOUT ME?
Hmmm...
...I'LL MANAGE IT SOMEHOW. I CAN DO IT!
...HUH?
...OH.
UH...ER, I MEAN, AT THE GAME!
I'M SERIOUS ABOUT WINNING!!
I mean, I haven't left the bench, but still.
GOOD LUCK.
SERIOUS, HUH?
ME, TOO. I JUST HAVE TO DO WHATEVER I CAN.
ANYWAY, I'LL TRY TALKING TO HIM. I DON'T WANT THINGS TO STAY AWKWARD LIKE THIS.

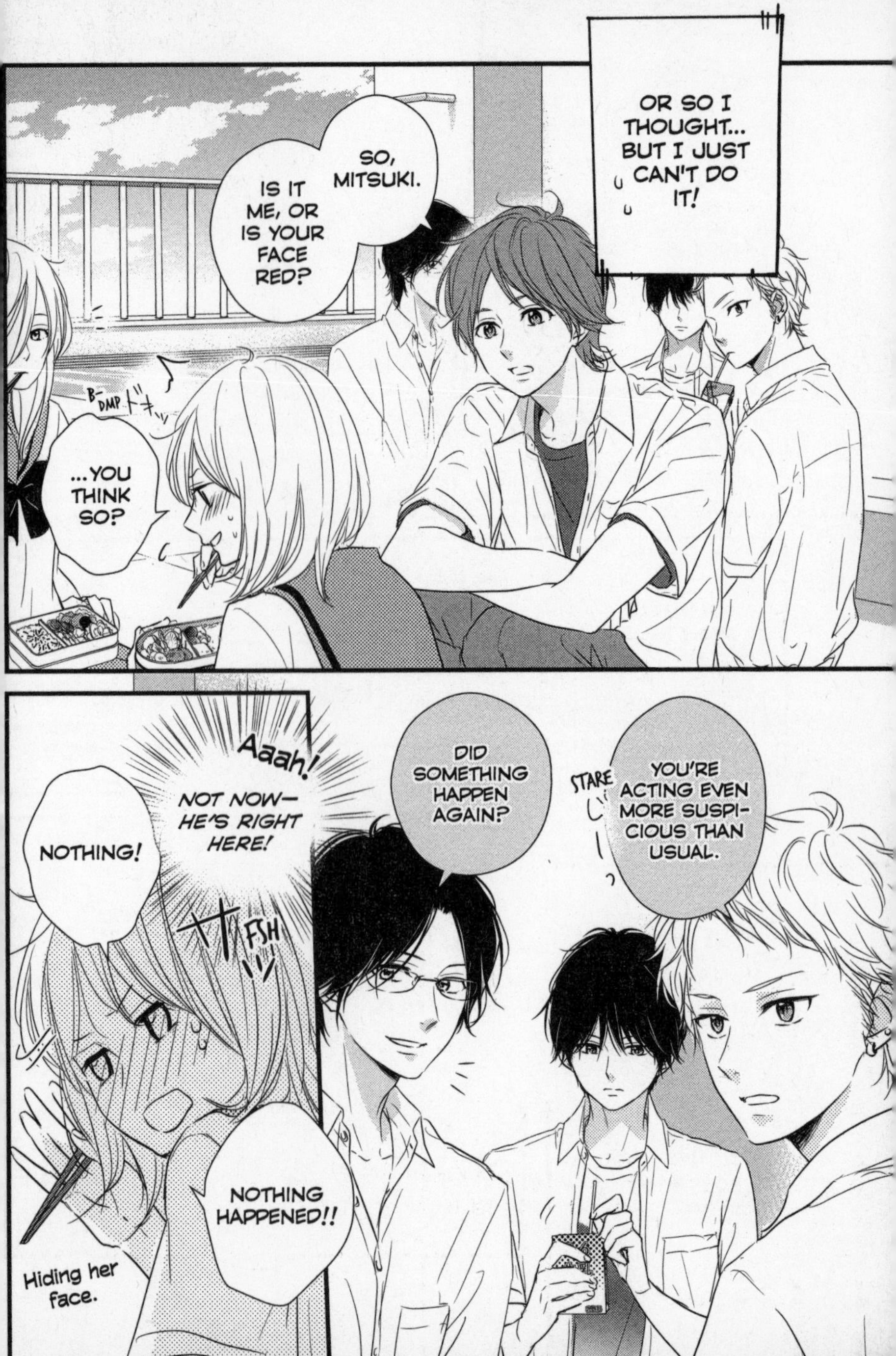
OR SO I THOUGHT... BUT I JUST CAN'T DO IT!
SO, MITSUKI.
IS IT ME, OR IS YOUR FACE RED?
B-DMP
...YOU THINK SO?
YOU'RE ACTING EVEN MORE SUSPICIOUS THAN USUAL.
STARE
DID SOMETHING HAPPEN AGAIN?
Aaah!
NOT NOW—HE'S RIGHT HERE!
NOTHING!
FSH
NOTHING HAPPENED!!
Hiding her face.

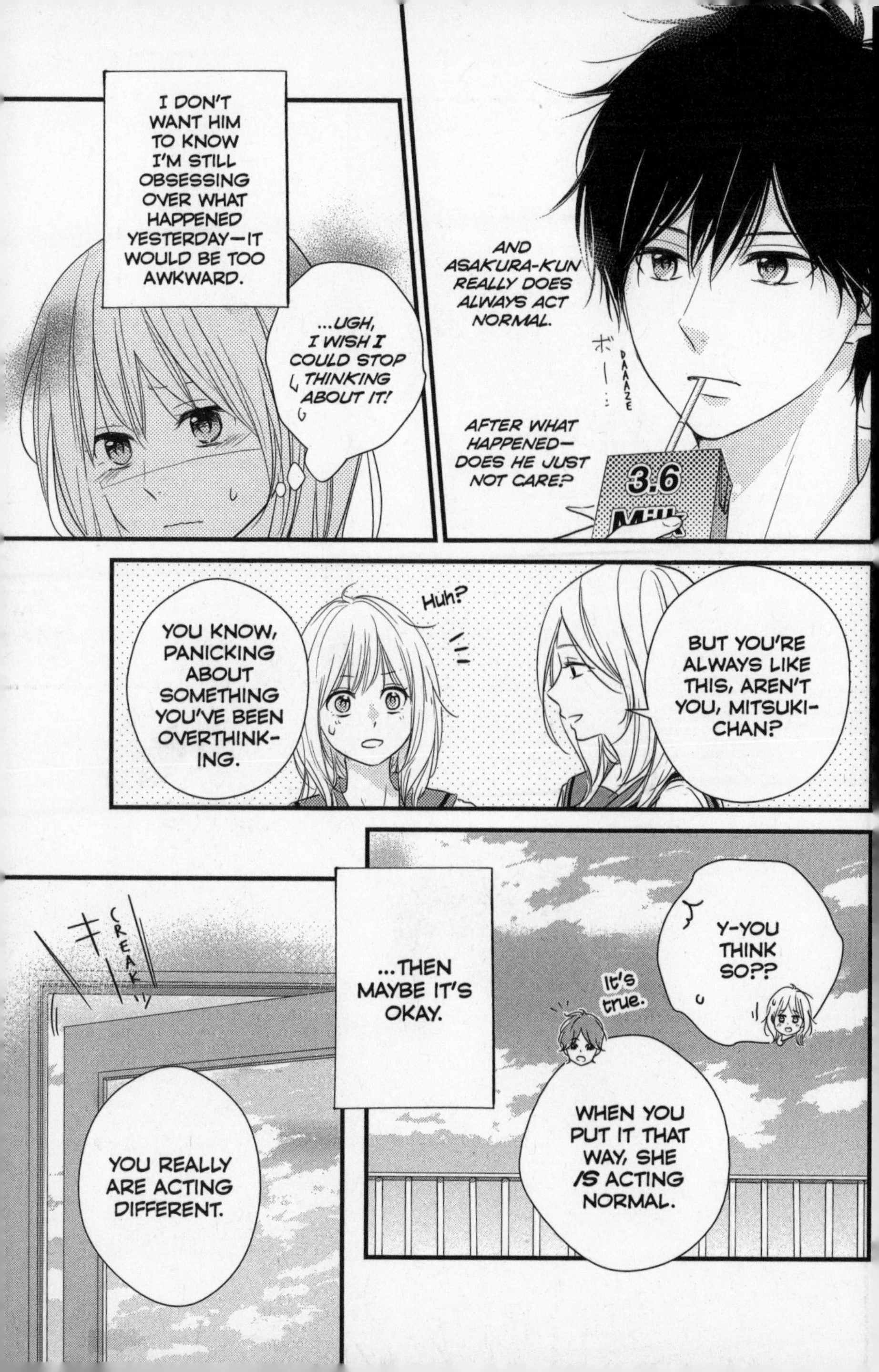
AND ASAKURA-KUN REALLY DOES ALWAYS ACT NORMAL.
ボー…
DAAAZE
AFTER WHAT HAPPENED—DOES HE JUST NOT CARE?
3.6
I DON'T WANT HIM TO KNOW I'M STILL OBSESSING OVER WHAT HAPPENED YESTERDAY—IT WOULD BE TOO AWKWARD.
...UGH, I WISH I COULD STOP THINKING ABOUT IT!
BUT YOU'RE ALWAYS LIKE THIS, AREN'T YOU, MITSUKI-CHAN?
Huh?
YOU KNOW, PANICKING ABOUT SOMETHING YOU'VE BEEN OVERTHINKING.
Y-YOU THINK SO??
It's true.
WHEN YOU PUT IT THAT WAY, SHE *IS* ACTING NORMAL.
...THEN MAYBE IT'S OKAY.
キ
CREAK
YOU REALLY ARE ACTING DIFFERENT.

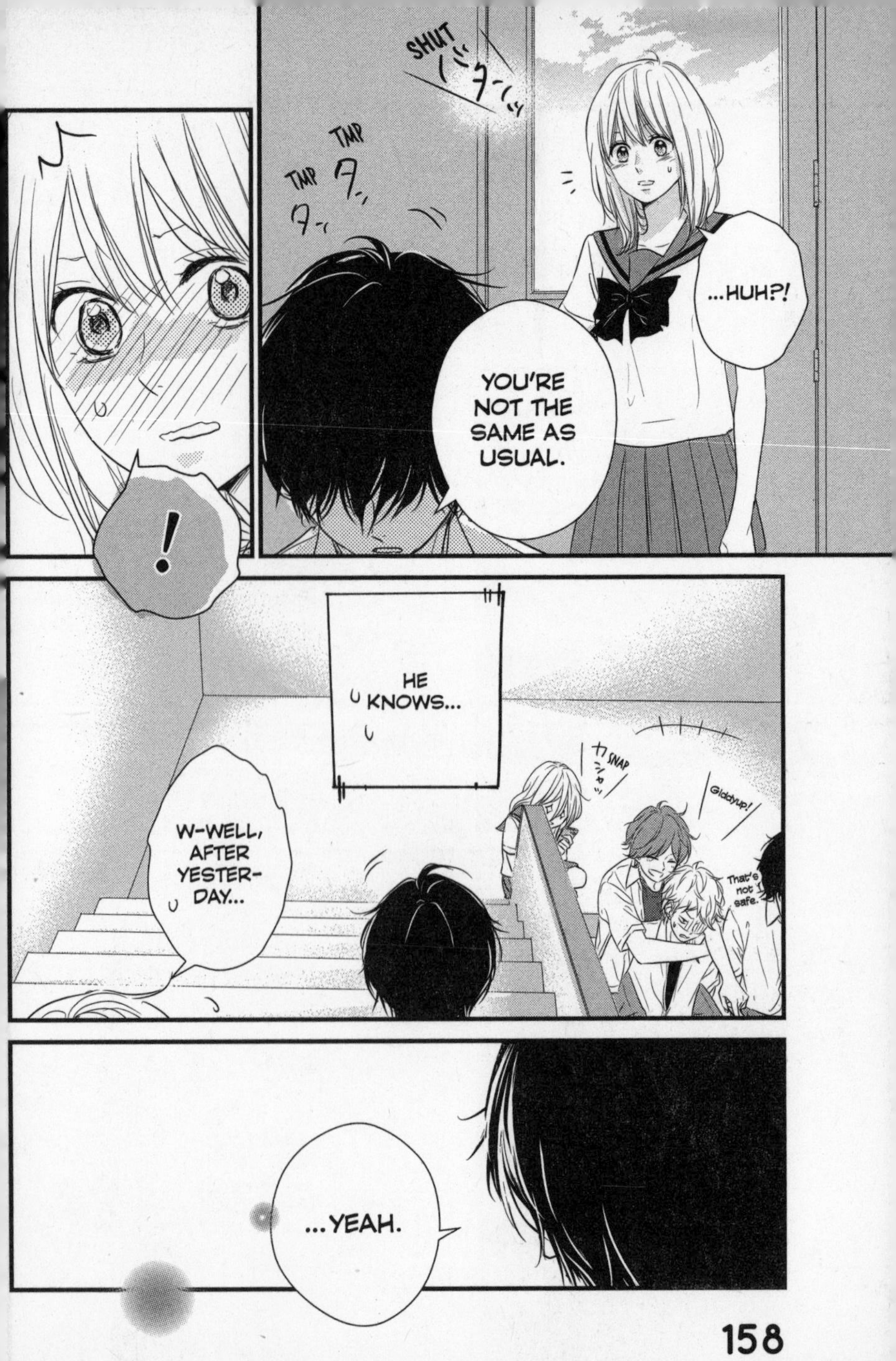
SHUT
TMP
TMP
...HUH?!
YOU'RE NOT THE SAME AS USUAL.
!
HE KNOWS...
SNAP
Giddyup!
That's not safe.
W-WELL, AFTER YESTER-DAY...
...YEAH.

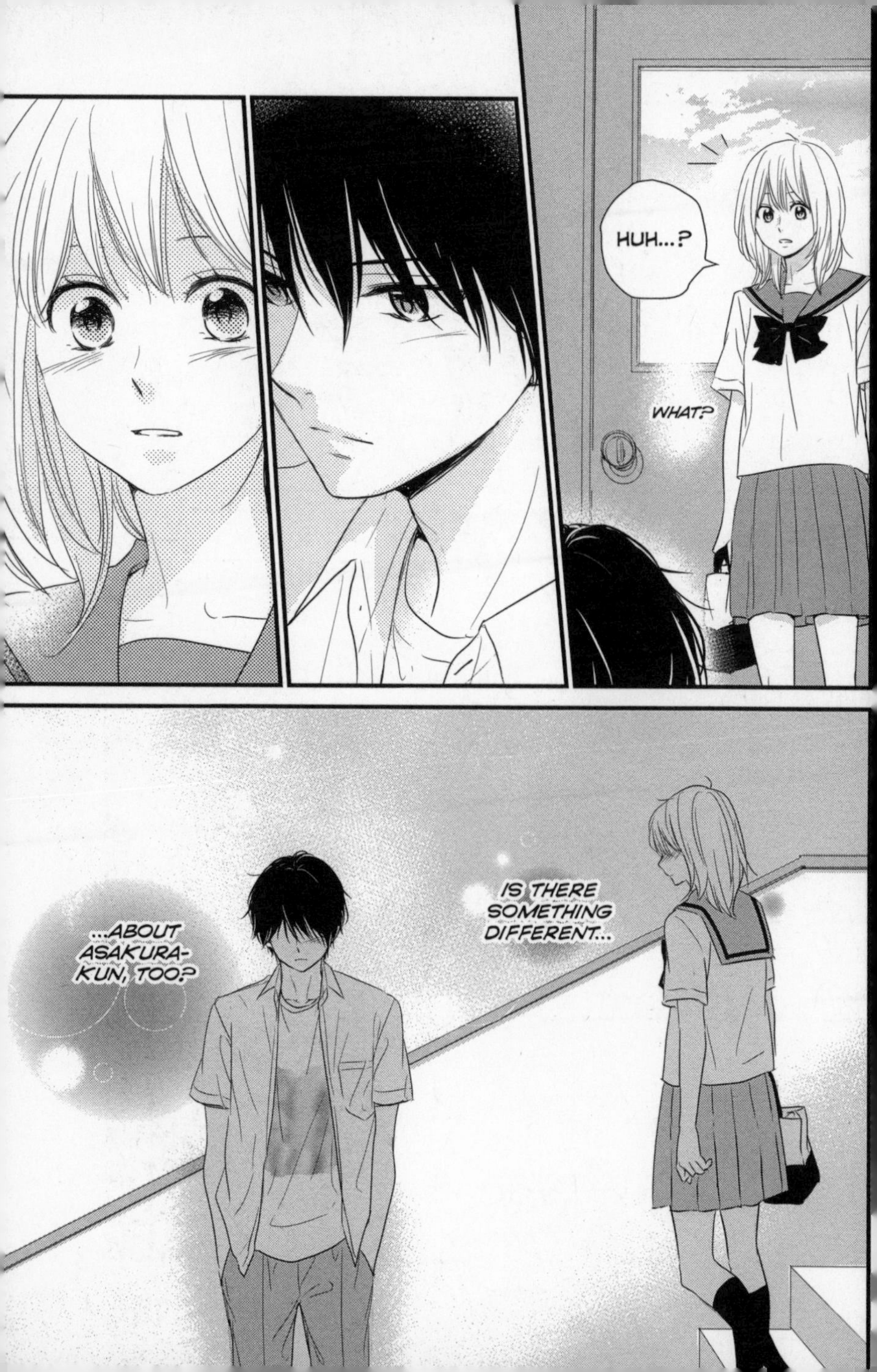
HUH...?
WHAT?
IS THERE SOMETHING DIFFERENT...
...ABOUT ASAKURA-KUN, TOO?

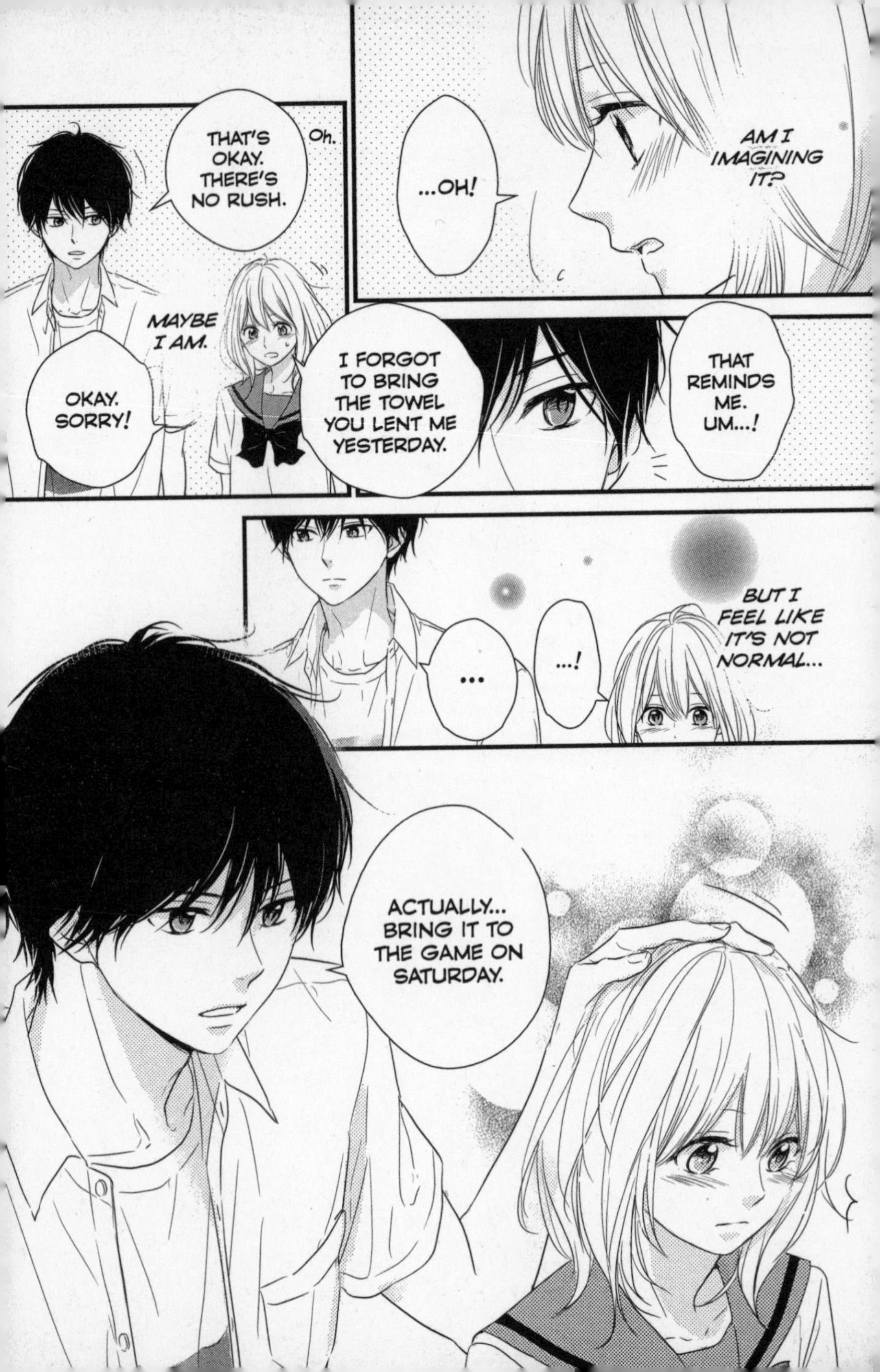
AM I IMAGINING IT?
...OH!
THAT REMINDS ME. UM...!
I FORGOT TO BRING THE TOWEL YOU LENT ME YESTERDAY.
Oh.
THAT'S OKAY. THERE'S NO RUSH.
MAYBE I AM.
OKAY. SORRY!
BUT I FEEL LIKE IT'S NOT NORMAL...
...!
...
ACTUALLY... BRING IT TO THE GAME ON SATURDAY.

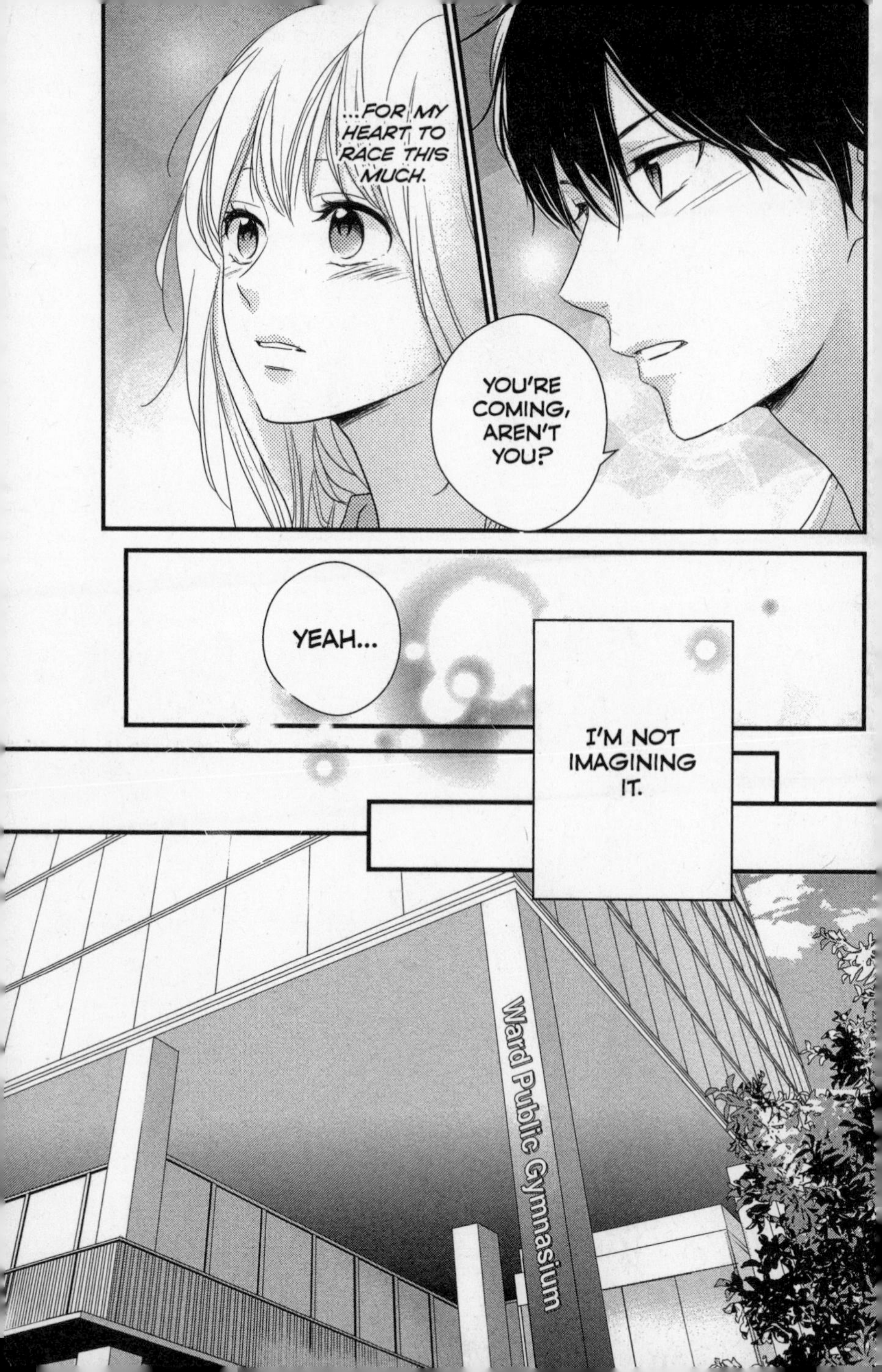
...FOR MY HEART TO RACE THIS MUCH.
YOU'RE COMING, AREN'T YOU?
YEAH...
I'M NOT IMAGINING IT.
Ward Public Gymnasium

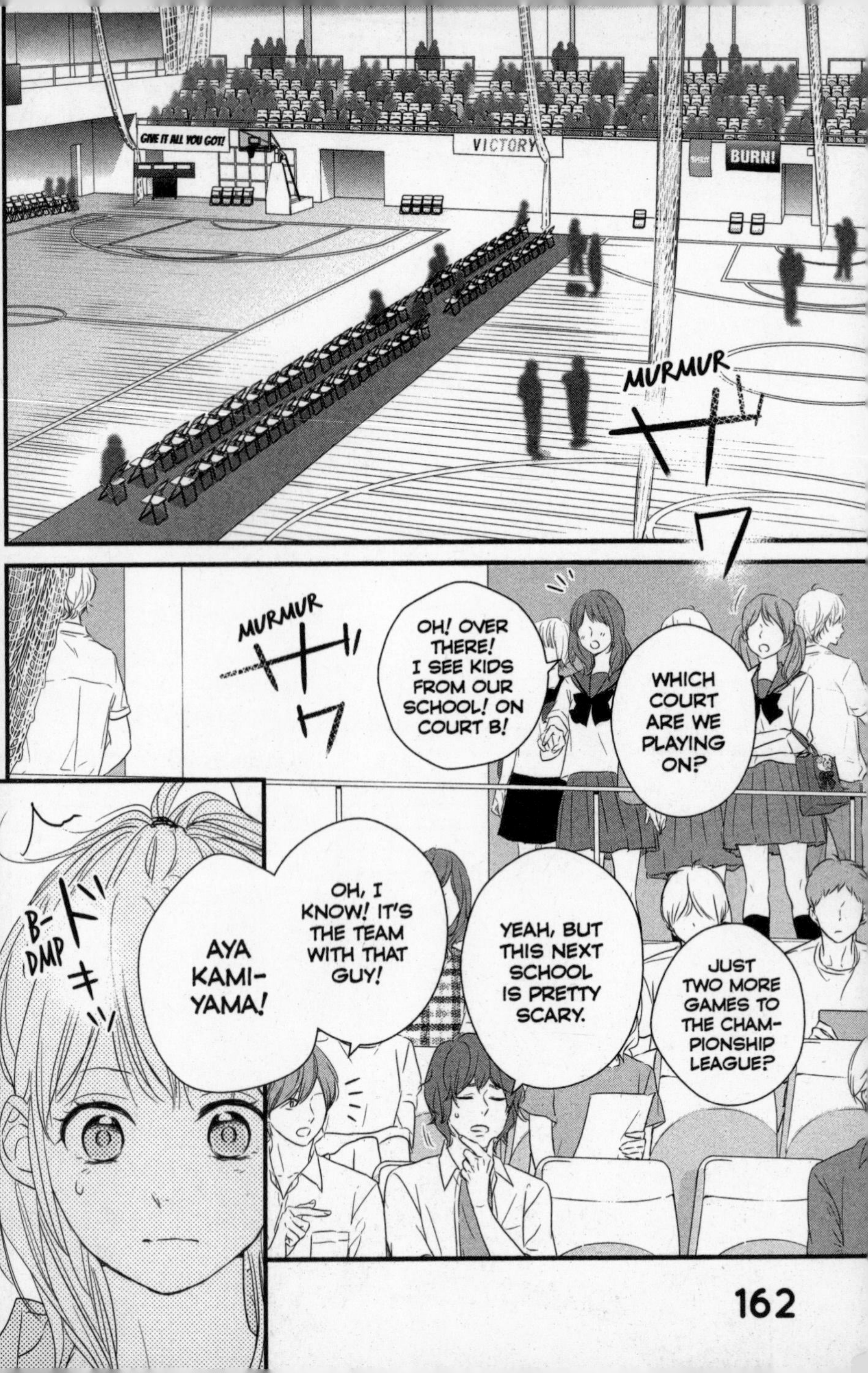
GIVE IT ALL YOU GOT!
VICTORY
BURN!
MURMUR
WHICH COURT ARE WE PLAYING ON?
OH! OVER THERE! I SEE KIDS FROM OUR SCHOOL! ON COURT B!
MURMUR
JUST TWO MORE GAMES TO THE CHAMPIONSHIP LEAGUE?
YEAH, BUT THIS NEXT SCHOOL IS PRETTY SCARY.
OH, I KNOW! IT'S THE TEAM WITH THAT GUY!
AYA KAMI-YAMA!
B-DMP

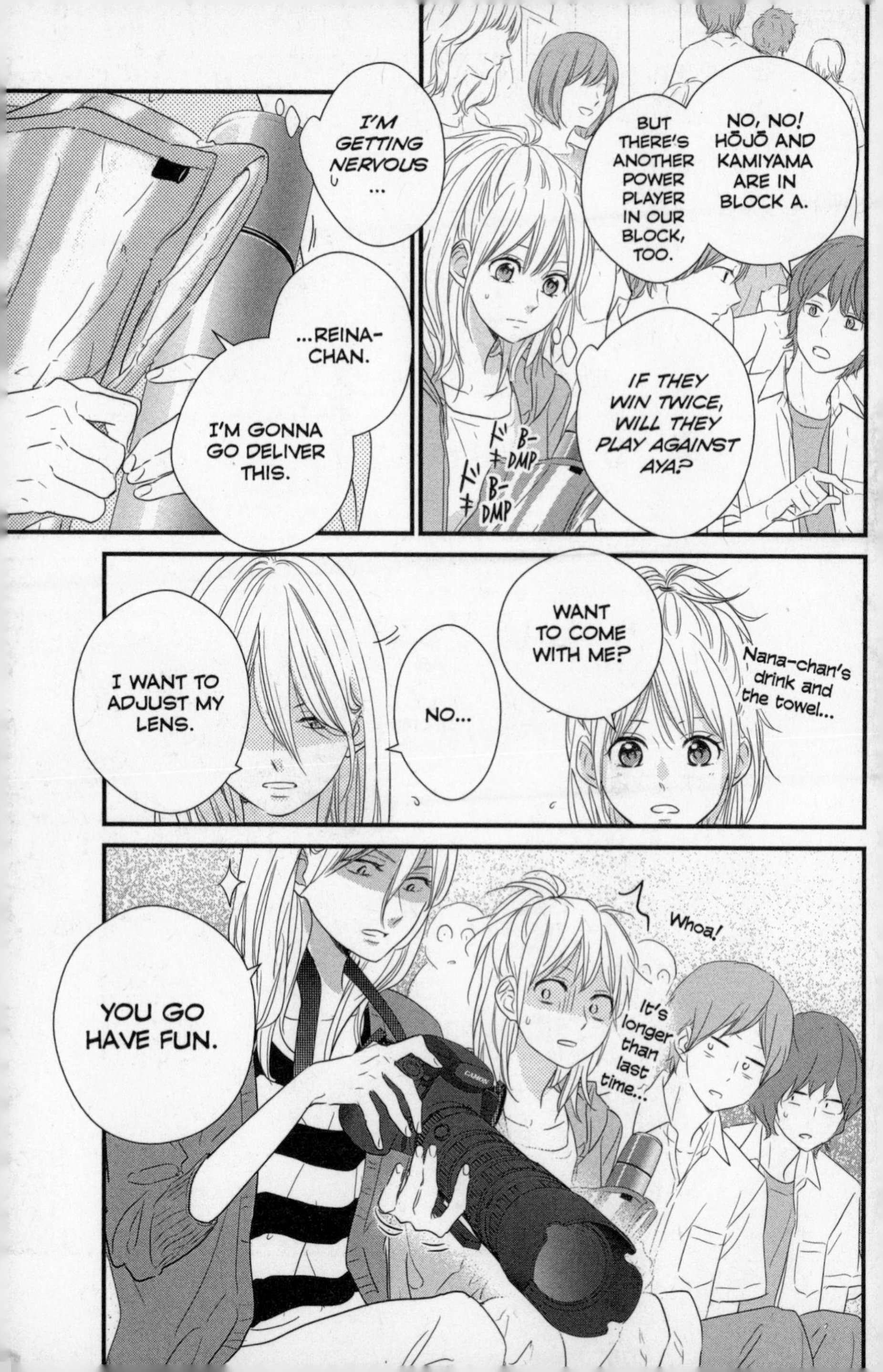
NO, NO! HŌJŌ AND KAMIYAMA ARE IN BLOCK A.
BUT THERE'S ANOTHER POWER PLAYER IN OUR BLOCK, TOO.
IF THEY WIN TWICE, WILL THEY PLAY AGAINST AYA?
B-DMP
B-DMP
I'M GETTING NERVOUS...
...REINA-CHAN.
I'M GONNA GO DELIVER THIS.
Nana-chan's drink and the towel...
WANT TO COME WITH ME?
NO...
I WANT TO ADJUST MY LENS.
Whoa!
It's longer than last time...
YOU GO HAVE FUN.

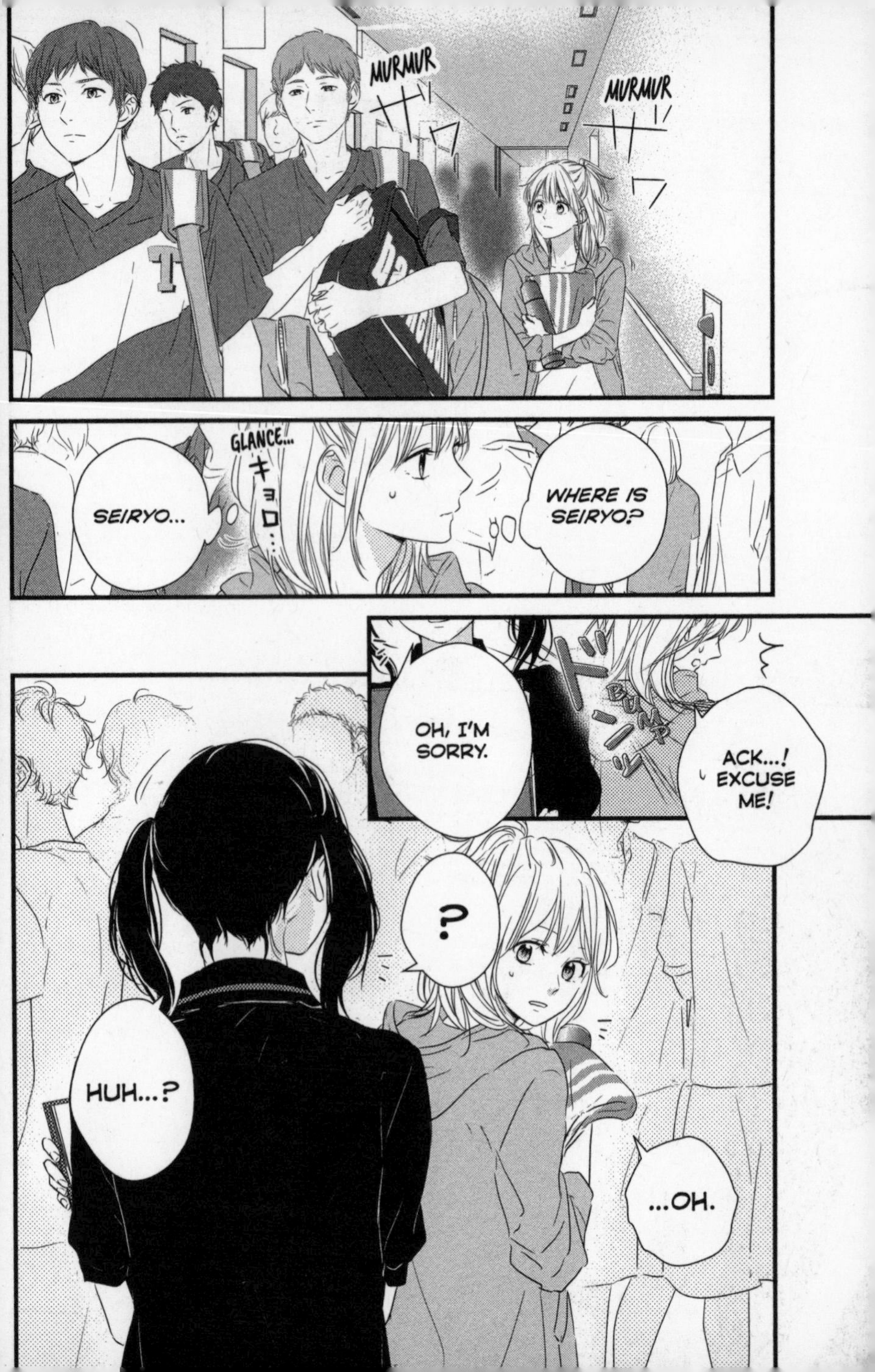
MURMUR
MURMUR
WHERE IS SEIRYO?
GLANCE...
SEIRYO...
ACK...! EXCUSE ME!
BUMP
OH, I'M SORRY.
...OH.
?
HUH...?

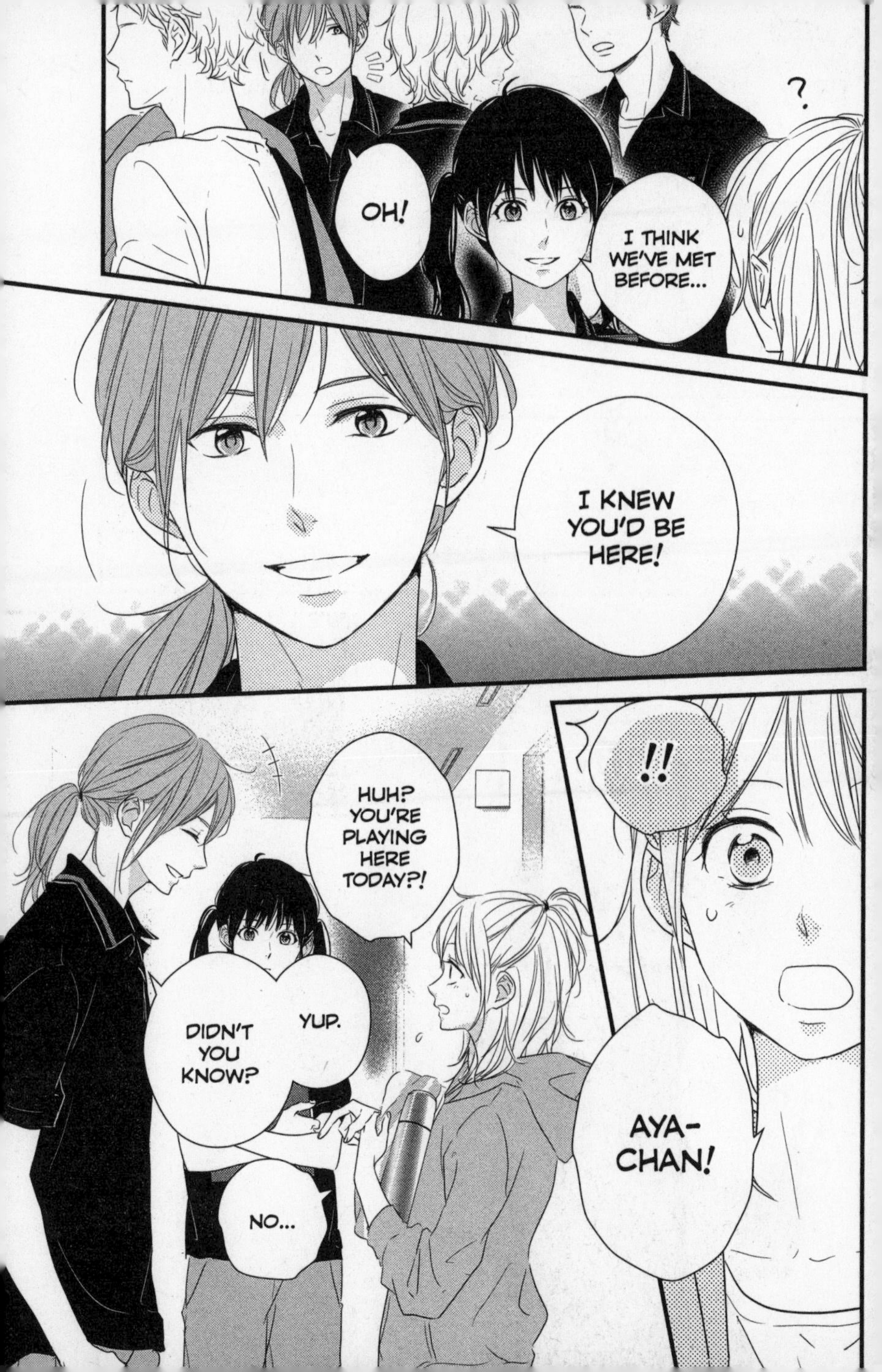
?
I THINK WE'VE MET BEFORE...
OH!
I KNEW YOU'D BE HERE!
!!
AYA-CHAN!
HUH? YOU'RE PLAYING HERE TODAY?!
YUP.
DIDN'T YOU KNOW?
NO...

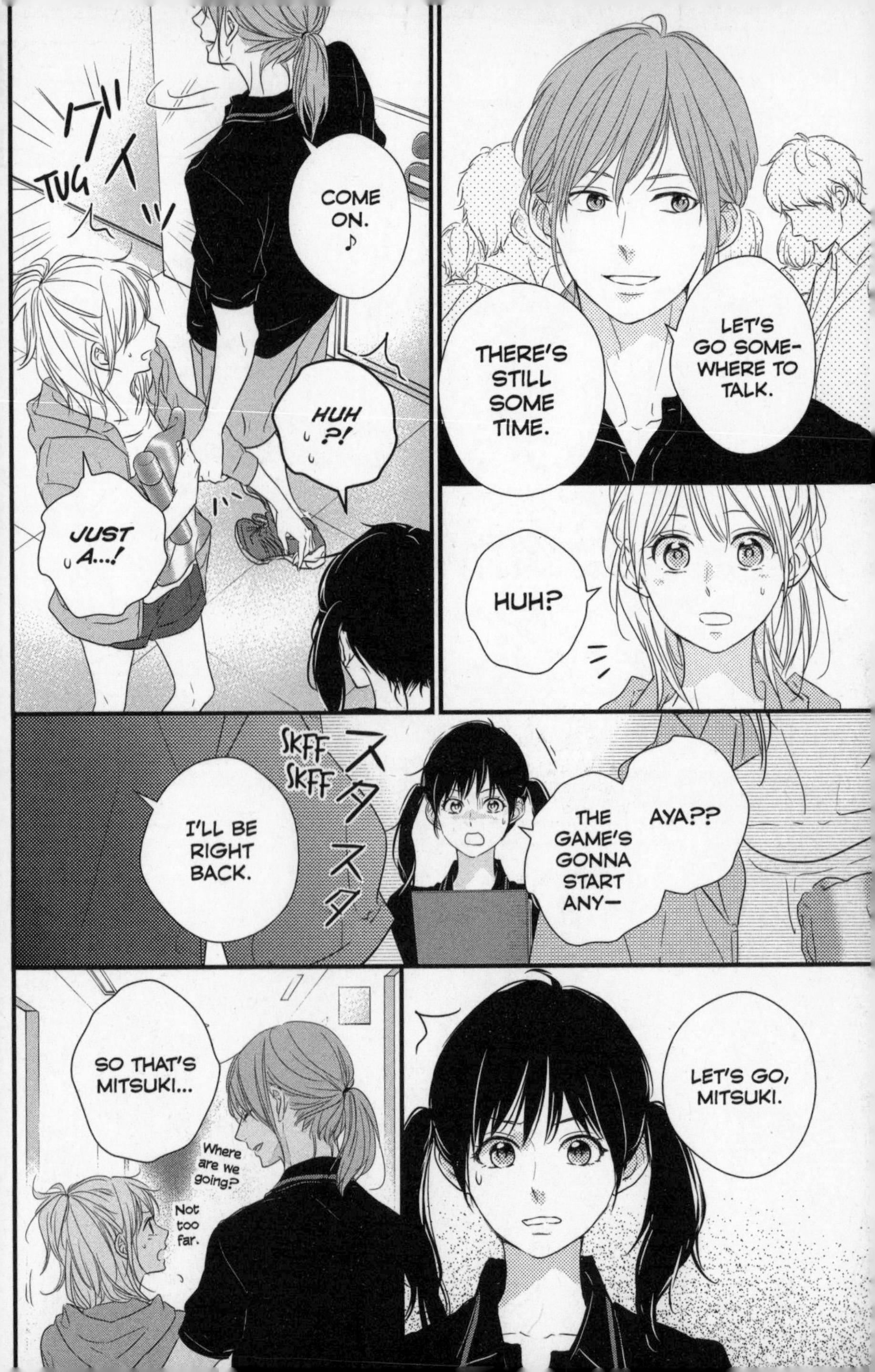
LET'S GO SOME-WHERE TO TALK.
THERE'S STILL SOME TIME.
HUH?
COME ON. ♪
TUG
HUH ?!
JUST A...!
THE GAME'S GONNA START ANY— AYA??
SKFF SKFF
I'LL BE RIGHT BACK.
LET'S GO, MITSUKI.
SO THAT'S MITSUKI...
Where are we going?
Not too far.

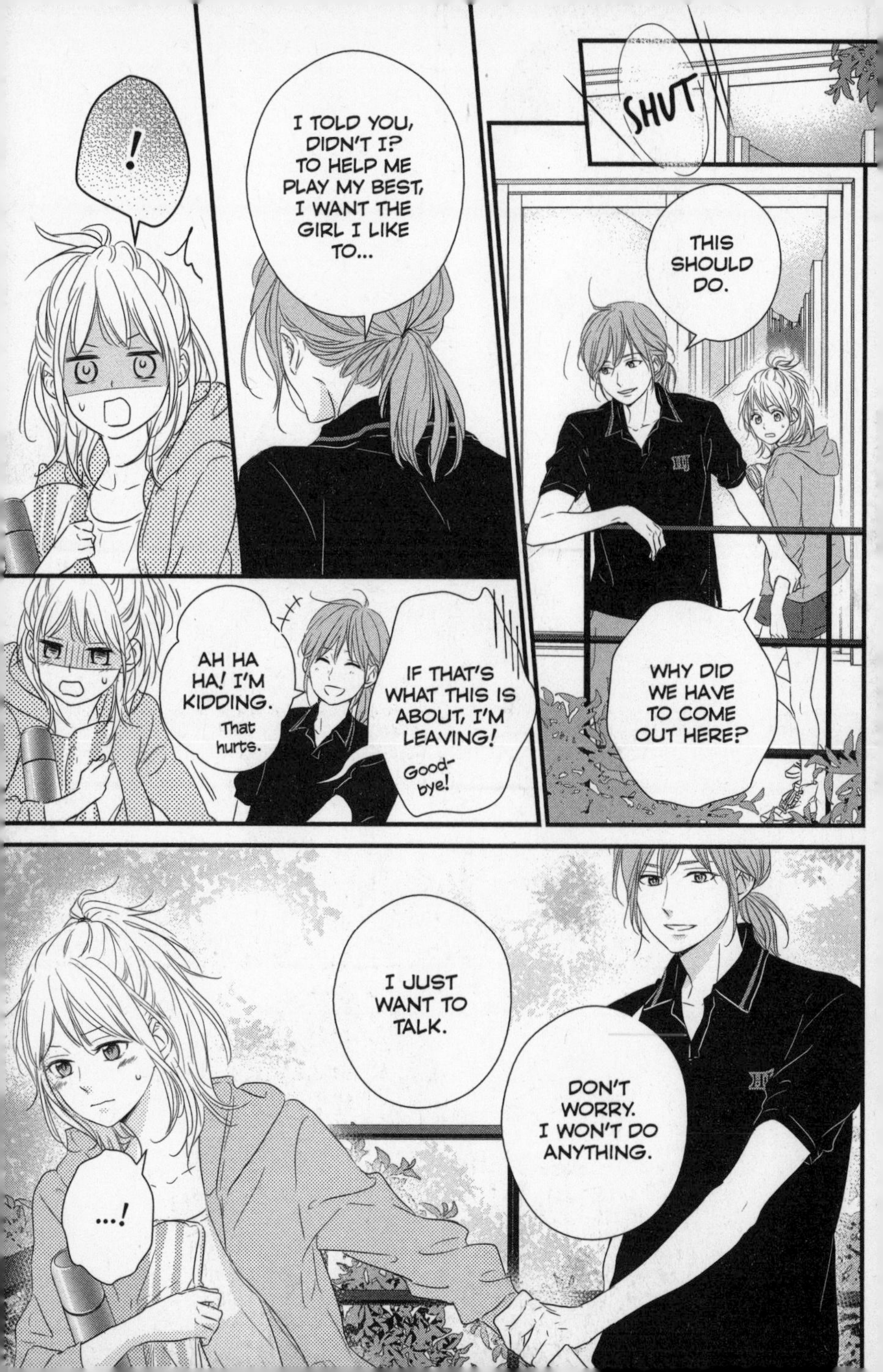
SHUT
THIS SHOULD DO.
WHY DID WE HAVE TO COME OUT HERE?
I TOLD YOU, DIDN'T I? TO HELP ME PLAY MY BEST, I WANT THE GIRL I LIKE TO...
!
IF THAT'S WHAT THIS IS ABOUT, I'M LEAVING!
Good-bye!
AH HA HA! I'M KIDDING.
That hurts.
I JUST WANT TO TALK.
DON'T WORRY. I WON'T DO ANYTHING.
...!

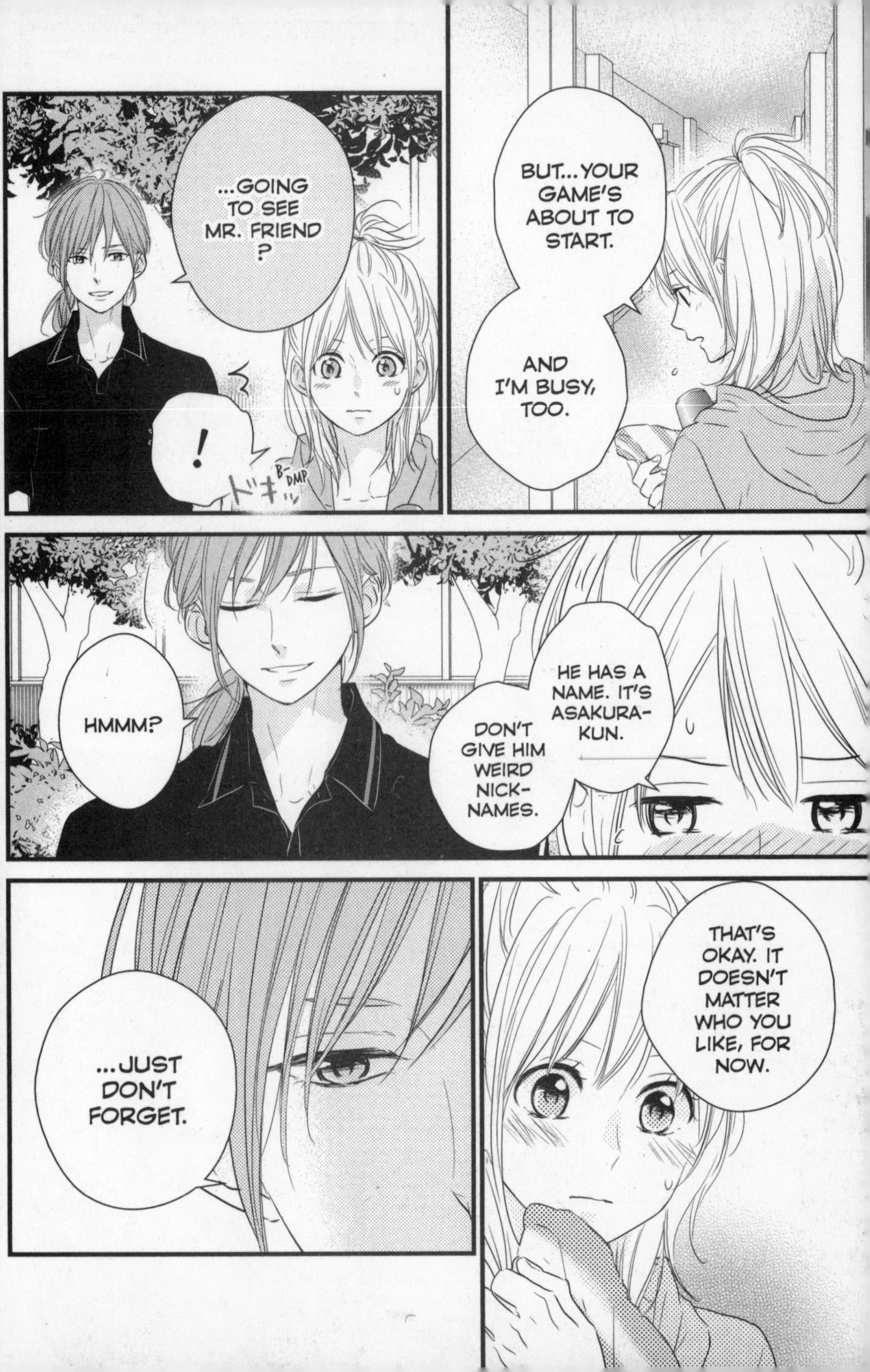
BUT...YOUR GAME'S ABOUT TO START.
AND I'M BUSY, TOO.
...GOING TO SEE MR. FRIEND?
!
B-DMP
ドキッ
HE HAS A NAME. IT'S ASAKURA-KUN.
DON'T GIVE HIM WEIRD NICK-NAMES.
HMMM?
THAT'S OKAY. IT DOESN'T MATTER WHO YOU LIKE, FOR NOW.
...JUST DON'T FORGET.

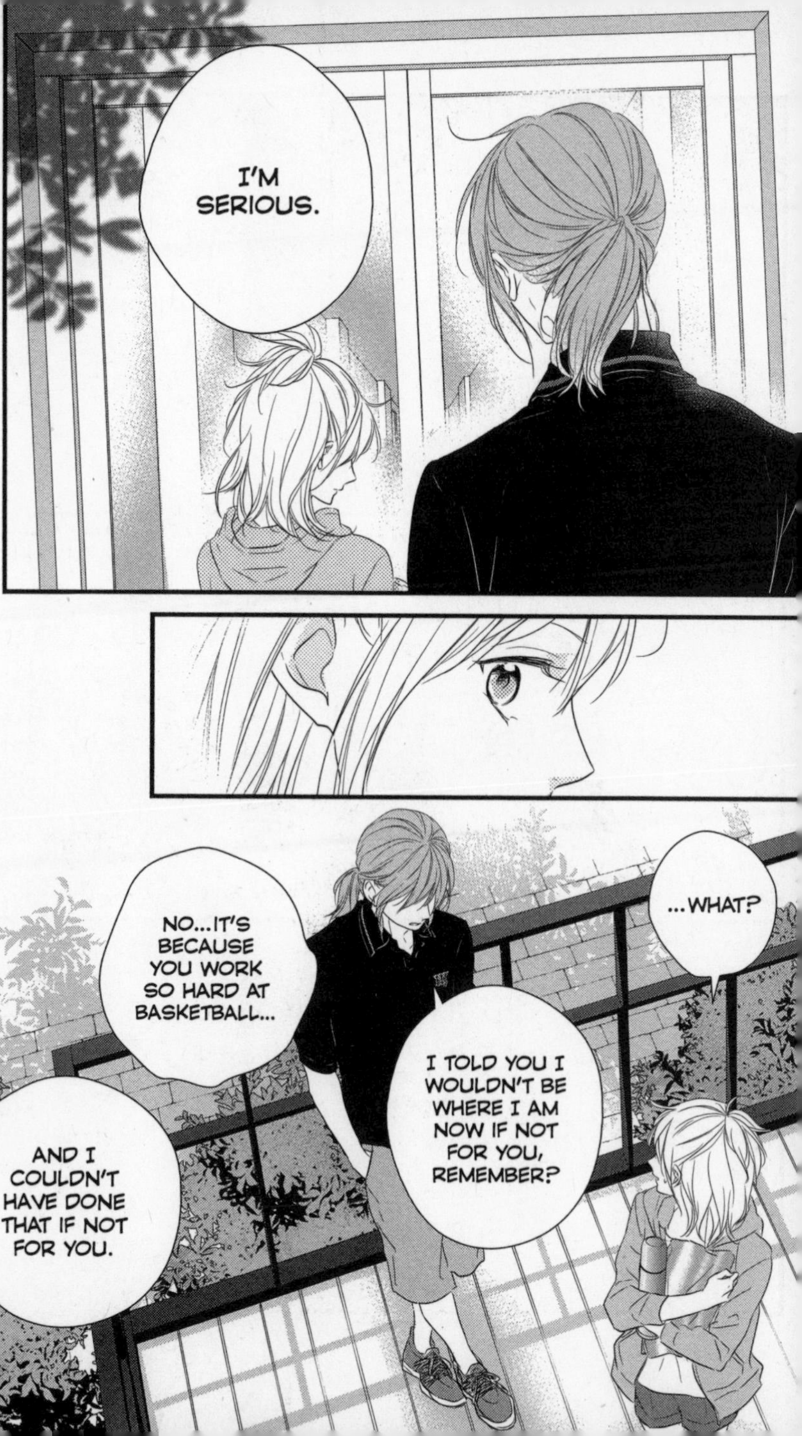
I'M SERIOUS.
...WHAT?
NO...IT'S BECAUSE YOU WORK SO HARD AT BASKETBALL...
I TOLD YOU I WOULDN'T BE WHERE I AM NOW IF NOT FOR YOU, REMEMBER?
AND I COULDN'T HAVE DONE THAT IF NOT FOR YOU.

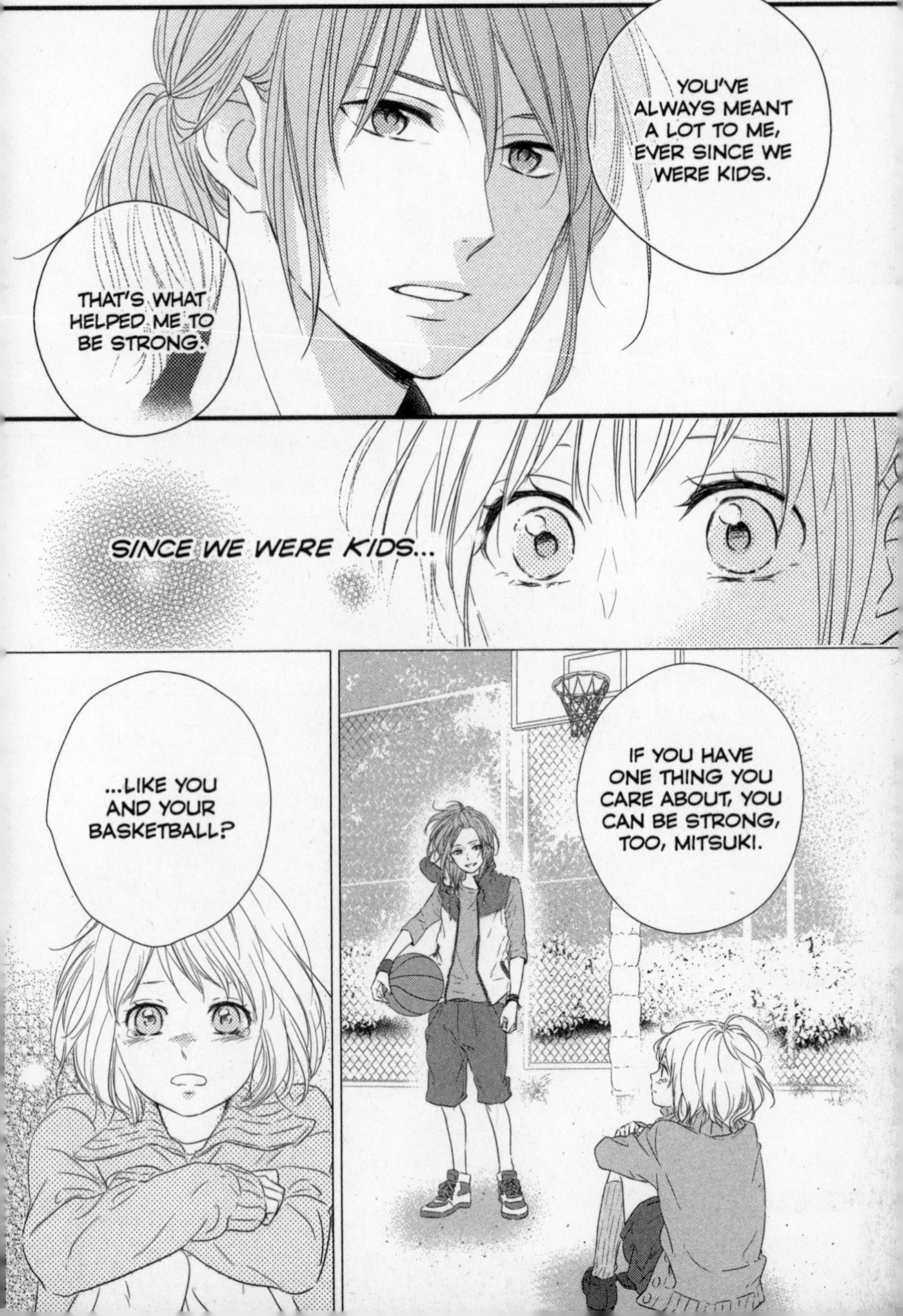
YOU'VE ALWAYS MEANT A LOT TO ME, EVER SINCE WE WERE KIDS.
THAT'S WHAT HELPED ME TO BE STRONG.
SINCE WE WERE KIDS...
IF YOU HAVE ONE THING YOU CARE ABOUT, YOU CAN BE STRONG, TOO, MITSUKI.
...LIKE YOU AND YOUR BASKETBALL?

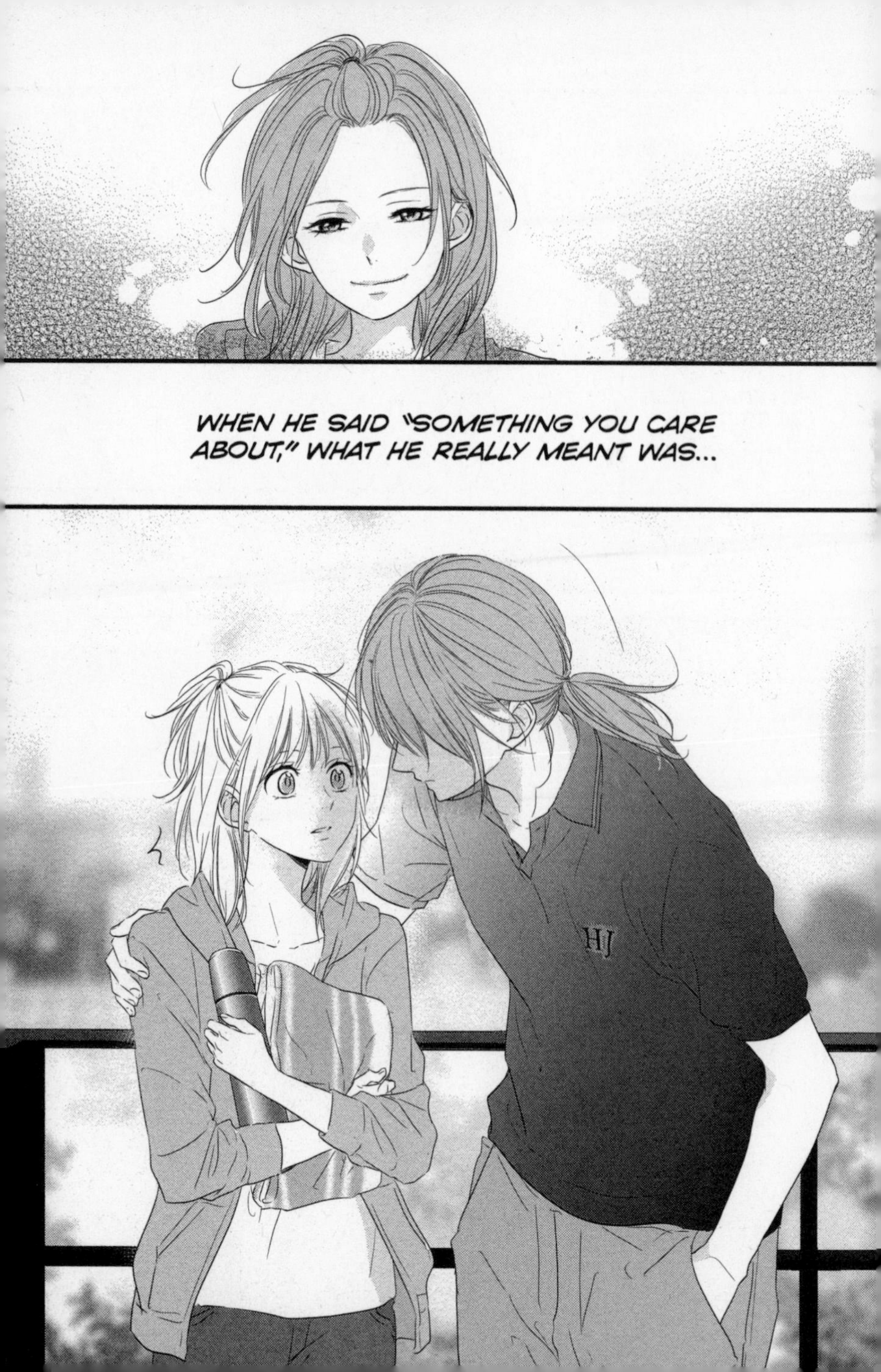
WHEN HE SAID "SOMETHING YOU CARE ABOUT," WHAT HE REALLY MEANT WAS...
HJ

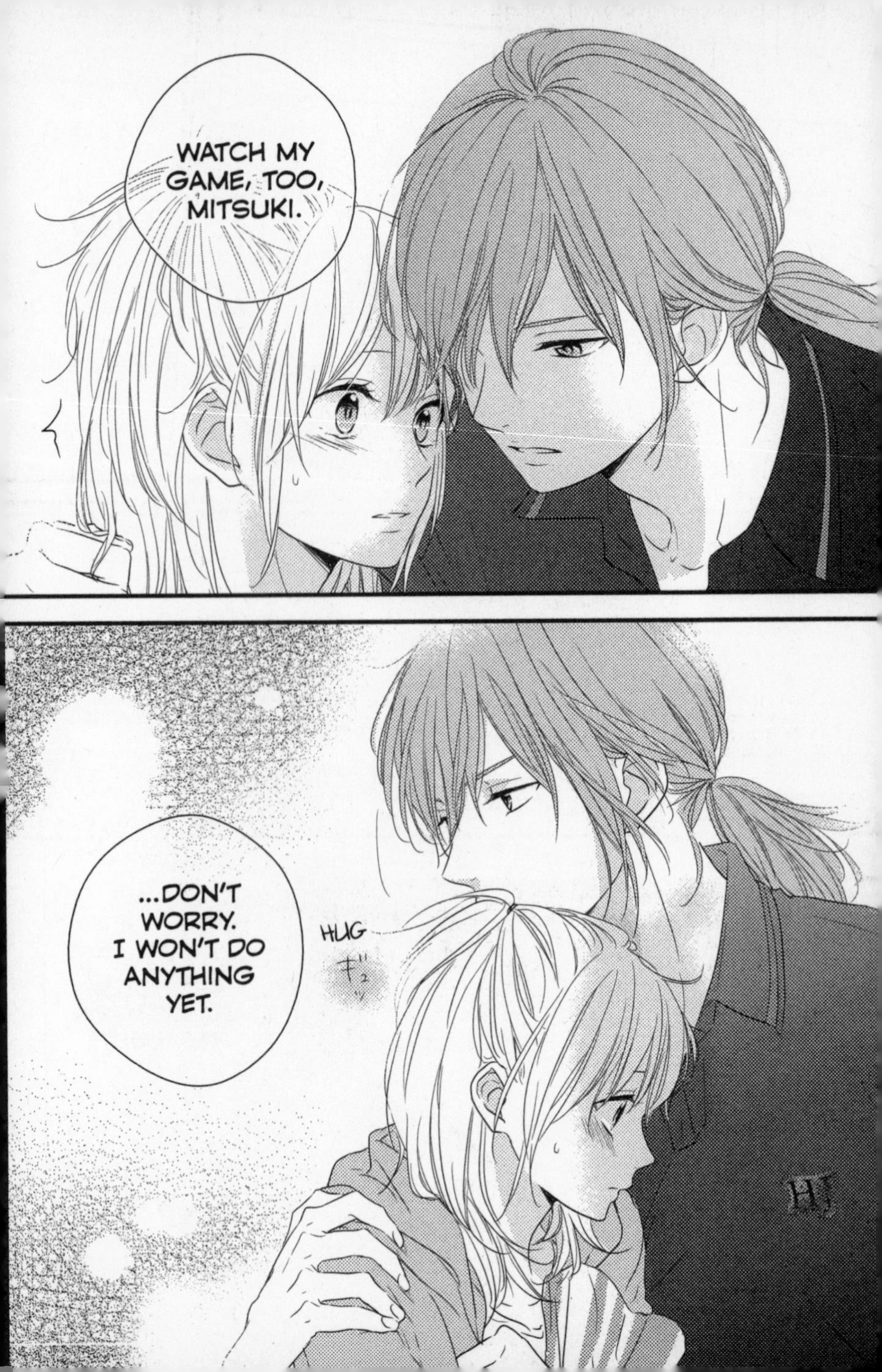
WATCH MY GAME, TOO, MITSUKI.
...DON'T WORRY. I WON'T DO ANYTHING YET.
HUG

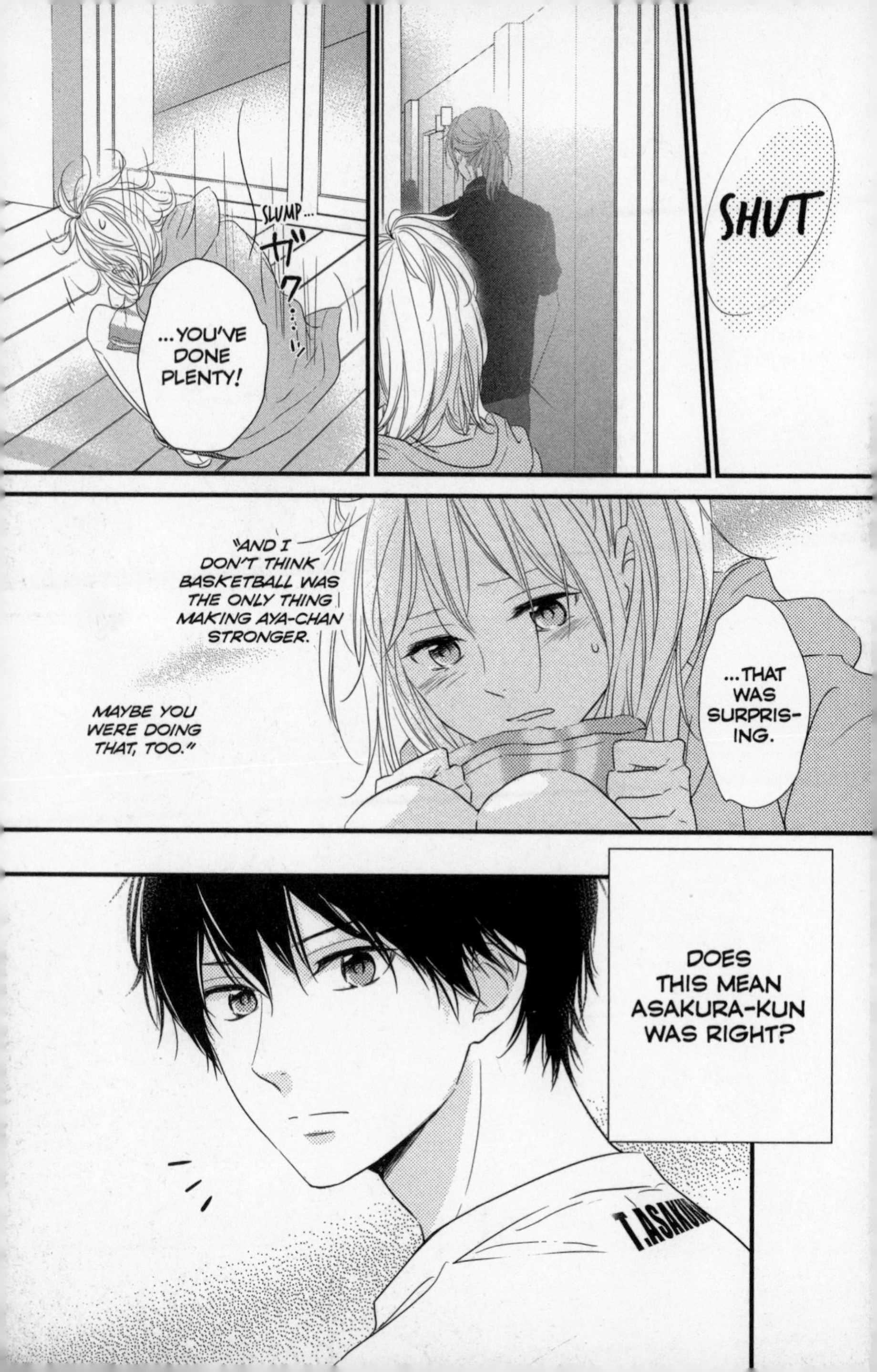
SHUT
SLUMP...
ガク…ッ
...YOU'VE DONE PLENTY!
...THAT WAS SURPRISING.
"AND I DON'T THINK BASKETBALL WAS THE ONLY THING MAKING AYA-CHAN STRONGER.
MAYBE YOU WERE DOING THAT, TOO."
DOES THIS MEAN ASAKURA-KUN WAS RIGHT?

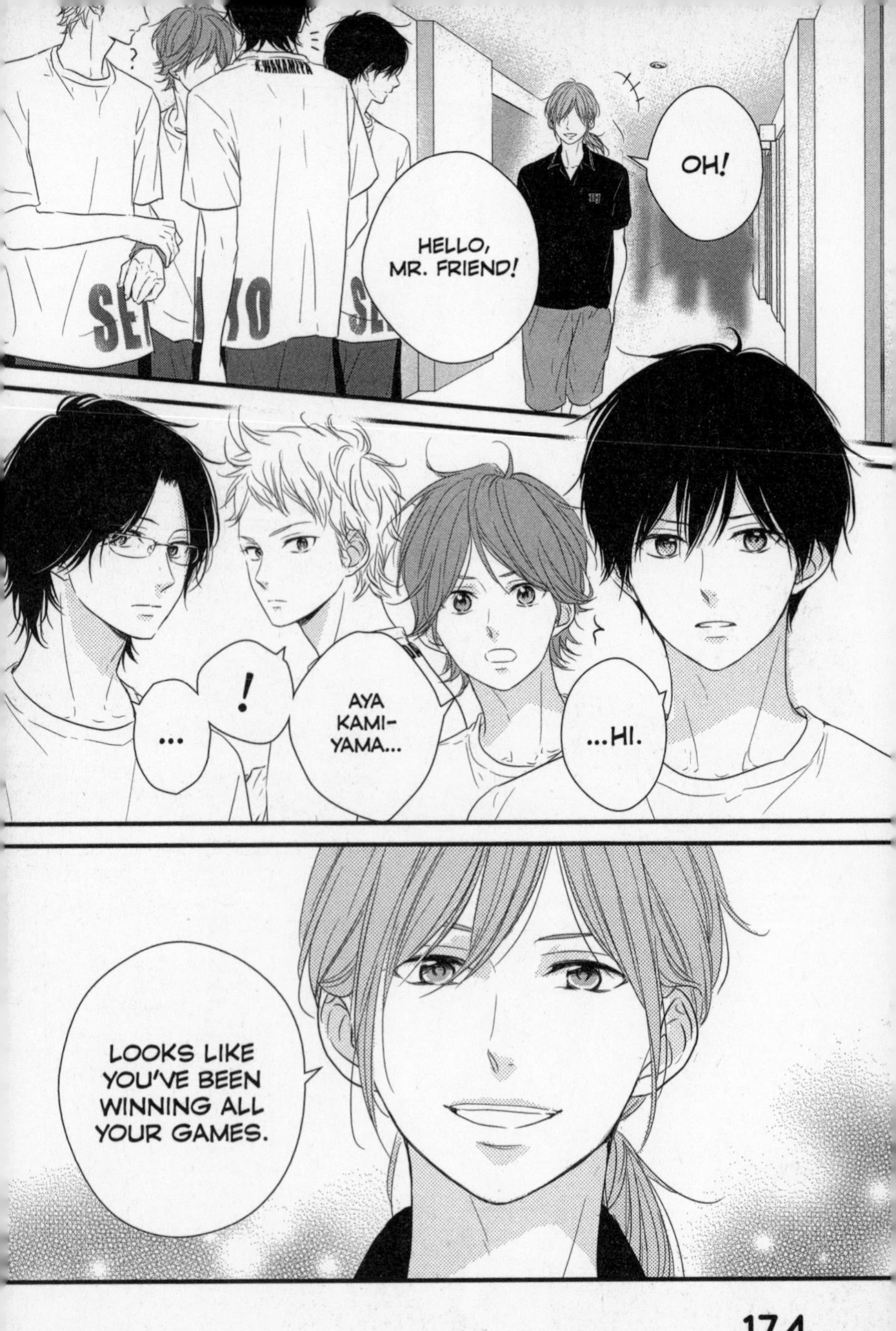
OH!
HELLO, MR. FRIEND!
...HI.
AYA KAMI-YAMA...
!
...
LOOKS LIKE YOU'VE BEEN WINNING ALL YOUR GAMES.

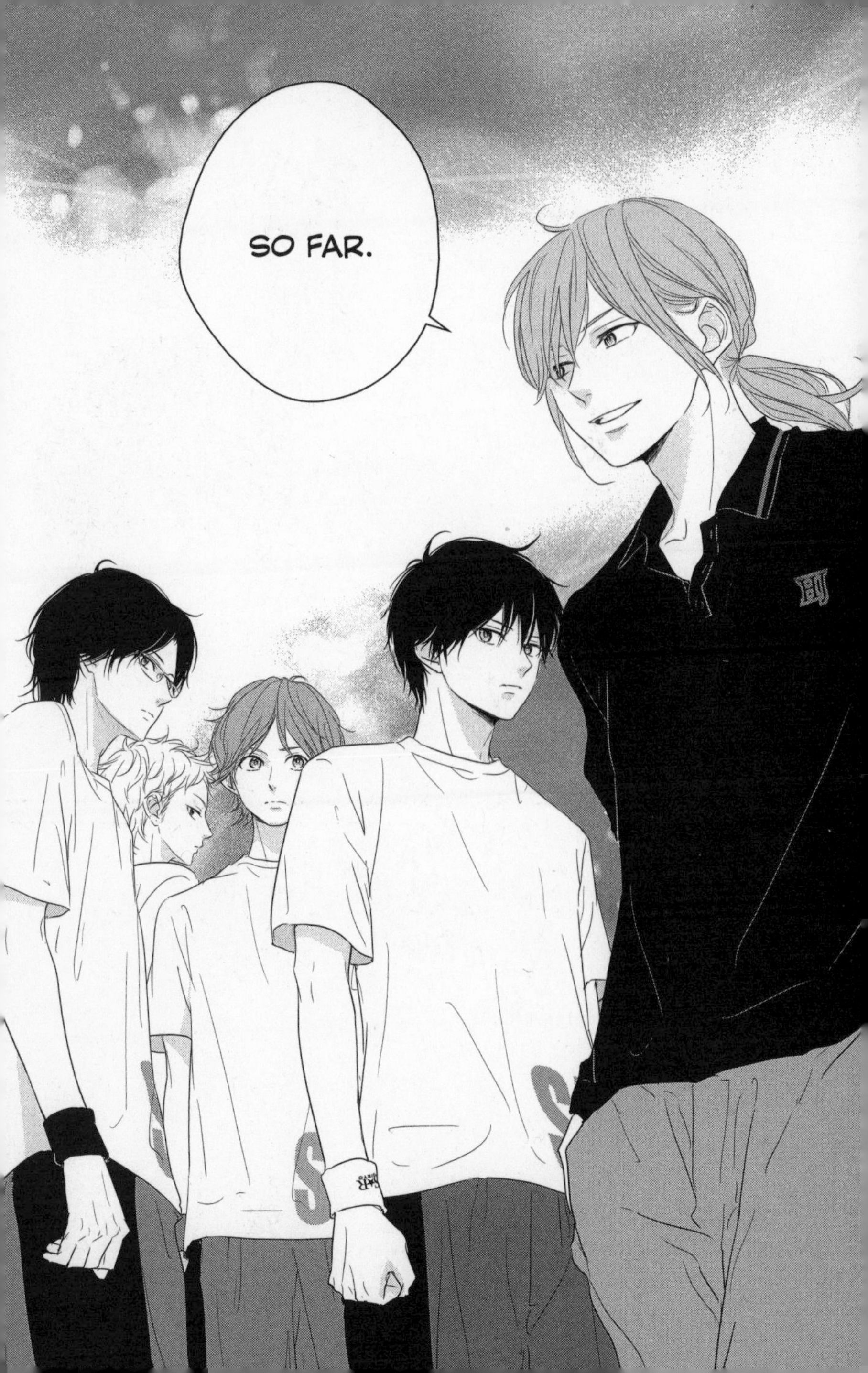
SO FAR.

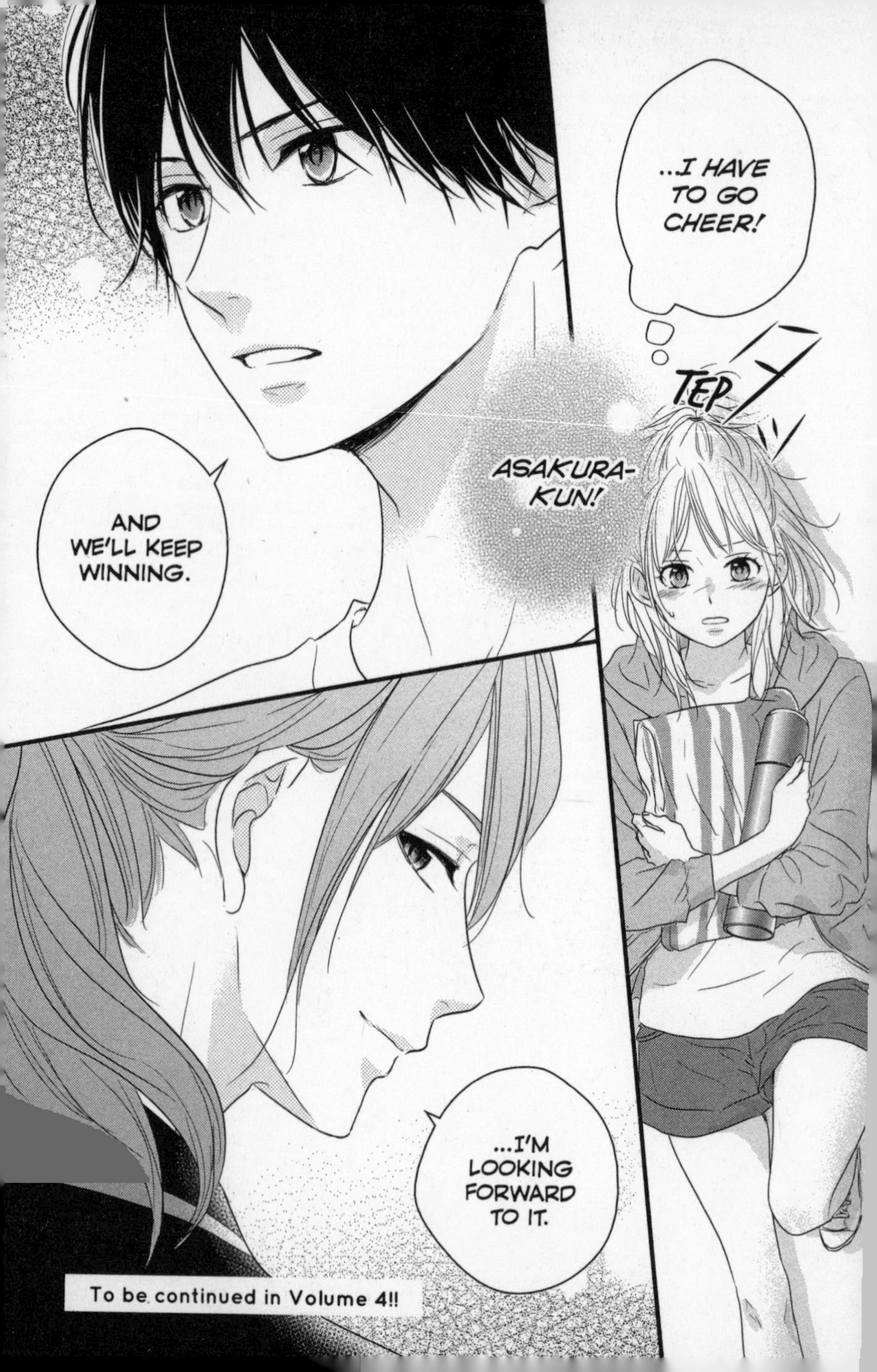
...I HAVE TO GO CHEER!
TEP
ASAKURA-KUN!
AND WE'LL KEEP WINNING.
...I'M LOOKING FORWARD TO IT.
To be continued in Volume 4!!

Bonus One-Shot Manga

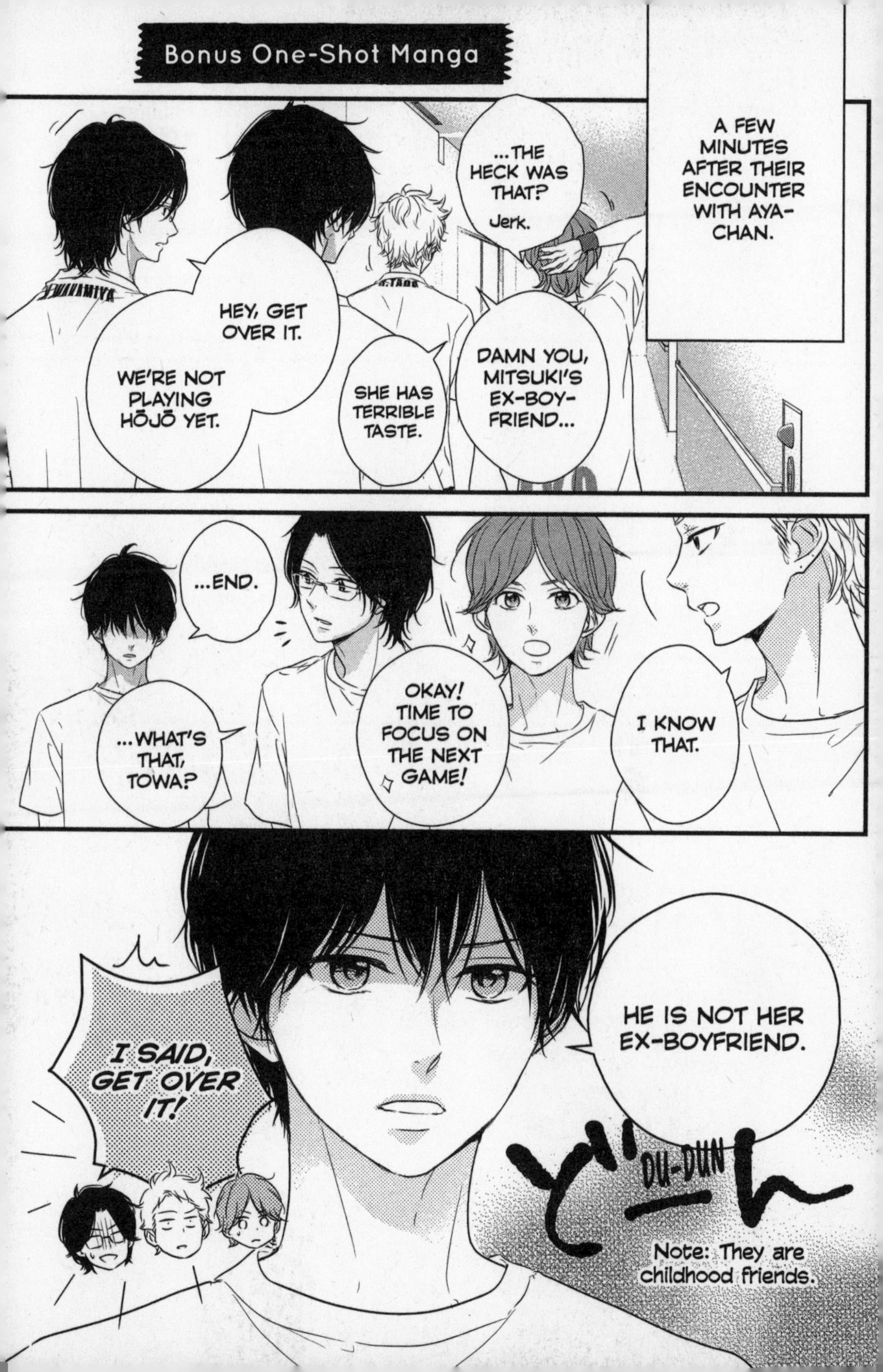

A FEW MINUTES AFTER THEIR ENCOUNTER WITH AYA-CHAN.
...THE HECK WAS THAT?
Jerk.
DAMN YOU, MITSUKI'S EX-BOY-FRIEND...
SHE HAS TERRIBLE TASTE.
HEY, GET OVER IT.
WE'RE NOT PLAYING HŌJŌ YET.
I KNOW THAT.
OKAY! TIME TO FOCUS ON THE NEXT GAME!
...END.
...WHAT'S THAT, TOWA?
HE IS NOT HER EX-BOYFRIEND.
DU-DUN
Note: They are childhood friends.
I SAID, GET OVER IT!

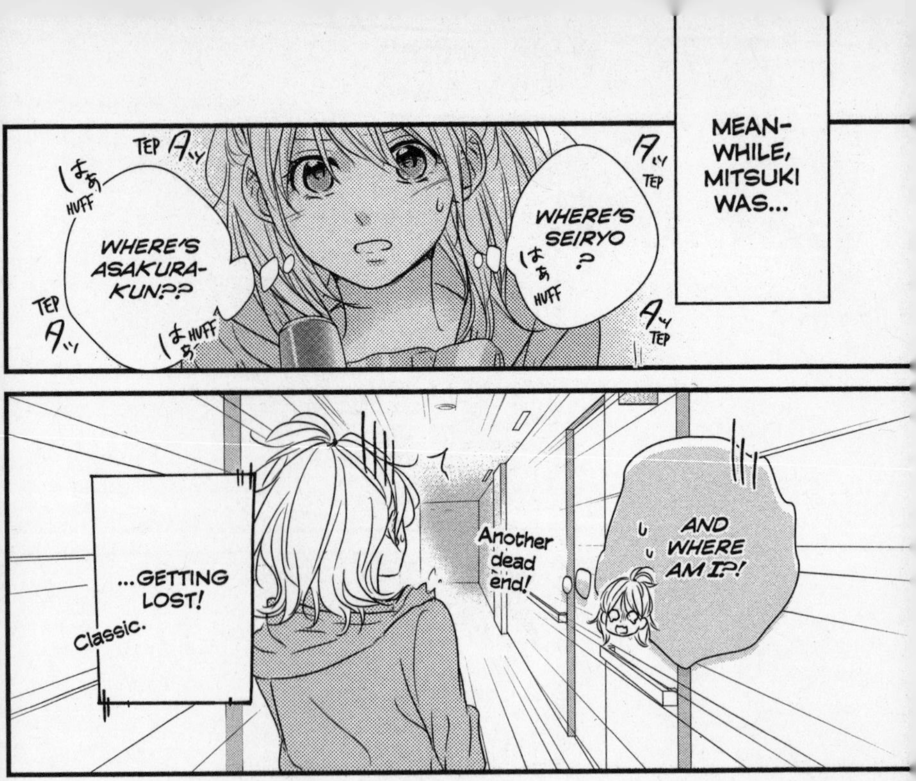
MEAN-WHILE, MITSUKI WAS...
TEP
WHERE'S SEIRYO?
HUFF
WHERE'S ASAKURA-KUN??
HUFF
TEP
AND WHERE AM I?!
Another dead end!
...GETTING LOST!
Classic.

SPECIAL THANKS ★*

To my editor, the Designer-sama, everyone on the DESSERT editorial team, everyone at the printing office, everyone who was involved in the creation of this work.

My assistants Masuda-san, Aki-chan
My family, friends
Words Café-sama
And to all my readers,
My sincerest gratitude ✧✧

July 2, 2015

Anashin

Kyōsuke, age 12 (Part 1)

OH, COME ON! STOP LYING!
IT'S TRUE.
BEEP-BOP
BEEP-BOP
HEY, WHO'S THAT?
THE GIRL WITH KYŌSUKE.
Is she in high school?
...PROBABLY HIS SISTER.
Kyōsuke's.
YEAH, I GUESS...
Hurry it up, Towa!
Yeah.
IS THAT WHAT SHE LOOKED LIKE?
MMMWAH ♥
!
...THAT IS *NOT* HIS SISTER!!
Also age 12 →
PLOP

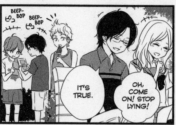

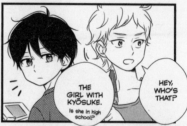

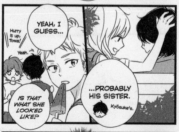

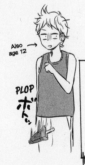

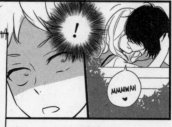

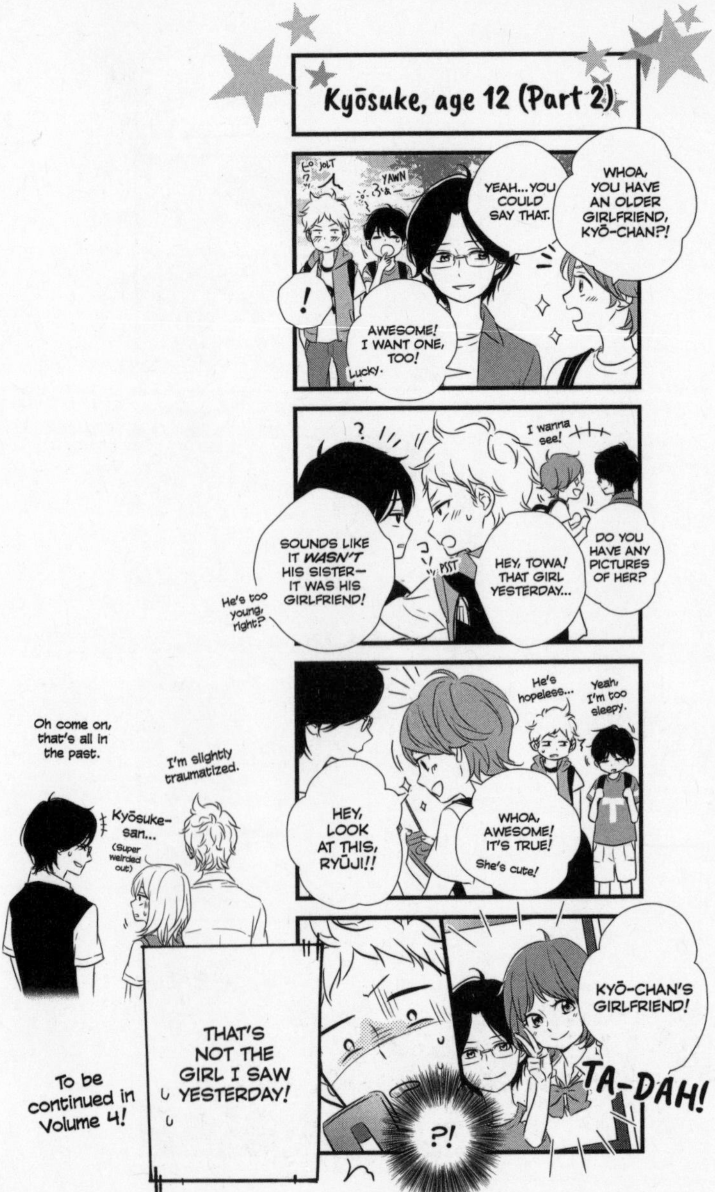
Kyōsuke, age 12 (Part 2)
WHOA, YOU HAVE AN OLDER GIRLFRIEND, KYŌ-CHAN?!
YEAH...YOU COULD SAY THAT.
YAWN
JOLT
!
AWESOME! I WANT ONE, TOO!
Lucky.
I wanna see!
DO YOU HAVE ANY PICTURES OF HER?
HEY, TOWA! THAT GIRL YESTERDAY...
PSST
SOUNDS LIKE IT *WASN'T* HIS SISTER—IT WAS HIS GIRLFRIEND!
He's too young, right?
Yeah, I'm too sleepy.
He's hopeless...
WHOA, AWESOME! IT'S TRUE!
She's cute!
HEY, LOOK AT THIS, RYŪJI!!
KYŌ-CHAN'S GIRLFRIEND!
TA-DAH!
?!
THAT'S NOT THE GIRL I SAW YESTERDAY!
I'm slightly traumatized.
Oh come on, that's all in the past.
Kyōsuke-san...
(Super weirded out)
To be continued in Volume 4!

Waiting for Spring

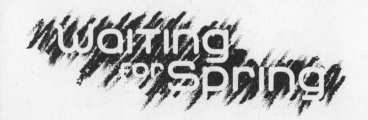

OPPOSITES ATTRACT...MAYBE?

Haru Yoshida is feared as an unstable and violent "monster." Mizutani Shizuku is a grade-obsessed student with no friends. Fate brings these two together to form the most unlikely pair. Haru firmly believes he's in love with Mizutani and she firmly believes he's insane.

KC KODANSHA

SAY I LOVE YOU.

KC
KODANSHA
COMICS

Mei Tachibana has no friends — and says she doesn't need them!
But everything changes when she accidentally roundhouse kicks the most popular boy in school! However, Yamato Kurosawa isn't angry in the slightest—in fact, he thinks his ordinary life could use an unusual girl like Mei. But winning Mei's trust will be a tough task. How long will she refuse to say, "I love you"?

NO.6

A PERFECT LIFE IN A PERFECT CITY

For Shion, an elite student in the technologically sophisticated city No. 6, life is carefully choreographed. One fateful day, he takes a misstep, sheltering a fugitive his age from a typhoon. Helping this boy throws Shion's life down a path to discovering the appalling secrets behind the "perfection" of No. 6.

KC/ KODANSHA COMICS

"I'm pleasantly surprised to find modern shojo using cross-dressing as a dramatic device to deliver social commentary... Recommended."

Otaku USA Magazine

The prince in his dark days

By Hico Yamanaka

A drunkard for a father, a household of poverty... For 17-year-old Atsuko, misfortune is all she knows and believes in. Until one day, a chance encounter with Itaru–the wealthy heir of a huge corporation–changes everything. The two look identical, uncannily so. When Itaru curiously goes missing, Atsuko is roped into being his stand-in. There, in his shoes, Atsuko must parade like a prince in a palace. She encounters many new experiences, but at what cost…?

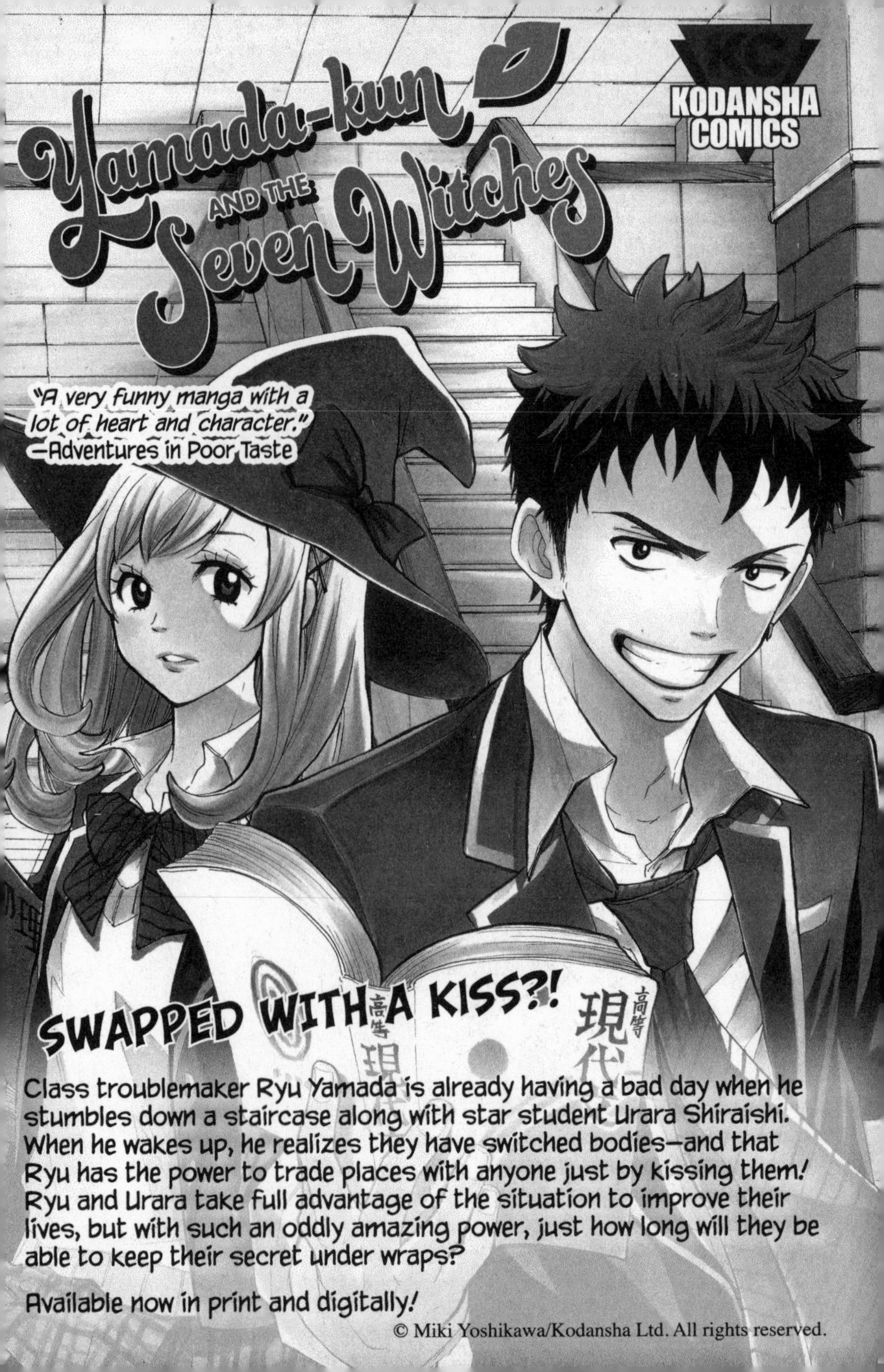
Yamada-kun AND THE Seven Witches
KODANSHA COMICS
"A very funny manga with a lot of heart and character."
—Adventures in Poor Taste
SWAPPED WITH A KISS?!
Class troublemaker Ryu Yamada is already having a bad day when he stumbles down a staircase along with star student Urara Shiraishi. When he wakes up, he realizes they have switched bodies—and that Ryu has the power to trade places with anyone just by kissing them! Ryu and Urara take full advantage of the situation to improve their lives, but with such an oddly amazing power, just how long will they be able to keep their secret under wraps?
Available now in print and digitally!
© Miki Yoshikawa/Kodansha Ltd. All rights reserved.

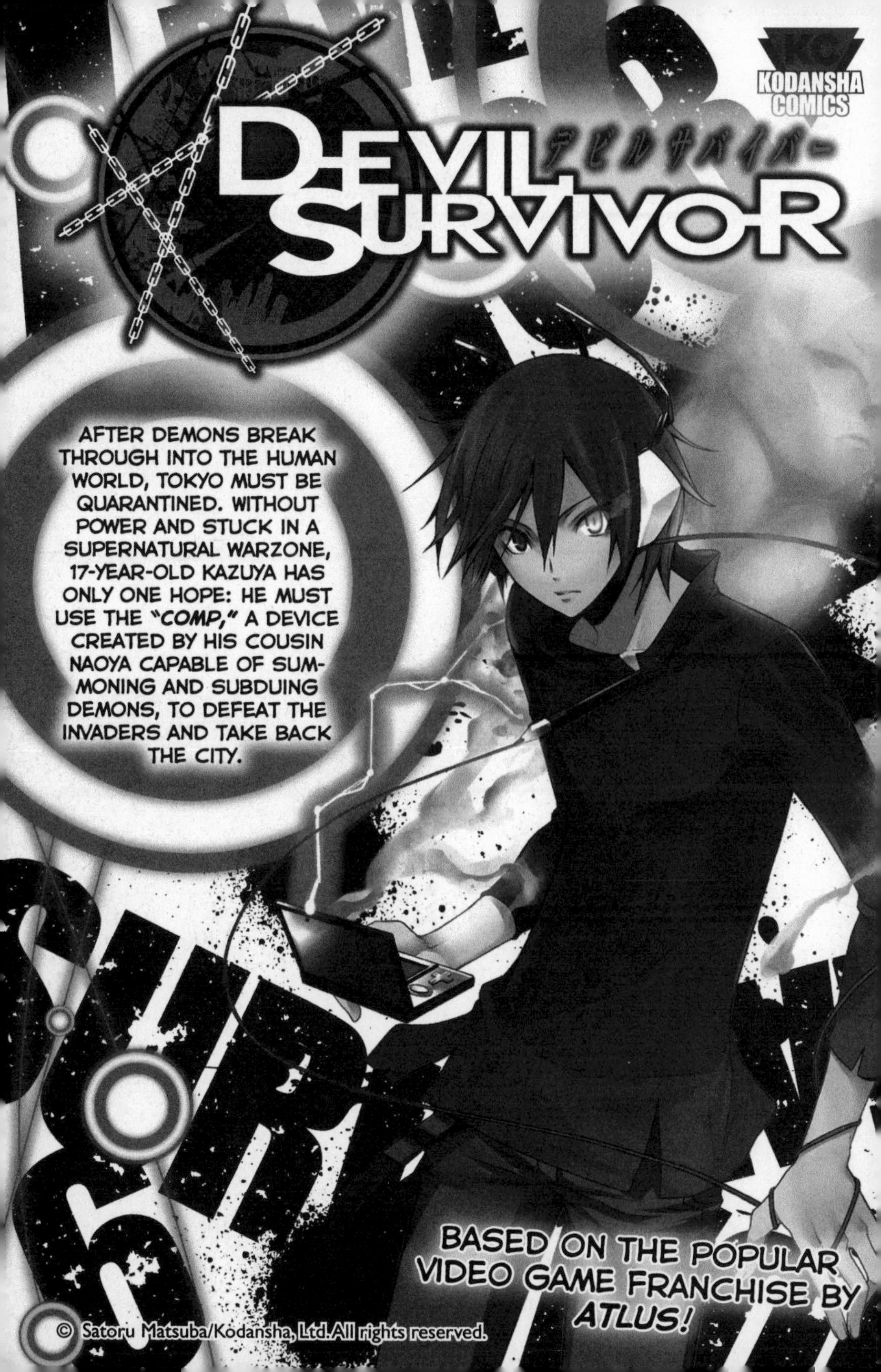
KODANSHA COMICS
DEVIL SURVIVOR
デビルサバイバー
AFTER DEMONS BREAK THROUGH INTO THE HUMAN WORLD, TOKYO MUST BE QUARANTINED. WITHOUT POWER AND STUCK IN A SUPERNATURAL WARZONE, 17-YEAR-OLD KAZUYA HAS ONLY ONE HOPE: HE MUST USE THE "COMP," A DEVICE CREATED BY HIS COUSIN NAOYA CAPABLE OF SUMMONING AND SUBDUING DEMONS, TO DEFEAT THE INVADERS AND TAKE BACK THE CITY.
BASED ON THE POPULAR VIDEO GAME FRANCHISE BY ATLUS!
© Satoru Matsuba/Kodansha, Ltd. All rights reserved.

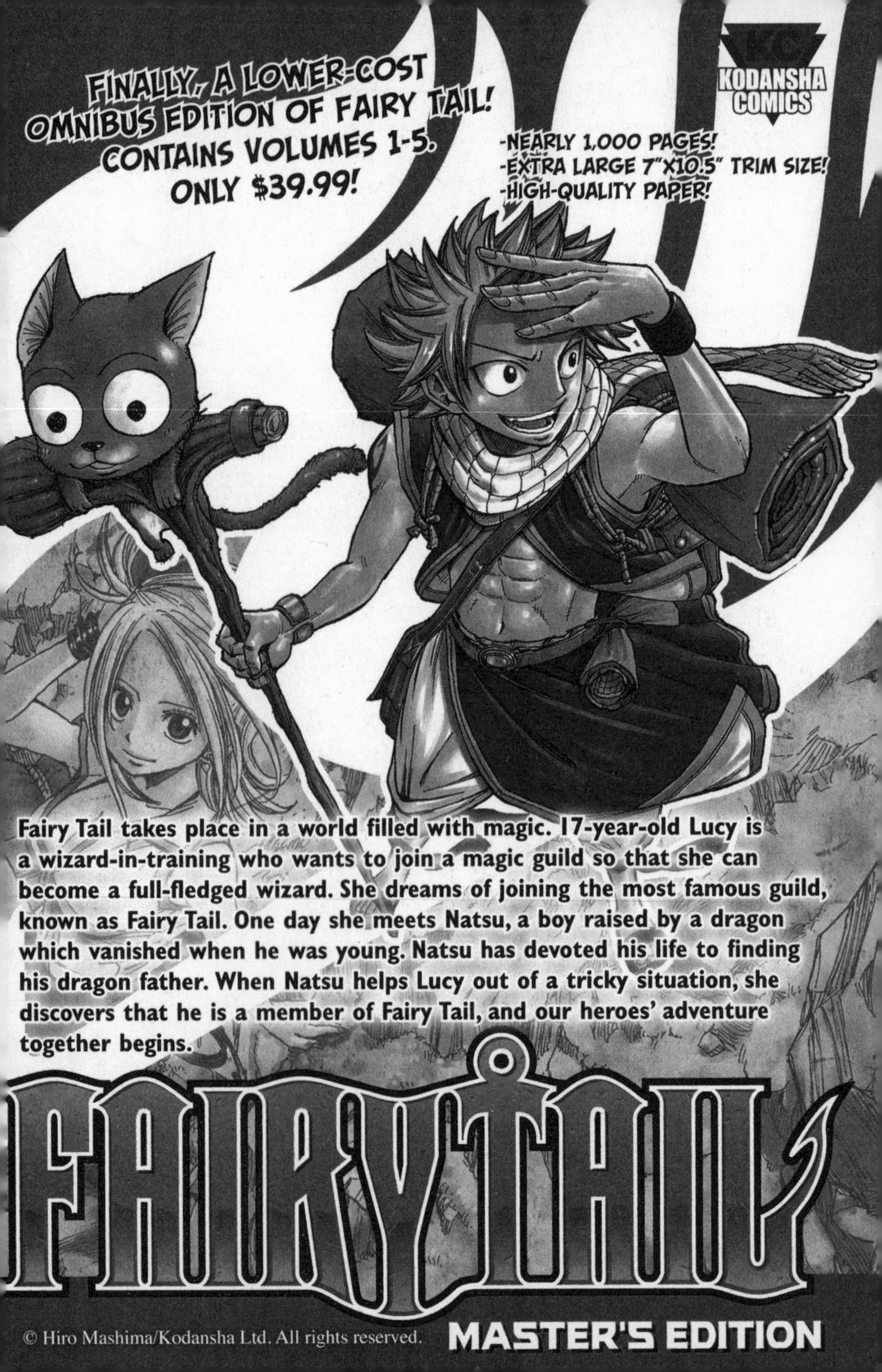
KODANSHA COMICS
FINALLY, A LOWER-COST OMNIBUS EDITION OF FAIRY TAIL! CONTAINS VOLUMES 1-5. ONLY $39.99!
-NEARLY 1,000 PAGES!
-EXTRA LARGE 7"X10.5" TRIM SIZE!
-HIGH-QUALITY PAPER!
Fairy Tail takes place in a world filled with magic. 17-year-old Lucy is a wizard-in-training who wants to join a magic guild so that she can become a full-fledged wizard. She dreams of joining the most famous guild, known as Fairy Tail. One day she meets Natsu, a boy raised by a dragon which vanished when he was young. Natsu has devoted his life to finding his dragon father. When Natsu helps Lucy out of a tricky situation, she discovers that he is a member of Fairy Tail, and our heroes' adventure together begins.
FAIRY TAIL
© Hiro Mashima/Kodansha Ltd. All rights reserved.
MASTER'S EDITION

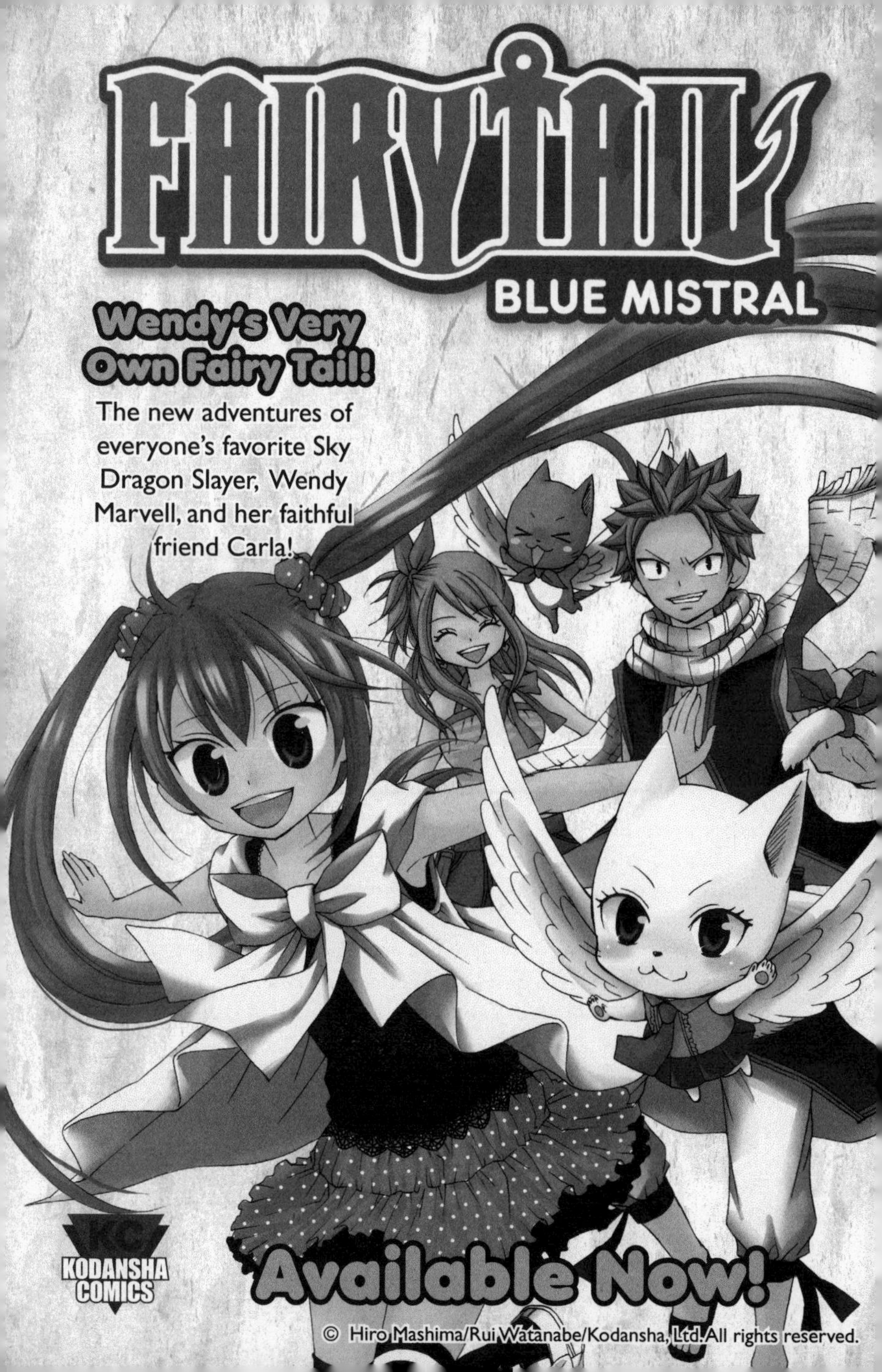
FAIRY TAIL
BLUE MISTRAL
Wendy's Very Own Fairy Tail!
The new adventures of everyone's favorite Sky Dragon Slayer, Wendy Marvell, and her faithful friend Carla!
KC KODANSHA COMICS
Available Now!
© Hiro Mashima/Rui Watanabe/Kodansha, Ltd. All rights reserved.

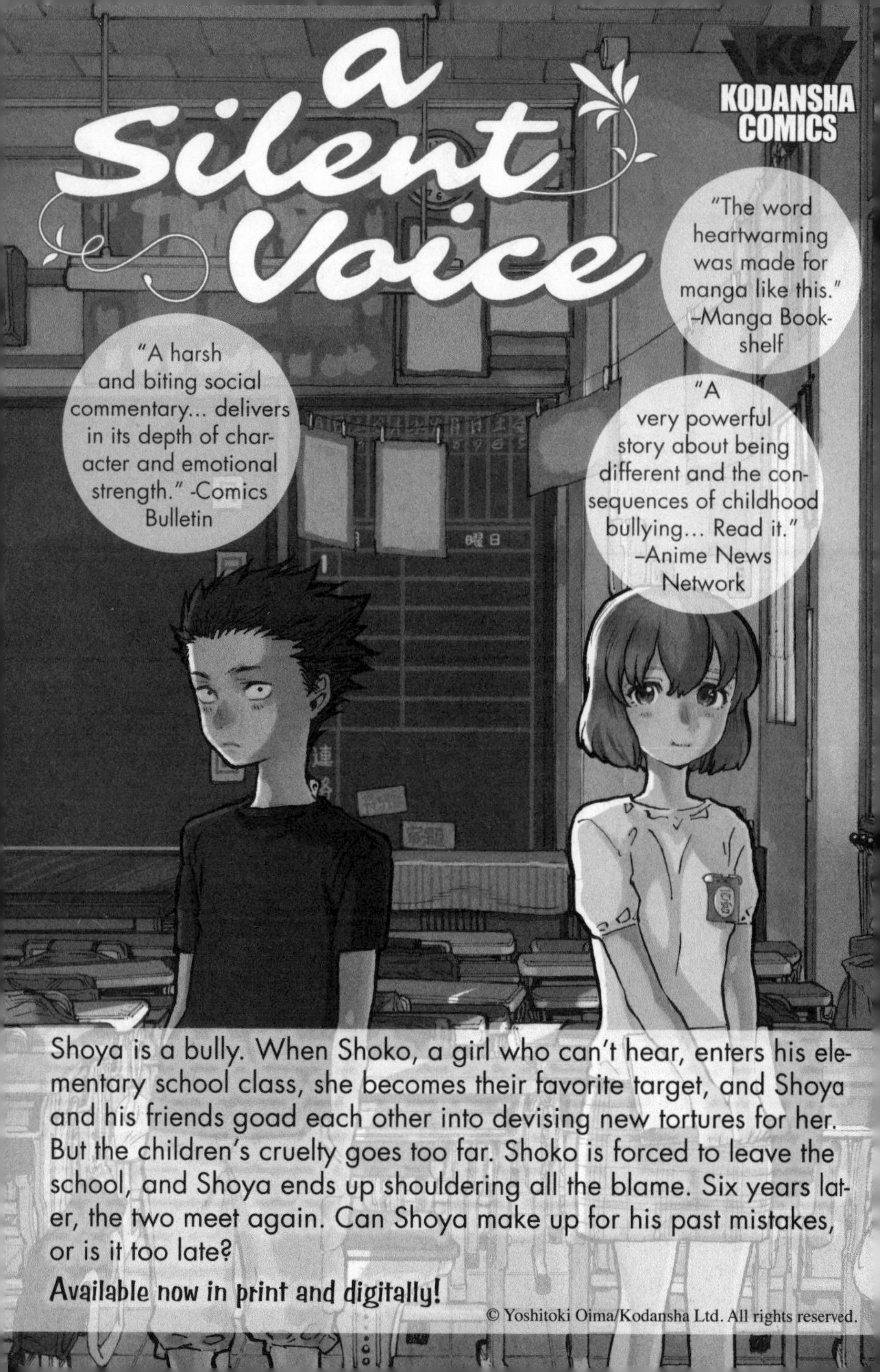
KC
KODANSHA COMICS
a Silent Voice
"The word heartwarming was made for manga like this." –Manga Bookshelf
"A harsh and biting social commentary... delivers in its depth of character and emotional strength." -Comics Bulletin
"A very powerful story about being different and the consequences of childhood bullying... Read it." –Anime News Network
Shoya is a bully. When Shoko, a girl who can't hear, enters his elementary school class, she becomes their favorite target, and Shoya and his friends goad each other into devising new tortures for her. But the children's cruelty goes too far. Shoko is forced to leave the school, and Shoya ends up shouldering all the blame. Six years later, the two meet again. Can Shoya make up for his past mistakes, or is it too late?
Available now in print and digitally!
© Yoshitoki Oima/Kodansha Ltd. All rights reserved.

A Kodansha Comics Trade Paperback Original
Waiting for Spring volume 3 copyright © 2015 Anashin
English translation copyright © 2017 Anashin

Published in the United States by Kodansha Comics, an imprint of
Kodansha USA Publishing, LLC, New York.

Publication rights for this English edition arranged through
Kodansha Ltd, Tokyo.

ISBN 978-1-63236-518-7

Printed in the United States of America.

www.kodanshacomics.com

9 8 7 6 5 4 3 2 1
Translation: Alethea and Athena Nibley
Lettering: Sara Linsley
Editing: Haruko Hashimoto
Kodansha Comics edition cover design by Phil Balsman